TOYOTA PRIUS
2001-08 REPAIR MANUAL

CHILTON'S

Covers all U.S. and Canadian models of
Toyota Prius

by Tim Imhoff

CHILTON *Automotive Books*

PUBLISHED BY **HAYNES NORTH AMERICA. Inc.**

AUTOMOTIVE
PARTS &
ACCESSORIES
ASSOCIATION MEMBER

Manufactured in USA
©2007 Haynes North America, Inc.
ISBN-13: 978-1-56392-691-4
ISBN-10: 1-56392-691-1
Library of Congress Control Number 2007940014

Haynes Publishing Group
Sparkford Nr Yeovil
Somerset BA22 7JJ England

Haynes North America, Inc
861 Lawrence Drive
Newbury Park
California 91320 USA

ABCDE
FGHIJ
KLMNO
PQRST

Chilton is a registered trademark of W.G. Nichols, Inc., and has been licensed to Haynes North America, Inc.

Contents

7

8

9

10

11

12

GLOSSARY

MASTER INDEX

Mechanic and photographer with a 2005 Toyota Prius

ACKNOWLEDGEMENTS

Wiring diagrams originated exclusively for the publisher by Solution Builders.

All rights reserved. No part of this book may be reproduced or transmitted in any form or by any means, electronic or mechanical, including photocopying, recording or by any information storage or retrieval system, without permission in writing from the copyright holder.

While every attempt is made to ensure that the information in this manual is correct, no liability can be accepted by the authors or publishers for loss, damage or injury caused by any errors in, or omissions from, the information given.

About this manual

ITS PURPOSE

The purpose of this manual is to help you get the best value from your vehicle. It can do so in several ways. It can help you decide what work must be done, even if you choose to have it done by a dealer service department or a repair shop; it provides information and procedures for routine maintenance and servicing; and it offers diagnostic and repair procedures to follow when trouble occurs.

We hope you use the manual to tackle the work yourself. For many simpler jobs, doing it yourself may be quicker than arranging an appointment to get the vehicle into a shop and making the trips to leave it and pick it up. More importantly, a lot of money can be saved by avoiding the expense the shop must pass on to you to cover its labor and overhead costs. An added benefit is the sense of satisfaction and accomplishment that you feel after doing the job yourself.

USING THE MANUAL

The manual is divided into Chapters. Each Chapter is divided into numbered Sections, which are headed in bold type between horizontal lines. Each Section consists of consecutively numbered paragraphs.

At the beginning of each numbered Section you will be referred to any illustrations which apply to the procedures in that Section. The reference numbers used in illustration captions pinpoint the pertinent Section and the Step within that Section. That is, illustration 3.2 means the illustration refers to Section 3 and Step (or paragraph) 2 within that Section.

Procedures, once described in the text, are not normally repeated. When it's necessary to refer to another Chapter, the reference will be given as Chapter and Section number. Cross references given without use of the word "Chapter" apply to Sections and/or paragraphs in the same Chapter. For example, "see Section 8" means in the same Chapter.

References to the left or right side of the vehicle assume you are sitting in the driver's seat, facing forward.

Even though we have prepared this manual with extreme care, neither the publisher nor the author can accept responsibility for any errors in, or omissions from, the information given.

➡NOTE

A *Note* provides information necessary to properly complete a procedure or information which will make the procedure easier to understand.

✳✳ CAUTION

A *Caution* provides a special procedure or special steps which must be taken while completing the procedure where the Caution is found. Not heeding a Caution can result in damage to the assembly being worked on.

✳✳ WARNING

A *Warning* provides a special procedure or special steps which must be taken while completing the procedure where the Warning is found. Not heeding a Warning can result in personal injury.

Introduction

The Toyota Prius models covered by this manual are four-door sedans. They are "hybrid" vehicles in that they are powered by a combination of a fuel-injected, transversely-mounted, internal combustion engine and two battery-powered electric motors.

The engine and electric motors drive the front wheels through an automatic transaxle/power-split device via independent driveaxles.

Independent suspension, featuring McPherson struts, is used on the front of the vehicle. The rack-and-pinion steering unit is mounted behind the engine and has electric power assist. The rear suspension uses coil-over shock absorber assemblies, connected to a pressed-steel beam-type axle.

The brakes are disc at the front and drums at the rear, with power assist standard. An Anti-lock Brake System (ABS) is standard on all models.

Vehicle Identification Numbers

Modifications are a continuing and unpublicized process in vehicle manufacturing. Since spare parts manuals and lists are compiled on a numerical basis, the individual vehicle numbers are essential to correctly identify the component required.

VEHICLE IDENTIFICATION NUMBER (VIN)

This very important identification number is stamped on a plate attached to the dashboard inside the windshield on the driver's side of the vehicle and on the Vehicle Safety Certification label in the driver's door opening (see illustration). The VIN also appears on the Vehicle Certificate of Title and Registration. It contains information such as where and when the vehicle was manufactured, the model year and the body style.

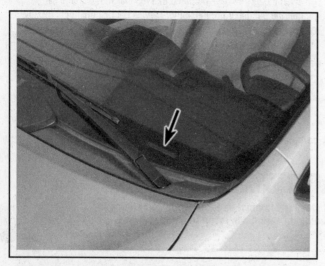

The Vehicle Identification Number (VIN) is visible through the driver's side of the windshield

The manufacturer's certification regulation label is affixed to the left door

MANUFACTURER'S CERTIFICATION REGULATION LABEL

The manufacturer's Certification Regulation label is attached to the driver's side door end or post. The plate contains the name of the manufacturer, the month and year of production, the Gross Vehicle Weight Rating (GVWR), the Gross Axle Weight Rating (GAWR) and the certification statement (see illustration).

VIN MODEL YEAR CODES

One particularly important piece of information found within the VIN is the model year code. Counting from the left, the model year code designation is the 10th character in the VIN.

On all models covered by this manual the model year codes are:

1	2001
2	2002
3	2003
4	2004
5	2005
6	2006
7	2007
8	2008

ENGINE AND TRANSAXLE IDENTIFICATION NUMBERS

The engine code number can be found on a pad on the front side of the block. It is only visible from beneath the vehicle. The transaxle identification number is located at the top front of the transaxle case (see illustration).

Location of the transaxle identification number; it is visible between the wiring harnesses and lines stamped into the case of the transaxle

Recall information

Vehicle recalls are carried out by the manufacturer in the rare event of a possible safety-related defect. The vehicle's registered owner is contacted at the address on file at the Department of Motor Vehicles and given the details of the recall. Remedial work is carried out free of charge at a dealer service department.

If you are the new owner of a used vehicle which was subject to a recall and you want to be sure that the work has been carried out, it's best to contact a dealer service department and ask about your indi-vidual vehicle - you'll need to furnish them your Vehicle Identification Number (VIN).

The table below is based on information provided by the National Highway Traffic Safety Administration (NHTSA), the body which over-sees vehicle recalls in the United States. The recall database is updated constantly. For the latest information on vehicle recalls, check the NHTSA website at www.nhtsa.gov, or call the NHTSA hotline at 1-888-327-4236.

Recall date	Recall campaign number	Model(s) affected	Concern
Oct 27, 2000	00V285000	2001 Prius	Insufficient electrical contact can occur in the torque sensor that controls the power assist operation of the electric power steering gear box. If this occurs, the power steering warning icon will be displayed on the center panel, and the driver could experience higher than normal steering effort depending upon vehicle speed.
Nov 18, 2004	04V558000	2004 Prius	Certain passenger vehicles may be equipped with an improperly designed brake light switch. A silicon oxide build-up occurs on the contacts inside the brake light switch, which can make it inoperable. If the switch is inoperable, the brake lights will not illuminate and can increase the risk of a crash.
Apr 6, 2006	06V096000	2004, 2005, 2006 Prius	On certain vehicles, due to improper assembly of the air bag inflator, which is used in the side air bag, the curtain shield air bag, and the knee air bag assembly, some inflators were produced with an insufficient amount of the heating agents necessary for proper air bag deployment. This may increase the risk of injury to the occupant in the involved seating position in the event of a crash.
Jun 9, 2006	06V188000	2004, 2005, 2006 Prius	The intermediate shaft and sliding yoke in the electric power steering system can crack when large forces are applied and the connection may separate or the sleeve may fracture. This could result in a loss of steering control of the vehicle.
Jul 26, 2006	06V266000	2001, 2002 Prius	On certain passenger vehicles, due to improper molding of the resin body of the crankshaft position sensor, engine oil may penetrate the seal and enter the sensor wiring connector. Engine oil inside the sensor wiring connector could cause expansion due to the heat of the engine and could deform the sensor wiring connector. The connector may become disconnected, which could cause the engine to stall while driving and not be able to be restarted, increasing the risk of a crash.

Buying parts

Replacement parts are available from many sources, which generally fall into one of two categories - authorized dealer parts departments and independent retail auto parts stores. Our advice concerning these parts is as follows:

Retail auto parts stores: Good auto parts stores will stock frequently needed components which wear out relatively fast, such as clutch components, exhaust systems, brake parts, tune-up parts, etc. These stores often supply new or reconditioned parts on an exchange basis, which can save a considerable amount of money. Discount auto parts stores are often very good places to buy materials and parts needed for general vehicle maintenance such as oil, grease, filters, spark plugs, belts, touch-up paint, bulbs, etc. They also usually sell

tools and general accessories, have convenient hours, charge lower prices and can often be found not far from home.

Authorized dealer parts department: This is the best source for parts which are unique to the vehicle and not generally available elsewhere (such as major engine parts, transmission parts, trim pieces, etc.).

Warranty information: If the vehicle is still covered under warranty, be sure that any replacement parts purchased - regardless of the source - do not invalidate the warranty!

To be sure of obtaining the correct parts, have engine and chassis numbers available and, if possible, take the old parts along for positive identification.

Maintenance techniques, tools and working facilities

MAINTENANCE TECHNIQUES

There are a number of techniques involved in maintenance and repair that will be referred to throughout this manual. Application of these techniques will enable the home mechanic to be more efficient, better organized and capable of performing the various tasks properly, which will ensure that the repair job is thorough and complete.

Fasteners

Fasteners are nuts, bolts, studs and screws used to hold two or more parts together. There are a few things to keep in mind when working with fasteners. Almost all of them use a locking device of some type, either a lockwasher, locknut, locking tab or thread adhesive. All threaded fasteners should be clean and straight, with undamaged threads and undamaged corners on the hex head where the wrench fits. Develop the habit of replacing all damaged nuts and bolts with new ones. Special locknuts with nylon or fiber inserts can only be used once. If they are removed, they lose their locking ability and must be replaced with new ones.

Rusted nuts and bolts should be treated with a penetrating fluid to ease removal and prevent breakage. Some mechanics use turpentine in a spout-type oil can, which works quite well. After applying the rust penetrant, let it work for a few minutes before trying to loosen the nut or bolt. Badly rusted fasteners may have to be chiseled or sawed off or removed with a special nut breaker, available at tool stores.

If a bolt or stud breaks off in an assembly, it can be drilled and removed with a special tool commonly available for this purpose. Most automotive machine shops can perform this task, as well as other repair procedures, such as the repair of threaded holes that have been stripped out.

Flat washers and lockwashers, when removed from an assembly, should always be replaced exactly as removed. Replace any damaged washers with new ones. Never use a lockwasher on any soft metal surface (such as aluminum), thin sheet metal or plastic.

Fastener sizes

For a number of reasons, automobile manufacturers are making wider and wider use of metric fasteners. Therefore, it is important to be able to tell the difference between standard (sometimes called U.S.

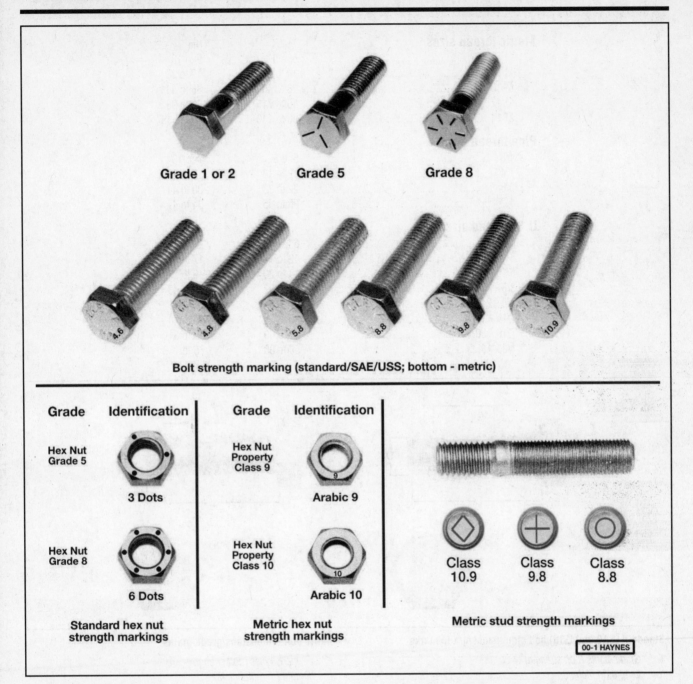

Grade 1 or 2   Grade 5   Grade 8

Bolt strength marking (standard/SAE/USS; bottom - metric)

Grade	Identification	Grade	Identification
Hex Nut Grade 5	3 Dots	Hex Nut Property Class 9	Arabic 9
Hex Nut Grade 8	6 Dots	Hex Nut Property Class 10	Arabic 10

Standard hex nut strength markings

Metric hex nut strength markings

Class 10.9   Class 9.8   Class 8.8

Metric stud strength markings

00-1 HAYNES

or SAE) and metric hardware, since they cannot be interchanged.

All bolts, whether standard or metric, are sized according to diameter, thread pitch and length. For example, a standard 1/2 - 13 x 1 bolt is 1/2 inch in diameter, has 13 threads per inch and is 1 inch long. An M12 - 1.75 x 25 metric bolt is 12 mm in diameter, has a thread pitch of 1.75 mm (the distance between threads) and is 25 mm long. The two bolts are nearly identical, and easily confused, but they are not interchangeable.

In addition to the differences in diameter, thread pitch and length, metric and standard bolts can also be distinguished by examining the bolt heads. To begin with, the distance across the flats on a standard bolt head is measured in inches, while the same dimension on a metric bolt is sized in millimeters (the same is true for nuts). As a result, a standard wrench should not be used on a metric bolt and a metric wrench should not be used on a standard bolt. Also, most standard bolts have slashes

radiating out from the center of the head to denote the grade or strength of the bolt, which is an indication of the amount of torque that can be applied to it. The greater the number of slashes, the greater the strength of the bolt. Grades 0 through 5 are commonly used on automobiles. Metric bolts have a property class (grade) number, rather than a slash, molded into their heads to indicate bolt strength. In this case, the higher the number, the stronger the bolt. Property class numbers 8.8, 9.8 and 10.9 are commonly used on automobiles.

Strength markings can also be used to distinguish standard hex nuts from metric hex nuts. Many standard nuts have dots stamped into one side, while metric nuts are marked with a number. The greater the number of dots, or the higher the number, the greater the strength of the nut.

Metric studs are also marked on their ends according to property class (grade). Larger studs are numbered (the same as metric bolts), while smaller studs carry a geometric code to denote grade.

Metric thread sizes

	Ft-lbs	Nm
M-6	6 to 9	9 to 12
M-8	14 to 21	19 to 28
M-10	28 to 40	38 to 54
M-12	50 to 71	68 to 96
M-14	80 to 140	109 to 154

Pipe thread sizes

	Ft-lbs	Nm
1/8	5 to 8	7 to 10
1/4	12 to 18	17 to 24
3/8	22 to 33	30 to 44
1/2	25 to 35	34 to 47

U.S. thread sizes

	Ft-lbs	Nm
1/4 - 20	6 to 9	9 to 12
5/16 - 18	12 to 18	17 to 24
5/16 - 24	14 to 20	19 to 27
3/8 - 16	22 to 32	30 to 43
3/8 - 24	27 to 38	37 to 51
7/16 - 14	40 to 55	55 to 74
7/16 - 20	40 to 60	55 to 81
1/2 - 13	55 to 80	75 to 108

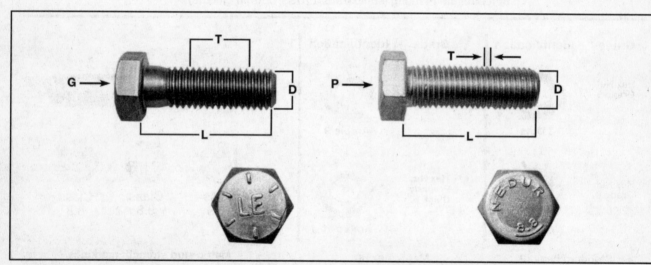

Standard (SAE and USS) bolt dimensions/grade marks

G   Grade marks (bolt strength)
L   Length (in inches)
T   Thread pitch (number of threads per inch)
D   Nominal diameter (in inches)

Metric bolt dimensions/grade marks

P   Property class (bolt strength)
L   Length (in millimeters)
T   Thread pitch (distance between threads in millimeters)
D   Diameter

It should be noted that many fasteners, especially Grades 0 through 2, have no distinguishing marks on them. When such is the case, the only way to determine whether it is standard or metric is to measure the thread pitch or compare it to a known fastener of the same size.

Standard fasteners are often referred to as SAE, as opposed to metric. However, it should be noted that SAE technically refers to a non-metric fine thread fastener only. Coarse thread non-metric fasteners are referred to as USS sizes.

Since fasteners of the same size (both standard and metric) may have different strength ratings, be sure to reinstall any bolts, studs or nuts removed from your vehicle in their original locations. Also, when replacing a fastener with a new one, make sure that the new one has a strength rating equal to or greater than the original.

Tightening sequences and procedures

Most threaded fasteners should be tightened to a specific torque value (torque is the twisting force applied to a threaded component such as a nut or bolt). Overtightening the fastener can weaken it and cause it to break, while undertightening can cause it to eventually come loose. Bolts, screws and studs, depending on the material they are made of and their thread diameters, have specific torque values, many of which are noted in the Specifications at the end of each Chapter. Be sure to follow the torque recommendations closely. For fasteners not assigned a specific torque, a general torque value chart is presented here as a guide. These torque values are for dry (unlubricated) fasteners threaded into steel or cast iron (not aluminum). As was previously mentioned, the size and grade of a fastener determine the amount of torque that can

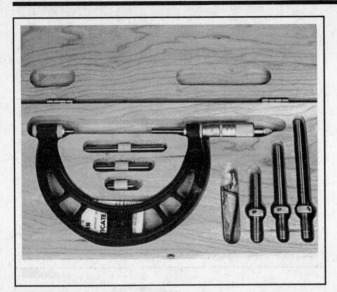

Micrometer set

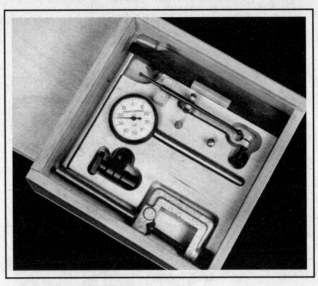

Dial indicator set

safely be applied to it. The figures listed here are approximate for Grade 2 and Grade 3 fasteners. Higher grades can tolerate higher torque values.

Fasteners laid out in a pattern, such as cylinder head bolts, oil pan bolts, differential cover bolts, etc., must be loosened or tightened in sequence to avoid warping the component. This sequence will normally be shown in the appropriate Chapter. If a specific pattern is not given, the following procedures can be used to prevent warping.

Initially, the bolts or nuts should be assembled finger-tight only. Next, they should be tightened one full turn each, in a criss-cross or diagonal pattern. After each one has been tightened one full turn, return to the first one and tighten them all one-half turn, following the same pattern. Finally, tighten each of them one-quarter turn at a time until each fastener has been tightened to the proper torque. To loosen and remove the fasteners, the procedure would be reversed.

Component disassembly

Component disassembly should be done with care and purpose to help ensure that the parts go back together properly. Always keep track of the sequence in which parts are removed. Make note of special characteristics or marks on parts that can be installed more than one way, such as a grooved thrust washer on a shaft. It is a good idea to lay the disassembled parts out on a clean surface in the order that they were removed. It may also be helpful to make sketches or take instant photos of components before removal.

When removing fasteners from a component, keep track of their locations. Sometimes threading a bolt back in a part, or putting the washers and nut back on a stud, can prevent mix-ups later. If nuts and bolts cannot be returned to their original locations, they should be kept in a compartmented box or a series of small boxes. A cupcake or muffin tin is ideal for this purpose, since each cavity can hold the bolts and nuts from a particular area (i.e. oil pan bolts, valve cover bolts, engine mount bolts, etc.). A pan of this type is especially helpful when working on assemblies with very small parts, such as the carburetor, alternator, valve train or interior dash and trim pieces. The cavities can be marked with paint or tape to identify the contents.

Whenever wiring looms, harnesses or connectors are separated, it is a good idea to identify the two halves with numbered pieces of masking tape so they can be easily reconnected.

Gasket sealing surfaces

Throughout any vehicle, gaskets are used to seal the mating surfaces between two parts and keep lubricants, fluids, vacuum or pressure contained in an assembly.

Many times these gaskets are coated with a liquid or paste-type gasket sealing compound before assembly. Age, heat and pressure can sometimes cause the two parts to stick together so tightly that they are very difficult to separate. Often, the assembly can be loosened by striking it with a soft-face hammer near the mating surfaces. A regular hammer can be used if a block of wood is placed between the hammer and the part. Do not hammer on cast parts or parts that could be easily damaged. With any particularly stubborn part, always recheck to make sure that every fastener has been removed.

Avoid using a screwdriver or bar to pry apart an assembly, as they can easily mar the gasket sealing surfaces of the parts, which must remain smooth. If prying is absolutely necessary, use an old broom handle, but keep in mind that extra clean up will be necessary if the wood splinters.

After the parts are separated, the old gasket must be carefully scraped off and the gasket surfaces cleaned. Stubborn gasket material can be soaked with rust penetrant or treated with a special chemical to soften it so it can be easily scraped off.

❋ CAUTION:

Never use gasket removal solutions or caustic chemicals on plastic or other composite components.

A scraper can be fashioned from a piece of copper tubing by flattening and sharpening one end. Copper is recommended because it is usually softer than the surfaces to be scraped, which reduces the chance of gouging the part. Some gaskets can be removed with a wire brush, but regardless of the method used, the mating surfaces must be left clean and smooth. If for some reason the gasket surface is gouged, then a gasket sealer thick enough to fill scratches will have to be used during reassembly of the components. For most applications, a non-drying (or semi-drying) gasket sealer should be used.

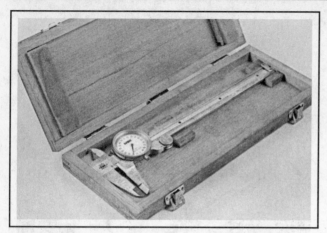

Dial caliper

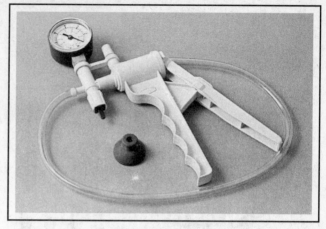

Hand-operated vacuum pump

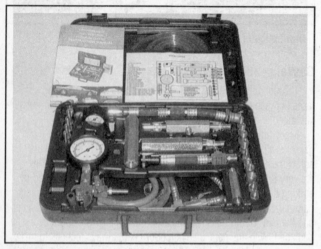

Fuel pressure gauge set

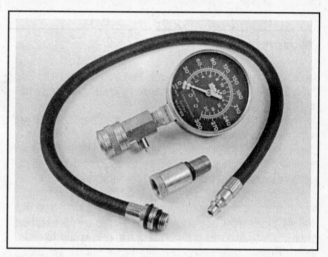

Compression gauge with spark plug hole adapter

Hose removal tips

✽✽ WARNING:

If the vehicle is equipped with air conditioning, do not disconnect any of the A/C hoses without first having the system depressurized by a dealer service department or a service station.

Hose removal precautions closely parallel gasket removal precautions. Avoid scratching or gouging the surface that the hose mates against or the connection may leak. This is especially true for radiator hoses. Because of various chemical reactions, the rubber in hoses can bond itself to the metal spigot that the hose fits over. To remove a hose, first loosen the hose clamps that secure it to the spigot. Then, with slip-joint pliers, grab the hose at the clamp and rotate it around the spigot. Work it back and forth until it is completely free, then pull it off. Silicone or other lubricants will ease removal if they can be applied between the hose and the outside of the spigot. Apply the same lubricant to the inside of the hose and the outside of the spigot to simplify installation.

As a last resort (and if the hose is to be replaced with a new one anyway), the rubber can be slit with a knife and the hose peeled from the spigot. If this must be done, be careful that the metal connection is not damaged.

If a hose clamp is broken or damaged, do not reuse it. Wire-type clamps usually weaken with age, so it is a good idea to replace them with screw-type clamps whenever a hose is removed.

TOOLS

A selection of good tools is a basic requirement for anyone who plans to maintain and repair his or her own vehicle. For the owner who has few tools, the initial investment might seem high, but when compared to the spiraling costs of professional auto maintenance and repair, it is a wise one.

To help the owner decide which tools are needed to perform the tasks detailed in this manual, the following tool lists are offered: *Maintenance and minor repair, Repair/overhaul* and *Special*.

The newcomer to practical mechanics should start off with the *maintenance and minor repair* tool kit, which is adequate for the simpler jobs performed on a vehicle. Then, as confidence and experience grow, the owner can tackle more difficult tasks, buying additional tools as they are needed. Eventually the basic kit will be expanded into the *repair and overhaul* tool set. Over a period of time, the experienced do-it-yourselfer will assemble a tool set complete enough for most repair and overhaul procedures and will add tools from the special category when it is felt that the expense is justified by the frequency of use.

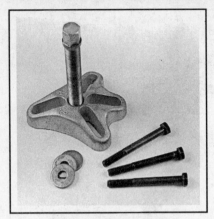

Damper/steering wheel puller

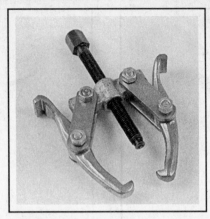

General purpose puller

Hydraulic lifter removal tool

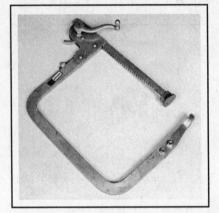

Valve spring compressor

Valve spring compressor

Ridge reamer

Maintenance and minor repair tool kit

The tools in this list should be considered the minimum required for performance of routine maintenance, servicing and minor repair work. We recommend the purchase of combination wrenches (box-end and open-end combined in one wrench). While more expensive than open end wrenches, they offer the advantages of both types of wrench.

Combination wrench set (1/4-inch to 1 inch or 6 mm to 19 mm)
Adjustable wrench, 8 inch
Spark plug wrench with rubber insert
Spark plug gap adjusting tool
Feeler gauge set
Brake bleeder wrench
Standard screwdriver (5/16-inch x 6 inch)
Phillips screwdriver (No. 2 x 6 inch)
Combination pliers - 6 inch
Hacksaw and assortment of blades
Tire pressure gauge
Grease gun
Oil can
Fine emery cloth
Wire brush
Battery post and cable cleaning tool
Oil filter wrench
Funnel (medium size)
Safety goggles
Jackstands (2)
Drain pan

➠Note: If basic tune-ups are going to be part of routine maintenance, it will be necessary to purchase a good quality stroboscopic timing light and combination tachometer/dwell meter. Although they are included in the list of special tools, it is mentioned here because they are absolutely necessary for tuning most vehicles properly.

Repair and overhaul tool set

These tools are essential for anyone who plans to perform major repairs and are in addition to those in the maintenance and minor repair tool kit. Included is a comprehensive set of sockets which, though expensive, are invaluable because of their versatility, especially when various extensions and drives are available. We recommend the 1/2-inch drive over the 3/8-inch drive. Although the larger drive is bulky and more expensive, it has the capacity of accepting a very wide range of large sockets. Ideally, however, the mechanic should have a 3/8-inch drive set and a 1/2-inch drive set.

Socket set(s)
Reversible ratchet
Extension - 10 inch
Universal joint
Torque wrench (same size drive as sockets)
Ball peen hammer - 8 ounce
Soft-face hammer (plastic/rubber)
Standard screwdriver (1/4-inch x 6 inch)
Standard screwdriver (stubby - 5/16-inch)
Phillips screwdriver (No. 3 x 8 inch)
Phillips screwdriver (stubby - No. 2)
Pliers - vise grip

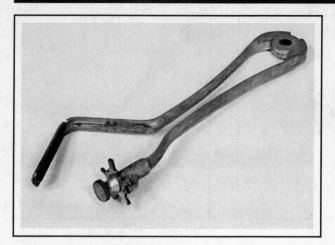

Piston ring groove cleaning tool

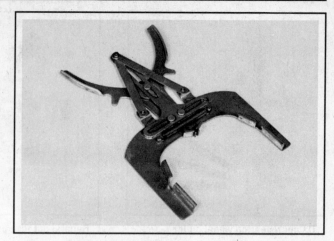

Ring removal/installation tool

Ring compressor

Cylinder hone

Brake hold-down spring tool

Pliers - lineman's
Pliers - needle nose
Pliers - snap-ring (internal and external)
Cold chisel - 1/2-inch
Scribe
Scraper (made from flattened copper tubing)
Centerpunch
Pin punches (1/16, 1/8, 3/16-inch)
Steel rule/straightedge - 12 inch
Allen wrench set (1/8 to 3/8-inch or 4 mm to 10 mm)
A selection of files
Wire brush (large)
Jackstands (second set)
Jack (scissor or hydraulic type)

➡**Note: Another tool which is often useful is an electric drill with a chuck capacity of 3/8-inch and a set of good quality drill bits.**

Special tools

The tools in this list include those which are not used regularly, are expensive to buy, or which need to be used in accordance with their manufacturer's instructions. Unless these tools will be used frequently, it is not very economical to purchase many of them. A consideration would be to split the cost and use between yourself and a friend or friends. In addition, most of these tools can be obtained from a tool rental shop on a temporary basis.

This list primarily contains only those tools and instruments widely available to the public, and not those special tools produced by the vehicle manufacturer for distribution to dealer service depart-

ments. Occasionally, references to the manufacturer's special tools are included in the text of this manual. Generally, an alternative method of doing the job without the special tool is offered. However, sometimes there is no alternative to their use. Where this is the case, and the tool cannot be purchased or borrowed, the work should be turned over to the dealer service department or an automotive repair shop.

Valve spring compressor
Piston ring groove cleaning tool
Piston ring compressor
Piston ring installation tool
Cylinder compression gauge
Cylinder ridge reamer
Cylinder surfacing hone
Cylinder bore gauge
Micrometers and/or dial calipers
Hydraulic lifter removal tool
Balljoint separator
Universal-type puller
Impact screwdriver
Dial indicator set
Stroboscopic timing light (inductive pick-up)
Hand operated vacuum/pressure pump
Tachometer/dwell meter
Universal electrical multimeter
Cable hoist
Brake spring removal and installation tools
Floor jack

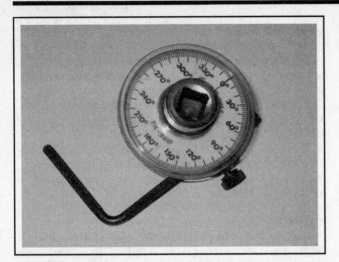

Torque angle gauge

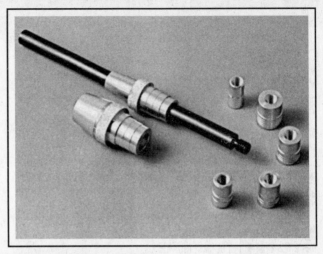

Clutch plate alignment tool

Buying tools

For the do-it-yourselfer who is just starting to get involved in vehicle maintenance and repair, there are a number of options available when purchasing tools. If maintenance and minor repair is the extent of the work to be done, the purchase of individual tools is satisfactory. If, on the other hand, extensive work is planned, it would be a good idea to purchase a modest tool set from one of the large retail chain stores. A set can usually be bought at a substantial savings over the individual tool prices, and they often come with a tool box. As additional tools are needed, add-on sets, individual tools and a larger tool box can be purchased to expand the tool selection. Building a tool set gradually allows the cost of the tools to be spread over a longer period of time and gives the mechanic the freedom to choose only those tools that will actually be used.

Tool stores will often be the only source of some of the special tools that are needed, but regardless of where tools are bought, try to avoid cheap ones, especially when buying screwdrivers and sockets, because they won't last very long. The expense involved in replacing cheap tools will eventually be greater than the initial cost of quality tools.

Care and maintenance of tools

Good tools are expensive, so it makes sense to treat them with respect. Keep them clean and in usable condition and store them properly when not in use. Always wipe off any dirt, grease or metal chips before putting them away. Never leave tools lying around in the work area. Upon completion of a job, always check closely under the hood for tools that may have been left there so they won't get lost during a test drive.

Some tools, such as screwdrivers, pliers, wrenches and sockets, can be hung on a panel mounted on the garage or workshop wall, while others should be kept in a tool box or tray. Measuring instruments, gauges, meters, etc. must be carefully stored where they cannot be damaged by weather or impact from other tools.

When tools are used with care and stored properly, they will last a very long time. Even with the best of care, though, tools will wear out if used frequently. When a tool is damaged or worn out, replace it. Subsequent jobs will be safer and more enjoyable if you do.

HOW TO REPAIR DAMAGED THREADS

Sometimes, the internal threads of a nut or bolt hole can become stripped, usually from overtightening. Stripping threads is an all-too-

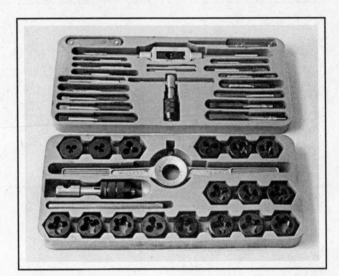

Tap and die set

common occurrence, especially when working with aluminum parts, because aluminum is so soft that it easily strips out.

Usually, external or internal threads are only partially stripped. After they've been cleaned up with a tap or die, they'll still work. Sometimes, however, threads are badly damaged. When this happens, you've got three choices:

1) Drill and tap the hole to the next suitable oversize and install a larger diameter bolt, screw or stud.

2) Drill and tap the hole to accept a threaded plug, then drill and tap the plug to the original screw size. You can also buy a plug already threaded to the original size. Then you simply drill a hole to the specified size, then run the threaded plug into the hole with a bolt and jam nut. Once the plug is fully seated, remove the jam nut and bolt.

3) The third method uses a patented thread repair kit like Heli-Coil or Slimsert. These easy-to-use kits are designed to repair damaged threads in straight-through holes and blind holes. Both are available as kits which can handle a variety of sizes and thread patterns. Drill the hole, then tap it with the special included tap. Install the Heli-Coil and the hole is back to its original diameter and thread pitch.

Regardless of which method you use, be sure to proceed calmly and carefully. A little impatience or carelessness during one of these relatively simple procedures can ruin your whole day's work and cost you a bundle if you wreck an expensive part.

WORKING FACILITIES

Not to be overlooked when discussing tools is the workshop. If anything more than routine maintenance is to be carried out, some sort of suitable work area is essential.

It is understood, and appreciated, that many home mechanics do not have a good workshop or garage available, and end up removing an engine or doing major repairs outside. It is recommended, however, that the overhaul or repair be completed under the cover of a roof.

A clean, flat workbench or table of comfortable working height is an absolute necessity. The workbench should be equipped with a vise that has a jaw opening of at least four inches.

As mentioned previously, some clean, dry storage space is also required for tools, as well as the lubricants, fluids, cleaning solvents, etc. which soon become necessary.

Sometimes waste oil and fluids, drained from the engine or cooling system during normal maintenance or repairs, present a disposal problem. To avoid pouring them on the ground or into a sewage system, pour the used fluids into large containers, seal them with caps and take them to an authorized disposal site or recycling center. Plastic jugs, such as old antifreeze containers, are ideal for this purpose.

Always keep a supply of old newspapers and clean rags available. Old towels are excellent for mopping up spills. Many mechanics use rolls of paper towels for most work because they are readily available and disposable. To help keep the area under the vehicle clean, a large cardboard box can be cut open and flattened to protect the garage or shop floor.

Whenever working over a painted surface, such as when leaning over a fender to service something under the hood, always cover it with an old blanket or bedspread to protect the finish. Vinyl covered pads, made especially for this purpose, are available at auto parts stores.

Booster battery (jump) starting

Observe these precautions when using a booster battery to start a vehicle:

a) *Before connecting the booster battery, make sure the ignition switch is in the Off position.*
b) *Turn off the lights, heater and other electrical loads.*
c) *Your eyes should be shielded. Safety goggles are a good idea.*
d) *Make sure the booster battery is the same voltage as the dead one in the vehicle.*
e) *The two vehicles MUST NOT TOUCH each other!*
f) *Make sure the transaxle is in Park.*
g) *If the booster battery is not a maintenance-free type, remove the vent caps and lay a cloth over the vent holes.*

Connect the red jumper cable to the positive (+) terminals of each battery (see illustration). Refer to Chapter 6 for information on access-ing the battery. On all models it is located beneath a cover in the lug-gage compartment.

➡Note: 2004 and later models have a jump-starting terminal located beneath a plastic cover in the engine compartment. This makes a convenient point for connecting the positive jumper cable (see illustration).

Connect one end of the black jumper cable to the negative (-) ter-minal of the booster battery. The other end of this cable should be con-nected to a good ground on the vehicle to be started, such as a bolt or bracket on the body.

Start the hybrid system using the booster battery, then disconnect the jumper cables in the reverse order of connection. The READY light must come on.

➡Note 1: If the vehicle does not start and the main high-voltage warning light comes on, then the main battery may be low as well. Contact a dealer or other service facility.

➡Note 2: The manufacturer strongly recommends that you do not use quick-chargers on the Prius battery.

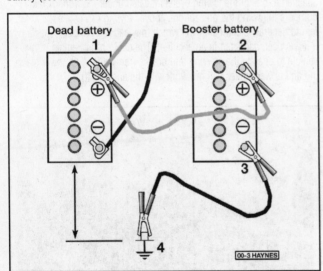

Make the booster battery cable connections in the numerical order shown (note that the negative cable of the booster battery is NOT attached to the negative terminal of the dead battery). Never attempt to connect cables to the high-voltage battery - only connect the booster battery to the small auxiliary battery of the Prius . . .

. . . or, on 2004 and later models, to the remote positive terminal located in the underhood fuse/relay box, under the red plastic cover

Jacking and towing

JACKING

The jack supplied with the vehicle should only be used for changing a tire or placing jackstands under the frame. Never work under the vehicle or start the engine while this jack is being used as the only means of support.

The vehicle should be on level ground. Place the shift lever in Park. Block the wheel diagonally opposite the wheel being changed. Set the parking brake.

Remove the spare tire and jack from stowage. Remove the wheel cover and trim ring (if so equipped) with the tapered end of the lug nut wrench by inserting and twisting the handle and then prying against the back of the wheel cover. Loosen, but do not remove, the lug nuts (one-half turn is sufficient).

Place the scissors-type jack under the side of the vehicle and adjust the jack height until it fits between the notches in the vertical rocker panel flange nearest the wheel to be changed. There is a front and rear jacking point on each side of the vehicle (see illustration).

Turn the jack handle clockwise until the tire clears the ground. Remove the lug nuts and pull the wheel off. Replace it with the spare.

Install the lug nuts with the beveled edges facing in. Tighten them snugly. Don't attempt to tighten them completely until the vehicle is lowered or it could slip off the jack. Turn the jack handle counterclockwise to lower the vehicle. Remove the jack and tighten the lug nuts in a diagonal pattern.

Install the cover (and trim ring, if used) and be sure it's snapped into place all the way around.

Stow the tire, jack and wrench. Unblock the wheels.

TOWING

The manufacturer does not recommend towing except with a flatbed car carrier or a towing dolly under the front wheels. In an emergency the vehicle can be towed a very short distance with a cable or chain attached to one of the towing eyelets located under the front or rear bumpers following the precautions above. Towing can cause the system to generate electrical power which may cause a danger, especially if it has been damaged in an accident. The driver must remain in the vehicle to operate the steering and brakes (remember that power steering and power brakes will not work with the engine off).

The jack fits at designated spots (there are two jacking points on each side of the vehicle)

Automotive chemicals and lubricants

A number of automotive chemicals and lubricants are available for use during vehicle maintenance and repair. They include a wide variety of products ranging from cleaning solvents and degreasers to lubricants and protective sprays for rubber, plastic and vinyl.

CLEANERS

Carburetor cleaner and choke cleaner is a strong solvent for gum, varnish and carbon. Most carburetor cleaners leave a dry-type lubricant film which will not harden or gum up. Because of this film it is not recommended for use on electrical components.

Brake system cleaner is used to remove brake dust, grease and brake fluid from the brake system, where clean surfaces are absolutely necessary. It leaves no residue and often eliminates brake squeal caused by contaminants.

Electrical cleaner removes oxidation, corrosion and carbon deposits from electrical contacts, restoring full current flow. It can also be used to clean spark plugs, carburetor jets, voltage regulators and other parts where an oil-free surface is desired.

Demoisturants remove water and moisture from electrical components such as alternators, voltage regulators, electrical connectors and fuse blocks. They are non-conductive and non-corrosive.

Degreasers are heavy-duty solvents used to remove grease from the outside of the engine and from chassis components. They can be sprayed or brushed on and, depending on the type, are rinsed off either with water or solvent.

LUBRICANTS

Motor oil is the lubricant formulated for use in engines. It normally contains a wide variety of additives to prevent corrosion and reduce foaming and wear. Motor oil comes in various weights (viscosity ratings) from 0 to 50. The recommended weight of the oil depends on the season, temperature and the demands on the engine. Light oil is used in cold climates and under light load conditions. Heavy oil is used in hot climates and where high loads are encountered. Multi-viscosity oils are designed to have characteristics of both light and heavy oils and are available in a number of weights from 5W-20 to 20W-50.

Gear oil is designed to be used in differentials, manual transmissions and other areas where high-temperature lubrication is required.

Chassis and wheel bearing grease is a heavy grease used where increased loads and friction are encountered, such as for wheel bearings, balljoints, tie-rod ends and universal joints.

High-temperature wheel bearing grease is designed to withstand the extreme temperatures encountered by wheel bearings in disc brake equipped vehicles. It usually contains molybdenum disulfide (moly), which is a dry-type lubricant.

White grease is a heavy grease for metal-to-metal applications where water is a problem. White grease stays soft under both low and high temperatures (usually from -100 to +190-degrees F), and will not wash off or dilute in the presence of water.

Assembly lube is a special extreme pressure lubricant, usually containing moly, used to lubricate high-load parts (such as main and rod bearings and cam lobes) for initial start-up of a new engine. The assembly lube lubricates the parts without being squeezed out or washed away until the engine oiling system begins to function.

Silicone lubricants are used to protect rubber, plastic, vinyl and nylon parts.

Graphite lubricants are used where oils cannot be used due to contamination problems, such as in locks. The dry graphite will lubricate metal parts while remaining uncontaminated by dirt, water, oil or acids. It is electrically conductive and will not foul electrical contacts in locks such as the ignition switch.

Moly penetrants loosen and lubricate frozen, rusted and corroded fasteners and prevent future rusting or freezing.

Heat-sink grease is a special electrically non-conductive grease that is used for mounting electronic ignition modules where it is essential that heat is transferred away from the module.

SEALANTS

RTV sealant is one of the most widely used gasket compounds. Made from silicone, RTV is air curing, it seals, bonds, waterproofs, fills surface irregularities, remains flexible, doesn't shrink, is relatively easy to remove, and is used as a supplementary sealer with almost all low and medium temperature gaskets.

Anaerobic sealant is much like RTV in that it can be used either to seal gaskets or to form gaskets by itself. It remains flexible, is solvent resistant and fills surface imperfections. The difference between an anaerobic sealant and an RTV-type sealant is in the curing. RTV cures when exposed to air, while an anaerobic sealant cures only in the absence of air. This means that an anaerobic sealant cures only after the assembly of parts, sealing them together.

Thread and pipe sealant is used for sealing hydraulic and pneumatic fittings and vacuum lines. It is usually made from a Teflon compound, and comes in a spray, a paint-on liquid and as a wrap-around tape.

CHEMICALS

Anti-seize compound prevents seizing, galling, cold welding, rust and corrosion in fasteners. High-temperature anti-seize, usually made with copper and graphite lubricants, is used for exhaust system and exhaust manifold bolts.

Anaerobic locking compounds are used to keep fasteners from vibrating or working loose and cure only after installation, in the absence of air. Medium strength locking compound is used for small nuts, bolts and screws that may be removed later. High-strength locking compound is for large nuts, bolts and studs which aren't removed on a regular basis.

Oil additives range from viscosity index improvers to chemical treatments that claim to reduce internal engine friction. It should be noted that most oil manufacturers caution against using additives with their oils.

Gas additives perform several functions, depending on their chemical makeup. They usually contain solvents that help dissolve gum and varnish that build up on carburetor, fuel injection and intake parts. They also serve to break down carbon deposits that form on the inside surfaces of the combustion chambers. Some additives contain upper cylinder lubricants for valves and piston rings, and others contain chemicals to remove condensation from the gas tank.

MISCELLANEOUS

Brake fluid is specially formulated hydraulic fluid that can withstand the heat and pressure encountered in brake systems. Care must be taken so this fluid does not come in contact with painted surfaces or plastics. An opened container should always be resealed to prevent contamination by water or dirt.

Weatherstrip adhesive is used to bond weatherstripping around doors, windows and trunk lids. It is sometimes used to attach trim pieces.

Undercoating is a petroleum-based, tar-like substance that is designed to protect metal surfaces on the underside of the vehicle from corrosion. It also acts as a sound-deadening agent by insulating the bottom of the vehicle.

Waxes and polishes are used to help protect painted and plated surfaces from the weather. Different types of paint may require the use of different types of wax and polish. Some polishes utilize a chemical or abrasive cleaner to help remove the top layer of oxidized (dull) paint on older vehicles. In recent years many non-wax polishes that contain a wide variety of chemicals such as polymers and silicones have been introduced. These non-wax polishes are usually easier to apply and last longer than conventional waxes and polishes.

CONVERSION FACTORS

LENGTH (distance)

Inches (in)	X	25.4	= Millimeters (mm)	X	0.0394 = Inches (in)
Feet (ft)	X	0.305	= Meters (m)	X	3.281 = Feet (ft)
Miles	X	1.609	= Kilometers (km)	X	0.621 = Miles

VOLUME (capacity)

Cubic inches (cu in; in³)	X	16.387	= Cubic centimeters (cc; cm³)	X	0.061 = Cubic inches (cu in; in³)
Imperial pints (Imp pt)	X	0.568	= Liters (l)	X	1.76 = Imperial pints (Imp pt)
Imperial quarts (Imp qt)	X	1.137	= Liters (l)	X	0.88 = Imperial quarts (Imp qt)
Imperial quarts (Imp qt)	X	1.201	= US quarts (US qt)	X	0.833 = Imperial quarts (Imp qt)
US quarts (US qt)	X	0.946	= Liters (l)	X	1.057 = US quarts (US qt)
Imperial gallons (Imp gal)	X	4.546	= Liters (l)	X	0.22 = Imperial gallons (Imp gal)
Imperial gallons (Imp gal)	X	1.201	= US gallons (US gal)	X	0.833 = Imperial gallons (Imp gal)
US gallons (US gal)	X	3.785	= Liters (l)	X	0.264 = US gallons (US gal)

MASS (weight)

Ounces (oz)	X	28.35	= Grams (g)	X	0.035 = Ounces (oz)
Pounds (lb)	X	0.454	= Kilograms (kg)	X	2.205 = Pounds (lb)

FORCE

Ounces-force (ozf; oz)	X	0.278	= Newtons (N)	X	3.6 = Ounces-force (ozf; oz)
Pounds-force (lbf; lb)	X	4.448	= Newtons (N)	X	0.225 = Pounds-force (lbf; lb)
Newtons (N)	X	0.1	= Kilograms-force (kgf; kg)	X	9.81 = Newtons (N)

PRESSURE

Pounds-force per square inch (psi; lbf/in²; lb/in²)	X	0.070	= Kilograms-force per square centimeter (kgf/cm²; kg/cm²)	X	14.223 = Pounds-force per square inch (psi; lbf/in²; lb/in²)
Pounds-force per square inch (psi; lbf/in²; lb/in²)	X	0.068	= Atmospheres (atm)	X	14.696 = Pounds-force per square inch (psi; lbf/in²; lb/in²)
Pounds-force per square inch (psi; lbf/in²; lb/in²)	X	0.069	= Bars	X	14.5 = Pounds-force per square inch (psi; lbf/in²; lb/in²)
Pounds-force per square inch (psi; lbf/in²; lb/in²)	X	6.895	= Kilopascals (kPa)	X	0.145 = Pounds-force per square inch (psi; lbf/in²; lb/in²)
Kilopascals (kPa)	X	0.01	= Kilograms-force per square centimeter (kgf/cm²; kg/cm²)	X	98.1 = Kilopascals (kPa)

TORQUE (moment of force)

Pounds-force inches (lbf in; lb in)	X	1.152	= Kilograms-force centimeter (kgf cm; kg cm)	X	0.868 = Pounds-force inches (lbf in; lb in)
Pounds-force inches (lbf in; lb in)	X	0.113	= Newton meters (Nm)	X	8.85 = Pounds-force inches (lbf in; lb in)
Pounds-force inches (lbf in; lb in)	X	0.083	= Pounds-force feet (lbf ft; lb ft)	X	12 = Pounds-force inches (lbf in; lb in)
Pounds-force feet (lbf ft; lb ft)	X	0.138	= Kilograms-force meters (kgf m; kg m)	X	7.233 = Pounds-force feet (lbf ft; lb ft)
Pounds-force feet (lbf ft; lb ft)	X	1.356	= Newton meters (Nm)	X	0.738 = Pounds-force feet (lbf ft; lb ft)
Newton meters (Nm)	X	0.102	= Kilograms-force meters (kgf m; kg m)	X	9.804 = Newton meters (Nm)

VACUUM

Inches mercury (in. Hg)	X	3.377	= Kilopascals (kPa)	X	0.2961 = Inches mercury
Inches mercury (in. Hg)	X	25.4	= Millimeters mercury (mm Hg)	X	0.0394 = Inches mercury

POWER

Horsepower (hp)	X	745.7	= Watts (W)	X	0.0013 = Horsepower (hp)

VELOCITY (speed)

Miles per hour (miles/hr; mph)	X	1.609	= Kilometers per hour (km/hr; kph)	X	0.621 = Miles per hour (miles/hr; mph)

FUEL CONSUMPTION *

Miles per gallon, Imperial (mpg)	X	0.354	= Kilometers per liter (km/l)	X	2.825 = Miles per gallon, Imperial (mpg)
Miles per gallon, US (mpg)	X	0.425	= Kilometers per liter (km/l)	X	2.352 = Miles per gallon, US (mpg)

TEMPERATURE

Degrees Fahrenheit = (°C x 1.8) + 32   Degrees Celsius (Degrees Centigrade; °C) = (°F - 32) x 0.56

*It is common practice to convert from miles per gallon (mpg) to liters/100 kilometers (l/100km), where mpg (Imperial) x l/100 km = 282 and mpg (US) x l/100 km = 235

FRACTION/DECIMAL/MILLIMETER EQUIVALENTS

DECIMALS TO MILLIMETERS

Decimal	mm	Decimal	mm
0.001	0.0254	0.500	12.7000
0.002	0.0508	0.510	12.9540
0.003	0.0762	0.520	13.2080
0.004	0.1016	0.530	13.4620
0.005	0.1270	0.540	13.7160
0.006	0.1524	0.550	13.9700
0.007	0.1778	0.560	14.2240
0.008	0.2032	0.570	14.4780
0.009	0.2286	0.580	14.7320
		0.590	14.9860
0.010	0.2540		
0.020	0.5080		
0.030	0.7620		
0.040	1.0160	0.600	15.2400
0.050	1.2700	0.610	15.4940
0.060	1.5240	0.620	15.7480
0.070	1.7780	0.630	16.0020
0.080	2.0320	0.640	16.2560
0.090	2.2860	0.650	16.5100
		0.660	16.7640
0.100	2.5400	0.670	17.0180
0.110	2.7940	0.680	17.2720
0.120	3.0480	0.690	17.5260
0.130	3.3020		
0.140	3.5560		
0.150	3.8100		
0.160	4.0640	0.700	17.7800
0.170	4.3180	0.710	18.0340
0.180	4.5720	0.720	18.2880
0.190	4.8260	0.730	18.5420
		0.740	18.7960
0.200	5.0800	0.750	19.0500
0.210	5.3340	0.760	19.3040
0.220	5.5880	0.770	19.5580
0.230	5.8420	0.780	19.8120
0.240	6.0960	0.790	20.0660
0.250	6.3500		
0.260	6.6040		
0.270	6.8580	0.800	20.3200
0.280	7.1120	0.810	20.5740
0.290	7.3660	0.820	21.8280
		0.830	21.0820
0.300	7.6200	0.840	21.3360
0.310	7.8740	0.850	21.5900
0.320	8.1280	0.860	21.8440
0.330	8.3820	0.870	22.0980
0.340	8.6360	0.880	22.3520
0.350	8.9000	0.890	22.6060
0.360	9.1440		
0.370	9.3980		
0.380	9.6520		
0.390	9.9060	0.900	22.8600
0.400	10.1600	0.910	23.1140
0.410	10.4140	0.920	23.3680
0.420	10.6680	0.930	23.6220
0.430	10.9220	0.940	23.8760
0.440	11.1760	0.950	24.1300
0.450	11.4300	0.960	24.3840
0.460	11.6840	0.970	24.6380
0.470	11.9380	0.980	24.8920
0.480	12.1920	0.990	25.1460
0.490	12.4460	1.000	25.4000

FRACTIONS TO DECIMALS TO MILLIMETERS

Fraction	Decimal	mm	Fraction	Decimal	mm
1/64	0.0156	0.3969	33/64	0.5156	13.0969
1/32	0.0312	0.7938	17/32	0.5312	13.4938
3/64	0.0469	1.1906	35/64	0.5469	13.8906
1/16	0.0625	1.5875	9/16	0.5625	14.2875
5/64	0.0781	1.9844	37/64	0.5781	14.6844
3/32	0.0938	2.3812	19/32	0.5938	15.0812
7/64	0.1094	2.7781	39/64	0.6094	15.4781
1/8	0.1250	3.1750	5/8	0.6250	15.8750
9/64	0.1406	3.5719	41/64	0.6406	16.2719
5/32	0.1562	3.9688	21/32	0.6562	16.6688
11/64	0.1719	4.3656	43/64	0.6719	17.0656
3/16	0.1875	4.7625	11/16	0.6875	17.4625
13/64	0.2031	5.1594	45/64	0.7031	17.8594
7/32	0.2188	5.5562	23/32	0.7188	18.2562
15/64	0.2344	5.9531	47/64	0.7344	18.6531
1/4	0.2500	6.3500	3/4	0.7500	19.0500
17/64	0.2656	6.7469	49/64	0.7656	19.4469
9/32	0.2812	7.1438	25/32	0.7812	19.8438
19/64	0.2969	7.5406	51/64	0.7969	20.2406
5/16	0.3125	7.9375	13/16	0.8125	20.6375
21/64	0.3281	8.3344	53/64	0.8281	21.0344
11/32	0.3438	8.7312	27/32	0.8438	21.4312
23/64	0.3594	9.1281	55/64	0.8594	21.8281
3/8	0.3750	9.5250	7/8	0.8750	22.2250
25/64	0.3906	9.9219	57/64	0.8906	22.6219
13/32	0.4062	10.3188	29/32	0.9062	23.0188
27/64	0.4219	10.7156	59/64	0.9219	23.4156
7/16	0.4375	11.1125	15/16	0.9375	23.8125
29/64	0.4531	11.5094	61/64	0.9531	24.2094
15/32	0.4688	11.9062	31/32	0.9688	24.6062
31/64	0.4844	12.3031	63/64	0.9844	25.0031
1/2	0.5000	12.7000	1	1.0000	25.4000

Safety first!

Regardless of how enthusiastic you may be about getting on with the job at hand, take the time to ensure that your safety is not jeopardized. A moment's lack of attention can result in an accident, as can failure to observe certain simple safety precautions. The possibility of an accident will always exist, and the following points should not be considered a comprehensive list of all dangers. Rather, they are intended to make you aware of the risks and to encourage a safety conscious approach to all work you carry out on your vehicle.

ESSENTIAL DOS AND DON'TS

DON'T rely on a jack when working under the vehicle. Always use approved jackstands to support the weight of the vehicle and place them under the recommended lift or support points.

DON'T attempt to loosen extremely tight fasteners (i.e. wheel lug nuts) while the vehicle is on a jack - it may fall.

DON'T start the engine without first making sure that the transmission is in Neutral (or Park where applicable) and the parking brake is set.

DON'T remove the radiator cap from a hot cooling system - let it cool or cover it with a cloth and release the pressure gradually.

DON'T attempt to drain the engine oil until you are sure it has cooled to the point that it will not burn you.

DON'T touch any part of the engine or exhaust system until it has cooled sufficiently to avoid burns.

DON'T siphon toxic liquids such as gasoline, antifreeze and brake fluid by mouth, or allow them to remain on your skin.

DON'T inhale brake lining dust - it is potentially hazardous (see *Asbestos* below).

DON'T allow spilled oil or grease to remain on the floor - wipe it up before someone slips on it.

DON'T use loose fitting wrenches or other tools which may slip and cause injury.

DON'T push on wrenches when loosening or tightening nuts or bolts. Always try to pull the wrench toward you. If the situation calls for pushing the wrench away, push with an open hand to avoid scraped knuckles if the wrench should slip.

DON'T attempt to lift a heavy component alone - get someone to help you.

DON'T rush or take unsafe shortcuts to finish a job.

DON'T allow children or animals in or around the vehicle while you are working on it.

DO wear eye protection when using power tools such as a drill, sander, bench grinder, etc. and when working under a vehicle.

DO keep loose clothing and long hair well out of the way of moving parts.

DO make sure that any hoist used has a safe working load rating adequate for the job.

DO get someone to check on you periodically when working alone on a vehicle.

DO carry out work in a logical sequence and make sure that everything is correctly assembled and tightened.

DO keep chemicals and fluids tightly capped and out of the reach of children and pets.

DO remember that your vehicle's safety affects that of yourself and others. If in doubt on any point, get professional advice.

ASBESTOS

Certain friction, insulating, sealing, and other products - such as brake linings, brake bands, clutch linings, torque converters, gaskets, etc. - may contain asbestos. Extreme care must be taken to avoid inhalation of dust from such products, since it is hazardous to health. If in doubt, assume that they do contain asbestos.

FIRE

Remember at all times that gasoline is highly flammable. Never smoke or have any kind of open flame around when working on a vehicle. But the risk does not end there. A spark caused by an electrical short circuit, by two metal surfaces contacting each other, or even by static electricity built up in your body under certain conditions, can ignite gasoline vapors, which in a confined space are highly explosive. Do not, under any circumstances, use gasoline for cleaning parts. Use an approved safety solvent.

Always disconnect the battery ground (-) cable at the battery before working on any part of the fuel system or electrical system. Never risk spilling fuel on a hot engine or exhaust component. It is strongly recommended that a fire extinguisher suitable for use on fuel and electrical fires be kept handy in the garage or workshop at all times. Never try to extinguish a fuel or electrical fire with water.

FUMES

Certain fumes are highly toxic and can quickly cause unconsciousness and even death if inhaled to any extent. Gasoline vapor falls into this category, as do the vapors from some cleaning solvents. Any draining or pouring of such volatile fluids should be done in a well ventilated area.

When using cleaning fluids and solvents, read the instructions on the container carefully. Never use materials from unmarked containers.

Never run the engine in an enclosed space, such as a garage. Exhaust fumes contain carbon monoxide, which is extremely poisonous. If you need to run the engine, always do so in the open air, or at least have the rear of the vehicle outside the work area.

If you are fortunate enough to have the use of an inspection pit, never drain or pour gasoline and never run the engine while the vehicle is over the pit. The fumes, being heavier than air, will concentrate in the pit with possibly lethal results.

THE BATTERY

Never create a spark or allow a bare light bulb near a battery. They normally give off a certain amount of hydrogen gas, which is highly explosive.

Always disconnect the battery ground (-) cable at the battery before working on the fuel or electrical systems.

If possible, loosen the filler caps or cover when charging the battery from an external source (this does not apply to sealed or maintenance-free batteries). Do not charge at an excessive rate or the battery may burst.

Take care when adding water to a non maintenance-free battery and when carrying a battery. The electrolyte, even when diluted, is very corrosive and should not be allowed to contact clothing or skin.

Always wear eye protection when cleaning the battery to prevent the caustic deposits from entering your eyes.

HOUSEHOLD CURRENT

When using an electric power tool, inspection light, etc., which operates on household current, always make sure that the tool is correctly connected to its plug and that, where necessary, it is properly grounded. Do not use such items in damp conditions and, again, do not create a spark or apply excessive heat in the vicinity of fuel or fuel vapor.

SECONDARY IGNITION SYSTEM VOLTAGE

A severe electric shock can result from touching certain parts of the ignition system (such as the spark plug wires) when the engine is running or being cranked, particularly if components are damp or the insulation is defective. In the case of an electronic ignition system, the secondary system voltage is much higher and could prove fatal.

Troubleshooting

CONTENTS

Hybrid system

※※ WARNING:

Due to the complexity of the hybrid drive system and the danger of working with its associated high-voltage circuits, all troubleshooting and repair procedures related to hybrid system problems must be left to a technician trained in hybrid vehicle repair. When performing any repair procedure near the high-voltage battery, the inverter/converter or any orange-colored wiring harnesses, the safety plug must be removed and special insulating gloves must be worn (see Chapter 5, Section 2).

This section provides an easy reference guide to the more common problems which may occur during the operation of your vehicle. These problems and their possible causes are grouped under headings denoting various components or systems, such as Engine, Cooling system, etc. They also refer you to the chapter and/or section which deals with the problem.

Remember that successful troubleshooting is not a mysterious art practiced only by professional mechanics. It is simply the result of the right knowledge combined with an intelligent, systematic approach to the problem. Always work by a process of elimination, starting with the simplest solution and working through to the most complex - and

never overlook the obvious. Anyone can run the gas tank dry or leave the lights on overnight, so don't assume that you are exempt from such oversights.

Finally, always establish a clear idea of why a problem has occurred and take steps to ensure that it doesn't happen again. If the electrical system fails because of a poor connection, check the other connections in the system to make sure that they don't fail as well. If a particular fuse continues to blow, find out why - don't just replace one fuse after another. Remember, failure of a small component can often be indicative of potential failure or incorrect functioning of a more important component or system.

ENGINE

1 Engine hard to start

1 Fuel tank empty.
2 Air filter clogged (Chapter 1).
3 Corroded battery connections, especially ground (Chapter 1).
4 Fuel not reaching fuel rail (Chapter 4).
5 Ignition components damp or damaged (Chapter 6).
6 Worn, faulty or incorrectly gapped spark plugs (Chapter 1).
7 Broken, loose or disconnected wires at the ignition coils (Chapter 6).
8 Faulty camshaft or crankshaft position sensor (Chapter 6).

2 Oil puddle under engine

1 Oil pan gasket and/or oil pan drain bolt washer leaking (Chapter 2).
2 Oil pressure sending unit leaking (Chapter 2).
3 Valve cover leaking (Chapter 2).
4 Engine oil seals leaking (Chapter 2).
5 Timing chain cover leaking (Chapter 2).

3 Engine lopes while idling or idles erratically

1 Vacuum leakage (Chapters 2 and 4).
2 Air filter clogged (Chapter 1).
3 Fuel pump not delivering sufficient fuel to the fuel injection system (Chapter 4).
4 Leaking head gasket (Chapter 2).
5 Timing chain and/or sprockets worn (Chapter 2).
6 Camshaft worn (Chapter 2).

4 Engine misses at idle speed

1 Spark plugs worn or not gapped properly (Chapter 1).
2 Faulty ignition coil (Chapter 5).
3 Vacuum leaks (Chapter 1).
4 Fault in engine management system (Chapter 6).
5 Uneven or low compression (Chapter 2B).

5 Engine misses throughout driving speed range

1 Fuel filter clogged and/or impurities in the fuel system (Chapter 1).
2 Low fuel output at the injector(s) (Chapter 4).
3 Faulty or incorrectly gapped spark plugs (Chapter 1).
4 Fault in engine management system (Chapter 6).
5 Faulty emission system components (Chapter 6).
6 Low or uneven cylinder compression pressures (Chapter 2B).
7 Faulty ignition coil (Chapter 5)
8 Vacuum leak in fuel injection system, intake manifold/plenum, air control valve or vacuum hoses (Chapter 4).

6 Engine surges

1 Intake air leak (Chapter 4).
2 Fuel pump faulty (Chapter 4).

3 Loose fuel injector wire harness connectors (Chapter 4).
4 Defective ECM or information sensor (Chapter 6).

7 Engine stalls

1 Fuel filter clogged and/or water and impurities in the fuel system (Chapter 4).
2 Ignition components damp or damaged (Chapter 5).
3 Faulty emissions system components (Chapter 6).
4 Faulty or incorrectly gapped spark plugs (Chapter 1).
5 Vacuum leak in the fuel injection system, intake manifold or vacuum hoses (Chapters 2 and 4).

8 Engine lacks power

1 Fault in engine management system (Chapter 6).
2 Faulty or incorrectly gapped spark plugs (Chapter 1).
3 Fuel injection system malfunction (Chapter 4).
4 Faulty coil(s) (Chapter 5).
5 Brakes binding (Chapter 9).
6 Fuel filter clogged and/or impurities in the fuel system (Chapter 4).
7 Low or uneven cylinder compression pressures (Chapter 2).
8 Obstructed exhaust system (Chapter 4).

9 Engine backfires

1 Emission control system not functioning properly (Chapter 6).
2 Fault in engine management system (Chapter 6).
3 Faulty secondary ignition system (cracked spark plug insulator, faulty ignition coil) (Chapters 1 and 5).
4 Fuel injection system malfunction (Chapter 4).
5 Vacuum leak at fuel injector(s), intake manifold, air control valve or vacuum hoses (Chapters 2 and 4).
6 Valve clearances incorrectly set (Chapter 2A) and/or valves sticking.

10 Pinging or knocking engine sounds during acceleration or uphill

1 Incorrect grade of fuel.
2 Fault in engine management system (Chapter 6).
3 Fuel injection system faulty (Chapter 4).
4 Improper or damaged spark plugs (Chapter 1).
5 Vacuum leak (Chapters 2 and 4).
6 Defective knock sensor (Chapter 6).

11 Engine runs with oil pressure light on

1 Low oil level (Chapter 1).
2 Idle rpm below specification (Chapter 4).
3 Short in wiring circuit (Chapter 12).
4 Faulty oil pressure sender (Chapter 2).
5 Worn engine bearings and/or oil pump (Chapter 2).

12 Engine diesels (continues to run) after switching off

1 Excessive engine operating temperature (Chapter 3).
2 Fault in engine management system (Chapter 6).

ENGINE ELECTRICAL SYSTEM

13   12-volt (auxiliary) battery will not hold a charge

1   Battery electrolyte level low (Chapter 1).
2   Battery terminals loose or corroded (Chapter 1).
3   Loose, broken or faulty wiring in the charging circuit (Chapter 6).
4   Short in vehicle wiring (Chapter 12).
5   Internally defective battery (Chapters 1 and 6).

FUEL SYSTEM

14   Excessive fuel consumption

1   Dirty or clogged air filter element (Chapter 1).
2   Fault in engine management system (Chapter 6).
3   Emissions systems not functioning properly (Chapter 6).
4   Fuel injection system not functioning properly (Chapter 4).
5   Low tire pressure or incorrect tire size (Chapter 1).
6   Hybrid drive system problem.

15   Fuel leakage and/or fuel odor

1   Leaking fuel feed line (Chapters 1 and 4).
2   Tank overfilled.
3   Evaporative emissions control system problem (Chapter 6).
4   Fuel injection system not functioning properly (Chapter 4).

COOLING SYSTEM

16   Overheating

1   Insufficient coolant in system (Chapter 1).
2   Water pump defective (Chapter 3).
3   Radiator core blocked or grille restricted (Chapter 3).
4   Thermostat faulty (Chapter 3).
5   Electric coolant fan blades broken or cracked (Chapter 3).
6   Radiator cap not maintaining proper pressure (Chapter 3).
7   Fault in engine management system (Chapter 6).

17   Overcooling

1   Faulty thermostat (Chapter 3).
2   Inaccurate temperature gauge sending unit (Chapter 3)

18   External coolant leakage

1   Deteriorated/damaged hoses; loose clamps (Chapters 1 and 3).
2   Water pump defective (Chapter 3).
3   Leakage from radiator core or coolant reservoir bottle (Chapter 3).
4   Engine drain or water jacket core plugs leaking (Chapter 2).

19   Internal coolant leakage

1   Leaking cylinder head gasket (Chapter 2).
2   Cracked cylinder bore or cylinder head (Chapter 2).

20   Coolant loss

1   Too much coolant in system (Chapter 1).
2   Coolant boiling away because of overheating (Chapter 3).
3   Internal or external leakage (Chapter 3).
4   Faulty radiator cap (Chapter 3).

21   Poor coolant circulation

1   Inoperative water pump (Chapter 3).
2   Restriction in cooling system (Chapters 1 and 3).
3   Drivebelt or tensioner defective (Chapter 1).
4   Thermostat sticking (Chapter 3).

TRANSAXLE

➡Note: It is difficult for the home mechanic to properly diagnose and service this component. For problems other than the following, the vehicle should be taken to a dealer or transaxle specialist.

22   Fluid leakage

1   Fluid leaks should not be confused with engine oil, which can easily be blown onto the transaxle/power-split device by air flow.
2   To pinpoint a leak, first remove all built-up dirt and grime from the housing with degreasing agents and/or steam cleaning. Then drive the vehicle at low speeds so air flow will not blow the leak far from its source. Raise the vehicle and determine where the leak is coming from.

DRIVEAXLES

23   Clicking noise in turns

Worn or damaged outboard CV joint (Chapter 8).

24   Shudder or vibration during acceleration

1   Excessive toe-in (Chapter 10).
2   Incorrect spring heights (Chapter 10).
3   Worn or damaged inboard or outboard CV joints (Chapter 8).
4   Sticking inboard CV joint assembly (Chapter 8).

25   Vibration at highway speeds

1   Out-of-balance front wheels and/or tires.
2   Out-of-round front tires.
3   Worn CV joint(s) (Chapter 8).

Brakes

➡Note: Before assuming that a brake problem exists, make sure that:

a) The tires are in good condition and properly inflated (Chapter 1).
b) The front end alignment is correct (Chapter 10).
c) The vehicle is not loaded with weight in an unequal manner.

26 Vehicle pulls to one side during braking

1 Incorrect tire pressures (Chapter 1).
2 Front end out of alignment (have the front end aligned).
3 Front or rear tires not matched to one another.
4 Restricted brake lines or hoses (Chapter 9).
5 Malfunctioning drum brake or caliper assembly (Chapter 9).
6 Loose suspension parts (Chapter 10).
7 Excessive wear of brake shoe or pad material or disc/drum on one side.

27 Noise (high-pitched squeal or grating sound when the brakes are applied)

1 Disc brake pads worn out. Replace pads with new ones immediately (Chapter 9).
2 Drum brake shoes worn out. Replace shoes with new ones immediately (Chapter 9).

28 Brake roughness or chatter (pedal pulsates)

1 Excessive disc lateral runout (Chapter 9).
2 Uneven pad wear (Chapter 9).
3 Brake drum out-of-round (Chapter 9).

29 Excessive brake pedal effort required to stop vehicle

1 Malfunctioning power brake system (Chapter 9).
2 Partial system failure (Chapter 9).
3 Excessively worn pads or shoes (Chapter 9).
4 Piston in caliper or wheel cylinder stuck or sluggish (Chapter 9).
5 Brake pads or shoes contaminated with oil or grease (Chapter 9).
6 New pads or shoes installed and not yet seated. It will take a while for the new material to seat against the disc or drum.

30 Excessive brake pedal travel

1 Partial brake system failure (Chapter 9).
2 Insufficient fluid in master cylinder (Chapters 1 and 9).
3 Air trapped in system (Chapters 1 and 9).

31 Dragging brakes

1 Incorrect adjustment of brake light switch (Chapter 9).
2 Master cylinder pistons not returning correctly (Chapter 9).
3 Restricted brakes lines or hoses (Chapters 1 and 9).
4 Incorrect parking brake adjustment (Chapter 9).

32 Grabbing or uneven braking action

1 Malfunction of proportioning valve (Chapter 9).
2 Malfunction of power brake system (Chapter 9).

33 Brake pedal feels spongy when depressed

1 Air in hydraulic lines (Chapter 9).
2 Master cylinder defective (Chapter 9).

34 Brake pedal travels to the floor with little resistance

1 Little or no fluid in the master cylinder reservoir caused by leaking caliper or wheel cylinder piston(s) (Chapter 9).
2 Loose or damaged brake lines (Chapter 9).

35 Parking brake does not hold

Parking brake linkage improperly adjusted (Chapter 9).

SUSPENSION AND STEERING SYSTEMS

➡Note: Before attempting to diagnose the suspension and steering systems, perform the following preliminary checks:

a) Tires for wrong pressure and uneven wear.
b) Steering universal joints from the column to the rack and pinion for loose connectors or wear.
c) Front and rear suspension and the rack and pinion assembly for loose or damaged parts.
d) Out-of-round or out-of-balance tires, bent rims and loose and/or rough wheel bearings.

36 Vehicle pulls to one side

1 Mismatched or uneven tires.
2 Broken or sagging springs (Chapter 10).
3 Wheels out of alignment (Chapter 10).
4 Front brake dragging (Chapter 9).

37 Abnormal or excessive tire wear

1 Wheels out of alignment (Chapter 10).
2 Sagging or broken springs (Chapter 10).
3 Tire out of balance (Chapter 10).
4 Worn strut or shock absorber (Chapter 10).
5 Overloaded vehicle.
6 Tires not rotated regularly (Chapter 1).

38 Wheel makes a thumping noise

1 Blister or bump on tire.
2 Improper strut or shock absorber action (Chapter 10).

39 Shimmy, shake or vibration

1 Tire or wheel out-of-balance or out-of-round.
2 Loose or worn wheel (hub) bearings (Chapter 10).
3 Worn tie-rod ends (Chapter 10).
4 Worn balljoints (Chapters 1 and 10).
5 Excessive wheel runout.
6 Blister or bump on tire.
7 Loose wheel lug nuts.

40 Hard steering

1 Lack of lubrication at balljoints, tie-rod ends and rack and pinion assembly (Chapter 10).

2 Front wheels out of alignment (Chapter 10).
3 Low tire pressure(s) (Chapter 1).

41 Poor returnability of steering to center

1 Lack of lubrication at balljoints and tie-rod ends (Chapter 10).
2 Binding in balljoints (Chapter 10).
3 Binding in steering column (Chapter 10).
4 Steering gear defective (Chapter 10).
5 Front wheels out of alignment (Chapter 10).

42 Abnormal noise at the front end

1 Lack of lubrication at balljoints and tie-rod ends (Chapter 10).
2 Damaged strut mounting (Chapter 10).
3 Worn control arm bushings or tie-rod ends (Chapter 10).
4 Loose stabilizer bar (Chapter 10).
5 Loose wheel nuts.
6 Loose suspension bolts (Chapter 10)

43 Wander or poor steering stability

1 Mismatched or uneven tires.
2 Lack of lubrication at balljoints and tie-rod ends (Chapter 10).
3 Worn strut assemblies (Chapter 10).
4 Loose stabilizer bar (Chapter 10).
5 Broken or sagging springs (Chapter 10).
6 Wheels out of alignment (Chapter 10).

44 Erratic steering when braking

1 Wheel bearings worn (Chapter 10).
2 Broken or sagging springs (Chapter 10).
3 Leaking wheel cylinder or caliper (Chapter 9).
4 Warped discs or drums (Chapter 9).

45 Excessive pitching and/or rolling around corners or during braking

1 Loose stabilizer bar (Chapter 10).
2 Worn strut/shock absorber or mounts (Chapter 10).
3 Broken or sagging springs (Chapter 10).
4 Overloaded vehicle.

46 Suspension bottoms

1 Overloaded vehicle.
2 Worn struts or shock absorbers (Chapter 10).
3 Incorrect, broken or sagging springs (Chapter 10).

47 Cupped tires

1 Front wheel or rear wheels out of alignment (Chapter 10).
2 Worn struts or shock absorbers (Chapter 10).
3 Wheel bearings worn (Chapter 10).
4 Excessive tire or wheel runout.
5 Worn balljoints (Chapter 10).

48 Excessive tire wear on outside edge

1 Inflation pressures incorrect (Chapter 1).
2 Excessive speed in turns.
3 Front end alignment incorrect (excessive toe-in or positive camber). Have professionally aligned.
4 Suspension arm bent or twisted (Chapter 10).

49 Excessive tire wear on inside edge

1 Inflation pressures incorrect (Chapter 1).
2 Front end alignment incorrect (toe-out or negative camber). Have professionally aligned.
3 Loose or damaged steering components (Chapter 10).

50 Tire tread worn in one place

1 Tires out of balance.
2 Damaged wheel. Inspect and replace if necessary.
3 Defective tire (Chapter 1).

51 Excessive play or looseness in steering system

1 Wheel bearing(s) worn (Chapter 10).
2 Tie-rod end loose (Chapter 10).
3 Steering gear loose or worn (Chapter 10).
4 Worn or loose steering intermediate shaft (Chapter 10).

52 Rattling or clicking noise in steering gear

1 Steering gear loose or defective (Chapter 10).

Notes

Section

Reference to other Chapters

CHECK ENGINE light on - See Chapter 6

1

TUNE-UP
AND ROUTINE
MAINTENANCE

1 Maintenance schedule

The maintenance intervals in this manual are provided with the assumption that you, not the dealer, will be doing the work. These are the minimum maintenance intervals recommended by the factory for vehicles that are driven daily. If you wish to keep your vehicle in peak condition at all times, you may wish to perform some of these procedures even more often. Because frequent maintenance enhances the efficiency, performance and resale value of your car, we encourage you to do so. If you drive in dusty areas, tow a trailer, idle or drive at low speeds for extended periods or drive for short distances (less than four miles) in below freezing temperatures, shorter intervals are also recommended.

When your vehicle is new, it should be serviced by a factory authorized dealer service department to protect the factory warranty. In many cases, the initial maintenance check is done at no cost to the owner.

EVERY 250 MILES OR WEEKLY, WHICHEVER COMES FIRST

Check the engine oil level (Section 4)
Check the engine/inverter coolant level (Section 4)
Check the windshield washer fluid level (Section 4)
Check the brake fluid level (Section 4)
Check the power steering fluid level (Section 4)
Check the transaxle fluid level (Section 4)
Check the tires and tire pressures (Section 5)

EVERY 5000 MILES OR 6 MONTHS, WHICHEVER COMES FIRST

All items listed above plus:
Change the engine oil and oil filter (Section 6)

EVERY 7500 MILES OR 6 MONTHS, WHICHEVER COMES FIRST

Inspect (and replace, if necessary) the windshield wiper blades (Section 7)
Check and service the auxiliary battery (Section 8)
Check/adjust the engine drivebelt (Section 9)
Inspect (and replace if, necessary) all underhood hoses (Section 10)
Check the cooling system (Section 11)
Rotate the tires (Section 12)
Check the seat belts (Section 13)

EVERY 15,000 MILES OR 12 MONTHS, WHICHEVER COMES FIRST

All items listed above plus:
Inspect the brake system (Section 14)*
Inspect the fuel system (Section 15)
Inspect the suspension, steering and driveaxle components (Section 16)*

EVERY 30,000 MILES OR 24 MONTHS, WHICHEVER COMES FIRST

All items listed above plus:
Replace the air filter (Section 17)*
Replace the cabin air filter (Section 18)*
Inspect the evaporative emissions control system (Section 19)
Inspect the exhaust system (Section 20)
Check and replace if necessary the PCV valve (Section 21)

EVERY 50,000 MILES OR 60 MONTHS, WHICHEVER COMES FIRST

All items listed above plus:
Service the cooling system (drain, flush and refill) (Section 22)

EVERY 100,000 MILES OR 60 MONTHS, WHICHEVER COMES FIRST

All items listed above plus:
Replace the spark plugs (Section 23)
This item is affected by "severe" operating conditions as described below. If your vehicle is operated under "severe" conditions, perform all maintenance indicated with an asterisk (*) at 3000 mile/3 month intervals. Severe conditions are indicated if you mainly operate your vehicle under one or more of the following conditions:
Operating in dusty areas
Towing a trailer
Idling for extended periods and/or low speed operation
Operating when outside temperatures remain below freezing and when most trips are less than 4 miles
** If operated under one or more of the following conditions, change the manual or automatic transaxle fluid and differential lubricant every 15,000 miles:
In heavy city traffic where the outside temperature regularly reaches 90-degrees F (32-degrees C) or higher
In hilly or mountainous terrain
Frequent trailer pulling

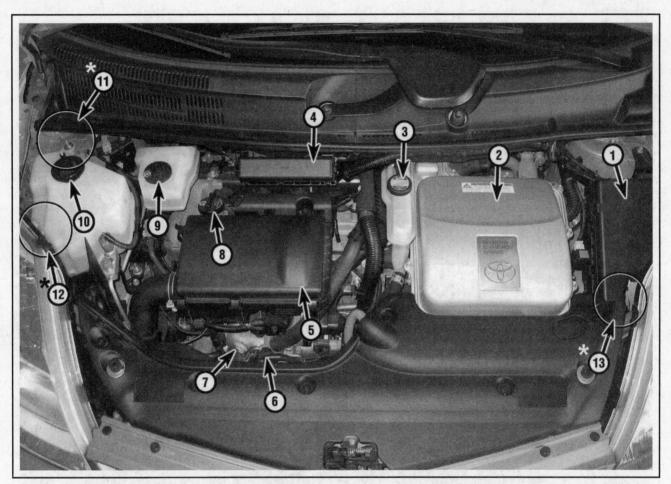

Engine compartment layout (2004 and later model shown. Where different, locations of 2003 and earlier model components are identified with an asterisk)

1   Main relay/fuse center
2   Inverter/converter
3   Coolant reservoir for transaxle and inverter/converter
4   Relay center
5   Air filter housing
6   Engine coolant reservoir
7   Engine oil dipstick
8   Engine oil fill cap
9   Brake fluid reservoir
10   Windshield washer fluid reservoir
*11   Fuse/relay center (2003 and earlier)
*12   Engine coolant reservoir (2003 and earlier)
*13   Windshield washer fluid reservoir (2003 and earlier)

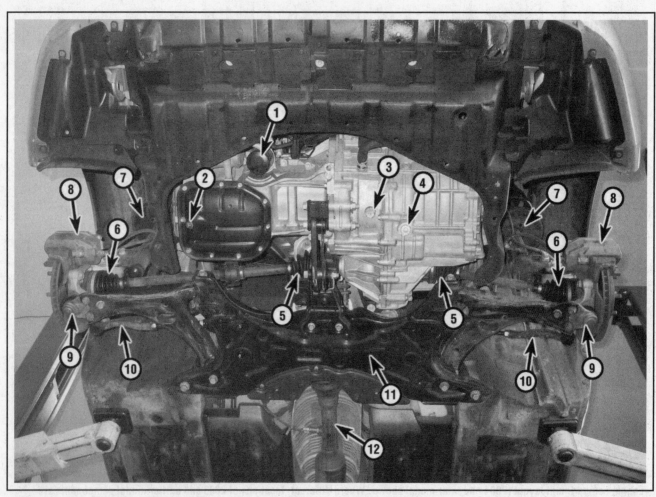

Typical front underside components (2004 and later models shown, earlier models similar)

1	Engine oil filter	5	Inner driveaxle boots	9	Balljoint
2	Engine oil drain plug	6	Outer driveaxle boots	10	Tie-rod ends
3	Transaxle coolant drain plug	7	Strut/coil spring assembly	11	Crossmember
4	Transaxle lubricant drain plug	8	Brake caliper	12	Exhaust pipe

Typical rear underside components (2004 and later models shown, earlier models similar)

1	Brake drums	3	Spring/shock absorber assemblies	5	Exhaust pipe
2	Muffler	4	Fuel tank	6	Parking brake cables

2 Introduction

This Chapter is designed to help the home mechanic maintain the Toyota Prius for peak performance, economy, safety and long life.

Included is a master maintenance schedule, followed by sections dealing specifically with each item on the schedule. Visual checks, adjustments, component replacement and other helpful items are included. Refer to the accompanying illustrations of the engine compartment and the underside of the vehicle for the location of various components.

Servicing your Prius in accordance with the mileage/time maintenance schedule and the following Sections will provide it with a planned maintenance program that should result in a long and reliable service life. This is a comprehensive plan, so maintaining some items but not others at the specified service intervals will not produce the same results.

As you service your Prius, you will discover that many of the procedures can - and should - be grouped together because of the nature of the particular procedure you're performing or because of the close proximity of two otherwise unrelated components to one another.

For example, if the vehicle is raised for any reason, you should inspect the exhaust, suspension, steering and fuel systems while you're under the vehicle. When you're rotating the tires, it makes good sense to check the brakes and wheel bearings since the wheels are already removed.

Finally, let's suppose you have to borrow or rent a torque wrench. Even if you only need to tighten the spark plugs, you might as well check the torque of as many critical fasteners as time allows.

The first step of this maintenance program is to prepare yourself before the actual work begins. Read through all Sections pertinent to the procedures you're planning to do, then make a list of and gather together all the parts and tools you will need to do the job. If it looks as if you might run into problems during a particular segment of some procedure, seek advice from your local parts counterperson or dealer service department.

✳✳ WARNING:

Make sure power to the hybrid system is turned Off before performing any work on this vehicle. Also, on models equipped with the Smart Key system, place the key in a secure spot at least 20 feet away from the work area.

3 Tune-up general information

The term tune-up is used in this manual to represent a combination of individual operations rather than one specific procedure.

If, from the time the vehicle is new, the routine maintenance schedule is followed closely and frequent checks are made of fluid levels and high wear items, as suggested throughout this manual, the engine will be kept in relatively good running condition and the need for additional work will be minimized.

More likely than not, however, there will be times when the engine is running poorly due to lack of regular maintenance. This is even more likely if a used vehicle, which has not received regular and frequent maintenance checks, is purchased. In such cases, an engine tune-up will be needed outside of the regular routine maintenance intervals.

Normally, the first step in any tune-up or engine diagnosis to help correct a poor running engine would be a cylinder compression check, but with the Prius, this cannot be performed without the use of an expensive proprietary scan tool. However, a leakdown test of the engine's cylinders (see Chapter 2 Part B) can be done, which will give valuable information regarding the overall performance of certain internal components and should be used as a basis for tune-up and repair procedures. If, for instance, a leakdown test indicates serious internal engine wear, a conventional tune-up will not help the running condition of the engine and would be a waste of time and money.

The following series of operations are those most often needed to bring a generally poor running engine back into a proper state of tune.

MINOR TUNE-UP

Check all engine related fluids (Section 4)
Clean, inspect and test the auxiliary battery (Section 8)
Check the drivebelt (Section 9)
Check all underhood hoses (Section 10)
Check the cooling system (Section 11)
Check the air filter (Section 17)

MAJOR TUNE-UP

All items listed under Minor tune-up, plus . . .
Check the fuel system (Section 15)
Replace the air filter (Section 17)
Replace the spark plugs at 100,000 miles (Section 23)

4 Fluid level checks (every 250 miles or weekly)

✳✳ WARNING:

Make sure power to the hybrid system is turned Off before performing any work on this vehicle. Also, on models equipped with the Smart Key system, place the key in a secure spot at least 20 feet away from the work area.

1 Fluids are an essential part of the lubrication, cooling, brake, clutch and other systems. Because these fluids gradually become depleted and/or contaminated during normal operation of the vehicle, they must be periodically replenished. See *Recommended lubricants and fluids and Capacities* at the end of this Chapter before adding fluid to any of the following components.

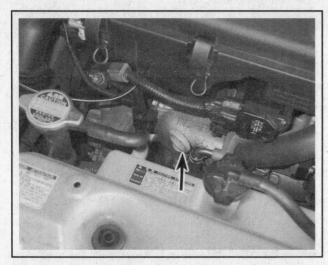

4.2 The engine oil dipstick is located between the engine and the radiator

➡Note: The vehicle must be on level ground before fluid levels can be checked.

ENGINE OIL

▶ **Refer to illustrations 4.2, 4.4 and 4.6**

2   The engine oil level is checked with a dipstick located at the front of the engine (see illustration). The dipstick extends through a metal tube from which it protrudes down into the engine oil pan.

3   The oil level should be checked before the vehicle has been driven, or about 5 minutes after the engine has been shut off. If the oil is checked immediately after driving the vehicle, some of the oil will remain in the upper engine components, producing an inaccurate reading on the dipstick.

4   Pull the dipstick from the tube and wipe all the oil from the end with a clean rag or paper towel. Insert the clean dipstick all the way back into its metal tube and pull it out again. Observe the oil at the end

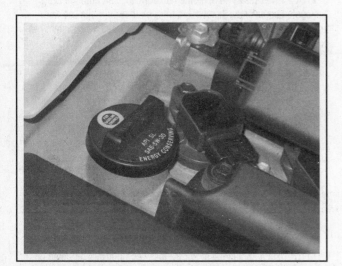

4.6 The oil filler cap is on the valve cover - to prevent dirt from entering the engine, always make sure the area around this opening is clean before unscrewing it

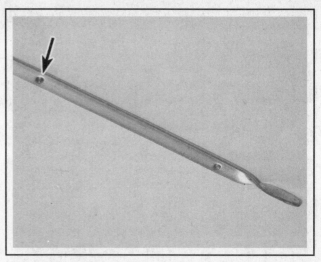

4.4 The oil level should be at or near the F mark on the dipstick - if it isn't, add enough oil to bring it to or near the F mark (it takes one quart to bring it from the L mark to the F mark)

of the dipstick. At its highest point, the level should be between the two dimples (see illustration).

5   It takes one quart of oil to raise the level from the lower dimple to the upper dimple on the dipstick. Do not allow the level to drop below the lower dimple or oil starvation may cause engine damage. Conversely, overfilling the engine (adding oil above the upper dimple) may cause oil fouled spark plugs, oil leaks or oil seal failures.

6   Remove the threaded cap from the valve cover to add oil (see illustration). Use a funnel to prevent spills. After adding the oil, install the filler cap hand tight. Start the engine and look carefully for any small leaks around the oil filter or drain plug. Stop the engine and check the oil level again after it has had sufficient time to drain from the upper block and cylinder head galleys.

7   Checking the oil level is an important preventive maintenance step. A continually dropping oil level indicates oil leakage through damaged seals, from loose connections, or past worn rings or valve guides. If the oil looks milky in color or has water droplets in it, a cylinder head gasket may be blown. The engine should be checked immediately. The condition of the oil should also be checked. Each time you check the oil level, slide your thumb and index finger up the dipstick before wiping off the oil. If you see small dirt or metal particles clinging to the dipstick, the oil should be changed (see Section 6).

ENGINE COOLANT

▶ **Refer to illustration 4.8**

✳✳ WARNING:

Do not allow antifreeze to come in contact with your skin or painted surfaces of the vehicle. Flush contaminated areas immediately with plenty of water. Don't store new coolant or leave old coolant lying around where it's accessible to children or pets - they're attracted by its sweet smell and may drink it. Ingestion of even a small amount of coolant can be fatal! Wipe up garage floor and drip pan spills immediately. Keep antifreeze containers covered and repair cooling system leaks as soon as they're noticed.

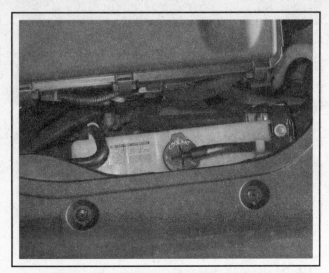

4.8 Make sure the coolant level is between the Full and Low lines - if it's below the Low line, add the specified mixture of antifreeze and water (2004 and later model shown)

8   All vehicles covered by this manual are equipped with a pressurized coolant recovery system. On 2001 through 2003 models the coolant reservoir is located behind the right headlight in the engine compartment. On later models it is located just behind the radiator (see illustration). It is connected by a hose to the radiator. If the coolant heats up during engine operation, coolant can escape through a pressurized filler cap, then through a connecting hose into the reservoir. As the engine cools, the coolant is automatically drawn back into the cooling system to maintain the correct level.

9   The coolant level should be checked regularly. It must be between the Full and Low lines on the tank. The level will vary with the temperature of the engine. When the engine is cold, the coolant level should be at or slightly above the Low mark on the tank. Once the engine has warmed up, the level should be at or near the Full mark. If it isn't, allow the fluid in the tank to cool, then remove the cap from the reservoir and add coolant to bring the level up to the Full line. Use only the coolant listed in this Chapter's Specifications, or its equivalent. Do not use supplemental inhibitor additives. If only a small amount of coolant is required to bring the system up to the proper level, water can be used.

4.14b . . . make sure it's filled to the FULL mark

4.14a There is a separate coolant reservoir for the inverter/ converter and the transaxle, mounted inboard of the inverter/ converter . . .

However, repeated additions of water will dilute the recommended antifreeze and water solution. In order to maintain the proper ratio of antifreeze and water, it is advisable to top up the coolant level with the correct mixture.

10   If the coolant level drops within a short time after replenishment, there may be a leak in the system. Inspect the radiator, hoses, engine coolant filler cap, drain plugs, air bleeder plugs and water pump. If no leak is evident, have the radiator cap pressure tested by your dealer.

❊❊ WARNING:

Never remove the radiator cap or the coolant recovery reservoir cap when the engine is running or has just been shut down, because the cooling system is hot. Escaping steam and scalding liquid could cause serious injury.

11   If it is necessary to open the radiator cap, wait until the system has cooled completely, then wrap a thick cloth around the cap and turn it to the first stop. If any steam escapes, wait until the system has cooled further, then remove the cap.

12   When checking the coolant level, always note its condition. It should be relatively clear. If it is brown or rust colored, the system should be drained, flushed and refilled. Even if the coolant appears to be normal, the corrosion inhibitors wear out with use, so it must be replaced at the specified intervals.

13   Do not allow antifreeze to come in contact with your skin or painted surfaces of the vehicle. Flush contacted areas immediately with plenty of water.

INVERTER/CONVERTER AND TRANSAXLE COOLANT

▸ Refer to illustrations 4.14a and 4.14b

14   There is a coolant reservoir for these components mounted on the inboard side of the inverter/converter (see illustration). This is a coolant system that is separate from the engine cooling system. On 2003 and earlier models it uses a separate radiator; on 2004 and later models

4.16 On 2004 and later models the windshield washer reservoir is next to the brake fluid reservoir - flip up the cap to add fluid

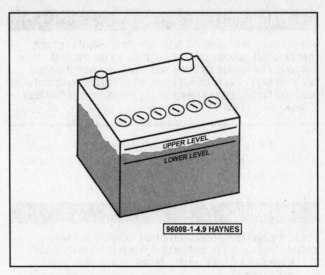

4.18 On non-maintenance-free batteries with a translucent case, the electrolyte level must be kept between the upper and lower lines

it uses a radiator that is mounted directly under and attached to the engine cooling radiator.

15 Follow Steps 9, 12 and 13 to check and service this cooling system.

WINDSHIELD WASHER FLUID

▸ **Refer to illustration 4.16**

16 Fluid for the windshield washer system is stored in a plastic reservoir, which is located on the left front corner of the engine compartment on 2001 through 2003 models. On 2004 and later models it is found at the right rear corner of the engine compartment (see illustration). In milder climates, plain water can be used to top up the reservoir, but the reservoir should be kept no more than two-thirds full to allow for expansion should the water freeze. In colder climates, the use of a specially designed windshield washer fluid, available at your dealer and any auto parts store, will help lower the freezing point of the fluid. Mix

the solution with water in accordance with the manufacturer's directions on the container. Do not use regular antifreeze. It will damage the vehicle's paint.

BATTERY ELECTROLYTE

▸ **Refer to illustration 4.18**

17 On all models the 12-volt auxiliary battery is mounted under floor panels in the luggage compartment. Refer to Chapter 6 for information on how to access it.

18 On models not equipped with a sealed battery, remove the filler/vent caps and check the electrolyte level. It must be above the plates, and up to the bottom of the split ring. Or, if the battery has a translucent case, it must be between the upper and lower levels (see illustration). If the level is low, add distilled water. Install and securely retighten the caps.

※ CAUTION:

Overfilling the cells may cause electrolyte to spill over during periods of heavy charging, causing corrosion or damage.

BRAKE FLUID

▸ **Refer to illustration 4.20**

19 The brake master cylinder reservoir is mounted near the right rear corner of the engine compartment.

20 To check the fluid level, simply look at the MAX and MIN marks on the reservoir (see illustration). The level should be at or near the maximum fill line.

21 If the level is low, wipe the top of the reservoir cover with a clean rag to prevent contamination of the brake or clutch system before lifting the cap.

22 Add only the specified brake fluid to the reservoir (refer to Recommended lubricants and fluids at the front of this Chapter, or to your owner's manual). Mixing different types of brake fluid can damage the system.

4.20 The brake fluid should be kept between the MIN and MAX lines on the reservoir

❊❊ WARNING:

Use caution when filling the reservoir - brake fluid can harm your eyes and damage painted surfaces. Do not use brake fluid that has been opened for more than one year (even if the cap has been on) or has been left open. Brake fluid absorbs moisture from the air. Excess moisture can cause a dangerous loss of braking.

23 While the reservoir cap is removed, inspect the master cylinder reservoir for contamination. If deposits, dirt particles or water droplets are present, the fluid in the brake system should be changed.

❊❊ WARNING:

Due to the special equipment required to safely and completely bleed the brake system, this is a procedure that must be entrusted to a dealer service department or other properly equipped repair shop.

24 After filling the reservoir to the proper level, make sure the cap is properly seated to prevent fluid leakage.

25 The brake fluid in the master cylinder will drop slightly as the brake pads wear down during normal operation. If the master cylinder requires repeated replenishing to keep it at the proper level, this is an indication of leakage in the brake system, which should be corrected immediately. Check all brake lines and connections, along with the calipers, wheel cylinders and hydraulic contro unit (see Chapter 9).

26 If, upon checking the master cylinder fluid level, you discover the reservoir empty or nearly empty, the brake system must be diagnosed immediately (see Chapter 9).

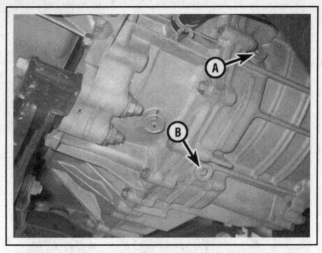

4.28 Transaxle check/fill plug (A) and drain plug (B)

TRANSAXLE FLUID

▶ **Refer to illustration 4.28**

27 Raise the vehicle and support it securely on jackstands. Both ends of the vehicle must be raised because it must be level for this check.

28 Remove the check/fill plug on the front side of the transaxle (see illustration). The fluid level should be within 3/16-inch of the bottom of the hole. If it isn't, add the specified type of fluid with a squeeze bottle or lubricant pump.

29 Reinstall the check/fill plug and tighten it to the torque listed in this Chapter's Specifications.

5 Tire and tire pressure checks (every 250 miles or weekly)

▶ **Refer to illustrations 5.2, 5.3, 5.4a, 5.4b and 5.8**

1 Periodic inspection of the tires may spare you from the inconvenience of being stranded with a flat tire. It can also provide you with vital information regarding possible problems in the steering and suspension systems before major damage occurs.

2 Normal tread wear can be monitored with a simple, inexpensive device known as a tread depth indicator (see illustration). When the tread depth reaches the specified minimum, replace the tire(s).

3 Note any abnormal tread wear (see illustration). Tread pattern irregularities such as cupping, flat spots and more wear on one side than the other are indications of front end alignment and/or balance problems. If any of these conditions are noted, take the vehicle to a tire shop or service station to correct the problem.

4 Look closely for cuts, punctures and embedded nails or tacks. Sometimes a tire will hold its air pressure for a short time or leak down very slowly even after a nail has embedded itself into the tread. If a slow leak persists, check the valve stem core to make sure it is tight (see illustration). Examine the tread for an object that may have embedded itself into the tire or for a "plug" that may have begun to leak (radial tire punctures are repaired with a plug that is installed in a puncture). If a puncture is suspected, it can be easily verified by spraying a solution of soapy water onto the puncture area (see illustration). The soapy solution will bubble if there is a leak. Unless the puncture is inordinately large, a tire shop or gas station can usually repair the punctured tire.

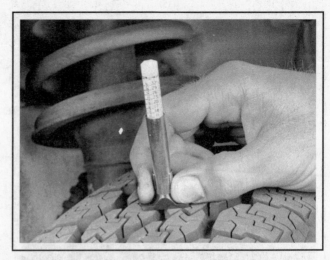

5.2 Use a tire tread depth gauge to monitor the wear - they are available at auto parts stores and service stations and cost very little

UNDERINFLATION

CUPPING

Cupping may be caused by:

- Underinflation and/or mechanical irregularities such as out-of-balance condition of wheel and/or tire, and bent or damaged wheel.
- Loose or worn steering tie-rod or steering idler arm.
- Loose, damaged or worn front suspension parts.

OVERINFLATION

INCORRECT TOE-IN OR EXTREME CAMBER

FEATHERING DUE TO MISALIGNMENT

5.3 This chart will help you determine the condition of your tires, the probable cause(s) of abnormal wear and the corrective action necessary

5   Carefully inspect the inner sidewall of each tire for evidence of brake fluid leakage. If you see any, inspect the brakes immediately.

6   Correct tire air pressure adds miles to the lifespan of the tires, improves mileage and enhances overall ride quality. Tire pressure cannot be accurately estimated by looking at a tire, particularly if it is a radial. A tire pressure gauge is therefore essential. Keep an accurate gauge in the glove box. The pressure gauges fitted to the nozzles of air hoses at gas stations are often inaccurate.

7   Always check tire pressure when the tires are cold. "Cold," in this case, means the vehicle has not been driven over a mile in the three

5.4a If a tire loses air on a regular basis, check the valve core first to make sure it's snug (a special inexpensive wrench is commonly available at auto parts stores)

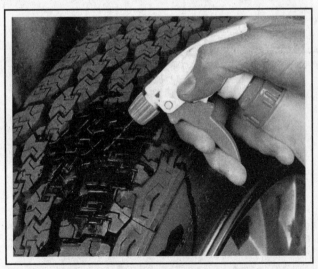

5.4b If the valve core is tight, raise the corner of the vehicle with the low tire and spray a soapy water solution onto the tread as the tire is turned slowly - leaks will cause small bubbles to appear

hours preceding a tire pressure check. A pressure rise of four to eight pounds is not uncommon once the tires are warm.

8   Unscrew the valve cap protruding from the wheel or hubcap and push the gage firmly onto the valve (see illustration). Note the reading on the gauge and compare this figure to the recommended tire pressure shown on the tire placard on the left door. Be sure to reinstall the valve cap to keep dirt and moisture out of the valve stem mechanism. Check all four tires and, if necessary, add enough air to bring them up to the recommended pressure levels.

9   Don't forget to keep the spare tire inflated to the specified pressure (consult your owner's manual). Note that the air pressure specified for the compact spare is significantly higher than the pressure of the regular tires.

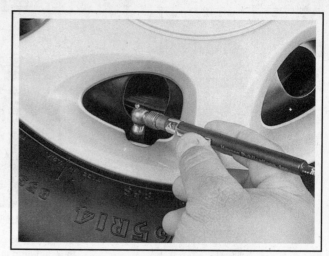

5.8 To extend the life of the tires, check the air pressure at least once a week with an accurate gauge (don't forget the spare)

6   Engine oil and oil filter change (every 5000 miles or 6 months)

▶ Refer to illustrations 6.2, 6.7, 6.13 and 6.15

✳✳ WARNING:

Make sure power to the hybrid system is turned Off before performing any work on this vehicle. Also, on models equipped with the Smart Key system, place the key in a secure spot at least 20 feet away from the work area.

1   Frequent oil changes are the best preventive maintenance the home mechanic can give the engine, because aging oil becomes diluted and contaminated, which leads to premature engine wear.

2   Make sure that you have all the necessary tools before you begin this procedure (see illustration). You should also have plenty of rags or newspapers handy for mopping up any spills. Also, since warm engine oil drains better, operate the vehicle under conditions which will cause the gasoline engine to run until it reaches normal operating temperature.

3   Access to the underside of the vehicle is greatly improved if the vehicle can be lifted on a hoist, driven onto ramps or supported by jackstands.

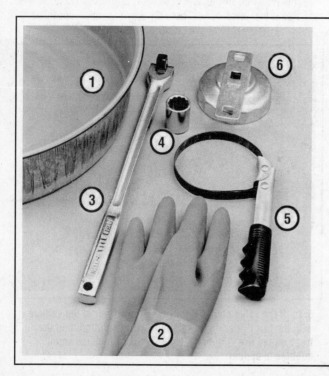

6.2 These tools are required when changing the engine oil and filter

1   *Drain pan* - It should be fairly shallow in depth, but wide in order to prevent spills

2   *Rubber gloves* - When removing the drain plug and filter, it is inevitable that you will get oil on your hands (the gloves will prevent burns)

3   *Breaker bar* - Sometimes the oil drain plug is pretty tight and a long breaker bar is needed to loosen it

4   *Socket* - To be used with the breaker bar or a ratchet (must be the correct size to fit the drain plug)

5   *Filter wrench* - This is a metal band-type wrench, which requires clearance around the filter to be effective

6   *Filter wrench* - This type fits on the bottom of the filter and can be turned with a ratchet or beaker bar (different size wrenches are available for different types of filters)

6.7 Use the proper size box-end wrench or socket to remove the oil drain plug without rounding off the corners

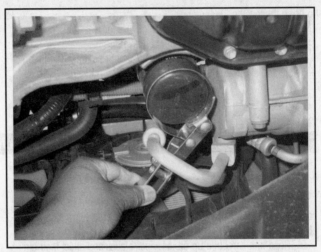

6.13 You will need a special wrench to remove the oil filter since it is usually very tight - DO NOT use the wrench to tighten the new filter

※ WARNING:

Do not work under a vehicle which is supported only by a bumper, hydraulic or scissors-type jack.

4   If this is your first oil change, get under the vehicle and familiarize yourself with the location of the oil drain plug. The engine and exhaust components will be warm during the actual work, so try to anticipate any potential problems before the engine and accessories are hot.

5   Park the vehicle on a level spot, push the Park button and turn the hybrid system Off. Remove the filler cap on the valve cover.

6   Raise the vehicle and support it on jackstands.

※ WARNING:

To avoid personal injury, never get beneath the vehicle when it is supported by only a jack. The jack provided with your vehicle is designed solely for raising the vehicle to remove and replace the wheels. Always use jackstands to support the vehicle when it becomes necessary to place your body underneath the vehicle.

7   Being careful not to touch the hot exhaust components, place the drain pan under the drain plug in the bottom of the pan and remove the plug (see illustration). You may want to wear gloves while unscrewing the plug the final few turns if the engine is really hot.

8   Allow the old oil to drain into the pan. It may be necessary to move the pan farther under the engine as the oil flow slows to a trickle. Inspect the old oil for the presence of metal shavings and chips.

9   After all the oil has drained, wipe off the drain plug with a clean rag. Even tiny metal particles clinging to the plug would immediately contaminate the new oil.

10 Clean the area around the drain plug opening, reinstall the plug and tighten it to the torque listed in this Chapter's Specifications.

11 Move the drain pan into position under the oil filter.

12 Remove all tools, rags, etc. from under the vehicle, being careful not to spill the oil in the drain pan, then lower the vehicle.

13 Loosen the oil filter (see illustration) by turning it counterclockwise with the filter wrench. Once the filter is loose, use your hands to unscrew it from the block.

14 With a clean rag, wipe off the mounting surface on the block. If a residue of old oil is allowed to remain, it will smoke when the block is

heated up. It will also prevent the new filter from seating properly. Also make sure that none of the old gasket remains stuck to the mounting surface. It can be removed with a scraper if necessary.

15 Compare the old filter with the new one to make sure they are the same type. Smear some engine oil on the rubber gasket of the new filter and screw it into place (see illustration). Because overtightening the filter will damage the gasket, do not use a filter wrench to tighten the filter. Tighten it by hand following the directions on the canister or packing box.

16 Add new oil to the engine through the oil filler cap in the valve cover. Use a funnel to prevent oil from spilling onto the top of the engine. Add the specified type and amount of oil to the engine. Wait a few minutes to allow the oil to drain into the pan, then check the level on the oil dipstick (see Section 4 if necessary). If the oil level is at or near the F mark, install the filler cap hand tight, start the engine (this can be done by depressing the brake pedal and turning on the air conditioning; you may have to wait awhile for the engine to start) and allow the new oil to circulate.

17 Allow the engine to run for about a minute, then turn it off.

18 Wait a few minutes to allow the oil to trickle down into the pan, then recheck the level on the dipstick and, if necessary, add enough oil

6.15 Lubricate the new filter gasket with clean engine oil before installing it on the engine

to bring the level to the F mark.

19 During the first few trips after an oil change, make it a point to check frequently for leaks and proper oil level.

20 The old oil drained from the engine cannot be reused in its present state and should be discarded. Check with your local refuse dis-

posal company, disposal facility or environmental agency to see if they will accept the oil for recycling. Don't pour used oil into drains or onto the ground. After the oil has cooled, it can be drained into a suitable container (capped plastic jugs, topped bottles, milk cartons, etc.) for transport to one of these disposal sites.

7 Windshield wiper blade inspection and replacement (every 7500 miles or 6 months)

▶ **Refer to illustrations 7.5a, 7.5b, 7.6a and 7.6b**

1 The windshield wiper and blade assembly should be inspected periodically for damage, loose components and cracked or worn blade elements.

2 Road film can build up on the wiper blades and affect their efficiency, so they should be washed regularly with a mild detergent solution.

3 The action of the wiping mechanism can loosen bolts, nuts and fasteners, so they should be checked and tightened, as necessary, at the

same time the wiper blades are checked.

4 If the wiper blade elements are cracked, worn or warped, or no longer clean adequately, they should be replaced with new ones.

5 Lift the arm assembly away from the glass for clearance, press on the release lever, then slide the wiper blade assembly out of the hook at the end of the arm (see illustrations).

6 The rear blades are removed by removing the cover at the lower end of the wiper arm, then lifting the arm up and rotating the blade assembly out of the arm (see illustrations).

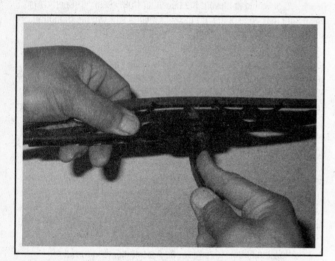

7.5a To release the blade holder, push the release lever . . .

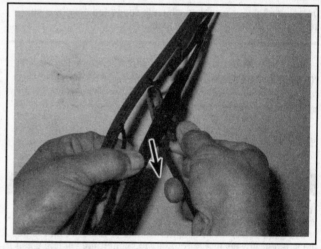

7.5b . . . and pull the wiper blade in the direction of the arrow to separate it from the arm

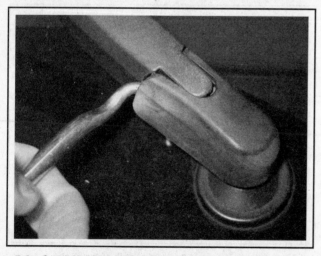

7.6a Carefully pry the cover from the wiper arm pivot . . .

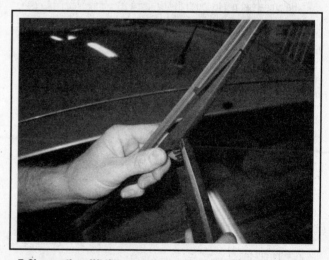

7.6b . . . then lift the rear wiper up and rotate the blade out of the arm

8   Battery check, maintenance and charging (every 7500 miles or 6 months)

▶ **Refer to illustrations 8.1, 8.8a, 8.8b, 8.9a, 8.9b and 8.10**

❊❊ WARNING 1:

This Section applies only to the 12-volt auxiliary battery. It does not apply to the large high-voltage battery. Both batteries are mounted under floor panels in the luggage compartment. Refer to Chapter 6 for more information on these batteries.

❊❊ WARNING 2:

Certain precautions must be followed when checking and servicing the battery. Hydrogen gas, which is highly flammable, is always present in the battery cells, so keep lighted tobacco and all other open flames and sparks away from the battery. The electrolyte inside the battery is actually dilute sulfuric acid, which will cause injury if splashed on your skin or in your eyes. It will also ruin clothes and painted surfaces. When removing the battery cables, always detach the negative cable first and hook it up last!

❊❊ WARNING 3:

Make sure power to the hybrid system is turned Off before performing any work on this vehicle. Also, on models equipped with the Smart Key system, place the key in a secure spot at least 20 feet away from the work area.

1   A routine preventive maintenance program for the battery in your vehicle is the only way to ensure quick and reliable starts. But before performing any battery maintenance, make sure that you have the proper equipment necessary to work safely around the battery (see illustration).

2   There are also several precautions that should be taken whenever battery maintenance is performed. Before servicing the battery, always turn the engine/hybrid system and all accessories off and disconnect the cable from the negative terminal of the battery.

3   The battery produces hydrogen gas, which is both flammable and explosive. Never create a spark, smoke or light a match around the battery. Always charge the battery in a ventilated area.

4   Electrolyte contains poisonous and corrosive sulfuric acid. Do not allow it to get in your eyes, on your skin or on your clothes. Never ingest it. Wear protective safety glasses when working near the battery. Keep children away from the battery.

5   The 12-volt auxiliary battery is located in the trunk. To access it, first raise the trunk lid. On 2001 through 2003 models it is in the left rear corner. On later models it is in the right side.

6   On 2004 and later models, release the two floor board knobs and lift out the rear floor board. Remove the floor box beneath the floor board and set it aside. Remove the smaller floor board on the right side by releasing the four clips.

7   Note the external condition of the battery. If the positive terminal and cable clamp on your vehicle's battery is equipped with a rubber protector, make sure that it's not torn or damaged. It should completely cover the terminal. Look for any corroded or loose connections, cracks in the case or cover or loose hold-down clamps. Also check the entire length of each cable for cracks and frayed conductors.

8   If corrosion, which looks like white, fluffy deposits (see illustration) is evident, particularly around the terminals, the battery should be removed for cleaning. Loosen the cable clamp bolts with a wrench,

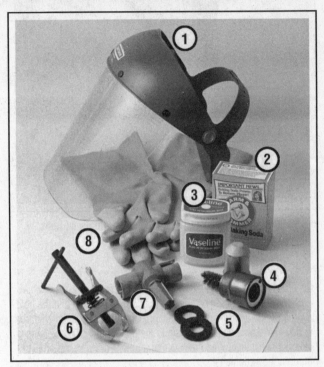

8.1 Tools and materials required for battery maintenance

1   *Face shield/safety goggles* - When removing corrosion with a brush, the acidic particles can easily fly up into your eyes
2   *Baking soda* - A solution of baking soda and water can be used to neutralize corrosion
3   *Petroleum jelly* - A layer of this on the battery posts will help prevent corrosion
4   *Battery post/cable cleaner* - This wire brush cleaning tool will remove all traces of corrosion from the battery posts and cable clamps
5   *Treated felt washers* - Placing one of these on each post, directly under the cable clamps, will help prevent corrosion
6   *Puller* - Sometimes the cable clamps are very difficult to pull off the posts, even after the nut/bolt has been completely loosened. This tool pulls the clamp straight up and off the post without damage
7   *Battery post/cable cleaner* - Here is another cleaning tool which is a slightly different version of number 4 above, but it does the same thing
8   *Rubber gloves* - Another safety item to consider when servicing the battery; remember that's acid inside the battery!

being careful to remove the ground cable first, and slide them off the terminals (see illustration). Disconnect the hold-down clamp bolt and nut, remove the clamp and lift the battery from the engine compartment.

9   Clean the cable clamps thoroughly with a battery brush or a terminal cleaner and a solution of warm water and baking soda (see illustration). Wash the terminals and the top of the battery case with the same solution, but make sure that the solution doesn't get into the battery. When cleaning the cables, terminals and battery top, wear safety goggles and rubber gloves to prevent any solution from coming in contact with your eyes or hands. Wear old clothes, too - even diluted, sulfuric acid splashed onto clothes will burn holes in them. If the terminals have been extensively corroded, clean them up with a terminal cleaner

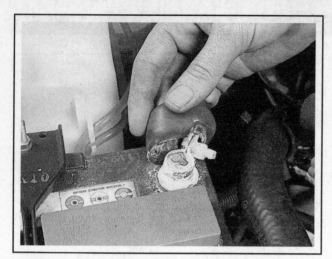

8.8a Battery terminal corrosion usually appears as light, fluffy powder

8.8b Loosen the battery clamp bolt with a wrench - sometimes special battery pliers are necessary for this if corrosion has deteriorated the hex nut - always remove the negative cable first and reconnect it last!

(see illustrations). Thoroughly wash all cleaned areas with plain water.

10 Make sure that the battery tray is in good condition and the hold-down fasteners are tight (see illustration). If the battery is removed from the tray, make sure no parts remain in the bottom of the tray when the battery is reinstalled. When reinstalling the hold-down clamp bolt or nut, do not overtighten it.

11 Information on removing and installing the battery can be found in Chapter 6. Information on jump starting can be found at the front of this manual. For more detailed battery checking procedures, refer to the Haynes Automotive Electrical Manual.

CLEANING

12 Corrosion on the hold-down components, battery case and surrounding areas can be removed with a solution of water and baking soda. Thoroughly rinse all cleaned areas with plain water.

13 Any metal parts of the vehicle damaged by corrosion should be covered with a zinc-based primer, then painted.

CHARGING

✴ WARNING:

When batteries are being charged, hydrogen gas, which is very explosive and flammable, is produced. Do not smoke or allow open flames near a charging or a recently charged battery. Wear eye protection when near the battery during charging. Also, make sure the charger is unplugged before connecting or disconnecting the battery from the charger.

14 Slow-rate charging is the best way to restore a battery that's discharged to the point where it will not start the engine. It's also a good way to maintain the battery charge in a vehicle that's only driven a few miles between starts. Maintaining the battery charge is particularly important in the winter when the battery must work harder to start the

8.9a When cleaning the cable clamps, all corrosion must be removed (the inside of the clamp is tapered to match the taper of the post, so don't remove too much material)

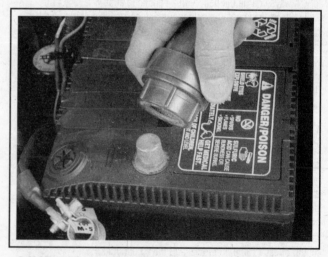

8.9b Regardless of the type of tool used on the battery posts, a clean, shiny surface should be the result

engine and electrical accessories that drain the battery are in greater use.

15 It's best to use a one or two-amp battery charger (sometimes called a "trickle" charger). They are the safest and put the least strain on the battery. They are also the least expensive. For a faster charge, you can use a higher amperage charger, but don't use one rated more than 1/10th the amp/hour rating of the battery. Rapid boost charges that claim to restore the power of the battery in one to two hours are hardest on the battery and can damage batteries not in good condition.

✳✳ CAUTION:

Toyota specifies that a "quick-charge" system not be used.

16 The average time necessary to charge a battery should be listed in the instructions that come with the charger. As a general rule, a trickle charger will charge a battery in 12 to 16 hours.

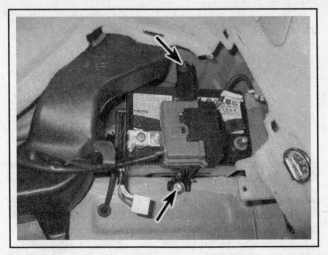

8.10 Battery (12-volt) hold-down nut and bolt

9   Drivebelt check, adjustment and replacement (every 7500 miles or 6 months)

✳✳ WARNING:

Make sure power to the hybrid system is turned Off before performing any work on this vehicle. Also, on models equipped with the Smart Key system, place the key in a secure spot at least 20 feet away from the work area.

CHECK

▶ **Refer to illustration 9.3**

1 The water pump, alternator and, on 2003 and earlier models, the air conditioning compressor, are driven by one serpentine belt. Because of their composition and the stresses they are subjected to, drivebelts stretch and deteriorate as they get older. They must therefore be inspected periodically.

2 The serpentine belt has an adjuster bolt which applies tension to the belt via an idler pulley.

3 With the engine off, open the hood and locate the drivebelt. With a flashlight, check the belt for separation of the adhesive rubber on both sides of the core, core separation from the belt side, a severed core, separation of the ribs from the adhesive rubber, cracking or separation of the ribs, and torn or worn ribs or cracks in the inner ridges of the ribs (see illustration). Also check for fraying and glazing, which gives the belt a shiny appearance. Both sides of the belt should be inspected, which means you will have to twist the belt to check the underside. Use your fingers to feel the belt where you can't see it. If any of the above conditions are evident, replace the belt (go to Step 4).

ADJUSTMENT/REPLACEMENT

▶ **Refer to illustrations 9.4**

4 Loosen the lock nut, then loosen the tension on the belt by turning the adjuster bolt (see illustration). Remove the belt.

9.3 Here are some of the more common problems associated with drivebelts (check the belts very carefully to prevent an untimely breakdown)

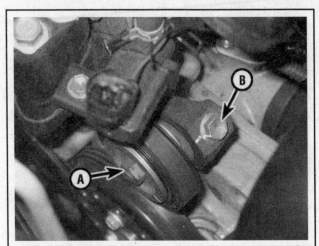

9.4 Drivebelt tensioner lock bolt (A) and adjuster bolt (B)

5   Route the new belt over the pulleys. Tighten the adjuster bolt until the belt is adequately tight (1/2" deflection when a 20 pound load is applied).

6   Tighten the lock nut to the torque value listed in this Chapter's Specifications. Make sure the belt is properly centered in the pulleys.

DRIVEBELT TENSIONER PULLEY REPLACEMENT

7   To replace a tensioner that exhibits binding or a worn-out bearing/pulley, remove the drivebelt (see Step 4) then unscrew the mounting nut.

8   Installation is the reverse of the removal procedure.

9   Install the drivebelt (see Steps 5 and 6), then tighten the nut to the torque value listed in this Chapter's Specifications

10 Underhood hose check and replacement (every 7500 miles or 6 months)

✳✳ WARNING:

Make sure power to the hybrid system is turned Off before performing any work on this vehicle. Also, on models equipped with the Smart Key system, place the key in a secure spot at least 20 feet away from the work area.

✳✳ CAUTION:

Replacement of air conditioning hoses must be left to a dealer service department or air conditioning shop that has the equipment to recover the refrigerant. Never remove air conditioning components or hoses until the system has been depressurized.

GENERAL

1   High temperatures in the engine compartment can cause the deterioration of the rubber and plastic hoses used for engine, accessory and emission systems operation. Periodic inspection should be made for cracks, loose clamps, material hardening and leaks.

2   Information specific to the cooling system hoses can be found in Section 11.

3   Some, but not all, hoses are secured to the fittings with clamps. Where clamps are used, check to be sure they haven't lost their tension, allowing the hose to leak. If clamps aren't used, make sure the hose has not expanded and/or hardened where it slips over the fitting, allowing it to leak.

VACUUM HOSES

4   It's quite common for vacuum hoses, especially those in the emissions system, to be color coded or identified by colored stripes molded into them. Various systems require hoses with different wall thickness, collapse resistance and temperature resistance. When replacing hoses, be sure the new ones are made of the same material.

5   Often the only effective way to check a hose is to remove it completely from the vehicle. If more than one hose is removed, be sure to label the hoses and fittings to ensure correct installation.

6   When checking vacuum hoses, be sure to include any plastic T-fittings in the check. Inspect the fittings for cracks and the hose where it fits over the fitting for distortion, which could cause leakage.

7   A small piece of vacuum hose (1/4-inch inside diameter) can be used as a stethoscope to detect vacuum leaks. Hold one end of the hose to your ear and probe around vacuum hoses and fittings, listening for the "hissing" sound characteristic of a vacuum leak.

✳✳ WARNING:

When probing with the vacuum hose stethoscope, be very careful not to come into contact with moving engine components such as the drivebelt, cooling fan, etc.

FUEL HOSE

✳✳ WARNING:

Gasoline is extremely flammable, so take extra precautions when you work on any part of the fuel system. Don't smoke or allow open flames or bare light bulbs near the work area, and don't work in a garage where a gas-type appliance (such as a water heater or a clothes dryer) is present. Since gasoline is carcinogenic, wear fuel-resistant gloves when there's a possibility of being exposed to fuel, and, if you spill any fuel on your skin, rinse it off immediately with soap and water. Mop up any spills immediately and do not store fuel-soaked rags where they could ignite. The fuel system is under constant pressure, so, if any fuel lines are to be disconnected, the fuel pressure in the system must be relieved first. When you perform any kind of work on the fuel system, wear safety glasses and have a Class B type fire extinguisher on hand.

8   Check all rubber fuel lines for deterioration and chafing. Check especially for cracks in areas where the hose bends and just before fittings, such as where a hose attaches to the fuel filter.

9   High quality fuel line, specifically designed for fuel injection systems, must be used for fuel line replacement.

✳✳ WARNING:

Never use anything other than the proper fuel line for fuel line replacement.

10 Spring-type clamps are commonly used on fuel lines. These clamps often lose their tension over a period of time, and can be "sprung" during removal. Replace all spring-type clamps with screw clamps whenever a hose is replaced.

METAL LINES

11 Sections of metal line are often used for fuel line between the fuel pump and fuel injection unit. Check carefully to be sure the line has not been bent or crimped and that cracks have not started in the line.

12 If a section of metal fuel line must be replaced, only seamless steel tubing should be used, since copper and aluminum tubing don't have the strength necessary to withstand normal engine vibration.

13 Check the metal brake lines where they enter the master cylinder and brake proportioning unit (if used) for cracks in the lines or loose fittings. Any sign of brake fluid leakage calls for an immediate thorough inspection of the brake system.

11 Cooling system check (every 7500 miles or 6 months)

▸ **Refer to illustrations 11.3 and 11.4**

✳ WARNING 1:

Wait until the engine is completely cool before beginning this procedure.

✳ WARNING 2:

Make sure power to the hybrid system is turned Off before performing any work on this vehicle. Also, on models equipped with the Smart Key system, place the key in a secure spot at least 20 feet away from the work area.

1   Many major engine failures can be attributed to a faulty cooling system. The cooling system also cools the transaxle fluid and thus plays an important role in prolonging transaxle life.

2   The cooling system should be checked with the engine cold. Do this before the vehicle is driven for the day or after the engine has been shut off for at least three hours.

3   Remove the radiator cover (see illustration), then remove the radiator cap by turning it to the left until it reaches a stop. If you hear a hissing sound (indicating there is still pressure in the system), wait until it stops. Now press down on the cap with the palm of your hand and continue turning to the left until the cap can be removed. Thoroughly clean the cap, inside and out, with clean water. Also clean the filler neck on the radiator. All traces of corrosion should be removed. The coolant inside the radiator should be relatively transparent. If it's rust colored, the system should be drained and refilled (see Section 22). If the coolant level isn't up to the top, add additional antifreeze/coolant mixture (see Section 4).

4   Carefully check the large upper and lower radiator hoses along with the smaller diameter heater hoses, which run from the engine to the firewall. Inspect each hose along its entire length, replacing any hose, which is cracked, swollen or shows signs of deterioration. Cracks may become more apparent if the hose is squeezed (see illustration). Regardless of condition, it's a good idea to replace hoses with new ones every two years.

Check for a chafed area that could fail prematurely.

Check for a soft area indicating the hose has deteriorated inside.

Overtightening the clamp on a hardened hose will damage the hose and cause a leak.

Check each hose for swelling and oil-soaked ends. Cracks and breaks can be located by squeezing the hose.

11.3 Remove the plastic fasteners and lift off the radiator cover for access to the radiator cap ("A" indicates cap location)

11.4 Hoses, like drivebelts, have a habit of failing at the worst possible time - to prevent the inconvenience of a blown hose, inspect them carefully as shown here

5 Make sure that all hose connections are tight. A leak in the cooling system will usually show up as white or rust colored deposits on the areas adjoining the leak. If wire-type clamps are used at the ends of the hoses, it may be a good idea to replace them with more secure screw-type clamps.

6 Use compressed air or a soft brush to remove bugs, leaves, etc.

from the front of the radiator or air conditioning condenser. Be careful not to damage the delicate cooling fins or cut yourself on them.

7 Every other inspection, or at the first indication of cooling system problems, have the cap and system pressure tested. If you don't have a pressure tester, most gas stations and repair shops will do this for a minimal charge.

12 Tire rotation (every 7500 miles or 6 months)

▶ **Refer to illustration 12.2**

1 The tires should be rotated at the specified intervals and whenever uneven wear is noticed. Since the vehicle will be raised and the tires removed anyway, check the brakes (see Section 14) at this time.

2 Radial tires must be rotated in a specific pattern (see illustration).

3 Refer to the information in *Jacking and towing* at the front of this manual for the proper procedures to follow when raising the vehicle and changing a tire. If the brakes are to be checked, do not apply the parking brake as stated. Make sure the tires are blocked to prevent the vehicle from rolling.

4 Preferably, the entire vehicle should be raised at the same time. This can be done on a hoist or by jacking up each corner and lowering the vehicle onto jackstands placed under the frame rails. Always use four jackstands and make sure the vehicle is firmly supported.

5 After rotation, check and adjust the tire pressures as necessary and be sure to check the lug nut tightness.

6 For further information on the wheels and tires, refer to Chapter 10.

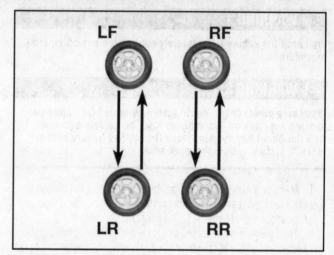

12.2 The recommended tire rotation pattern for these vehicles

13 Seat belt check (every 7500 miles or 6 months)

1 Check the seat belts, buckles, latch plates and guide loops for obvious damage and signs of wear. Seat belts that exhibit fraying along the edges should be replaced.

2 Where the seat belt receptacle bolts to the floor of the vehicle,

check that the bolts are secure.

3 See if the seat belt reminder light blinks when the On button is depressed (with your foot on the brake pedal); a chime should also sound.

14 Brake check (every 15,000 miles or 12 months)

✳✳ WARNING 1:

Dust created by the brake system is harmful to your health. Never blow it out with compressed air and don't inhale any of it. An approved filtering mask should be worn when working on the brakes. Do not, under any circumstances, use petroleum-based solvents to clean brake parts. Use brake system cleaner only!

✳✳ WARNING 2:

Make sure power to the hybrid system is turned Off before performing any work on this vehicle. Also, on models equipped with the Smart Key system, place the key in a secure spot at least 20 feet away from the work area.

➡**Note: For detailed photographs of the brake system, refer to Chapter 9.**

1 In addition to the specified intervals, the brakes should be inspected every time the wheels are removed or whenever a defect is suspected. Any of the following symptoms could indicate a potential brake system defect: The vehicle pulls to one side when the brake pedal is depressed; the brakes make squealing or dragging noises when applied; brake travel is excessive; the pedal pulsates; brake fluid leaks, usually onto the inside of the tire or wheel.

2 The disc brake pads have built-in wear indicators which should make a high-pitched squealing or scraping noise when they are worn to the replacement point. When you hear this noise, replace the pads immediately or expensive damage to the discs can result.

14.6 You'll find an inspection hole like this (A) in each caliper through which you can view the inner brake pad linings; the outer pad is more easily viewed from the edge of the caliper (B)

14.13 A quick check of the drum brake shoe lining material can be made by removing the rubber plug in the backing plate and looking through the inspection hole

3   Loosen the wheel lug nuts.

4   Raise the vehicle and place it securely on jackstands.

5   Remove the wheels (see *Jacking and towing* at the front of this book, or your owner's manual, if necessary).

DISC BRAKES

▶ **Refer to illustration 14.6**

6   There are two pads - an outer and an inner - in each caliper. The pads are visible through a small inspection hole in each caliper, as well as from the ends of the caliper (see illustration).

7   Check the pad thickness by looking at each end of the caliper and through the inspection hole in the caliper body. If the lining material is less than the thickness listed in this Chapter's Specifications, replace the pads.

➡ **Note: Keep in mind that the lining material is riveted or bonded to a metal backing plate and the metal portion is not included in this measurement.**

8   If it is difficult to determine the exact thickness of the remaining pad material by the above method, or if you are at all concerned about the condition of the pads, remove the caliper(s), then remove the pads for further inspection (see Chapter 9).

9   Once the pads are removed from the calipers, clean them with brake cleaner and re-measure them.

10   Measure the disc thickness with a micrometer to make sure that it still has service life remaining. If any disc is thinner than the specified minimum thickness, replace it (see Chapter 9). Even if the disc has service life remaining, check its condition. Look for scoring, gouging and burned spots. If these conditions exist, remove the disc and have it resurfaced (see Chapter 9).

11   Before installing the wheels, check all brake lines and hoses for damage, wear, deformation, cracks, corrosion, leakage, bends and twists, particularly in the vicinity of the rubber hoses at the calipers.

12   Check the clamps for tightness and the connections for leakage. Make sure that all hoses and lines are clear of sharp edges, moving parts and the exhaust system. If any of the above conditions are noted, repair, reroute or replace the lines and/or fittings as necessary (see Chapter 9).

REAR DRUM BRAKES

▶ **Refer to illustrations 14.13, 14.15 and 14.17**

13   To check the brake shoe lining thickness without removing the brake drums, remove the rubber plug from the backing plate and use a flashlight to inspect the linings (see illustration). For a more thorough brake inspection, follow the procedure below.

14   Refer to Chapter 9 and remove the rear brake drums.

15   Note the thickness of the lining material on the rear brake shoes (see illustration) and look for signs of contamination by brake fluid and grease. If the lining material is within 1/16-inch of the recessed rivets or metal shoes, replace the brake shoes with new ones. The shoes should also be replaced if they' are cracked, glazed (shiny lining surfaces) or contaminated with brake fluid or grease. See Chapter 9 for the replacement procedure.

16   Check the shoe return and hold-down springs and the adjusting mechanism to make sure they're installed correctly and in good condi-

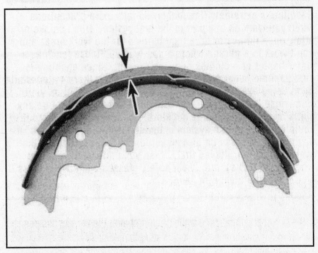

14.15 If the lining is bonded to the brake shoe, measure the lining thickness from the outer surface to the metal shoe as shown here; if the lining is riveted to the shoe, measure from the lining inner surface to the rivet head

tion. Deteriorated or distorted springs, if not replaced, could allow the linings to drag and wear prematurely.

17 Check the wheel cylinders for leakage by carefully peeling back the rubber boots (see illustration). If brake fluid is noted behind the boots, the wheel cylinders must be replaced (see Chapter 9).

18 Check the drums for cracks, score marks, deep scratches and hard spots, which will appear as small discolored areas. If imperfections cannot be removed with emery cloth, the drums must be resurfaced by an automotive machine shop (see Chapter 9 for more detailed information).

19 Install the brake drums.

20 Install the wheels and lug nuts.

21 Remove the jackstands and lower the vehicle.

22 Tighten the wheel lug nuts to the torque listed in this Chapter's Specifications.

PARKING BRAKE

23 Slowly pull up on the parking brake and count the number of clicks you hear until the handle is up as far as it will go. The adjustment is correct if you hear the specified number of clicks. If you hear more or fewer clicks, it's time to adjust the parking brake (see Chapter 9).

24 An alternative method of checking the parking brake is to park the vehicle on a steep hill with the parking brake set and the transaxle in

14.17 Carefully peel back the wheel cylinder boot and check for leaking fluid indicating that the cylinder must be replaced or rebuilt

Neutral (be sure to stay in the vehicle for this procedure). If the parking brake cannot prevent the vehicle from rolling, it is in need of adjustment (see Chapter 9).

15 Fuel system check (every 15,000 miles or 12 months)

✳✳ WARNING 1:

Make sure power to the hybrid system is turned Off before performing any work on this vehicle. Also, on models equipped with the Smart Key system, place the key in a secure spot at least 20 feet away from the work area.

✳✳ WARNING 2:

Gasoline is extremely flammable, so take extra precautions when you work on any part of the fuel system. Don't smoke or allow open flames or bare light bulbs near the work area, and don't work in a garage where a gas-type appliance (such as a water heater or a clothes dryer) is present. Since gasoline is carcinogenic, wear fuel-resistant gloves when there's a possibility of being exposed to fuel, and, if you spill any fuel on your skin, rinse it off immediately with soap and water. Mop up any spills immediately and do not store fuel-soaked rags where they could ignite. The fuel system is under constant pressure, so, if any fuel lines are to be disconnected, the fuel pressure in the system must be relieved first. When you perform any kind of work on the fuel system, wear safety glasses and have a Class B type fire extinguisher on hand.

1 If you smell gasoline while driving or after the vehicle has been sitting in the sun, inspect the fuel system immediately.

2 Remove the fuel filler cap and inspect it for damage and corrosion. The gasket should have an unbroken sealing imprint. If the gasket

is damaged or corroded, remove it and install a new one.

3 Inspect the fuel lines for cracks. Make sure that the threaded flare-nut type connectors which secure the metal fuel lines to the fuel injection system are tight.

4 Since some components of the fuel system - the fuel tank and part of the fuel feed and return lines, for example - are underneath the vehicle, they can be inspected more easily with the vehicle raised on a hoist. If that's not possible, raise the vehicle and support it securely on jackstands.

5 With the vehicle raised and safely supported, inspect the gas tank and filler neck for punctures, cracks and other damage. The connection between the filler neck and the tank is particularly critical. Sometimes a rubber filler neck will leak because of loose clamps or deteriorated rubber. These are problems a home mechanic can usually rectify.

✳✳ WARNING:

Do not, under any circumstances, try to repair a fuel tank (except rubber components). A welding torch or any open flame can easily cause fuel vapors inside the tank to explode.

6 Carefully check all rubber hoses and metal lines leading away from the fuel tank. Check for loose connections, deteriorated hoses, crimped lines and other damage. Carefully inspect the lines from the tank to the fuel injection system. Repair or replace damaged sections as necessary (see Chapter 4).

16 Steering, suspension and driveaxle boot check (every 15,000 miles or 12 months)

✳✳ WARNING:

Make sure power to the hybrid system is turned Off before performing any work on this vehicle. Also, on models equipped with the Smart Key system, place the key in a secure spot at least 20 feet away from the work area.

➡Note: For detailed illustrations of the steering and suspension components, refer to Chapter 10.

STEERING AND SUSPENSION CHECK

With the wheels on the ground

1 With the vehicle stopped and the front wheels pointed straight ahead, rock the steering wheel gently back and forth. If freeplay (see illustration) is excessive, a front wheel bearing, main shaft yoke, intermediate shaft yoke, lower arm balljoint or steering system joint is worn or the steering gear is out of adjustment or broken. Refer to Chapter 10 for the appropriate repair procedure.

2 Other symptoms, such as excessive vehicle body movement over rough roads, swaying (leaning) around corners and binding as the steering wheel is turned, may indicate faulty steering and/or suspension components.

3 Check the shock absorbers and struts by pushing down and releasing the vehicle several times at each corner. If the vehicle does not come back to a level position within one or two bounces, the shocks/struts are worn and must be replaced. When bouncing the vehicle up and down, listen for squeaks and noises from the suspension components. Additional information on suspension components can be found in Chapter 10.

Under the vehicle

▶ Refer to illustrations 16.7 and 16.8

4 Raise the vehicle with a floor jack and support it securely on jackstands. See *Jacking and towing* at the front of this book for the proper jacking points.

5 Check the tires for irregular wear patterns and proper inflation. See Section 5 in this Chapter for information regarding tire wear and Chapter 10 for the wheel bearing replacement procedures.

6 Inspect the universal joint between the steering shaft and the steering gear housing. Check the steering gear housing for grease leakage or oozing. Make sure that the dust seals and boots are not damaged and that the boot clamps are not loose. Check the steering linkage for looseness or damage. Check the tie-rod ends for excessive play. Look for loose bolts, broken or disconnected parts and deteriorated rubber bushings on all suspension and steering components. While an assistant turns the steering wheel from side to side, check the steering components for free movement, chafing and binding. If the steering components do not seem to be reacting with the movement of the steering wheel, try to determine where the slack is located.

7 Move each control arm up and down with a prybar (see illustration) to ensure that its balljoint has no play. If any balljoint does have play, replace it. See Chapter 10 for the balljoint replacement procedure.

8 Inspect the balljoint boots for damage and leaking grease (see illustration). Replace the balljoints with new ones if they are damaged (see Chapter 10).

DRIVEAXLE BOOT CHECK

▶ Refer to illustration 16.10

9 The driveaxle boots are very important because they prevent dirt, water and foreign material from entering and damaging the constant velocity (CV) joints. Oil and grease can cause the boot material to deteriorate prematurely, so it's a good idea to wash the boots with soap and water. Because it constantly pivots back and forth following the steering action of the front hub, the outer CV boot wears out sooner and should be inspected regularly.

10 Inspect the boots for tears and cracks as well as loose clamps (see illustration). If there is any evidence of cracks or leaking lubricant, they must be replaced as described in Chapter 8.

16.7 To check the balljoints, attempt to move the lower control arm up and down with a prybar to make sure there is no play in the balljoint - if there is, replace it

16.8 Push on the balljoint boot to check for tears and grease leaks

16.10 Flex the driveaxle boots by hand to check for tears, cracks and leaking grease

17 Air filter replacement (every 30,000 miles or 24 months)

▶ Refer to illustrations 17.2a, 17.2b and 17.2c

❋❋ WARNING:

Make sure power to the hybrid system is turned Off before performing any work on this vehicle. Also, on models equipped with the Smart Key system, place the key in a secure spot at least 20 feet away from the work area.

1   The air filter is located inside a housing at the center of the engine compartment.

2   To remove the air filter, release the spring clips that keep the two halves of the air cleaner housing together, then lift the cover up and remove the air filter element (see illustrations).

3   Inspect the outer surface of the filter element. If it is dirty, replace it. If it is only moderately dusty, it can be reused by blowing it clean from the back to the front surface with compressed air. Because it is a pleated paper type filter, it cannot be washed or oiled. If it cannot be cleaned satisfactorily with compressed air, discard and replace it. While the cover is off, be careful not to drop anything down into the housing.

❋❋ CAUTION:

Never drive the vehicle with the air cleaner removed. Excessive engine wear could result and backfiring could even cause a fire under the hood.

17.2a The top of the air filter housing is retained by clips that can be removed without tools

4   Wipe out the inside of the air cleaner housing.
5   Place the new filter into its frame, making sure it seats properly.
6   Installation of the cover is the reverse of removal.

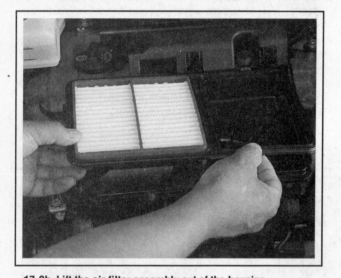

17.2b Lift the air filter assembly out of the housing . . .

17.2c . . . then remove the air filter element

18 Cabin air filter - replacement (every 30,000 miles or 24 months)

▶ Refer to illustrations 18.2a, 18.2b, 18.3a and 18.3b

1   The covered models are equipped with a cabin air filter in the blower housing. The filter traps dust and pollen before the air enters the passenger compartment.

2   For access to the cabin air filter, swing the glove box down. On 2001 through 2003 models this requires rotating and pulling out the pins on each inner wall of the glove box. On 2004 and later models

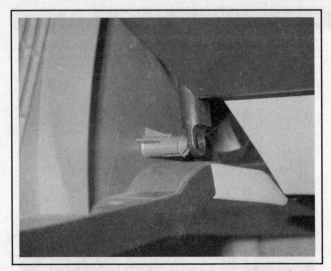

18.2a The glove box door supports must be pried off of their pins in order to fully lower the door

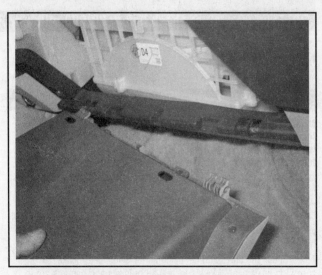

18.2b Remove the glove box door by lowering it fully

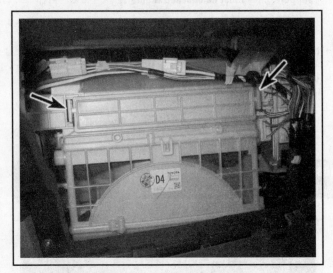

18.3a Release the tabs at each end of the filter . . .

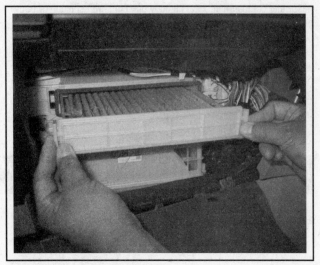

18.3b . . . then slide the filter rearward

disconnect the damper from the right side of the open glove box, then push inward on both sides to lower the door (see illustrations).

3   Pull out the filter case and lift out the filter (see illustrations).
4   Installation is the reverse of the removal procedure.

19 Evaporative emissions control system check (every 30,000 miles or 24 months)

❊❊ WARNING:

Make sure power to the hybrid system is turned Off before performing any work on this vehicle. Also, on models equipped with the Smart Key system, place the key in a secure spot at least 20 feet away from the work area.

1   The function of the evaporative emissions control system is to draw fuel vapors from the gas tank and fuel system, store them in a charcoal canister, then burn them during normal engine operation.

2   The most common symptom of a fault in the evaporative emissions control system is a strong fuel odor from the rear of the vehicle. If a fuel odor is detected, inspect the charcoal canister duct. On all models it is located on or above the fuel tank. Check the canister and all hoses for damage and deterioration.

3   The evaporative emissions control system is explained in more detail in Chapter 6.

20 Exhaust system check (every 30,000 miles or 24 months)

▶ Refer to illustration 20.4

✽✽ WARNING:

Make sure power to the hybrid system is turned Off before performing any work on this vehicle. Also, on models equipped with the Smart Key system, place the key in a secure spot at least 20 feet away from the work area.

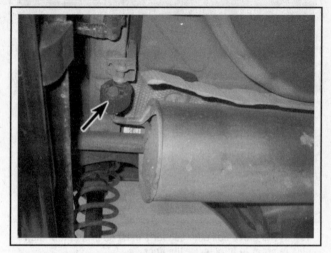

1   With the engine cold (at least three hours after the vehicle has been driven), check the complete exhaust system from its starting point at the engine to the end of the tailpipe. This should be done on a hoist where unrestricted access is available.

2   Check the pipes and connections for evidence of leaks, severe corrosion or damage. Make sure that all brackets and hangers are in good condition and tight.

3   At the same time, inspect the underside of the body for holes, corrosion, open seams, etc. which may allow exhaust gases to enter the passenger compartment. Seal all body openings with silicone or body putty.

4   Rattles and other noises can often be traced to the exhaust system, especially the mounts and hangers. Try to move the pipes, muffler and catalytic converter. If the components can come in contact with the body or suspension parts, secure the exhaust system with new mounts (see illustration).

20.4 The exhaust system relies on rubber mounts for its support - they must be checked regularly

5   Check the running condition of the engine by inspecting inside the end of the tailpipe. The exhaust deposits here are an indication of engine state-of-tune. If the pipe is black and sooty or coated with white deposits, the engine is in need of a tune-up, including a thorough engine control system inspection.

21 Positive Crankcase Ventilation (PCV) valve and hose check and replacement (every 30,000 miles or 24 months)

▶ Refer to illustration 21.1

1   The PCV valve is threaded into the left (driver's) end of the valve cover (see illustration).

2   On 2004 and later models it is necessary to remove several components to get access to the PCV valve. Refer to Chapter 6 and disconnect the negative cable from the auxiliary (12-volt) battery.

3   Remove the two mounting bolts from the interfering engine compartment relay block. Also unclip the wiring harness retainers.

4   Refer to Chapter 4 and remove the air filter housing.

5   Disconnect the two interfering injector and coil wiring harnesses. Set them out of the way.

6   Remove the plastic cover from the wiring harness between the valve cover and the inverter/converter coolant reservoir.

7   Disconnect the PCV valve hose and remove the PCV valve. Reattach the hose to the PCV valve. Reconnect the wiring harnesses.

8   With the engine idling at normal operating temperature, place your finger over the end of the valve. If there's no vacuum at the valve, check for a plugged hose or valve. Replace any plugged or deteriorated hoses.

9   Turn off the engine. Remove the PCV valve from the hose. Connect a clean piece of hose and blow through the valve from the valve cover (cylinder head) end. If air will not pass through the valve in this direction, replace it with a new one.

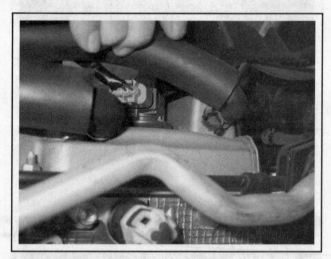

21.1 The PCV system valve is installed in the end of the valve cover

10   When purchasing a replacement PCV valve, make sure it's for your particular vehicle and engine size. Compare the old valve with the new one to make sure they're the same.

22 Cooling system servicing (draining, flushing and refilling) (every 50,000 miles or 60 months)

✳✳ WARNING 1:

Wait until the engine is completely cool before beginning this procedure.

✳✳ WARNING 2:

Do not allow engine coolant (antifreeze) to come in contact with your skin or painted surfaces of the vehicle. Rinse off spills immediately with plenty of water. Antifreeze is highly toxic if ingested. Never leave antifreeze lying around in an open container or in puddles on the floor; children and pets are attracted by its sweet smell and may drink it. Check with local authorities on disposing of used antifreeze. Many communities have collection centers which will see that antifreeze is disposed of safely. Antifreeze is flammable under certain conditions - be sure to read the precautions on the container.

➡ Note: Non-toxic antifreeze is available at most auto parts stores. Although the antifreeze is non-toxic when fresh, proper disposal is still required.

1 Periodically, the cooling system should be drained, flushed and refilled to replenish the antifreeze mixture and prevent formation of rust and corrosion, which can impair the performance of the cooling system and cause engine damage. When the cooling system is serviced, all hoses and the radiator cap should be checked and replaced if necessary.

DRAINING

▶ Refer to illustrations 22.3, 22.4 and 22.6

✳✳ WARNING 1:

On 2004 and later models the coolant may still be hot even if the engine is cool. This is because some of the coolant is contained in a heat storage tank.

22.4 On most models you will have to remove a panel for access to the radiator drain fitting

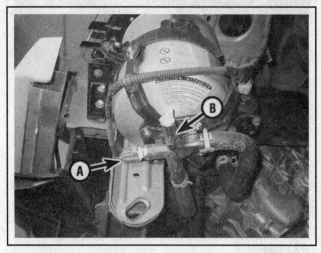

22.3 Heat storage tank details (bumper cover removed for clarity

   A Electrical connector   *B Drain fitting*

✳✳ WARNING 2:

Make sure power to the hybrid system is turned Off before performing any work on this vehicle. Also, on models equipped with the Smart Key system, place the key in a secure spot at least 20 feet away from the work area.

2 Apply the parking brake and block the wheels. If the vehicle has just been driven, wait several hours to allow the engine to cool down before beginning this procedure. On 2004 and later models, remove the front portion of the left inner fender panel (see Chapter 11).

3 Once the engine is completely cool, remove the radiator cap. On 2004 and later models, pull back the left inner fender panel and disconnect the electrical connector for the heat storage tank (see illustration).

✳✳ WARNING:

Read all of the labels on the tank, and wait until the heat storage tank cools down before proceeding.

4 Move a large container under the radiator drain to catch the coolant. Attach a 3/8-inch inner diameter hose to the drain fitting to direct the coolant into the container (some models are already equipped with a hose), then open the drain fitting (a pair of pliers may be required to turn it) (see illustration).

5 After the coolant stops flowing out of the radiator, move the container under the engine block drain plug. Loosen the plug and allow the coolant in the block to drain. When a sufficient amount of time has passed for the heat storage tank to cool down, move the drain pan under the tank, attach a hose to the drain fitting, then open the drain valve and let the coolant drain (see illustration 22.3).

6 While the coolant is draining, check the condition of the radiator hoses, heater hoses and clamps (see Section 12 if necessary). Replace any damaged clamps or hoses. If you wish to drain the coolant from the inverter/converter and transaxle cooling system remove the drain plug

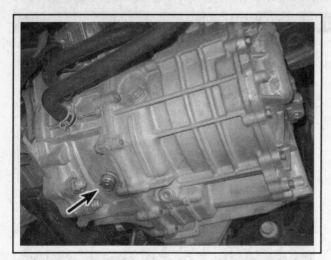

22.6 There is a hex-shape drain plug for the cooling system of the transaxle and the inverter/converter at the bottom of the transaxle

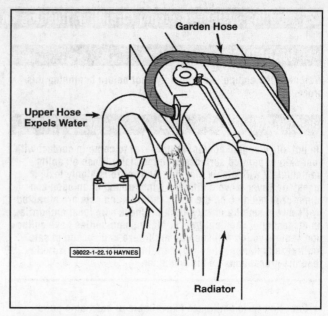

22.9 With the thermostat removed, disconnect the upper radiator hose and flush the radiator and engine block with a garden hose

from the bottom of the transaxle (see illustration). Once the coolant has drained, reinstall the drain plug (use a new sealing washer) and tighten it to the torque listed in this Chapter's Specifications.

FLUSHING

♦ **Refer to illustration 22.9**

7   Once the system is completely drained, remove the thermostat from the engine (see Chapter 3). Then reinstall the thermostat housing without the thermostat. This will allow the system to be thoroughly flushed.

8   Tighten the radiator drain plug. Turn your heating system controls to Hot, so that the heater core will be flushed at the same time as the rest of the cooling system.

9   Disconnect the upper radiator hose from the radiator, then place a garden hose in the upper radiator inlet and flush the system until the water runs clear at the upper radiator hose (see illustration).

10   In severe cases of contamination or clogging of the radiator, remove the radiator (see Chapter 3) and have a radiator repair facility clean and repair it if necessary.

11   Many deposits can be removed by the chemical action of a cleaner available at auto parts stores. Follow the procedure outlined in the manufacturer's instructions.

➡**Note: When the coolant is regularly drained and the system refilled with the correct antifreeze/water mixture, there should be no need to use chemical cleaners or descalers.**

12   Remove the overflow hose from the coolant recovery reservoir. Drain the reservoir and flush it with clean water, then reconnect the hose.

REFILLING

13   Close and tighten the radiator drain. Install and/or tighten the block drain plug. On 2004 and later models close the heat storage tank drain and reconnect the electrical connector. Reinstall the thermostat (see Chapter 3). On 2004 and later models remove the radiator upper cover (see illustration 11.3).

Engine cooling system
2003 and earlier models

14   Slowly add new coolant (a 50/50 mixture of water and antifreeze)

to the radiator until it's full.

15   Install the radiator cap and run the engine in a well-ventilated area for about two minutes, revving up the engine repeatedly, then turn the engine off and allow it to cool completely.

16   Remove the radiator cap and top up the coolant. Squeeze the radiator hoses, then add more coolant, if possible.

17   Install the radiator cap, then activate the vehicle's Inspection Mode. The following sequence of events must take place within one minute:

a) *Turn the ignition to the On position.*
b) *With the shifter in Park, push the accelerator pedal to the floor two times.*
c) *Place the shifter in Neutral, then push the accelerator pedal to the floor two times.*
d) *Place the shifter back into Park, then push the accelerator pedal to the floor two times.*

At this point the hybrid error warning light on the instrument panel should be flashing. The engine can now be started and run until it is turned off with the ignition switch.

18   Run the engine until the radiator fan comes on, then turn the engine Off.

19   Allow the engine to cool completely, then remove the radiator cap and check the coolant level. If it has dropped, perform Steps 16 through 18. Reinstall the radiator cap.

20   Set the blower knob to the LO position and the temperature knob to the MAX HOT position. Turn the ignition switch to the On position to operate the water pump; do this until aerated coolant can't be heard circulating through the heater core.

21   Check the coolant level in the radiator once again, adding as necessary. Reinstall the radiator cap.

22   Refill the coolant reservoir to the proper level.

2004 and later models

23   Place the heater temperature control in the maximum heat position.

24   Attach a hose to the bleeder valve at the left end (driver's side) of

the radiator and direct the other end into the coolant reservoir. Loosen the bleeder valve screw with a 6 mm hex bit inserted through the hole in the radiator support.

25 Slowly add new coolant (a 50/50 mixture of water and antifreeze) to the radiator until it's full. Squeeze the radiator hoses, then add more coolant, if possible. Add coolant to the reservoir up to the lower mark. Tighten the bleeder valve screw securely, then remove the bleeder hose.

26 Install the radiator cap and run the engine in a well-ventilated area until the thermostat opens (coolant will begin flowing through the radiator and the upper radiator hose will become hot).

27 Turn the engine off and let it cool. Add more coolant mixture to bring the level back up to the lip on the radiator filler neck.

28 Squeeze the upper radiator hose to expel air, then add more coolant mixture if necessary. Reinstall the radiator cap.

29 Start the engine, allow it to reach normal operating temperature and check for leaks.

Inverter/converter and transaxle cooling system

♦ Refer to illustration 22.30

30 Loosen the bleeder valve at the front of the inverter/converter and attach a hose to it (see illustration). Direct the other end of the hose into the coolant reservoir for the inverter/converter/transaxle.

➡Note: On 2003 and earlier models there are two bleeder valves; loosen and attach hoses to both of them.

31 Add coolant of the proper type to the reservoir, until coolant flows up the bleeder hose and reaches the same level as the FULL line on the side of the reservoir (at which time the coolant in the reservoir will also be at the FULL line). Close the bleeder valve but leave the hose attached.

32 Inside the vehicle, turn the power switch On and let the water

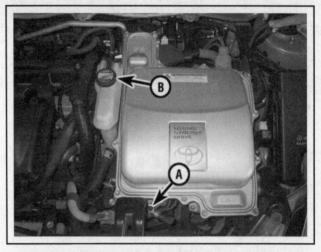

22.30 Loosen the bleeder valve (A) and attach a hose to it, then direct the other end of the hose into the inverter/converter/transaxle coolant reservoir (B)

pump run for about 30 seconds, then turn the power switch Off.

33 Loosen the bleeder valve again to bleed out any air, then tighten it securely.

34 Add coolant to the reservoir to bring it up to the FULL mark.

35 Repeat Steps 31 through 34.

36 Turn the power switch On and allow the water pump to run for five minutes.

37 If necessary, add coolant to the reservoir to bring it up to the FULL mark.

23 Spark plug check and replacement (every 100,000 miles or 72 months)

♦ Refer to illustrations 23.1, 23.4, 23.6a, 23.6b, 23.8, 23.9, 23.10a and 23.10b

❊❊ WARNING:

Make sure power to the hybrid system is turned Off before performing any work on this vehicle. Also, on models equipped with the Smart Key system, place the key in a secure spot at least 20 feet away from the work area.

1 Spark plug replacement requires a spark plug socket which fits onto a ratchet wrench. This socket is lined with a rubber grommet to protect the porcelain insulator of the spark plug and to hold the plug while you insert it into the spark plug hole. You will also need a wire-type feeler gauge to check and adjust the spark plug gap and a torque wrench to tighten the new plugs to the specified torque (see illustration).

2 If you are replacing the plugs, purchase the new plugs, adjust them to the proper gap, then replace each plug one at a time.

➡Note: When buying new spark plugs, it's essential that you obtain the correct plugs for your specific vehicle. This information can be found in the Specifications Section at the beginning of this Chapter, on the Vehicle Emissions Control Information (VECI) label located on the underside of the hood or in the owner's manual. If these sources specify different plugs, purchase the spark plug type specified on the VECI label because that information is provided specifically for your engine.

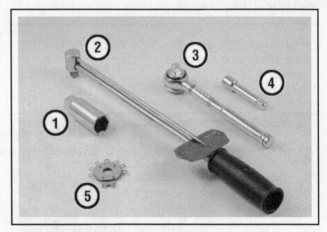

23.1 Tools required for changing spark plugs

1 *Spark plug socket* - This will have special padding inside to protect the spark plug porcelain insulator
2 *Torque wrench* - Although not mandatory, use of this tool is the best way to ensure that the plugs are tightened properly
3 *Ratchet* - Standard hand tool to fit the plug socket
4 *Extension* - Depending on model and accessories, you may need special extensions and universal joints to reach one or more of the plugs
5 *Spark plug gap gauge* - This gauge for checking the gap comes in a variety of styles. Make sure the gap for your engine is included

23.4 Spark plug manufacturers recommend using a wire-type gauge when checking the gap - if the wire does not slide between the electrodes with a slight drag, spark plug adjustment or replacement is required

23.6a Each coil is secured with a bolt - remove the bolts . . .

3   Inspect each of the new plugs for defects. If there are any signs of cracks in the porcelain insulator of a plug, don't use it.

4   Check the electrode gaps of the new plugs. Check the gap by inserting the wire gauge of the proper thickness between the electrodes at the tip of the plug (see illustration). The gap between the electrodes should be identical to that listed in this Chapter's Specifications or on the VECI label. If the gap is incorrect, use the notched adjuster on the feeler gauge body to bend the curved side electrode slightly.

✳✳ **CAUTION:**

Don't attempt to adjust the gap on a used iridium-coated plug.

5   If the side electrode is not exactly over the center electrode, use the notched adjuster to align them.

✳✳ **CAUTION:**

If the gap of a new plug must be adjusted, bend only the base of the ground electrode - do not touch the tip.

REMOVAL

6   Remove the ignition coils (see illustration).

7   If compressed air is available, blow any dirt or foreign material away from the spark plug area before proceeding.

8   Remove the spark plugs (see illustration).

9   Whether you are replacing the plugs at this time or intend to reuse the old plugs, compare the spark plug to those shown in this illustration to get an indication of the general running condition of the engine.

23.6b . . . and lift the coils off of the spark plugs

23.8 Use a special spark plug socket that grips the plug when removing spark plugs

A normally worn spark plug should have light tan or gray deposits on the firing tip.

A carbon fouled plug, identified by soft, sooty, black deposits, may indicate an improperly tuned vehicle. Check the air cleaner, ignition components and engine control system.

An oil fouled spark plug indicates an engine with worn piston rings and/or bad valve seals allowing excessive oil to enter the chamber.

This spark plug has been left in the engine too long, as evidenced by the extreme gap- Plugs with such an extreme gap can cause misfiring and stumbling accompanied by a noticeable lack of power.

A physically damaged spark plug may be evidence of severe detonation in that cylinder. Watch that cylinder carefully between services, as a continued detonation will not only damage the plug, but could also damage the engine.

A bridged or almost bridged spark plug, identified by a build-up between the electrodes caused by excessive carbon or oil build-up on the plug.

23.9 Inspect the spark plug to determine engine running conditions

INSTALLATION

10 Prior to installation, it's a good idea to coat the spark plug threads with anti-seize compound (see illustration). Also, it's often difficult to insert spark plugs into their holes without cross-threading them. To avoid this possibility, fit a length of snug-fitting rubber hose over the end of the spark plug (see illustration). The flexible hose acts as a universal joint to help align the plug with the plug hole. Should the plug begin to cross-thread, the hose will slip on the spark plug, preventing thread damage. Tighten the plug to the torque listed in this Chapter's Specifications.

11 Install the ignition coils.

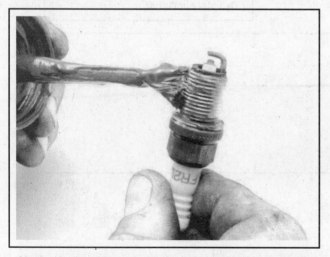
23.10a Apply a thin coat of anti-seize compound to the spark plug threads - DO NOT get any on the electrodes!

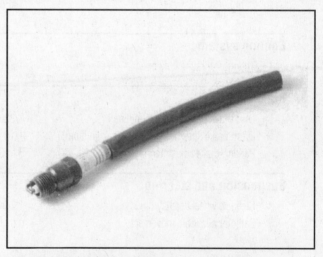
23.10b A length of snug-fitting rubber hose will save time and prevent damaged threads when installing the spark plugs

Specifications

Recommended lubricants and fluids

→Note: Listed here are manufacturer recommendations at the time this manual was written. Manufacturers occasionally upgrade their fluid and lubricant specifications, so check with your local auto parts store for current recommendations.

Engine oil
    Type   API "Certified for gasoline engines"
    Viscosity   SAE 5W-30
Fuel   Unleaded gasoline, 87 octane or higher
Coolant   Toyota Genuine Long Life Coolant or equivalent
Transaxle fluid   Toyota ATF WS automatic transmission fluid
Brake fluid   DOT 3 brake fluid

Capacities*

Engine oil (with filter change)	3.7 quarts
Coolant	
2001 through 2003	
Engine	5.2 quarts
Inverter/converter	2.7 quarts
2004 and later	
Engine	9.1 quarts
Inverter/converter	3.9 quarts
Transaxle (drain and refill)	
2001 through 2003	4.9 quarts
2004 and later	3.8 quarts

All capacities approximate. Add as necessary to bring up to appropriate level.

Ignition system

Spark plug type	Denso SK16R11 or NGK IFR5-A11
Gap	0.043 inch
Firing order	1-3-4-2

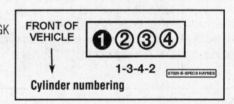

FRONT OF VEHICLE → ❶ ② ③ ④ 1-3-4-2 Cylinder numbering

Cooling system

Thermostat rating fully open	199-degrees F

Brakes

Disc brake pad thickness (minimum)	3/32 inch
Drum brake shoe lining thickness (minimum)	1/16 inch
Parking brake adjustment	5 to 8 clicks

Suspension and steering

Steering wheel freeplay limit	1.2 inches
Balljoint allowable movement	0 inch

Torque specifications	Ft-lbs (unless otherwise indicated)
Wheel lug nuts	76
Spark plugs	156 in-lbs
Drivebelt tensioner nut	30
Engine oil pan drain plug	28
Transaxle check/fill and drain plugs	
(including coolant drain plug)	29

Notes

2A
ENGINE

Section

Reference to other Chapters

1 General information

This Part of Chapter 2 is devoted to in-vehicle repair procedures for the 1.5L four-cylinder engine. Information concerning engine removal and overhaul or replacement can be found in Chapter 2, Part B.

The following repair procedures are based on the assumption that the engine is installed in the vehicle. If the engine has been removed from the vehicle and mounted on a stand, many of the steps outlined in this Part of Chapter 2 will not apply.

The Specifications included in this Part of Chapter 2 apply only to the procedures contained in this Part.

The four-cylinder engine in the Prius models covered by this manual is designated 1NZ-FXE (1.5L). It incorporates an aluminum cylinder block with a bedplate to strengthen the lower half of the block. The camshafts are driven from a single timing chain off the crankshaft, and all models are equipped with Variable Valve Timing (VVT) on the intake camshaft.

Because of the high compression ratio and the unique camshaft design, this engine is known as an Atkinson-Miller cycle engine rather than the typical Otto cycle engine used in almost all other vehicles. This engine design produces very high efficiency in a narrow engine rpm band, although at substantially reduced power. It is an ideal design for a hybrid vehicle such as the Prius.

✳✳ WARNING:

Make sure power to the hybrid system is turned Off before performing any work on this vehicle. Also, on models equipped with the Smart Key system, place the key in a secure spot at least 20 feet away from the work area.

2 Repair operations possible with the engine in the vehicle

Many major repair operations can be accomplished without removing the engine from the vehicle.

Clean the engine compartment and the exterior of the engine with some type of degreaser before any work is done. It will make the job easier and help keep dirt out of the internal areas of the engine.

Depending on the components involved, it may be helpful to remove the hood to improve access to the engine as repairs are performed (refer to Chapter 11 if necessary). Cover the fenders to prevent damage to the paint. Special pads are available, but an old bedspread or blanket will also work.

If vacuum, exhaust, oil or coolant leaks develop, indicating a need for gasket or seal replacement, the repairs can generally be made with the engine in the vehicle. The intake and exhaust manifold gaskets, oil pan gasket, crankshaft oil seals and cylinder head gasket are all accessible with the engine in place.

Exterior engine components, such as the intake and exhaust manifolds, the oil pan, the oil pump, the water pump and the fuel system components can be removed for repair with the engine in place.

Since the cylinder head can be removed without pulling the engine, camshaft and valve component servicing can also be accomplished with the engine in the vehicle. Replacement of the timing chain and sprockets is also possible with the engine in the vehicle.

In extreme cases caused by a lack of necessary equipment, repair or replacement of piston rings, pistons, connecting rods and rod bearings is possible with the engine in the vehicle. However, this practice is not recommended because of the cleaning and preparation work that must be done to the components involved.

3 Top Dead Center (TDC) for number one piston - locating

▶ **Refer to illustration 3.5**

✳✳ WARNING:

Make sure power to the hybrid system is turned Off before performing any work on this vehicle. Also, on models equipped with the Smart Key system, place the key in a secure spot at least 20 feet away from the work area.

1 Top Dead Center (TDC) is the highest point in the cylinder that each piston reaches as it travels up the cylinder bore. Each piston reaches TDC on the compression stroke and again on the exhaust stroke, but TDC generally refers to piston position on the compression stroke.

2 Positioning the piston(s) at TDC is an essential part of many procedures such as valve timing, camshaft and timing chain/sprocket removal.

3 Before beginning this procedure, be sure to place the transmission in Neutral and apply the parking brake or block the rear wheels. Disconnect the cable from the negative terminal of the 12-volt battery (see Chapter 6). Be sure to perform the initialization procedure when reconnecting it. Remove the ignition coils and the spark plugs (see Chapter 1).

4 When looking at the front of the engine, normal crankshaft rotation is clockwise. When performing Step 6, turn the crankshaft with a socket and ratchet attached to the bolt threaded into the front of the crankshaft. Turn the bolt in a clockwise direction only.

5 Install a compression gauge in the number one spark plug hole (see illustration). It should be a gauge with a screw-in fitting and a hose at least six inches long.

6 Rotate the crankshaft while observing for pressure on the compression gauge. The moment the gauge shows pressure indicates that the number one cylinder has begun the compression stroke.

7 Once the compression stroke has begun, TDC for the compression stroke is reached by bringing the piston to the top of the cylinder.

8   Continue turning the crankshaft until the notch in the crankshaft damper is aligned with the "TDC" or the "0" mark on the timing chain cover. At this point, the number one cylinder is at TDC on the compression stroke. If the marks are aligned but there was no compression, the piston was on the exhaust stroke; continue rotating the crankshaft 360-degrees (1-turn) and realign the marks.

➡Note: If a compression gauge is not available, you can simply place a blunt object over the spark plug hole and listen for compression as the engine is rotated. Once compression at the No.1 spark plug hole is noted the remainder of the Step is the same.

9   After the number one piston has been positioned at TDC on the compression stroke, TDC for any of the remaining cylinders can be located by turning the crankshaft 180-degrees (clockwise) and following the firing order (refer to the Specifications). Rotating the engine 180-degrees past TDC #1 will put the engine at TDC compression for cylinder #3.

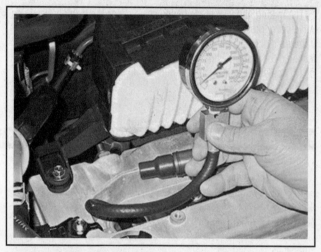

3.5 A compression gauge can be used in the number one spark plug hole to assist in finding TDC

4   Valve cover - removal and installation

※※ WARNING:

Make sure power to the hybrid system is turned Off before performing any work on this vehicle. Also, on models equipped with the Smart Key system, place the key in a secure spot at least 20 feet away from the work area.

※※ CAUTION:

Don't pry at the valve cover-to-cylinder head joint or damage to the sealing surfaces may occur, leading to oil leaks after the valve cover is reinstalled.

REMOVAL

1   Refer to Chapter 6 and disconnect the cable from the negative terminal of the 12-volt battery. Be sure to perform the initialization procedure when reconnecting it.

2   Refer to Chapter 12 and remove both windshield wiper arms.

3   Remove the cowl rubber seal. Release the clips and lift off both plastic cowl covers.

4   Remove the wiper linkage assembly. On 2001 through 2003 models, refer to Chapter 12 and remove the wiper motor as well as the ABS relay block.

5   Unbolt the engine compartment relay block on 2004 and later models, disconnect its wiring harness clips and lay it out of the way. Remove the bolts and remove the cowl panel assembly.

6   Release the clips and lift off the radiator upper cover (see illustration 11.3 in Chapter 1).

7   Refer to Chapter 4 and remove the air filter housing.

8   Unbolt the brake fluid reservoir and position it aside (do not disconnect the hoses).

9   Disconnect the wiring from the fuel injectors and the coils (refer to Chapters 4 and 6). Unbolt and move their wiring harness out of the way.

10 Disconnect the ventilation hoses from the valve cover as well as any interfering wiring.

11 Refer to Chapter 6 and remove the ignition coils.

12 Remove the valve cover mounting bolts and nuts, then detach the valve cover and gasket from the cylinder head. If the valve cover is stuck to the cylinder head, bump the end with a wood block and a hammer to jar it loose. If that doesn't work, try to slip a flexible putty knife between the cylinder head and valve cover to break the seal.

INSTALLATION

▶ Refer to illustration 4.14

13 Remove the valve cover gasket from the valve cover and clean the mating surfaces with lacquer thinner or acetone. Install a new rubber gasket, pressing it evenly into the grooves around the underside of the valve cover.

➡Note: Make sure the spark plug tube seals are in place on the underside of the valve cover before reinstalling it.

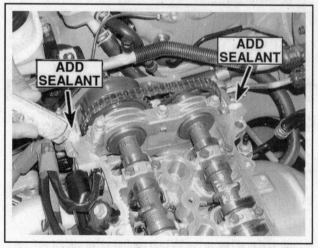

4.14 Apply sealant at the timing chain cover-to-cylinder head joint before installing the valve cover

The mating surfaces of the timing chain cover, the cylinder head and valve cover must be perfectly clean when the valve cover is installed. If there's residue or oil on the mating surfaces when the valve cover is installed, oil leaks may develop.

14 Apply RTV sealant at the timing chain cover-to-cylinder head joint, then install the valve cover and fasteners (see illustration).

15 Tighten the nuts/bolts to the torque listed in this Chapter's Specifications in three or four equal steps.

16 Reinstall the remaining parts, run the engine and check for oil leaks.

5 Variable Valve Timing (VVT) system - description and component check

1 The VVT system is used on all models.

2 The VVT system varies intake camshaft timing by directing oil pressure to advance or retard the intake camshaft sprocket/actuator assembly. Changing the intake camshaft timing during certain engine conditions increases engine power output, fuel economy and reduces emissions.

3 System components include the Powertrain Control Module (PCM), the VVT oil control valve (OCV), the VVT oil control valve filter and the intake camshaft sprocket/actuator assembly.

4 The PCM uses inputs from the following sensors to turn the oil control valve ON or OFF:

　　a) Vehicle Speed Sensor (VSS)
　　b) Throttle Position Sensor (TPS)
　　c) Mass Air Flow (MAF) sensor
　　d) Engine Coolant Temperature (ECT) sensor

5 Once the VVT oil control valve is actuated by the PCM it directs the specified amount of oil pressure from the engine to advance or retard the intake camshaft sprocket/actuator assembly.

6 The intake camshaft sprocket/actuator assembly is equipped with an inner hub that is attached to the camshaft. The inner hub consists of a series of fixed vanes that use oil pressure as a wedge against the vanes to rotate the camshaft. The higher the oil pressure (or flow) the more the actuator assembly will rotate, thereby advancing or retarding the camshaft.

7 When oil is applied to the advance side of the vanes, the actuator can advance the camshaft up to 21-degrees in a clockwise direction. When oil is applied to the retard side of the vanes, the actuator will start to rotate the camshaft counterclockwise back to 0-degrees which is the normal position of the actuator during engine operation under no load or at idle. The PCM can also send a signal to the oil control valve to stop oil flow to both (advance and retard) passages to hold camshaft advance in its current position.

COMPONENT CHECKS

❋❋ WARNING:

Make sure power to the hybrid system is turned Off before performing any work on this vehicle. Also, on models equipped with the Smart Key system, place the key in a secure spot at least 20 feet away from the work area.

VVT oil control valve and filter

▸ Refer to illustration 5.8

➡Note 1: A problem in the VVT oil control valve circuit will set a diagnostic trouble code and turn on the Check Engine light on the dash. Refer to Chapter 6 for accessing trouble codes.

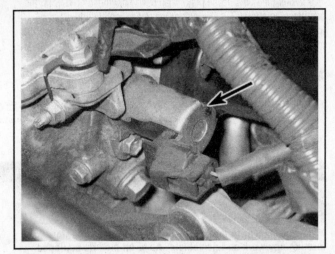

5.8 The Variable Valve Timing (VVT) oil control valve and filter are located at the front of the cylinder head

➡Note 2: Most problems in the VVT system are with the oil control valve and its filter. Regular engine oil and filter changes are necessary for trouble-free operation of the valve.

➡Note 3: Some checks and inspections of the VVT system require removal of the valve cover, the intake camshaft sprocket/actuator assembly and the intake camshaft.

8 The first check of the VVT system components begins with removing the oil control valve filter from the cylinder head and checking the filter/O-ring for clogging (see illustration). Clean and reinstall the filter with a new O-ring. A clogged filter screen is often the cause of system problems.

9 The second and third checks of the VVT system involve checking the operation of the oil control valve. Disconnect the electrical connector from the oil control valve and measure the resistance between the terminals of the control valve. There should be 6.9 to 7.9 ohms (approximately); if not, replace the VVT oil control valve.

10 If the resistance figures check out OK, remove the oil control valve from the cylinder head and check the operation of the control valve plunger. Using a pair of fused jumper wires, apply battery voltage to terminal No. 1 on the control valve, then apply ground to terminal No. 2 on the oil control valve. With battery voltage applied to the oil control valve, check for free movement of the plunger. The plunger should move out when voltage is applied and move back inward when voltage is not applied. If the oil control valve does not operate as described, replace the VVT oil control valve. Always use a new O-ring when reinstalling the control valve.

VVT camshaft sprocket/actuator assembly

11 The fourth and final check of the VVT system requires removing

the valve cover, the intake camshaft and the camshaft sprocket/actuator assembly from the engine. Refer to Section 8 and perform Steps 1 through 10, removing the intake camshaft and sprocket from the engine only. Do not remove the exhaust camshaft or sprocket from the engine.

12 Clean the snout of the intake camshaft with lacquer thinner or acetone to remove all traces of oil from the front journals and the VVT oil control orifices. Apply vinyl tape over all the oil control orifices at the front of the camshaft, except the advance side oil port. Do not apply tape over the front of the camshaft where the sprocket fits.

13 Install the intake camshaft sprocket/actuator assembly onto the intake camshaft and tighten the bolt. Check that the actuator assembly will not rotate from the locked position. The locked position is a neutral position in which the actuator is placed during idle and no load conditions or when the VVT system is not activated by the PCM.

14 Apply 14 psi of air pressure to the advance side oil port and try to rotate the actuator assembly by hand. The actuator should rotate approximately 30-degrees in a counterclockwise direction from the locked position. Also check that it rotates freely with no obvious binding.

➡Note: It is critical to have an airtight seal between the air gun nozzle and the advance oil port hole to accomplish this task, as the lock pin in the actuator may not be forced out of its locating hole. If leakage at the air gun nozzle occurs, it may be necessary to apply a greater amount of air pressure to the advance side oil port in order to force the lock pin from the locating hole.

15 If the actuator does not rotate freely as described, replace the intake camshaft sprocket/actuator assembly.

16 Reassembly is the reverse of removal.

6   Valve springs, retainers and seals - replacement

▶ **Refer to illustrations 6.4, 6.8, 6.10, 6.15 and 6.17**

❊❊ WARNING:

Make sure power to the hybrid system is turned Off before performing any work on this vehicle. Also, on models equipped with the Smart Key system, place the key in a secure spot at least 20 feet away from the work area.

➡Note: Broken valve springs and defective valve stem seals can be replaced without removing the cylinder head. Two special tools and a compressed air source are normally required to perform this operation, so read through this Section carefully. The universal shaft-type valve spring compressor required for the tight valve spring pockets of this vehicle may not be available at all tool rental yards, so check on the availability before beginning the job.

1   Remove the valve cover (see Section 4). Refer to Section 7 and remove the timing chain, then refer to Section 8 and remove the camshafts and lifters from the cylinder head.

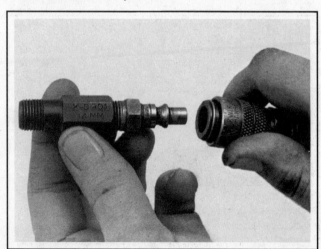

6.4 This is what the air hose adapter that threads into the spark plug hole looks like - they're usually available at auto parts stores

2   Remove the spark plug from the cylinder that has the defective component. If all of the valve stem seals are being replaced, all of the spark plugs should be removed.

3   Turn the crankshaft until the piston in the affected cylinder is at Top Dead Center (TDC) on the compression stroke (see Section 3 for instructions). If you're replacing all of the valve stem seals, begin with cylinder number one and work on the valves for one cylinder at a time. Move from cylinder-to-cylinder following the firing order sequence (see this Chapter's Specifications).

4   Thread an adapter into the spark plug hole (see illustration) and connect an air hose from a compressed air source to it. Most auto parts stores can supply the air hose adapter.

➡Note: Many cylinder compression gauges utilize a screw-in fitting that may work with your air hose quick-disconnect fitting.

5   Apply compressed air to the cylinder. The valves should be held in place by the air pressure.

❊❊ WARNING:

If the cylinder isn't exactly at TDC, air pressure may force the piston down, causing the engine to quickly rotate. DO NOT leave a wrench on the crankshaft drive sprocket bolt or you may be injured by the tool.

6   Stuff shop rags into the cylinder head holes around the valves to prevent parts and tools from falling into the engine.

7   Using a socket and a hammer, gently tap on the top of each valve spring retainer several times. This will break the bond between the valve keepers and the spring retainer and allow the keepers to separate from the valve spring retainer as the valve spring is compressed.

8   Use a valve spring compressor to compress the spring, then remove the keepers with small needle-nose pliers or a magnet (see illustration).

➡Note: Several different types of tools are available for compressing the valve springs with the head in place. Be sure to purchase or rent the "import type" that bolts to the top of the cylinder head. This type uses a support bar across the cylinder head for leverage as the valve spring is compressed. The lack of clearance surrounding the valve springs on these engines prohibits typical types of valve spring compressors from being used.

6.8 Compress the valve spring enough to release the keepers, then lift out the keepers with a magnet or needlenose pliers

6.10 Remove the valve guide seal with a pair of pliers

9 Remove the valve spring and retainer.

➥**Note: If air pressure fails to retain the valve in the closed position during this operation, the valve face or seat may be damaged. If so, the cylinder head will have to be removed for repair.**

10 Remove the old valve stem seals, noting differences between the intake and exhaust seals (see illustration).

11 Wrap a rubber band or tape around the top of the valve stem so the valve won't fall into the combustion chamber, then release the air pressure.

12 Inspect the valve stem for damage. Rotate the valve in the guide and check the end for eccentric movement, which would indicate that the valve is bent.

13 Move the valve up-and-down in the guide and make sure it doesn't bind. If the valve stem binds, either the valve is bent or the guide is damaged. In either case, the head will have to be removed for repair.

14 Reapply air pressure to the cylinder to retain the valve in the closed position, then remove the tape or rubber band from the valve stem.

15 Lubricate the valve stem with engine oil and install a new seal on the valve guide (see illustration).

16 Install the valve spring and the spring retainer in position over the valve.

17 Compress the valve spring and carefully position the keepers in the groove. Apply a small dab of grease to the inside of each keeper to hold it in place (see illustration).

18 Remove the pressure from the spring tool and make sure the keepers are seated.

19 Disconnect the air hose and remove the adapter from the spark plug hole.

20 Install the camshaft, lifters, timing chain and the valve cover by referring to the appropriate Sections.

21 Install the spark plugs and the ignition coils.

22 Start and run the engine, then check for oil leaks and unusual sounds coming from the valve cover area.

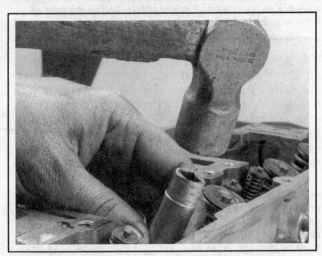

6.15 Gently tap the new seal into place with a hammer and a deep socket

6.17 Apply a small dab of grease to each keeper before installation to hold it in place on the valve stem until the spring is released

7   Timing chain and sprockets - removal, inspection and installation

※※ WARNING 1:

Make sure power to the hybrid system is turned Off before performing any work on this vehicle. Also, on models equipped with the Smart Key system, place the key in a secure spot at least 20 feet away from the work area.

※※ WARNING 2:

Wait until the engine is completely cool before beginning this procedure.

➡Note: Special tools are required for this procedure. Read through the entire procedure and acquire the necessary tools and equipment before beginning work.

REMOVAL

▶ Refer to illustration 7.23

1   Refer to Chapter 6 and disconnect the cable from the negative terminal of the 12-volt battery. Be sure to perform the initialization procedure when reconnecting it.

2   Remove the drivebelt (see Chapter 1).

3   Unbolt the brake fluid reservoir and secure it out of the way (do not disconnect the hoses). Remove the reservoir bracket.

4   Remove the valve cover (see Section 4).

5   With the parking brake applied and the shifter in Park, loosen the lug nuts from the right front wheel, then raise the front of the vehicle and support it securely on jackstands. Remove the right front wheel.

6   On 2001 through 2003 models, remove the right hand engine bottom cover. On 2004 and later models, remove the right and center engine bottom covers.

7   Drain the cooling system (see Chapter 1).

8   Remove the air cleaner intake.

9   Remove the windshield washer reservoir (see Chapter 3).

10   Refer to Chapter 3 and remove the water pump.

11   Disconnect and label the wiring connectors for the various sensors and controllers that interfere with timing chain cover removal.

12   Remove the vacuum switching valve from the engine mount.

13   Put a block of wood on top of a floor jack and put the jack under the oil pan. Jack the engine up just enough to take some weight off of the engine mounts. Remove the engine mount and the engine mount bracket. On later models, remove the engine mount spacer.

14   Refer to Chapter 6 and remove the crankshaft position sensor.

15   Remove the camshaft timing oil control valve assembly (see illustration 5.8).

16   Position the number one piston at TDC on the compression stroke (see Section 3). Confirm the engine is at TDC on the compression stroke.

17   Remove the crankshaft pulley/vibration damper, being careful not to rotate the engine from TDC (see Section 12). If the engine rotates off TDC during this step, reposition the engine back to TDC before proceeding. The engine should be left at TDC for the No. 1 piston during this entire procedure.

18   Remove the timing chain cover fasteners and pry the cover off the engine.

19   There are two O-rings that must be removed and replaced.

7.23 Hold the lug on the camshaft with a wrench to keep it from rotating as the sprocket bolts are loosened - on the intake camshaft, loosen the center bolt securing the VVT sprocket to the camshaft only

20   Remove the timing chain tensioner as follows: Lift the lever and push the plunger in. Lower the lever. Insert a small rod into the lever hole to lock the lever in position. Unbolt the tensioner and remove it.

21   Remove the timing chain tensioner slipper and the damper.

22   Lift the timing chain off the camshaft sprockets and remove the timing chain and the crankshaft sprocket as an assembly from the engine. The crankshaft sprocket should slip off the crankshaft by hand. If not, use several flat bladed screwdrivers to evenly pry the sprocket off the crankshaft.

➡Note: If you intend to reuse the timing chain, use white paint or chalk to make a mark indicating the front of the chain. If a used timing chain is reinstalled with the wear pattern in the opposite direction, noise and increased wear may occur.

23   To remove the camshaft sprockets, loosen the bolts while holding the lug on the camshaft with a wrench (see illustration). Note the identification marks on the camshaft sprockets before removal, then remove the bolts. Pull on the sprockets by hand until they slip off the dowels. If necessary, use a small puller, with the legs inserted in the relief holes, to pull the sprockets off.

➡Note: All models are equipped with variable valve timing, which consists of an actuator assembly attached to the intake camshaft sprocket. When removing the intake camshaft sprocket only loosen and remove the center bolt, which fastens the sprocket to the camshaft. Do not loosen the outer four bolts that secure the actuator to the sprocket.

INSPECTION

▶ Refer to illustrations 7.24a, 7.24b and 7.25

24   Visually inspect all parts for wear and damage. Check the timing chain for loose pins, cracks, worn rollers and side plates. Check the sprockets for hook-shaped, chipped and broken teeth. Also check the timing chain for stretching and the diameter of the timing sprockets for

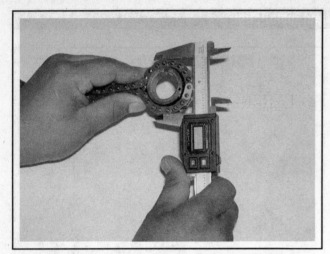

7.24a Wrap the chain around each of the timing sprockets and measure the diameter of the sprockets across the chain rollers - if the measurement exceeds the minimum sprocket diameter, the chain and the timing sprockets must be replaced

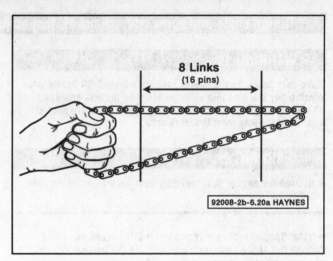

7.24b Timing chain stretch is measured by checking the length of the chain between 8 links (16 pins) at three or more places around the chain

wear with the chain assembled on the sprockets (see illustration). Be sure to measure across the chain rollers when checking the sprocket diameter and to measure chain stretch at three or more places around the chain; if chain stretch exceeds the specifications between any 8 links, the chain must be replaced (see illustration). Maximum chain elongation and minimum sprocket diameter (with chain) should not exceed the amount listed in this Chapter's Specifications. Replace the timing chain and sprockets as a set if the engine has high mileage or fails inspection.

25 Check the chain guides for excessive wear (see illustration). Replace the chain guides if scoring or wear exceeds the amount listed in this Chapter's Specifications. Note that some scoring of the timing chain guide shoes is normal. If excessive wear is indicated, it will also be necessary to inspect the chain guide oil hole on the front of the oil pump for clogging (see Section 15).

INSTALLATION

▶ **Refer to illustrations 7.33a and 7.33b**

26 Remove all traces of old sealant from the timing chain cover and the mating surfaces of the engine block and cylinder head.

27 Make sure the camshafts are positioned with the dowel pins at the top in the 12 o'clock position, then install both camshaft sprockets in their original locations by aligning the dowel pin hole on the rear of the sprockets with the dowel pin on the camshaft.

28 Apply medium strength thread locking compound to the camshaft sprocket bolt threads and make sure the washers are in place. Hold the camshaft from turning and tighten the bolts to the torque listed in this Chapter's Specifications.

❊❊ CAUTION:

Be very careful in the following Steps to avoid having the pistons contact the valves. If you feel any resistance while turning the crankshaft or the camshafts, stop and make certain there is no interference between the valves and pistons before proceeding. If the valves hit the pistons they will bend slightly and will require cylinder head removal to repair.

29 If the timing components get moved during this procedure, set the timing mark on the crankshaft at 40-degrees clockwise from Top Dead Center.

30 Position the timing marks for both camshafts at 20-degrees clockwise from Top Dead Center.

31 Turn the crankshaft counterclockwise to position it at 20-degrees past Top Dead Center.

32 Install the stationary timing chain guide.

33 Loop the timing chain around the crankshaft sprocket and align the No.1 colored link with the mark on the crankshaft sprocket. Install the chain and crankshaft sprocket as an assembly on the engine (see illustrations).

➡**Note: There are three colored links on the timing chain. The No.1 colored link is the link farthest away from the two colored links that are closest together.**

34 Slip the timing chain into the lip of the stationary timing chain guide and over the intake camshaft sprocket, then around the exhaust camshaft sprocket making sure to align the remaining two colored links with the marks on the camshaft sprockets. Be sure to remove all slack from the right side of the chain when doing so.

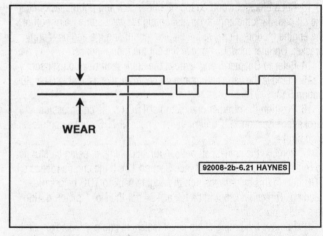

7.25 Timing chain guide wear is measured from the top of the chain contact surface to the bottom of the wear grooves

7.33a Loop the timing chain around the crankshaft sprocket and align the No.1 colored link with the mark on the crankshaft sprocket, then install the chain and crankshaft sprocket as an assembly on the engine

7.33b Install the timing chain on the camshaft sprockets aligning the two colored links on the marks on the sprockets - the other colored link mates with the mark on the crankshaft sprocket

➡Note: The exhaust camshaft will attempt to rotate out of place. Use a wrench to turn it to align the correct sprocket tooth with the colored chain link.

35 Use one hand to remove the slack from the left side of the chain and install the timing chain tensioner pivot arm/chain guide.

36 Reconfirm that the number one piston is still at TDC on the compression stroke and that the timing marks on the crankshaft and camshaft sprockets are aligned with the colored links on the chain.

37 Apply a bead of RTV sealant to the timing chain cover sealing surfaces. Place the timing chain cover in position on the engine and install the bolts in their original locations. Tighten the bolts evenly in

several steps to the torque values listed in this Chapter's Specifications. Be sure to follow the sealant manufacturer's recommendations for assembly and sealant curing times.

38 Install the crankshaft pulley/vibration damper (see Section 12).

39 Rotate the engine clockwise several turns and reposition the number one piston at TDC on the compression stroke (see Section 3). Visually confirm that the timing mark on the crankshaft pulley/vibration damper is aligned with the "O" mark on the timing chain cover and the camshaft sprocket marks are aligned.

40 The remainder of the installation is the reverse of removal.

8 Camshafts and lifters - removal, inspection and installation

❊❊ WARNING:

Make sure power to the hybrid system is turned Off before performing any work on this vehicle. Also, on models equipped with the Smart Key system, place the key in a secure spot at least 20 feet away from the work area.

➡Note: The camshafts should always be thoroughly inspected before installation and camshaft endplay should always be checked prior to camshaft removal (see Step 13).

REMOVAL

1 Refer to Chapter 6 and disconnect the cable from the negative terminal of the 12-volt battery. Be sure to perform the initialization procedure when reconnecting it.

2 Remove the valve cover (see Section 4).

3 Refer to Section 3 and place the engine on TDC for number 1 cylinder. Visually confirm the engine is at TDC on the compression stroke by verifying that the timing mark on the crankshaft pulley/vibration damper is aligned with the "O" mark on the timing chain cover and the

camshaft sprocket marks are aligned with the colored chain links.

4 If the camshaft sprockets are removed, then the timing chain tensioner will automatically tighten the chain preventing installation of the sprockets. To solve this problem: the timing cover must be removed and the tensioner manually retracted and locked (refer to Section 7).

5 Some auto parts stores sell a wedge-shaped tool that can be forced down between the timing chain to hold the tensioner in the partially retracted position. This will eliminate the need for front cover removal, but care must be taken to ensure that the wedge doesn't become loosened later in the procedure.

6 Using a wrench on the camshaft lugs to hold the camshaft sprockets from turning (see illustration 7.23), loosen the camshaft sprocket bolts several turns. If the camshaft sprockets have rotated during the bolt loosening process, rotate the engine clockwise until the "TDC" marks on the cam sprockets are realigned.

7 Remove the camshaft sprocket retaining bolts. Disengage the timing chain from the sprockets and remove the camshaft sprockets from the engine. Make sure to note that the sprockets are marked "IN" for intake or "EX" for exhaust and cannot be interchanged. After removing the sprockets, hang the timing chain up with a piece of wire and attach it to an object on the firewall. This will prevent the timing chain from

8.13 Mount a dial indicator as shown to measure camshaft endplay - pry the camshaft forward and back, then measure the difference on the dial indicator

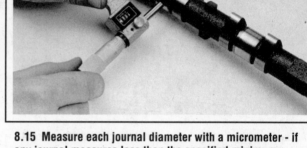

8.15 Measure each journal diameter with a micrometer - if any journal measures less than the specified minimum, replace the camshaft

falling into the engine as the remaining steps in this procedure are performed. Also place a rag into the opening of the timing chain cover to prevent any foreign objects from falling into the engine.

➡**Note: At this time, skip to Step 13 to check the camshaft endplay.**

8 Verify the markings on the camshaft bearing caps. The caps should be marked from 1 to 5 with an "I" or an "E" mark on the cap indicating whether they're for the intake or exhaust camshaft.

9 Loosen the camshaft bearing caps in two or three steps, starting with the outer bolts and working toward the center bolts.

❋❋ **CAUTION:**

Keep the caps in order. They must go back in the same locations from which they were removed.

10 Detach the bearing caps, then remove the camshaft(s) from the cylinder head.

➡**Note: When looking at the engine from the front of the vehicle, the forward facing cam is the intake camshaft and the cam nearest the firewall is the exhaust camshaft. It is very important that the camshafts are returned to their original locations during installation.**

11 Remove the lifters from the cylinder head, keeping them in order with their respective valve and cylinder.

❋❋ **CAUTION:**

Keep the lifters in order. They must go back in the position from which they were removed.

12 Inspect the camshafts and lifters as described below. Also inspect the camshaft sprockets for wear on the teeth. Inspect the chains for cracks or excessive wear of the rollers, and for stretching (see Section 7). If any of the components show signs of excessive wear they must be replaced.

INSPECTION

➡ **Refer to illustrations 8.13, 8.15 and 8.16**

13 Before the camshafts are removed from the engine, check the camshaft endplay by placing a dial indicator with the stem in line with the camshaft and touching the snout (see illustration). Push the camshaft all the way to the rear and zero the dial indicator. Next, pry the camshaft to the front as far as possible and check the reading on the dial indicator. The distance it moves is the endplay. If it's greater than the Specifications listed in this Chapter, check the bearing caps for wear. If the bearing caps are worn, the cylinder head must be replaced.

14 With the camshafts removed, visually check the camshaft bearing surfaces in the cylinder head for pitting, score marks, galling and abnormal wear. If the bearing surfaces are damaged, the cylinder head may have to be replaced.

15 Measure the outside diameter of each camshaft bearing journal and record your measurements (see illustration). Compare them to the journal outside diameter specified in this Chapter, then measure the inside diameter of each corresponding camshaft bearing and record the measurements. Subtract each cam journal outside diameter from its respective cam bearing bore inside diameter to determine the oil clearance for each bearing. Compare the results to the specified journal-to-bearing clearance. If any of the measurements fall outside the standard specified wear limits in this Chapter, either the camshaft or the cylinder head, or both, must be replaced.

➡**Note: If precision measuring tools are not available, Plastigage may be used to determine the bearing journal oil clearance (see Chapter 2B).**

16 Using a micrometer, measure the height of each camshaft lobe (see illustration). Compare your measurements with this Chapter's Specifications. If the height for any one lobe is less than the specified minimum, replace the camshaft.

17 Check the camshaft runout by placing the camshaft back into the cylinder head and set up a dial indicator on the center journal. Zero the dial indicator. Turn the camshaft slowly and note the dial indicator readings. Runout should not exceed 0.0012 inch. If the measured runout exceeds the specified runout, replace the camshaft.

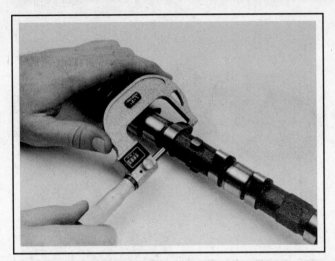

8.16 Measure each lobe height - if any is less than the minimum specified, replace the camshaft

18 Inspect each lifter for scuffing and score marks.

19 Measure the outside diameter of each lifter and the corresponding lifter bore inside diameter. Subtract the lifter diameter from the lifter bore diameter to determine the oil clearance. Compare it to this Chapter's Specifications. If the oil clearance is excessive, a new cylinder head and/or new lifters will be required.

INSTALLATION

▶ **Refer to illustration 8.22**

20 Apply moly-based engine assembly lubricant or camshaft installation lubricant to the camshaft lobes and journals and install the camshaft into the cylinder head with the No.1 cylinder camshaft lobes pointing inward toward each other and the dowel pins facing upward. If the old camshafts are being used, make sure they're installed in the exact location from which they came.

21 Install the bearing caps and bolts and tighten them hand tight. Make sure that the caps are on the intake camshaft and the E caps are

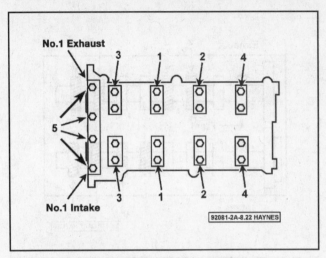

8.22 Camshaft bearing cap tightening sequence

on the exhaust camshaft. In addition, the arrows must point toward the timing sprockets, the number 5 caps must be farthest away from the sprockets and the number 2 caps closest.

22 Tighten the bearing cap bolts in several equal steps, to the torque listed in this Chapter's Specifications, using the proper tightening sequence (see illustration). Start with the front cap (with three bolts), then tighten the rest in sequence.

23 Install the camshaft sprockets and timing chain (see Section 7).

VALVE CLEARANCE CHECK

▶ **Refer to illustrations 8.25a, 8.25b and 8.26**

24 Refer to Section 3 and position the number 1 piston at TDC on the compression stroke.

25 Measure the clearances of the indicated valves with feeler gauges (see illustrations). Record the measurements which are out of specification. They will be used later to determine the required replacement lifters.

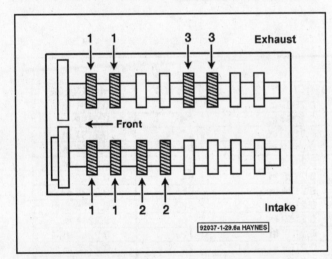

8.25a When the No. 1 piston is at TDC on the compression stroke, the valve clearance for the No. 1 and No. 3 cylinder exhaust valves and the No. 1 and No. 2 intake valves can be measured

8.25b Check the clearance for each valve with a feeler gauge of the specified thickness - if the clearance is correct, you should feel a slight drag on the gauge as you pull it out

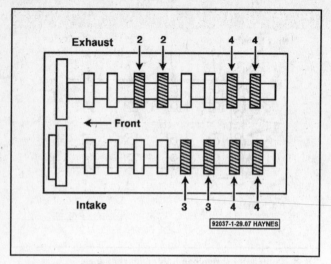

8.26 When the No. 4 piston is at TDC on the compression stroke, the valve clearance for the No. 2 and No. 4 exhaust valves and the No. 3 and No. 4 intake valves can be measured

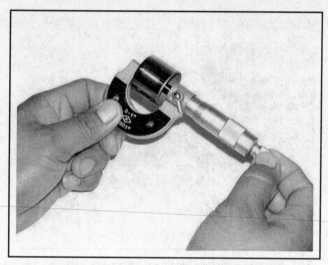

8.28 Measure the thickness of each lifter head with a micrometer

26 Turn the crankshaft one complete revolution and realign the timing marks. Measure the remaining valves (see illustration).

ADJUSTMENT

▶ **Refer to illustrations 8.28 and 8.29**

27 If any of the valve clearances were out of adjustment, remove the camshaft(s) from over the lifter(s) that was/were out of the specified clearance range (see Chapter 2, Part B).

28 Measure the thickness of the lifter with a micrometer (see illustration). To calculate the correct thickness of a replacement shim or lifter that will place the valve clearance within the specified value, use the following formula:

$$N = T + (A - V)$$

T = thickness of the old shim or lifter
A = valve clearance measured
N = thickness of the new shim or lifter
V = desired valve clearance (see this Chapter's Specifications)

29 Select a lifter with a thickness as close as possible to the valve clearance calculated. The lifters are available in 35 sizes in increments of 0.0008-inch (0.020 mm), range in size from 0.1992-inch (5.060 mm) to 0.2260-inch (5.740 mm) (see illustration).

➡**Note: Through careful analysis of the lifter sizes needed to bring the out-of-specification valve clearance within specification, it is often possible to simply move a lifter that has to come out anyway to another location requiring a lifter of that particular size, thereby reducing the number of new lifters that must be purchased.**

30 Install the proper thickness lifter(s) in position, making sure to lubricate them with camshaft installation lube first.

➡**Note: Apply the lubricant to the underside of the lifter where it contacts the valve stem, the walls of the lifter and the face of the lifter.**

31 Install the camshaft(s) (see Chapter 2A).
32 Recheck the valve clearances.

LIFTER NO.	THICKNESS	LIFTER NO.	THICKNESS	LIFTER NO.	THICKNESS
06	0.1992 in.	30	0.2087 in.	54	0.2181 in.
08	0.2000 in.	32	0.2094 in.	56	0.2189 in.
10	0.2008 in.	34	0.2102 in.	58	0.2197 in.
12	0.2016 in.	36	0.2110 in.	60	0.2205 in.
14	0.2024 in.	38	0.2118 in.	62	0.2213 in.
16	0.2031 in.	40	0.2126 in.	64	0.2220 in.
18	0.2039 in.	42	0.2134 in.	66	0.2228 in.
20	0.2047 in.	44	0.2142 in.	68	0.2236 in.
22	0.2055 in.	46	0.2150 in.	70	0.2244 in.
24	0.2063 in.	48	0.2157 in.	72	0.2252 in.
26	0.2071 in.	50	0.2165 in.	74	0.2260 in.
28	0.2079 in.	52	0.2173 in.		

8.29 Valve lifter thickness chart

9 Intake manifold - removal and installation

WARNING 1:

Make sure power to the hybrid system is turned Off before performing any work on this vehicle. Also, on models equipped with the Smart Key system, place the key in a secure spot at least 20 feet away from the work area.

WARNING 2:

Wait until the engine is completely cool before beginning this procedure.

REMOVAL

1 Relieve the fuel system pressure (see Chapter 4).

2 Refer to Chapter 6 and disconnect the cable from the negative terminal of the 12-volt battery. Be sure to perform the initialization procedure when reconnecting it.

3 Refer to Chapter 4 and remove the throttle body.

4 Label and detach the PCV and vacuum hoses connected to the rear of the intake manifold. Label and disconnect all interfering wiring.

5 Remove the intake manifold mounting nuts, bolts and support bracket bolts and remove the manifold and the gasket from the engine (see illustrations).

INSTALLATION

6 Clean the mating surfaces of the intake manifold and the cylinder head mounting surface with lacquer thinner or acetone. If the gasket shows signs of leaking, have the manifold checked for warpage at an automotive machine shop and resurfaced if necessary.

7 Install a new gasket over the manifold studs, then position the manifold on the cylinder head and install the nuts/bolts and brackets.

8 Tighten the manifold-to-cylinder head nuts/bolts in three or four equal steps to the torque listed in this Chapter's Specifications. Work from the center out towards the ends to avoid warping the manifold. After the manifold-to-cylinder head bolts have been tightened to the proper torque, tighten the lower bracket bolts.

9 Install the remaining parts in the reverse order of removal. Check the coolant level, adding as necessary (see Chapter 1).

10 Before starting the engine, check the throttle linkage for smooth operation.

11 Run the engine and check for coolant and vacuum leaks.

12 Road test the vehicle and check for proper operation of all accessories, including the cruise control system, if equipped.

10 Exhaust manifold - removal and installation

WARNING 1:

Make sure power to the hybrid system is turned Off before performing any work on this vehicle. Also, on models equipped with the Smart Key system, place the key in a secure spot at least 20 feet away from the work area.

WARNING 2:

The engine must be completely cool before beginning this procedure.

REMOVAL

1 Refer to Chapter 6 and disconnect the cable from the negative terminal of the 12-volt battery. Be sure to perform the initialization procedure when reconnecting it.

2 Raise the front of the vehicle and support it securely on jackstands.

3 Working below the vehicle, apply penetrating oil to the bolts and springs retaining the exhaust pipe to the manifold. After the bolts have soaked, remove the bolts retaining the exhaust pipe to the manifold. Separate the front exhaust pipe from the manifold, being careful not to damage the oxygen sensor.

➡Note: It may be necessary to remove the inner heat shield from above the right driveaxle to access one of the exhaust pipe-to-manifold bolts.

4 Unbolt the lower exhaust manifold brace and remove it from the engine.

5 Working in the engine compartment, remove the heat shield from the manifold.

6 Remove the nuts/bolts and detach the manifold and gasket. Remove the manifold.

INSTALLATION

7 Use a scraper to remove all traces of old gasket material and carbon deposits from the manifold and cylinder head mating surfaces. If the gasket was leaking, have the manifold checked for warpage at an automotive machine shop and resurfaced if necessary.

➡Note: If the manifold is being replaced with a new one it will be necessary to remove the lower heat shield and fasten it to the new manifold.

8 Position a new gasket over the cylinder head studs noting any directional marks or arrows on the gasket if equipped.

9 Install the manifold and thread the mounting nuts into place.

10 Working from the center out, tighten the nuts/bolts to the torque listed in this Chapter's Specifications in three or four equal steps.

11 Reinstall the remaining parts in the reverse order of removal.

12 Run the engine and check for exhaust leaks.

11 Cylinder head - removal and installation

☀☀ WARNING 1:

Make sure power to the hybrid system is turned Off before performing any work on this vehicle. Also, on models equipped with the Smart Key system, place the key in a secure spot at least 20 feet away from the work area.

☀☀ WARNING 2:

The engine must be completely cool before beginning this procedure.

REMOVAL

1   Relieve the fuel system pressure (see Chapter 4), then refer to Chapter 6 and disconnect the cable from the negative terminal of the 12-volt battery. Be sure to perform the initialization procedure when reconnecting it. Remove the service plug (refer to Chapter 6).

2   Drain the cooling system (see Chapter 1) including the transaxle coolant.

3   Refer to Chapter 5 and remove the inverter/converter assembly.

4   Remove the valve cover (see Section 4).

5   Remove the throttle body, fuel injectors and fuel rail (see Chapter 4).

6   Remove the intake manifold (see Section 9).

7   Remove the exhaust manifold (see Section 10).

➡Note: The cylinder head can be removed with the exhaust manifold attached, but remember to disconnect the oxygen sensor first.

8   Remove the timing chain and camshaft sprockets (see Section 7).

9   Remove the camshafts and lifters (see Section 8).

10 Refer to Section 5 and remove the variable valve timing control valve and filter.

11 Label and remove the coolant hoses, tubes and electrical connections from the cylinder head. Also remove the PCV valve and the oil control valve on 2001 through 2003 engines.

12 On 2004 and later models, remove the dipstick guide.

13 Loosen the cylinder head bolts in 1/4-turn increments until they can be removed by hand. Loosen the cylinder head bolts in the reverse order of the recommended tightening sequence (see illustration 11.26) to avoid warping or cracking the cylinder head.

14 On 2001 through 2003 models, be sure to remove the bolt that holds the water tube to the cylinder head.

15 Lift the cylinder head off the engine block. If it's stuck, very carefully pry up at the transaxle end, beyond the gasket surface.

16 Remove any remaining external components from the cylinder head to allow for thorough cleaning and inspection.

INSTALLATION

▶ Refer to illustration 11.26

17 The mating surfaces of the cylinder head and block must be perfectly clean when the cylinder head is installed.

18 Use a gasket scraper to remove all traces of carbon and old gasket material, then clean the mating surfaces with lacquer thinner or acetone. If there's oil on the mating surfaces when the cylinder head is installed, the gasket may not seal correctly and leaks could develop.

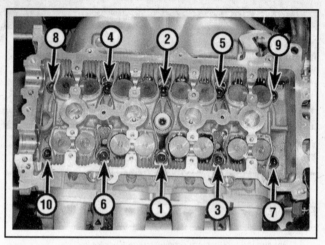

11.26 Cylinder head bolt tightening sequence

When working on the block, stuff the cylinders with clean shop rags to keep out debris. Use a vacuum cleaner to remove material that falls into the cylinders.

19 Check the block and cylinder head mating surfaces for nicks, deep scratches and other damage. If damage is slight, it can be removed with a file; if it's excessive, machining may be the only alternative.

20 Use a tap of the correct size to chase the threads in the cylinder head bolt holes, then clean the holes with compressed air - make sure that nothing remains in the holes.

☀☀ WARNING:

Wear eye protection when using compressed air!

21 Using a wire brush, clean the threads on each bolt to remove corrosion and restore the threads. Dirt, corrosion, sealant and damaged threads will affect torque readings. Also check the cylinder head bolts for stretching. Measure the entire length of each bolt from the underside of the head to the tip of the threads. If the length of any bolt exceeds 5.791 inches, it must be replaced.

22 Install the components that were removed from the cylinder head.

23 Position the new gasket over the dowel pins in the block. Position the gasket with the "Lot #" mark facing up and near the timing chain end of the engine.

24 Carefully set the cylinder head on the block without disturbing the gasket.

25 Before installing the cylinder head bolts, apply a small amount of clean engine oil to the threads and under the bolt heads.

26 Install the bolts in their original locations and tighten them finger tight. Following the recommended sequence, tighten the bolts in three steps to the torque listed in this Chapter's Specifications (see illustration). Step 3 of the tightening sequence requires each bolt to be tightened an additional 90 degrees. If you don't have an angle-torque attachment for your torque wrench, simply apply a paint mark at one edge of each cylinder head bolt and tighten the bolt until that mark is 90 degrees (1/4-turn) from where you started at the beginning of Step 3.

27 The remaining installation steps are the reverse of removal.

28 Change the engine oil and filter (see Chapter 1).

29 Refill the cooling system (see Chapter 1), run the engine and check for leaks.

12 Crankshaft pulley/vibration damper - removal and installation

▶ Refer to illustrations 12.4 and 12.5

※※ WARNING:

Make sure power to the hybrid system is turned Off before performing any work on this vehicle. Also, on models equipped with the Smart Key system, place the key in a secure spot at least 20 feet away from the work area.

1   Refer to Chapter 6 and disconnect the cable from the negative terminal of the 12-volt battery. Be sure to perform the initialization procedure when reconnecting it.

2   Remove the drivebelt (see Chapter 1).

3   With the parking brake applied and the shifter in Park, loosen the lug nuts from the right front wheel, then raise the front of the vehicle and support it securely on jackstands. Remove the right front wheel and the right splash shield from the wheelwell. There are some crankshaft pulley removal tools that don't require the removal of these parts. Test your puller before you do this work.

4   Remove the bolt from the front of the crankshaft. A breaker bar will probably be necessary, since the bolt is very tight (see illustration).

➡Note: To prevent the pulley from turning when the bolt is loosened, a strap wrench can be used; just be sure to wrap the outside of the pulley with an old drivebelt to prevent damaging it.

5   Using a puller that bolts to the crankshaft pulley hub, remove the crankshaft pulley from the crankshaft (see illustration).

※※ CAUTION:

Use the proper adapter on the end of the puller screw to prevent damaging the crankshaft threads.

➡Note: Depending on the type of puller you have it may be necessary to support the engine from above, remove the right side engine mount and lower the engine to gain sufficient clearance to use the puller.

6   To install the crankshaft pulley, slide the pulley onto the crankshaft as far as it will slide on, then use a vibration damper installation tool to press the pulley onto the crankshaft. Note that the slot (keyway) in the hub must be aligned with the Woodruff key in the end of the crankshaft and that the crankshaft bolt can also be used to press the crankshaft pulley into position.

7   Tighten the crankshaft bolt to the torque listed in this Chapter's Specifications.

8   The remaining installation steps are the reverse of removal.

12.4 A puller base and several spacers can be mounted to the center hub of the pulley to keep the crankshaft from turning as the pulley retaining bolt is loosened - install the socket over the crankshaft bolt head before installing the puller, then insert the extension through the center hole of the puller

12.5 Use the correct puller with spacers between it and the pulley - this will allow you to insert a bar through the spacers to keep the assembly from turning as the pulley is removed

13 Crankshaft front oil seal - replacement

▶ Refer to illustrations 13.2 and 13.3

※※ WARNING:

Make sure power to the hybrid system is turned Off before performing any work on this vehicle. Also, on models equipped with the Smart Key system, place the key in a secure spot at least 20 feet away from the work area.

1   Remove the crankshaft pulley (see Section 12).

2   Note how the seal is installed - the new one must be installed to the same depth and facing the same way. Carefully pry the oil seal out

13.2 Carefully pry the old seal out of the timing chain cover - don't damage the crankshaft in the process

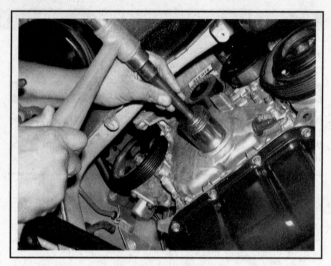

13.3 Drive the new seal into place with a seal driver or a large socket and hammer

of the cover with a seal puller or a large screwdriver (see illustration). Cut the lip of the seal with a utility knife to make removal easier. Be very careful not to distort the cover or scratch the crankshaft! Wrap electrician's tape around the tip of the screwdriver to avoid damage to the crankshaft.

3   Apply clean engine oil or multi-purpose grease to the outer edge of the new seal, then install it in the cover with the lip (spring side) facing IN. Drive the seal into place with a seal driver or a large socket and a hammer (see illustration). Make sure the seal enters the bore squarely

and stop when the front face is at the proper depth.

4   Check the surface on the pulley hub that the oil seal rides on. If the surface has been grooved from long-time contact with the seal, replace the pulley.

5   Lubricate the pulley hub with clean engine oil and reinstall the crankshaft pulley (see Section 12).

6   Install the crankshaft pulley retaining bolt and tighten it to the torque listed in this Chapter's Specifications.

7   The remainder of installation is the reverse of removal.

14 Oil pan - removal and installation

❋❋ WARNING:

Make sure power to the hybrid system is turned Off before performing any work on this vehicle. Also, on models equipped with the Smart Key system, place the key in a secure spot at least 20 feet away from the work area.

➧Note: This procedure is for the stamped sheet metal lower oil pan only. There is a larger cast aluminum upper oil pan that is also used on these vehicles. It is normally removed during an engine teardown. Refer to Chapter 2B for information on this component.

REMOVAL

▸ **Refer to illustrations 14.6a and 14.6b**

1   Disconnect the cable from the negative terminal of the 12-volt battery (see Chapter 6). Be sure to perform the initialization procedure when reconnecting it.

2   Set the parking brake and block the rear wheels.

3   Raise the front of the vehicle and support it securely on jackstands.

4   Remove the two plastic splash shields under the engine, if equipped.

5   Drain the engine oil and remove the oil filter (see Chapter 1). Remove the oil dipstick.

6   Remove the bolts and detach the oil pan (see illustration). If it's stuck, pry it loose very carefully with a small screwdriver or putty knife

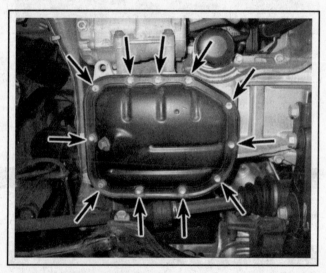

14.6a Oil pan bolt locations

(see illustration). Don't damage the mating surfaces of the pan and block or oil leaks could develop.

INSTALLATION

7   Use a scraper to remove all traces of old sealant from the block and oil pan. Clean the mating surfaces with lacquer thinner or acetone.

8   Make sure the threaded bolt holes in the block are clean.

9   Check the oil pan flange for distortion, particularly around the bolt holes. Remove any nicks or burrs as necessary.

10   Inspect the oil pump pick-up tube assembly for cracks and a blocked strainer. If the pick-up was removed, clean it thoroughly and install it now, using a new gasket. Tighten the nuts/bolts to the torque listed in this Chapter's Specifications.

11   Apply a 3/16-inch wide bead of RTV sealant to the mating surface of the oil pan.

➡Note: Be sure to follow the sealant manufacturer's recommendations for assembly and sealant curing times.

12   Carefully position the oil pan on the engine block and install the oil pan-to-engine block bolts loosely.

13   Working from the center out, tighten the oil pan-to-engine block bolts to the torque listed in this Chapter's Specifications in three or four steps.

14   The remainder of installation is the reverse of removal. Be sure to

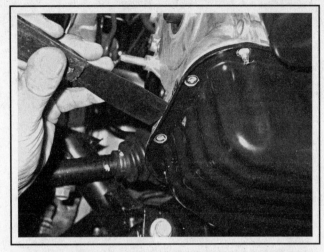

14.6b   Pry the oil pan loose with a screwdriver or putty knife - be careful not to damage the mating surfaces of the pan and block as oil leaks may develop

wait at least one hour before adding oil to allow the sealant to properly cure.

15   Run the engine and check for oil pressure and leaks.

15   Oil pump - removal, inspection and installation

❊❊ WARNING:

Make sure power to the hybrid system is turned Off before performing any work on this vehicle. Also, on models equipped with the Smart Key system, place the key in a secure spot at least 20 feet away from the work area.

REMOVAL

1   Refer to Section 7 and remove the timing chain and the crankshaft sprocket.

2   Remove the five bolts and detach the oil pump body from the inside of the timing chain cover.

3   Use a scraper to remove all traces of sealant and old gasket material from the pump body and engine block, then clean the mating surfaces with lacquer thinner or acetone.

4   Remove the oil pressure relief valve from the pump body.

5   Remove the screws and bolt and separate the pump body from the timing cover. Observe the marks on the two rotors. Lift out the drive and driven rotors.

INSPECTION

♦ **Refer to illustrations 15.8a, 15.8b, 15.8c, 15.8d and 15.8e**

6   Clean all components with solvent, then inspect them for wear and damage.

7   Check the oil pressure relief valve piston sliding surface and valve spring. If either the spring or the valve is damaged, they must be replaced as a set.

8   Check the driven rotor-to-body clearance, rotor-to-cover clearance and drive rotor tip clearance with a feeler gauge (see illustrations) and compare the results to this Chapter's Specifications. If any clearance is excessive, replace the rotors as a set. If necessary, replace the oil pump body.

9   Check the timing chain guide oil jet for blockage.

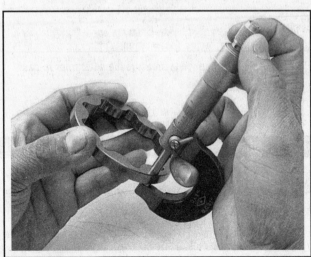

15.8a   Measure the outer rotor thickness

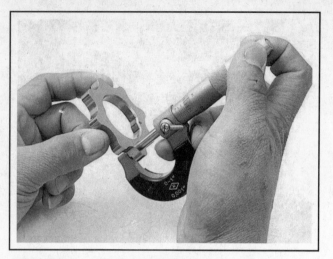

15.8b Measure the inner rotor thickness

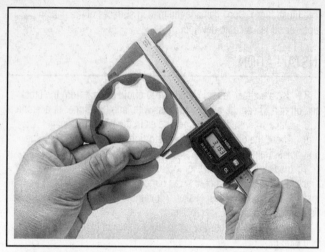

15.8c Use a caliper to measure the outer diameter of the outer rotor

INSTALLATION

10 Lubricate the drive and driven rotors with clean engine oil and place them in the pump body with the marks facing toward the timing chain cover as they were originally.

11 Pack the pump cavity with petroleum jelly and attach the pump

cover, tighten the bolt and screws to the torque listed in this Chapter's Specifications.

12 Lubricate the oil pressure relief valve piston with clean engine oil and reinstall the valve components in the pump body.

13 Reinstall the remaining parts in the reverse order of removal.

14 Add oil if necessary, start the engine and check for oil pressure and leaks.

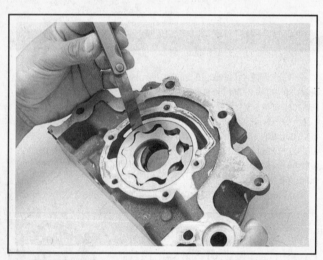

15.8d Use a feeler gauge to measure the outer rotor-to-case clearance

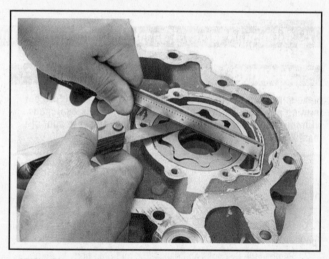

15.8e Place a precision straightedge over the rotors and measure the clearance between the rotors and the cover

16 Flywheel - removal and installation

REMOVAL

▶ **Refer to illustration 16.3**

1 If you're working on a 2003 or earlier model, remove the engine/transaxle assembly (see Chapter 2B), the separate the transaxle from the engine. If you're working on a 2004 or later model, remove the transaxle (see Chapter 7).

2 Remove the six bolts and lift off the transaxle damper from the flywheel.

3 Use a center punch or paint to make alignment marks on the flywheel and crankshaft to ensure correct alignment during reinstallation (see illustration).

4 Remove the bolts that secure the flywheel to the crankshaft. To prevent the crankshaft from turning a strap wrench can be used to hole the crankshaft pulley; just be sure to wrap the outside of the pulley with

an old drivebelt to prevent damaging it.

5   Remove the flywheel from the crankshaft.

INSTALLATION

6   Clean the flywheel to remove grease and oil. Inspect the surface for cracks, rivet grooves, burned areas and score marks. Light scoring can be removed with emery cloth.

7   Clean and inspect the mating surfaces of the flywheel and the crankshaft. If the crankshaft rear seal is leaking, replace it before reinstalling the flywheel (see Section 17).

8   Position the flywheel against the crankshaft. Be sure to align the marks made during removal. Note that some engines have an alignment dowel or staggered bolt holes to ensure correct installation. Before installing the bolts, apply thread-locking compound to the threads.

9   Hold the flywheel from turning and tighten the bolts to the torque listed in this Chapter's Specifications. Follow a criss-cross pattern and work up to the final torque in three or four steps.

10 The remainder of installation is the reverse of the removal procedure.

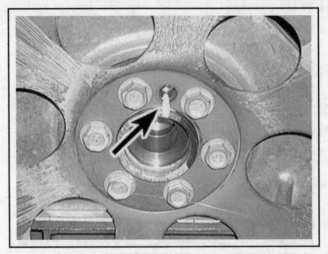

16.3 Before removing the flywheel, mark its relationship to the crankshaft with paint or a center punch (typical)

17 Rear main oil seal - replacement

▶ **Refer to illustration 17.3**

1   Remove the transaxle (see Chapter 7).

2   Remove the flywheel (see Section 16).

3   Pry the oil seal from the rear of the engine with a screwdriver (see illustration). If the seal can't be pried out, try carefully screwing a sheet metal screw into it, then pulling on it. Be careful not to nick or scratch the crankshaft or the seal bore. Be sure to note how far it's recessed into the bore before removal so the new seal can be installed to the same depth. Thoroughly clean the seal bore in the block with a shop towel. Remove all traces of oil and dirt.

4   Lubricate the outside diameter of the seal and, using a seal installation tool, install the seal over the end of the crankshaft. Drive the new seal squarely into the seal bore and flush with the edge of the seal retainer.

5   Install the flywheel and damper (see Section 16).

6   Install the transaxle (see Chapter 7).

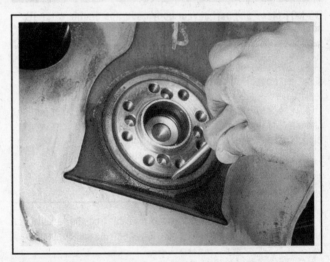

17.3 Carefully pry the seal out of its bore - DO NOT nick or scratch the crankshaft

18 Powertrain mounts - check and replacement

✷✷ WARNING:

Make sure power to the hybrid system is turned Off before performing any work on this vehicle. Also, on models equipped with the Smart Key system, place the key in a secure spot at least 20 feet away from the work area.

1   Engine mounts seldom require attention, but broken or deteriorated mounts should be replaced immediately or the added strain placed on the driveline components may cause damage or wear.

CHECK

▶ **Refer to illustrations 18.3a and 18.3b**

➡ **Note: During the check, the engine must be raised slightly to remove the weight from the mounts.**

2   Raise the vehicle and support it securely on jackstands, then position a jack under the engine oil pan. Place a large wood block between the jack head and the oil pan, then carefully raise the engine

18.3a Driver's side transaxle mounting fasteners

18.3b Be sure to check the engine movement rod by prying on it with a large screwdriver or a bar

just enough to take the weight off the mounts. Do not position the wood block under the drain plug.

✳✳ WARNING:

DO NOT place any part of your body under the engine when it's supported only by a jack!

3   Check the mounts to see if the rubber is cracked, hardened or separated from the metal casing, which would indicate the need for replacement (see illustrations).

4   Check for relative movement between the inner and outer portions of the mount (use a large screwdriver or pry bar to attempt to move the mounts). If movement is noted, replace the mount.

5   Check the mount fasteners to make sure they are tight.

REPLACEMENT

6   Refer to Chapter 6 and disconnect the cable from the negative terminal of the 12-volt battery. Be sure to perform the initialization pro- cedure when reconnecting it. Raise the vehicle and support it securely on jackstands (if not already done). The engine should be supported from above, preferably with an engine support fixture available from tool rental yards.

7   To remove the right (passenger side) engine mount, remove the three bolts securing the mount to the body, then remove the three bolts and two nuts securing the mount bracket to the engine bracket. Detach the refrigerant line bracket-retaining nut and remove the mount from the engine compartment. Be sure to remove the mount bracket from the old mount and install it on the new mount.

8   To remove the left (driver's side) engine mount, remove the four bolts securing the mount to the body, then remove the through-bolt securing the mount to the transaxle bracket.

9   To remove the front and rear engine mounts, remove the bolts securing the mount to the lower frame crossmember, then remove the through-bolt securing the mount to the engine bracket.

10 Installation is the reverse of removal. Use thread-locking com- pound on the mount bolts/nuts and be sure to tighten them securely.

Specifications

General

Engine type	DOHC, inline four-cylinder, four valves per cylinder
Engine designation	1NZ-FXE
Cylinder numbers (drivebelt end-to-transaxle end)	1-2-3-4
Firing order	1-3-4-2
Displacement	1.5 liters (92 cu. in.)

Timing chain

Timing chain sprocket wear limit (minimum diameter)	
Camshaft sprocket(s) (w/chain)	3.787 inches
Crankshaft sprocket (w/chain)	1.988 inches
Timing chain stretch limit	
8 links (16 pins)	4.890 inches
Timing chain guide wear limit	0.039 inch

Camshaft and lifters

Journal diameter	
No. 1 journal	1.3563 to 1.3569 inch
All others	0.9035 to 0.9041 inches
Bearing oil clearance	
Standard	0.0016 to 0.0037 inch
Service limit (maximum)	0.0045 inch
Runout limit	0.0012 inch
Thrust clearance (endplay)	
Standard	0.0016 to 0.0037 inch
Service limit (maximum)	0.0043 inch
Lobe height	
Intake camshaft	
2001 through 2003	
Standard	1.626 to 1.670 inches
Service limit	1.660 inches
2004 and later	
Standard	1.6657 to 1.6697 inches
Service limit (minimum)	1.6598 inches
Exhaust camshaft	
Standard	1.7341 to 1.7380 inches
Service limit (minimum)	1.7283 inches
Valve lifter	
Diameter	1.2191 to 1.2195 inches
Bore diameter	1.2208 to 1.2215 inches
Lifter oil clearance	
Standard	0.0013 to 0.0023 inch
Service limit	0.0039 inch
Valve clearance (cold)	
Intake	0.007 to 0.009-inch
Exhaust	0.011 to 0.013-inch

Oil pump

Rotor-to-body clearance	
Standard	0.0098 to 0.0128 inch
Service limit	0.0128 inch
Rotor tip clearance	
Standard	0.0024 to 0.0071 inch
Service limit	0.0138 inch

Torque specifications — Ft-lbs (unless otherwise indicated)

Camshaft bearing cap bolts	
Journal No.1	17
All others	110 in-lbs
Camshaft sprocket bolts	47
Crankshaft pulley/vibration damper bolt	95
Cylinder head bolts	
Step 1	21
Step 2	Tighten an additional 90-degrees
Step 3	Tighten an additional 90-degrees
Damper-to-flywheel bolts	15
Drivebelt tensioner	30
Engine mounts	44
Engine mount bracket-to timing chain cover bolts	35
Exhaust manifold nuts	20
Exhaust manifold heat shield bolts	71 in-lbs
Exhaust pipe-to-exhaust manifold bolts	32
Flywheel bolt	
2001 through 2002 models	
Step 1	62
Step 2	Tighten an additional 90-degrees
2003 and later models	
Step 1	36
Step 2	Tighten an additional 90-degrees
Intake manifold fasteners	15
Oil pump cover bolt	78 in-lbs
Oil pump cover screws	88 in-lbs
Oil pick-up/strainer nuts/bolts	80 in-lbs
Oil pan (bedplate) bolts	18
Oil pan (lower)-to-bedplate bolts	80 in-lbs
Timing chain guide bolts (stationary)	80 in-lbs
Timing chain tensioner pivot arm bolt	80 in-lbs
Timing chain cover bolts	
10 mm head	96 in-lbs
12 mm head	18
Timing chain tensioner nuts/bolts	168 in-lbs
Valve cover bolts/nuts	84 in-lbs

Section

Reference to other Chapters

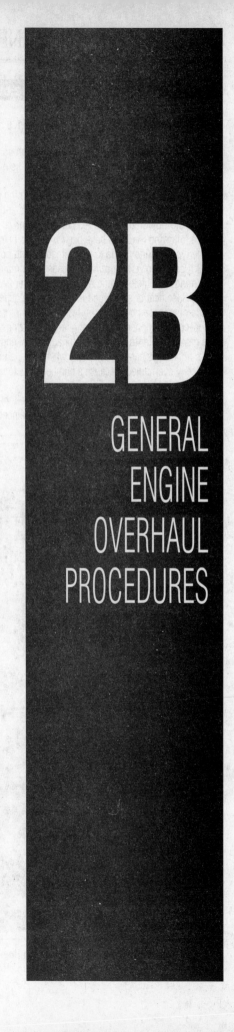

2B

GENERAL ENGINE OVERHAUL PROCEDURES

1 General information - engine overhaul

▶ **Refer to illustrations 1.2, 1.3, 1.4, 1.5, 1.6 and 1.7**

Included in this portion of Chapter 2 are general information and diagnostic testing procedures for determining the overall mechanical condition of your engine.

The information ranges from advice concerning preparation for an overhaul and the purchase of replacement parts and/or components to detailed, step-by-step procedures covering removal and installation.

The following Sections have been written to help you determine whether your engine needs to be overhauled and how to remove and install it once you've determined it needs to be rebuilt. For information concerning in-vehicle engine repair, see Chapter 2A.

The Specifications included in this Part are general in nature and include only those necessary for testing the oil pressure and checking the top-end components of the engine (piston rings, valves, cylinder head gasket). Refer to Chapter 2A for additional engine Specifications.

It's not always easy to determine when, or if, an engine should be completely overhauled, because a number of factors must be considered.

High mileage is not necessarily an indication that an overhaul is needed, while low mileage doesn't preclude the need for an overhaul.

The Prius engine only operates part of the time and at relatively low loads. Frequency of servicing is probably the most important consideration. An engine that's had regular and frequent oil and filter changes, as well as other required maintenance, will most likely give many thousands of miles of reliable service. Conversely, a neglected engine may require an overhaul very early in its service life.

Excessive oil consumption is an indication that piston rings, valve seals and/or valve guides are in need of attention. Make sure that oil leaks aren't responsible before deciding that the rings and/or guides are bad. Perform a leak-down check to determine the extent of the work required (see Section 3). Also check the vacuum readings under various conditions (see Section 4).

Check the oil pressure with a gauge installed in place of the oil pressure sending unit and compare it to this Chapter's Specifications (see Section 2). If it's extremely low, the bearings and/or oil pump are probably worn out.

Loss of power, rough running, knocking or metallic engine noises, excessive valve train noise and high fuel consumption rates may also point to the need for an overhaul, especially if they're all present at the same time. If a complete tune-up doesn't remedy the situation, major mechanical work is the only solution.

1.2 An engine block being bored - an engine rebuilder will use special machinery to recondition the cylinder bores

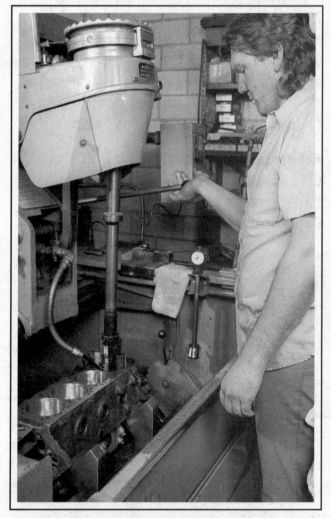

1.3 If the cylinders are bored, the machine shop will normally hone the engine on a machine like this

1.4 A crankshaft having a main bearing journal ground

1.5 A machinist checks for a bent connecting rod, using specialized equipment

An engine overhaul involves restoring the internal parts to the specifications of a new engine. During an overhaul, the piston rings are replaced and the cylinder walls are reconditioned (rebored and/or honed) (see illustrations 1.2 and 1.3). If a rebore is done by an automotive machine shop, new oversize pistons will also be installed. The main bearings, connecting rod bearings and camshaft bearings are generally replaced with new ones and, if necessary, the crankshaft may be reground to restore the journals (see illustration 1.4). Generally, the valves are serviced as well, since they're usually in less-than-perfect condition at this point. While the engine is being overhauled, other components, such as the distributor, starter and alternator, can be rebuilt as well. The end result should be a like-new engine that will give many trouble-free miles.

➡**Note: Critical cooling system components such as the hoses, drivebelts, thermostat and water pump should be replaced with new parts when an engine is overhauled. The radiator should be checked carefully to ensure that it isn't clogged or leaking (see Chapter 3). If you purchase a rebuilt engine or short block, some rebuilders will not warranty their engines unless the radiator has been professionally flushed. Also, we don't recommend**

overhauling the oil pump - always install a new one when an engine is rebuilt.

Overhauling the internal components on today's engines is a difficult and time-consuming task which requires a significant amount of specialty tools and is best left to a professional engine rebuilder (see illustrations 1.5, 1.6 and 1.7). A competent engine rebuilder will handle the inspection of your old parts and offer advice concerning the reconditioning or replacement of the original engine. Never purchase parts or have machine work done on other components until the block has been thoroughly inspected by a professional machine shop. As a general rule, time is the primary cost of an overhaul, especially since the vehicle may be tied up for a minimum of two weeks or more. Be aware that some engine builders only have the capability to rebuild the engine you bring them while other rebuilders have a large inventory of rebuilt exchange engines in stock. Also be aware that many machine shops could take as much as two weeks time to completely rebuild your engine depending on shop workload. Sometimes it makes more sense to simply exchange your engine for another engine that's already rebuilt to save time.

1.6 A bore gauge being used to check the main bearing bore

1.7 Uneven piston wear like this indicates a bent connecting rod

2 Oil pressure check

▶ Refer to illustration 2.2

☀☀ WARNING:

Make sure power to the hybrid system is turned Off before performing any work on this vehicle. Also, on models equipped with the Smart Key system, place the key in a secure spot at least 20 feet away from the work area.

1   Low engine oil pressure can be a sign of an engine in need of rebuilding. A 'low oil pressure' indicator (often called an 'idiot light') is not a test of the oiling system. Such indicators only come on when the oil pressure is dangerously low. Even a factory oil pressure gauge in the instrument panel is only a relative indication, although much better for driver information than a warning light. A better test is with a mechanical (not electrical) oil pressure gauge.

2   Locate the oil pressure indicator sending unit on the engine block. It is generally near the oil filter (see illustration).

3   Unscrew and remove the oil pressure sending unit and then screw in the hose for your oil pressure gauge. If necessary, install an adapter fitting. Use Teflon tape or thread sealant on the threads of the adapter and/or the fitting on the end of your gauge's hose.

4   Connect an accurate tachometer to the engine, according to the tachometer manufacturer's instructions.

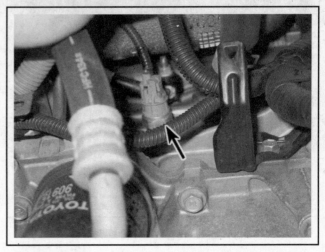

2.2 The oil pressure sending unit is located above the engine oil filter

5   Check the oil pressure with the engine running (normal operating temperature) at the specified engine speed, and compare it to this Chapter's Specifications. If it's extremely low, the bearings and/or oil pump are probably worn out.

3 Cylinder compression and leak-down tests

☀☀ WARNING:

Make sure power to the hybrid system is turned Off before performing any work on this vehicle. Also, on models equipped with the Smart Key system, place the key in a secure spot at least 20 feet away from the work area.

COMPRESSION TEST - GENERAL INFORMATION

➡Note: The starter cannot be used to crank the engine on this vehicle. Performing a compression test requires a special diagnostic scan tool. See a dealer or a properly equipped repair shop to have this done.

1   A compression check will tell you what mechanical condition the upper end of your engine (pistons, rings, valves, head gaskets) is in. Specifically, it can tell you if the compression is down due to leakage caused by worn piston rings, defective valves and seats or a blown head gasket.

2   If two adjacent cylinders have equally low compression, there's a strong possibility that the head gasket between them is blown. The appearance of coolant in the combustion chambers or the crankcase would verify this condition.

3   If one cylinder is slightly lower than the others, and the engine has a slightly rough idle, a worn lobe on the camshaft could be the cause.

4   If the compression is unusually high, the combustion chambers are probably coated with carbon deposits. If that's the case, the cylinder head(s) should be removed and decarbonized.

5   If compression is way down or varies greatly between cylinders, it would be a good idea to have a leak-down test performed. This test will pinpoint exactly where the leakage is occurring and how severe it is.

LEAK-DOWN TEST

6   A leak-down test can be performed at home if you buy or rent a leak-down tester and have access to an air compressor.

➡Note: The engine must be at normal operating temperature for this check.

7   Begin by cleaning the areas around the spark plugs before you remove them (compressed air should be used, if available). The idea is to prevent dirt from falling into cylinders as the test is being done.

8   Remove the spark plugs (see Chapter 1).

9   Refer to Chapter 2A and put number one cylinder at Top Dead Center on the compression stroke. Be sure to remove the wrench from the crankshaft before proceeding!

10   Screw the leak-down tester in the spark plug hole for number one cylinder.

11   Attach a supply of compressed air to the tester and adjust it so that the inlet pressure is exactly 100 psi.

✳✳ WARNING:

If the engine is not at TDC, the compressed air will make the engine rotate very quickly. If the wrench has been left attached to the crankshaft, it will swing and possibly break something or cause injury.

➡Note: Leak-down testers can operate differently than the one described here. Always follow the tool manufacturer's instructions.

12 Observe the reading on the second gauge. A reading of 85 psi indicates a leakage rate of fifteen percent.

13 A very low reading coupled with a sound of compressed air rushing through the engine indicates a problem. "Normal" readings can vary widely; from almost zero leakage to about thirty percent. A cylinder that needs repair will usually give a reading from 50-100 percent leakage.

14 To verify a bad exhaust valve, listen for air coming from the exhaust. To verify a bad intake valve, listen for air coming from the throttle body.

15 Remove the oil filler cap. If there is air coming out of the crankcase, the problem is with the rings. If air comes out of the radiator, there is probably a head gasket blown into a water passage.

16 If two adjacent cylinders have high leakage, there is probably a head gasket blown between them.

17 When you are finished with cylinder number one, carefully rotate the crankshaft clockwise exactly 180-degrees with a wrench or ratchet. You can now test the next cylinder in the firing order (number 3). Continue this processes until all cylinders have been checked.

18 All cylinders should give approximately equal results, but don't rely on leak-down testing to give you precise percentages. As long as the readings are fairly consistent, there is probably no problem. A low cylinder accompanied by the sound of moving air is the clue to an engine problem.

4   Vacuum gauge diagnostic checks

▶ **Refer to illustrations 4.1a and 4.1b**

✳✳ WARNING:

Make sure power to the hybrid system is turned Off before performing any work on this vehicle. Also, on models equipped with the Smart Key system, place the key in a secure spot at least 20 feet away from the work area.

A vacuum gauge provides inexpensive but valuable information about what is going on in the engine. You can check for worn rings or cylinder walls, leaking head or intake manifold gaskets, incorrect carburetor adjustments, restricted exhaust, stuck or burned valves, weak valve springs, improper ignition or valve timing and ignition problems.

Unfortunately, vacuum gauge readings are easy to misinterpret, so they should be used in conjunction with other tests to confirm the diagnosis.

Both the absolute readings and the rate of needle movement are important for accurate interpretation. Most gauges measure vacuum in inches of mercury (in-Hg). The following references to vacuum assume the diagnosis is being performed at sea level. As elevation increases (or atmospheric pressure decreases), the reading will decrease. For every 1,000 foot increase in elevation above approximately 2000 feet, the gauge readings will decrease about one inch of mercury.

Connect the vacuum gauge directly to the intake manifold vacuum, not to ported (throttle body) vacuum. Be sure no hoses are left disconnected during the test or false readings will result.

Before you begin the test, allow the engine to warm up completely. Block the wheels and set the parking brake. With the transmission in Park, start the engine and allow it to run at normal idle speed.

✳✳ WARNING:

Keep your hands and the vacuum gauge clear of the fans.

Read the vacuum gauge; an average, healthy engine should normally produce about 17 to 22 in-Hg with a fairly steady needle. Refer to

4.1a A simple vacuum gauge can tell a lot about an engine's condition

the following vacuum gauge readings and what they indicate about the engine's condition:

1   A low steady reading usually indicates a leaking gasket between the intake manifold and cylinder head(s) or throttle body, a leaky vacuum hose, late ignition timing or incorrect camshaft timing (see illustrations).

2   If the reading is three to eight inches below normal and it fluctuates at that low reading, suspect an intake manifold gasket leak at an intake port or a faulty fuel injector.

3   If the needle has regular drops of about two-to-four inches at a steady rate, the valves are probably leaking. Perform a compression check or leak-down test to confirm this.

4   An irregular drop or down-flick of the needle can be caused by a sticking valve or an ignition misfire. Perform a compression check or leak-down test and read the spark plugs.

5   A rapid vibration of about four in-Hg vibration at idle combined with exhaust smoke indicates worn valve guides. Perform a leak-down test to confirm this. If the rapid vibration occurs with an increase in

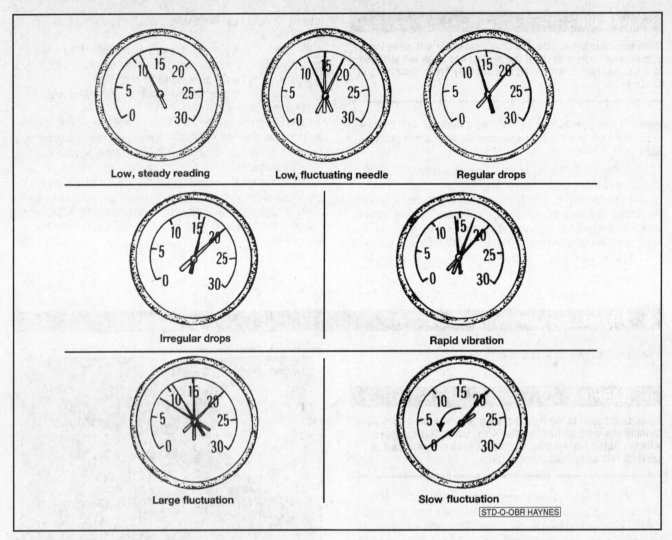

Low, steady reading   Low, fluctuating needle   Regular drops

Irregular drops   Rapid vibration

Large fluctuation   Slow fluctuation

STD-O-OBR HAYNES

4.1b Typical vacuum gauge readings

engine speed, check for a leaking intake manifold gasket or head gasket, weak valve springs, burned valves or ignition misfire.

6 A slight fluctuation, say one inch up and down, may mean ignition problems. Check all the usual tune-up items and, if necessary, run the engine on an ignition analyzer.

7 If there is a large fluctuation, perform a compression or leakdown test to look for a weak or dead cylinder or a blown head gasket.

8 If the needle moves slowly through a wide range, check for a clogged PCV system, incorrect idle fuel mixture, throttle body or intake manifold gasket leaks.

9 Check for a slow return after revving the engine by quickly snapping the throttle open until the engine reaches about 2,500 rpm and let it shut. Normally the reading should drop to near zero, rise above normal idle reading (about 5 in-Hg over) and then return to the previous idle reading. If the vacuum returns slowly and doesn't peak when the throttle is snapped shut, the rings may be worn. If there is a long delay, look for a restricted exhaust system (often the muffler or catalytic converter). An easy way to check this is to temporarily disconnect the exhaust ahead of the suspected part and redo the test.

5 Engine rebuilding alternatives

The do-it-yourselfer is faced with a number of options when purchasing a rebuilt engine. The major considerations are cost, warranty, parts availability and the time required for the rebuilder to complete the project. The decision to replace the engine block, piston/connecting rod assemblies and crankshaft depends on the final inspection results of your engine. Only then can you make a cost effective decision whether to have your engine overhauled or simply purchase an exchange engine for your vehicle.

Some of the rebuilding alternatives include:

Individual parts - If the inspection procedures reveal that the engine block and most engine components are in reusable condition, purchasing individual parts and having a rebuilder rebuild your engine may be the most economical alternative. The block, crankshaft and piston/connecting rod assemblies should all be inspected carefully by a machine shop first.

Short block - A short block consists of an engine block with a crankshaft and piston/connecting rod assemblies already installed. All new bearings are incorporated and all clearances will be correct. The existing camshafts, valve train components, cylinder head and external parts can be bolted to the short block with little or no machine shop work necessary.

Long block - A long block consists of a short block plus an oil pump, oil pan, cylinder head, valve cover, camshaft and valve train components, timing sprockets and chain or gears and timing cover. All components are installed with new bearings, seals and gaskets incorporated throughout. The installation of manifolds and external parts is all that's necessary.

Low mileage used engines - Some companies now offer low mileage used engines which is a very cost effective way to get your vehicle up and running again. These engines often come from vehicles that have been in totaled in accidents or come from other countries that have a higher vehicle turn over rate. A low mileage used engine also usually has a similar warranty like the newly remanufactured engines.

Give careful thought to which alternative is best for you and discuss the situation with local automotive machine shops, auto parts dealers and experienced rebuilders before ordering or purchasing replacement parts.

6 Engine removal - methods and precautions

▶ **Refer to illustrations 6.1, 6.2, 6.3, 6.4 and 6.5**

If you've decided that an engine must be removed for overhaul or major repair work, several preliminary steps should be taken. Read all removal and installation procedures carefully prior to committing this job. These engines are removed by lowering the engine to the floor, along with the transaxle, and then raising the vehicle sufficiently to slide the assembly out; this will require a vehicle hoist as well as an engine hoist.

Locating a suitable place to work is extremely important. Adequate work space, along with storage space for the vehicle, will be needed. If a shop or garage isn't available, at the very least a flat, level, clean work surface made of concrete or asphalt is required. Cleaning the engine compartment and engine before beginning the removal procedure will help keep tools clean and organized (see illustrations 6.1 and 6.2).

An engine hoist or A-frame will also be necessary. Make sure the equipment is rated in excess of the combined weight of the engine and transaxle. Safety is of primary importance, considering the potential hazards involved in lifting the engine out of the vehicle.

6.1 After wrapping water-vulnerable components in plastic, use a spray cleaner with concentration on the greasiest areas, usually around the valve cover and the lower edges of the block. If a section dries, apply more cleaner

6.2 Let the cleaner soak in according to directions and then hose off the grime. Dry using compressed air and rags

6.3 Get an engine hoist that's strong enough to easily lift your engine in and out of the engine compartment; an adapter like the one shown here (arrow) can be used to change the angle of the engine

6.4 Use an engine stand sturdy and stable enough to support the engine while you're working on it. Stay away from three-wheeled models as they have a tendency to tip over more easily - get a four-wheel unit

6.5 A clutch alignment tool will be necessary to align the transaxle input damper

tions 6.3, 6.4 and 6.5). Some of the equipment necessary to perform engine removal and installation safely and with relative ease are (in addition to an engine hoist) a heavy duty floor jack, complete sets of wrenches and sockets as described in the front of this manual, wooden blocks, plenty of rags and cleaning solvent for mopping up spilled oil, coolant and gasoline. If the hoist must be rented, make sure that you arrange for it in advance and have everything disconnected and/or removed before bringing the hoist home. This will save you money and time.

Plan for the vehicle to be out of use for quite a while. A machine shop can do the work that is beyond the scope of the home mechanic. Machine shops often have a busy schedule, so before removing the engine, consult the shop for an estimate of how long it will take to rebuild or repair the components that may need work.

If you're a novice at engine removal, get at least one helper. One person cannot easily do all the things you need to do to lift a big heavy engine out of the engine compartment. It is also helpful to seek advice and assistance from someone who's experienced in engine removal.

Plan the operation ahead of time. Arrange for or obtain all of the tools and equipment you'll need prior to beginning the job (see illustra-

7   Engine - removal and installation

▶ Refer to illustration 7.13

❄❄ WARNING 1:

The models covered by this manual are equipped with Supplemental Restraint systems (SRS), more commonly known as airbags. Always disable the airbag system before working in the vicinity of the impact sensors, steering column or instrument panel to avoid the possibility of accidental deployment of the airbag, which could cause personal injury (see Chapter 12).

❄❄ WARNING 2:

Gasoline is extremely flammable, so take extra precautions when you work on any part of the fuel system. Don't smoke or allow open flames or bare light bulbs near the work area, and don't work in a garage where a gas-type appliance (such as a water heater or a clothes dryer) is present. Since gasoline is carcinogenic, wear fuel-resistant gloves when there's a possibility of being exposed to fuel, and, if you spill any fuel on your skin, rinse it off immediately with soap and water. Mop up any spills immediately and do not store fuel-soaked rags where they could ignite. The fuel system is under constant pressure, so, if

any fuel lines are to be disconnected, the fuel pressure in the system must be relieved first (see Chapter 4 for more information). When you perform any kind of work on the fuel system, wear safety glasses and have a Class B type fire extinguisher on hand.

❄❄ WARNING 3:

Wait until the engine is completely cool before beginning this procedure.

❄❄ WARNING 4:

Make sure power to the hybrid system is turned Off before performing any work on this vehicle. Also, on models equipped with the Smart Key system, place the key in a secure spot at least 20 feet away from the work area.

➡Note 1: Engine removal on these vehicles is a difficult job, especially for the do-it-yourself mechanic working at home. Because of the vehicle's design, the manufacturer states that the engine and transaxle have to be removed as a unit from the bottom of the vehicle, not the top. With a floor jack and jackstands, the vehicle can't be raised high enough or supported safely enough for the engine/transaxle assembly to slide out from underneath. The manufacturer recommends that removal of the engine/transaxle assembly only be performed with the use of a frame-contact type vehicle hoist.

➡Note 2: Keep in mind that during this procedure you'll have to adjust the height of the vehicle with the vehicle hoist to perform certain operations.

REMOVAL

1 Park the vehicle on a frame-contact type vehicle hoist, then engage the arms of the hoist with the jacking points of the vehicle. Raise the hoist arms until they contact the vehicle, but not so much that the wheels come off the ground.

2 Loosen the wheel lug nuts and the driveaxle/hub nuts (see Chapter 8).

3 Disconnect both low and high voltage battery systems (see Chapters 5 and 6).

4 Refer to Chapter 12 and remove the wiper motor. Remove the wiring relay block, then remove the outer front cowl top panel.

5 Remove the air filter housing and air intake duct (see Chapter 4).

6 Drain the engine coolant and the transaxle/inverter/converter coolant (see Chapter 1). Drain the engine oil (see Chapter 1).

7 Remove the secondary radiator and the vacuum switching valve on 2004 and later models (see Chapters 3 and 6).

8 Drain the transaxle fluid (see Chapter 1). Relieve the fuel system pressure (see Chapter 4).

9 Remove the engine cooling fan and the radiator(s) (see Chapter 3).

10 Disconnect the fluid cooler lines from the transaxle.

11 Disconnect the fuel feed hose from the rigid line on the left (driver's) side of the engine compartment (see Chapter 4). Plug the line and fitting.

12 Refer to Chapter 5 and remove the converter/inverter.

13 Detach all hoses from the engine and label them (see illustration). Disconnect all interfering wiring and label each connector for future reference.

14 Remove the heater water pump (see Chapter 3).

15 Remove the air filter housing and the air intake duct (see Chapter 4).

16 Disconnect the engine wiring harness from the underhood fuse/relay box. Also label and detach any remaining electrical connectors/wiring harnesses and vacuum hoses between the engine and the vehicle.

17 On 2001 through 2003 models remove the engine coolant reservoir (see Chapter 3) and disconnect the shift cable from the transaxle.

18 Unbolt the brake fluid reservoir and position it out of the way without disconnecting the hose.

19 On 2001 through 2003 models remove the ECM (see Chapter 6). Pull the wiring harness from the ECM through the cowl and into the engine compartment. Remove the wiring junction box from the fender cover.

20 Remove the drivebelt (see Chapter 1).

21 Remove the plastic engine bottom covers.

22 Remove the air conditioning compressor without disconnecting the refrigerant lines (see Chapter 3). Tie the compressor out of the way.

23 Disconnect the tie-rod ends from the steering knuckles (see Chapter 10).

24 Disconnect the stabilizer bar links (see Chapter 10) and remove

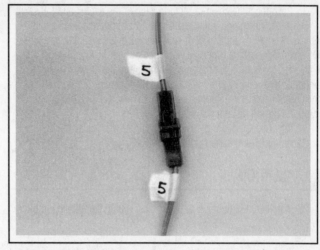

7.13 Label both ends of each wire and hose before disconnecting them

the driveaxles (see Chapter 8).

25 Remove the lower engine torque rod on 2001 through 2003 models.

26 Disconnect the steering column intermediate shaft from the steering gear (see Chapter 10).

27 Raise the vehicle on the hoist.

28 Remove the front exhaust pipe completely (see Chapter 4).

29 Remove the crossmember, then lower the vehicle.

30 Support the engine/transaxle assembly from above with an engine hoist. Attach the hoist chain to the lifting brackets. If no lifting brackets or hooks are present, lifting hooks may be available from your local auto parts store or dealer parts department. If not, you will have to fasten the chains to some substantial parts of the engine - ones that are strong enough to take the weight, but in locations that will provide good balance. If you're attaching a chain to a stud on the engine, or are using a bolt passing through the chain and into a threaded hole, place a washer between the nut or bolt head and the chain and tighten the nut or bolt securely.

❄❄ WARNING:

Do not place any part of your body under the engine/transaxle when it's supported only by a hoist or other lifting device.

31 Take up the slack until there is slight tension on the engine hoist. Position the chain on the hoist so it balances the engine and the transaxle level with the vehicle.

➡Note 1: Depending on the design of the engine hoist, it may be helpful to position the hoist from the side of the vehicle, so that when the engine/transaxle assembly is lowered, it will fit between the legs of the hoist.

➡Note 2: The sling or chain must be long enough to allow the engine hoist to lower the engine/transaxle assembly to the ground, without letting the hoist arm contact the vehicle.

32 Remove the bolts from the engine mounts.

33 Recheck to be sure nothing is still connecting the engine or transaxle to the vehicle. Disconnect and label anything still remaining.

34 Lower the engine/transaxle assembly. Once the assembly is on the floor, disconnect the engine lifting hoist and raise the vehicle until it clears the engine/transaxle assembly.

35 Reconnect the chain or sling to support the engine and transaxle.

36 Raise the engine/transaxle assembly. Support the engine with blocks of wood or another floor jack, while leaving the sling or chain attached. Support the transaxle with another floor jack, preferably one with a transaxle jack head adapter. At this point the transaxle can be unbolted and removed from the engine. Be very careful to ensure that the components are supported securely so they won't topple off their supports during disconnection.

37 Reconnect the lifting chain to the engine, then raise the engine and attach it to an engine stand.

INSTALLATION

38 Installation is the reverse of removal, noting the following points:

a) Check the powertrain mounts. If they're worn or damaged, replace them.
b) Attach the transaxle to the engine following the procedure described in Chapter 7.
c) When installing the crossmember, tighten the mounting bolts to the torque listed in the Chapter 10 Specifications.
d) Tighten the driveaxle/hub nuts to the torque listed in the Chapter 8 Specifications. Tighten all steering and suspension fasteners to the torque listed in the Chapter 10 Specifications. Tighten the wheel lug nuts to the torque listed in the Chapter 1 Specifications.
e) Refill the engine coolant, oil, power steering and transaxle fluids (see Chapter 1).
f) Run the engine and check for proper operation and leaks. Shut off the engine and recheck fluid levels.

8 Engine overhaul - disassembly sequence

1 It's much easier to remove the external components if it's mounted on a portable engine stand. A stand can often be rented quite cheaply from an equipment rental yard. Before the engine is mounted on a stand, the flywheel/driveplate should be removed from the engine.

2 If a stand isn't available, it's possible to remove the external engine components with it blocked up on the floor. Be extra careful not to tip or drop the engine when working without a stand.

3 If you're going to obtain a rebuilt engine, all external components must come off first, to be transferred to the replacement engine. These components include:

Driveplate
Ignition system components
Emissions-related components
Engine mounts and mount brackets
Fuel injection components
Intake/exhaust manifolds

Oil filter
Thermostat and housing assembly
Water pump

➡Note: When removing the external components from the engine, pay close attention to details that may be helpful or important during installation. Note the installed position of gaskets, seals, spacers, pins, brackets, washers, bolts and other small items.

4 If you're going to obtain a short block (assembled engine block, crankshaft, pistons and connecting rods), then you should remove the timing belt, cylinder head, oil pan, oil pump pick-up tube, oil pump and water pump from your engine so that you can turn in your old short block to the rebuilder as a core. See *Engine rebuilding alternatives* for additional information regarding the different possibilities to be considered.

9 Pistons and connecting rods - removal and installation

9.1 Before trying to remove the pistons, use a ridge reamer to remove the raised material (ridge) from the tops of the cylinders

REMOVAL

♦ **Refer to illustrations 9.1, 9.2, 9.3 and 9.4**

➡Note: Prior to removing the piston/connecting rod assemblies, remove the cylinder head, upper (aluminum) oil pan section and oil pan (see Chapter 2A).

1 Use your fingernail to feel if a ridge has formed at the upper limit of ring travel (about 1/4-inch down from the top of each cylinder). If carbon deposits or cylinder wear have produced ridges, they must be completely removed with a special tool (see illustration). Follow the manufacturer's instructions provided with the tool. Failure to remove the ridges before attempting to remove the piston/connecting rod assemblies may result in piston breakage.

2 After the cylinder ridges have been removed, turn the engine so the crankshaft is facing up. Remove the upper oil pan (see illustration 10.37).

9.3 Checking the connecting rod side clearance

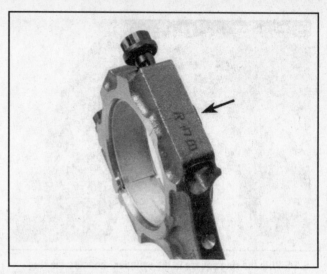

9.4 If the connecting rods and caps are not marked, use a center-punch or numbered stamps to mark the caps to the rods by cylinder number - don't confuse the numbers shown here with rod numbers; these are bearing size identifications

3   Before the connecting rods are removed, check the connecting rod endplay with feeler gauges. Slide them between the first connecting rod and the crankshaft throw until the play is removed (see illustration). Repeat this procedure for each connecting rod. The endplay is equal to the thickness of the feeler gauge(s). Check with an automotive machine shop for the endplay service limit. If the play exceeds the service limit, new connecting rods will be required. If new rods (or a new crankshaft) are installed, the endplay may fall under the minimum allowable clearance. If it does, the rods will have to be machined to restore it. If necessary, consult an automotive machine shop for advice.

4   Check the connecting rods and caps for identification marks (see illustration). If they aren't plainly marked, use a small center-punch to make the appropriate number of indentations on each rod and cap (1, 2, 3, etc., depending on the cylinder they're associated with).

5   Loosen each of the connecting rod cap bolts 1/2-turn at a time until they can be removed by hand. Remove the number one connecting

rod cap and bearing insert. Don't drop the bearing insert out of the cap.

➡**Note: Use new bolts when reassembling the engine, but save the old ones for use when checking the bearing oil clearance.**

6   Remove the bearing insert and push the connecting rod/piston assembly out through the top of the engine. Use a wooden or plastic hammer handle to push on the upper bearing surface in the connecting rod. If resistance is felt, double-check to make sure that all of the ridge was removed from the cylinder.

7   Repeat the procedure for the remaining cylinders.

8   After removal, reassemble the connecting rod caps and bearing inserts in their respective connecting rods and install the cap bolts finger tight.

9   Leaving the old bearing inserts in place until reassembly will help prevent the connecting rod bearing surfaces from being accidentally nicked or gouged.

10   The pistons and connecting rods are now ready for inspection and overhaul at an automotive machine shop.

PISTON RING INSTALLATION

♦ **Refer to illustrations 9.13, 9.14, 9.15, 9.19a, 9.19b and 9.22**

11   Before installing the new piston rings, the ring end gaps must be checked. It's assumed that the piston ring side clearance has been checked and verified correct.

➡**Note: Pistons and rods can only be installed after the crankshaft has been installed (see Section 10).**

12   Lay out the piston/connecting rod assemblies and the new ring sets so the ring sets will be matched with the same piston and cylinder during the end gap measurement and engine assembly.

13   Insert the top (number one) ring into the first cylinder and square it up with the cylinder walls by pushing it in with the top of the piston (see illustration). The ring should be near the bottom of the cylinder, at the lower limit of ring travel.

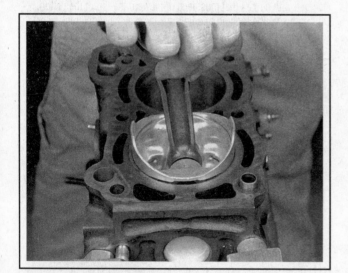

9.13 Install the piston ring into the cylinder and then push it down into position using a piston so the ring will be square in the cylinder

9.14 With the ring square in the cylinder, measure the ring end gap with a feeler gauge

14 To measure the end gap, slip feeler gauges between the ends of the ring until a gauge equal to the gap width is found (see illustration). The feeler gauge should slide between the ring ends with a slight amount of drag. Check with an automotive machine shop for the correct end gap for your engine. If the gap is larger or smaller than specified, double-check to make sure you have the correct rings before proceeding.

15 If the gap is too small, it must be enlarged or the ring ends may come in contact with each other during engine operation, which can cause serious damage to the engine. The end gap can be increased by filing the ring ends very carefully with a fine file. Mount the file in a vise equipped with soft jaws, slip the ring over the file with the ends contacting the file face and slowly move the ring to remove material from the ends. When performing this operation, file only by pushing the ring from the outside end of the file towards the vise (see illustration).

16 Excess end gap isn't critical unless it's greater than approximately 0.040-inch. Again, double-check to make sure you have the correct ring type and that you are referencing the correct section and category of specifications.

17 Repeat the procedure for each ring that will be installed in the first cylinder and for each ring in the remaining cylinders. Remember to keep rings, pistons and cylinders matched up.

9.15 If the ring end gap is too small, clamp a file in a vise and file the piston ring ends - be sure to file the ends square and finish by removing all raised material or burrs with a fine stone

18 Once the ring end gaps have been checked/corrected, the rings can be installed on the pistons.

19 The oil control ring (lowest one on the piston) is usually installed first. It's composed of three separate components. Slip the spacer/expander into the groove (see illustration). If an anti-rotation tang is used, make sure it's inserted into the drilled hole in the ring groove. Next, install the upper side rail in the same manner (see illustration). Don't use a piston ring installation tool on the oil ring side rails, as they may be damaged. Instead, place one end of the side rail into the groove between the spacer/expander and the ring land, hold it firmly in place and slide a finger around the piston while pushing the rail into the groove. Finally, install the lower side rail.

20 After the three oil ring components have been installed, check to make sure that both the upper and lower side rails can be rotated smoothly inside the ring grooves.

21 The number two (middle) ring is installed next. It's usually stamped with a mark that must face up, toward the top of the piston. Do not mix up the top and middle rings, as they have different cross-sections.

9.19a Installing the spacer/expander in the oil ring groove

9.19b DO NOT use a piston ring installation tool when installing the oil control side rails

9.22 Use a piston ring installation tool to install the number 2 and number 1 (top) rings - be sure the directional mark on the piston rings is facing toward the top of the engine

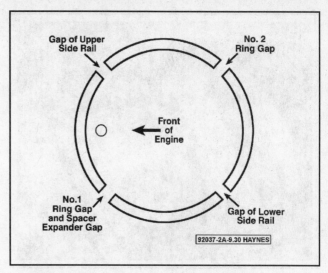

9.29 Position the piston ring end gaps as shown

➡Note: Always follow the instructions printed on the ring package or box - different manufacturers may require different approaches.

22 Use a piston ring installation tool and make sure the identification mark is facing the top of the piston, then slip the ring into the middle groove on the piston (see illustration). Don't expand the ring any more than necessary to slide it over the piston.

23 Install the number one (top) ring in the same manner. Make sure the mark is facing up. Be careful not to confuse the number one and number two rings.

24 Repeat the procedure for the remaining pistons and rings.

INSTALLATION

25 Before installing the piston/connecting rod assemblies, the cylinder walls must be perfectly clean, the top edge of each cylinder bore must be chamfered, and the crankshaft must be in place.

26 Remove the cap from the end of the number one connecting rod (refer to the marks made during removal). Remove the original bearing inserts and wipe the bearing surfaces of the connecting rod and cap with a clean, lint-free cloth. They must be kept spotlessly clean.

Connecting rod bearing oil clearance check

▸ **Refer to illustrations 9.29, 9.34, 9.36 and 9.40**

27 Clean the back side of the new upper bearing insert, then lay it in place in the connecting rod. Make sure the tab on the bearing fits into the recess in the rod. Don't hammer the bearing insert into place and be very careful not to nick or gouge the bearing face. Don't lubricate the bearing at this time.

28 Clean the back side of the other bearing insert and install it in the rod cap. Again, make sure the tab on the bearing fits into the recess in the cap, and don't apply any lubricant. It's critically important that the mating surfaces of the bearing and connecting rod are perfectly clean and oil free when they're assembled.

29 Position the piston ring gaps at 90-degree intervals around the piston as shown (see illustration).

30 Lubricate the piston and rings with clean engine oil and attach a piston ring compressor to the piston. Leave the skirt protruding about

1/4-inch to guide the piston into the cylinder. The rings must be compressed until they're flush with the piston.

31 Rotate the crankshaft until the number one connecting rod journal is at BDC (bottom dead center) and apply a liberal coat of engine oil to the cylinder walls.

32 With the mark (dot, arrow or letter R or L) on top of the piston facing the front (timing chain end) of the engine, gently insert the piston/connecting rod assembly into the number one cylinder bore and rest the bottom edge of the ring compressor on the engine block.

➡Note: The connecting rod also has a mark on it that must face the correct direction. On all models, the marks on the connecting rods face the front (timing chain) of the engine.

33 Tap the top edge of the ring compressor to make sure it's contacting the block around its entire circumference.

34 Gently tap on the top of the piston with the end of a wooden or plastic hammer handle (see illustration) while guiding the end of the connecting rod into place on the crankshaft journal. The piston rings may try to pop out of the ring compressor just before entering the cylinder bore, so keep some downward pressure on the ring compressor. Work slowly, and if any resistance is felt as the piston enters the

9.34 Use a plastic or wooden hammer to push the pistons into the bores

9.36 Put Plastigage on each connecting rod journal parallel to the crankshaft centerline

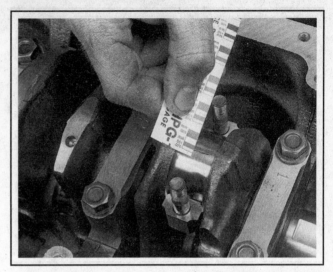

9.40 Use the scale on the Plastigage wrapper to find the bearing oil clearances - be sure to measure the widest part of the Plastigage and use the correct scale; it comes with both standard and metric scales

cylinder, stop immediately. Find out what's hanging up and fix it before proceeding. Do not, for any reason, force the piston into the cylinder - you might break a ring and/or the piston.

35 Once the piston/connecting rod assembly is installed, the connecting rod bearing oil clearance must be checked before the rod cap is permanently installed.

36 Cut a piece of the appropriate size Plastigage slightly shorter than the width of the connecting rod bearing and lay it in place on the number one connecting rod journal, parallel with the journal axis (see illustration).

37 Clean the connecting rod cap bearing face and install the rod cap. Make sure the mating mark on the cap is on the same side as the mark on the connecting rod.

38 Install the old rod bolts, at this time, and tighten them to the torque listed in this Chapter's Specifications, working up to it in three steps.

➡Note: Use a thin-wall socket to avoid erroneous torque readings that can result if the socket is wedged between the rod cap and the bolt. If the socket tends to wedge itself between the fastener and the cap, lift up on it slightly until it no longer contacts the cap. DO NOT rotate the crankshaft at any time during this operation.

39 Remove the fasteners and detach the rod cap, being very careful not to disturb the Plastigage. Discard the cap bolts at this time as they should not be reused.

40 Compare the width of the crushed Plastigage to the scale printed on the Plastigage envelope to obtain the oil clearance (see illustration). The connecting rod oil clearance is usually about 0.001 to 0.002 inch. Consult an automotive machine shop for the clearance specified for the rod bearings on your engine.

41 If the clearance is not as specified, the bearing inserts may be the wrong size (which means different ones will be required). Before deciding that different inserts are needed, make sure that no dirt or oil was between the bearing inserts and the connecting rod or cap when the clearance was measured. Also, recheck the journal diameter. If the Plastigage was wider at one end than the other, the journal may be tapered. If the clearance still exceeds the limit specified, the bearing will have to be replaced with an undersize bearing.

✳✳✳ **CAUTION:**

When installing a new crankshaft always use a standard size bearing.

Final installation

42 Carefully scrape all traces of the Plastigage material off the rod journal and/or bearing face. Be very careful not to scratch the bearing - use your fingernail or the edge of a plastic card.

43 Make sure the bearing faces are perfectly clean, then apply a uniform layer of clean moly-base grease or engine assembly lube to both of them. You'll have to push the piston into the cylinder to expose the face of the bearing insert in the connecting rod.

44 Slide the connecting rod back into place on the journal, install the rod cap, install the new bolts and tighten them to the torque listed in this Chapter's Specifications. Again, work up to the torque in three steps.

45 Repeat the entire procedure for the remaining pistons/connecting rods.

46 The important points to remember are:
 a) Keep the back sides of the bearing inserts and the insides of the connecting rods and caps perfectly clean when assembling them.
 b) Make sure you have the correct piston/rod assembly for each cylinder.
 c) The mark on the piston must face the front (timing chain end) of the engine.
 d) Lubricate the cylinder walls liberally with clean oil.
 e) Lubricate the bearing faces when installing the rod caps after the oil clearance has been checked.

47 After all the piston/connecting rod assemblies have been correctly installed, rotate the crankshaft a number of times by hand to check for any obvious binding.

48 As a final step, check the connecting rod endplay again. If it was correct before disassembly and the original crankshaft and rods were reinstalled, it should still be correct. If new rods or a new crankshaft were installed, the endplay may be inadequate. If so, the rods will have to be removed and taken to an automotive machine shop for resizing.

10 Crankshaft - removal and installation

REMOVAL

▶ **Refer to illustrations 10.1 and 10.3**

➥**Note: The crankshaft can be removed only after the engine has been removed from the vehicle. It's assumed that the flywheel or driveplate, crankshaft pulley, timing chain, oil pan, oil pump body, oil filter and piston/connecting rod assemblies have already been removed.**

1   Remove the upper oil pan, if not already done (see illustration 10.37). Before the crankshaft is removed, measure the endplay. Mount a dial indicator with the indicator in line with the crankshaft and touching the end of the crankshaft (see illustration).

2   Pry the crankshaft all the way to the rear and zero the dial indicator. Next, pry the crankshaft to the front as far as possible and check the reading on the dial indicator. The distance traveled is the endplay. A typical crankshaft endplay will fall between 0.003 to 0.010-inch. If it's greater than that, check the crankshaft thrust surfaces for wear after it's removed. If no wear is evident, new main bearings should correct the endplay.

3   If a dial indicator isn't available, feeler gauges can be used. Gently pry the crankshaft all the way to the front of the engine. Slip feeler gauges between the crankshaft and the front face of the thrust bearing or washer to determine the clearance (see illustration).

4   Loosen the main bearing cap bolts 1/4-turn at a time each, until they can be removed by hand.

➥**Note: The main bearing cap bolts can be re-used, provided that the necked-down area of the bolt is not less than 0.287-inch. However, considering the amount of work involved with an engine overhaul, it's a good idea to replace them as a matter of course.**

5   Remove the main bearing caps. The bolts can be reinserted into the caps part-way to be used as handles if the caps are stuck. Try not to drop the bearing inserts if they come out with the caps. Be sure to keep the caps in order - they must be returned to their original locations.

6   Carefully lift the crankshaft out of the engine. It may be a good idea to have an assistant available, since the crankshaft is quite heavy and awkward to handle.

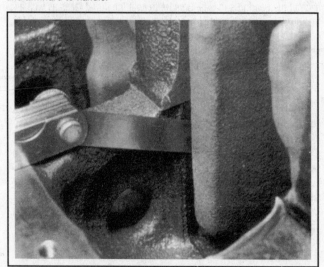

10.3 Checking crankshaft endplay with feeler gauges at the thrust bearing

10.1 Checking crankshaft endplay with a dial indicator

INSTALLATION

7   Crankshaft installation is the first step in engine reassembly. It's assumed at this point that the engine block and crankshaft have been cleaned, inspected and repaired or reconditioned.

8   Position the engine block with the bottom facing up.

9   If they're still in place, remove the original bearing inserts from the block and from the main bearing caps.

10   Wipe the bearing surfaces of the block and main bearing caps with a clean, lint-free cloth. They must be kept spotlessly clean. This is critical for determining the correct bearing oil clearance.

MAIN BEARING OIL CLEARANCE CHECK

▶ **Refer to illustrations 10.17 and 10.21**

11   Without mixing them up, clean the back sides of the new upper main bearing inserts (with grooves and oil holes) and lay one in each main bearing saddle in the block. Each upper bearing has an oil groove and oil hole in it.

✳✳ **CAUTION:**

The oil holes in the block must line up with the oil holes in the upper bearing inserts.

The thrust bearings (washers) must be installed in the number three (center) cap. Install the thrust bearings with the oil grooves facing out. Install the thrust washers with the grooved side facing out. Install the thrust washers so that one set is located in the block and the other set is with the main bearing cap assembly. Clean the back sides of the lower main bearing inserts (without grooves) and lay them in the corresponding location in the main bearing caps. Make sure the tab on the bearing insert fits into the recess in the block or main bearing cap assembly.

10.17 Place the Plastigage onto the crankshaft bearing journal as shown

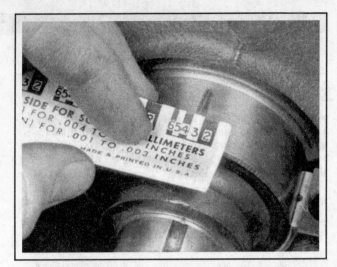

10.21 Use the scale on the Plastigage wrapper to determine the bearing oil clearance - be sure to measure the widest part of the Plastigage and use the correct scale; it comes with both standard and metric scales

✳✳ CAUTION:

Do not hammer the bearing insert into place and don't nick or gouge the bearing faces. DO NOT apply any lubrication at this time.

12 Clean the faces of the bearing inserts in the block and the crankshaft main bearing journals with a clean, lint-free cloth.

13 Check or clean the oil holes in the crankshaft, as any dirt here can go only one way - straight through the new bearings.

14 Once you're certain the crankshaft is clean, carefully lay it in position in the cylinder block.

15 Before the crankshaft can be permanently installed, the main bearing oil clearance must be checked.

16 Cut several strips of the appropriate size of Plastigage (they must be slightly shorter than the width of the main bearing journal).

17 Place one piece on each crankshaft main bearing journal, parallel with the journal axis (see illustration).

18 Clean the faces of the bearing inserts in the main bearing caps, then install the caps. DO NOT disturb the Plastigage.

19 Apply clean engine oil to all bolt threads prior to installation, then install all bolts finger-tight. Tighten main bearing cap bolts, progressing in two steps, to the torque listed in this Chapter's Specifications. DO NOT rotate the crankshaft at any time during this operation.

20 Remove the bolts and carefully lift the main bearing caps straight up and off the block. Do not disturb the Plastigage or rotate the crankshaft.

21 Compare the width of the crushed Plastigage on each journal to the scale printed on the Plastigage envelope to determine the main bearing oil clearance (see illustration). A typical main bearing oil clearance should fall between 0.0015 to 0.0023-inch. Check with an automotive machine shop for the clearance specified for your engine.

22 If the clearance is not as specified, the bearing inserts may be the wrong size (which means different ones will be required). Before deciding if different inserts are needed, make sure that no dirt or oil was between the bearing inserts and the caps or block when the clearance was measured. If the Plastigage was wider at one end than the other, the crankshaft journal may be tapered. If the clearance still exceeds the limit specified, the bearing insert(s) will have to be replaced with an undersize bearing insert(s).

✳✳ CAUTION:

When installing a new crankshaft always install a standard bearing insert set.

23 Carefully scrape all traces of the Plastigage material off the main bearing journals and/or the bearing insert faces. Be sure to remove all residue from the oil holes. Use your fingernail or the edge of a plastic card - don't nick or scratch the bearing faces.

FINAL INSTALLATION

▶ **Refer to illustration 10.37**

24 Carefully lift the crankshaft out of the cylinder block.

25 Clean the bearing insert faces in the cylinder block, then apply a thin, uniform layer of moly-base grease or engine assembly lube to each of the bearing surfaces. Be sure to coat the thrust faces as well as the journal face of the thrust bearing.

26 Make sure the crankshaft journals are clean, then lay the crankshaft back in place in the cylinder block.

27 Clean the bearing insert faces and then apply the same lubricant to them.

28 Install the main bearing caps in their original locations.

29 Apply clean engine oil to the bolt threads, wipe off any excess oil and then install the bolts finger-tight.

30 Tighten the main bearing cap bolts to 10 or 12 foot-pounds.

31 Gently tap the crankshaft back-and-forth with a soft face mallet to seat the thrust bearing.

32 Tighten the main bearing cap bolts in two steps to the torque and angle of rotation listed in this Chapter's Specifications.

33 Recheck crankshaft endplay with a feeler gauge or a dial indicator. The endplay should be correct if the crankshaft thrust faces aren't worn or damaged and if new bearings have been installed.

34 Rotate the crankshaft a number of times by hand to check for any obvious binding. It should rotate with a running torque of 50 in-lbs or less. If the running torque is too high, correct the problem at this time.

35 If everything checks out, prepare to install the cast aluminum oil

pan by carefully cleaning all sealing surfaces of dirt and oil with acetone or lacquer thinner.

36 Replace both O-rings that fit into the bottom of the block. Apply a thin bead of RTV silicone along the sealing surface of the block and then install the upper oil pan.

37 Tighten the upper oil pan fasteners to the torque listed in this Chapter's Specifications and in the proper sequence (see illustration).

38 Install the new rear main oil seal (see Chapter 2A).

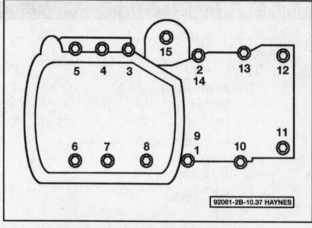

92081-2B-10.37 HAYNES

10.37 Upper oil pan bolt tightening sequence

11 Engine overhaul - reassembly sequence

1 Before beginning engine reassembly, make sure you have all the necessary new parts, gaskets and seals as well as the following items on hand:

Common hand tools
A 1/2-inch drive torque wrench
New engine oil
Gasket sealant
Thread locking compound

2 If you obtained a short block it will be necessary to install the cylinder head, the oil pump and pick-up tube, the oil pan, the water pump, the timing chain and cover, and the valve cover (see Chapter 2A). In order to save time and avoid problems, the external components must be installed in the following general order:

Thermostat and housing cover
Water pump
Intake and exhaust manifolds
Fuel injection components
Emission control components
Spark plugs
Ignition coils
Oil filter
Engine mounts and mount brackets
Driveplate

12 Initial start-up and break-in after overhaul

✳✳ WARNING:

Have a fire extinguisher handy when starting the engine for the first time.

1 Once the engine has been installed in the vehicle, double-check the engine oil and coolant levels.

2 Start the engine. It may take a few moments for the fuel system to build up pressure, but the engine should start quickly.

3 After the engine starts, it should be allowed to warm up to normal operating temperature. While the engine is warming up, make a thorough check for fuel, oil and coolant leaks.

4 Shut the engine off and recheck the engine oil and coolant levels.

5 Drive the vehicle to an area with minimum traffic, accelerate from 30 to 50 mph, then allow the vehicle to slow to 30 mph with the throttle closed. Repeat the procedure 10 or 12 times. This will load the piston rings and cause them to seat properly against the cylinder walls. Check again for oil and coolant leaks.

6 Drive the vehicle gently for the first 500 miles (no sustained high speeds) and keep a constant check on the oil level. It is not unusual for an engine to use oil during the break-in period.

7 At approximately 500 to 600 miles, change the oil and filter.

8 For the next few hundred miles, drive the vehicle normally. Do not pamper it or abuse it.

9 After 2000 miles, change the oil and filter again and consider the engine broken in.

Specifications

General

Displacement	92 cubic inches
Cylinder compression pressure	
Standard	128 psi
Minimum	99 psi
Maximum variation between cylinders	14 psi
Oil pressure	
At curb idle	5.7 psi or more
At 3000 rpm	43 to 78 psi

Torque specifications   Ft-lbs (unless otherwise indicated)

Connecting rod bearing cap bolts	
Step 1	132 in-lbs
Step 2	Tighten an additional 90-degrees (1/4-turn)
Main bearing cap bolts	
Step 1	16
Step 2	Tighten an additional 90-degrees (1/4-turn)
Upper oil pan bolts	18

Section

Reference to other Chapters

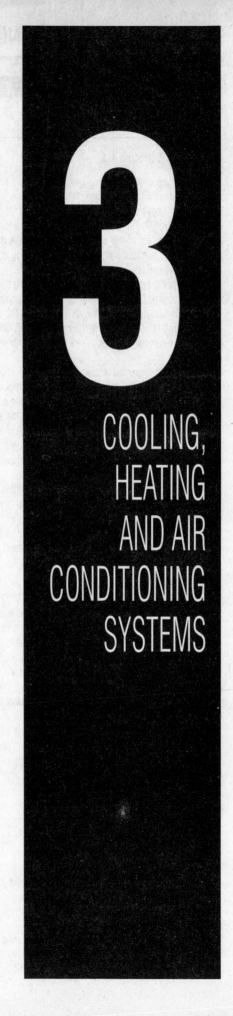

3

COOLING, HEATING AND AIR CONDITIONING SYSTEMS

1   General information

ENGINE COOLING SYSTEM

▶ **Refer to illustration 1.2**

All vehicles covered by this manual employ a pressurized engine cooling system with thermostatically-controlled coolant circulation. An impeller type water pump mounted on the front of the block pumps coolant through the engine. The coolant flows around each cylinder and toward the rear of the engine. Cast-in coolant passages direct coolant around the exhaust ports, near the spark plug areas and over the exhaust valve guides.

A wax-pellet type thermostat is located in the thermostat housing (see illustration). During warm up, the closed thermostat prevents coolant from circulating through the radiator. When the engine reaches normal operating temperature, the thermostat opens and allows hot coolant to travel through the radiator, where it is cooled before returning to the engine.

The cooling system is sealed by a pressure-type radiator cap. This raises the boiling point of the coolant, and the higher boiling point of the coolant increases the cooling efficiency of the radiator. If the system pressure exceeds the cap pressure-relief value, the excess pressure in the system forces the spring-loaded valve inside the cap off its seat and allows the coolant to escape through the overflow tube into a coolant reservoir. When the system cools, the excess coolant is automatically drawn from the reservoir back into the radiator.

The coolant reservoir serves as both the point at which fresh coolant is added to the cooling system to maintain the proper fluid level and as a holding tank for coolant.

This type of cooling system is known as a closed design because coolant that escapes past the pressure cap is saved and reused.

HEATING SYSTEM

The heating system consists of a blower and heater core located under the dashboard, the inlet and outlet hoses connecting the heater core to the engine cooling system and the heater/air conditioning control head on the dashboard. Hot engine coolant is circulated through the heater core by an electric water pump. This is done because the heater is often required when the engine is not running. When the heater mode is activated, a flap door opens to expose the heater box to the passenger compartment. A fan switch in a computer module activates the blower motor, which forces air through the core, heating the air.

Electric PTC heater elements are also used to provide a heat source in the heater unit under conditions when the engine cannot provide sufficiently warm coolant.

AIR CONDITIONING SYSTEM

The air conditioning system consists of a condenser (that is a part of the radiator/condenser module on 2001 through 2003 models), an evaporator mounted adjacent to the heater core, a compressor, a filter-drier and the plumbing connecting all of the above.

A blower forces the warmer air of the passenger compartment through the evaporator core (sort of a radiator-in-reverse), transferring the heat from the air to the refrigerant. The liquid refrigerant boils off into low pressure vapor, taking the heat with it when it leaves the evaporator. The compressor keeps refrigerant circulating through the system, pumping the warmed coolant through the condenser where it is cooled

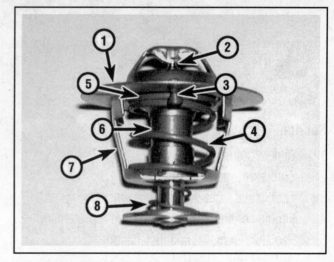

1.2 Typical thermostat

1	Flange	5	Valve seat
2	Piston	6	Valve
3	Jiggle valve	7	Frame
4	Main coil spring	8	Secondary coil spring

and then circulated back to the evaporator. 2001 through 2003 models use a conventional compressor that is operated by the engine by means of the drivebelt. Later models use a compressor that is driven by an electric AC motor so it can be used while the engine is not running.

HEAT STORAGE SYSTEM

2004 and later models use a vacuum-insulated coolant storage tank which can keep a supply of coolant warm for several days. When the engine is started, an auxiliary electric pump pumps this warm coolant through the engine. This warms the engine quickly and thereby greatly decreases hydrocarbon emissions.

The system components are: the heated coolant storage tank, a coolant temperature sensor specifically for this tank, a flow control valve and a coolant pump. The pump and the valve are computer controlled.

INVERTER/CONVERTER AND TRANSAXLE COOLING SYSTEM

These vehicles have a separate cooling system that controls the heat build-up in the electrical components of the hybrid system as well as the transaxle. These cooled electrical components are the inverter/converter, the #1 motor/generator and the #2 motor/generator.

On 2001 through 2003 models there is a small auxiliary radiator mounted in front of the conventional radiator. On 2004 and later models the vehicle radiator is partitioned into two sections. The lower part is for the electrical system only; the upper part handles the cooling of the internal combustion engine.

There is a small high-mounted coolant reservoir that is used to fill the system and to check the coolant level. An electric coolant pump circulates the coolant through the system components. It operates only when needed as determined by a computer. The pump receives power through a relay in the engine compartment.

2 Antifreeze - general information

♦ **Refer to illustration 2.4**

❋❋ **WARNING:**

Do not allow antifreeze to come in contact with your skin or painted surfaces of the vehicle. Rinse off spills immediately with plenty of water. Antifreeze is highly toxic if ingested. Never leave antifreeze lying around in an open container or in puddles on the floor; children and pets are attracted by its sweet smell and may drink it. Check with local authorities about disposing of used anti-freeze. Many communities have collection centers that will see that antifreeze is disposed of safely. Never dump used antifreeze on the ground or into drains.

➡**Note:** Non-toxic antifreeze is now manufactured and available at local auto parts stores, but even these types should be disposed of properly.

The cooling system should be filled with a water/ethylene-glycol based antifreeze solution, which will prevent freezing down to at least -20 degrees F, or lower if local climate requires it. It also provides protection against corrosion and increases the coolant boiling point.

The cooling system should be drained, flushed and refilled every 30,000 miles or every two years (see Chapter 1). The use of antifreeze solutions for periods of longer than two years is likely to cause damage and encourage the formation of rust and scale in the system. If your tap water is hard, i.e. contains a lot of dissolved minerals, use distilled water with the antifreeze.

Before adding antifreeze to the system, check all hose connections, because antifreeze tends to leak through very minute openings. Engines do not normally consume coolant. Therefore, if the level goes down,

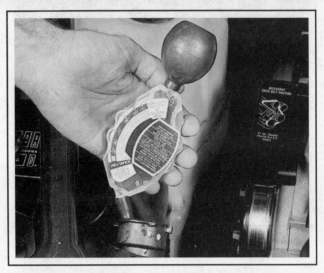

2.4 An inexpensive hydrometer can be used to test the condition of your coolant

find the cause and correct it.

The exact mixture of antifreeze-to-water you should use depends on the relative weather conditions. The mixture should contain at least 50-percent antifreeze, but should never contain more than 70-percent antifreeze. Consult the mixture ratio chart on the antifreeze container before adding coolant. Hydrometers are available at most auto parts stores to test the ratio of antifreeze to water (see illustration). Use antifreeze that meets the vehicle manufacturer's specifications.

3 Thermostat - check and replacement

❋❋ **WARNING 1:**

Do not attempt to remove the radiator cap, coolant or thermostat until the engine has cooled completely.

❋❋ **WARNING 2:**

Make sure power to the hybrid system is turned Off before performing any work on this vehicle. Also, on models equipped with the Smart Key system, place the key in a secure spot at least 20 feet away from the work area.

CHECK

1   Before assuming the thermostat is responsible for a cooling system problem, check the coolant level (see Chapter 1), drivebelt tension (see Chapter 1) and temperature gauge (or light) operation.

2   If the engine takes a long time to warm up (as indicated by the temperature gauge), the thermostat is probably stuck open. Replace the thermostat with a new one.

3   If the engine runs hot, use your hand to check the temperature of the right (passenger's side) radiator hose. If the hose is not hot, but the engine is, the thermostat is probably stuck in the closed position, preventing the coolant inside the engine from traveling through the radiator. Replace the thermostat.

❋❋ **CAUTION:**

Do not drive the vehicle without a thermostat. The computer may stay in open loop and emissions and fuel economy will suffer.

4   If the hose is hot, it means that the coolant is flowing and the thermostat is open. Consult the *Troubleshooting* Section at the front of this manual for further diagnosis.

REPLACEMENT

♦ **Refer to illustrations 3.5 and 3.7**

5   On 2004 and later models remove the radiator cover (see illustra-

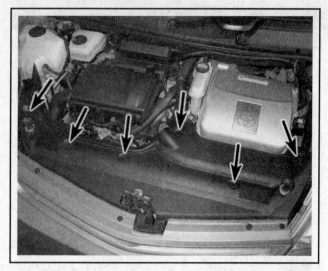

3.5 Radiator cover retainer locations (2004 and later models)

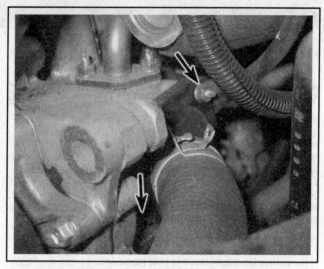

3.7 Thermostat housing fasteners (lower nut not visible in photo); the thermostat is installed with the spring end towards the engine, and the jiggle pin in the 12 o'clock position

tion). Also remove the plastic lower engine covers.

6   Drain the coolant from the radiator (see Chapter 1).

7   Detach the thermostat housing from the engine (see illustration). Be prepared for some coolant to spill as the gasket seal is broken. The radiator hose can be left attached to the housing, unless the housing itself is to be replaced.

8   Remove the thermostat, noting the direction in which it was installed in the housing, and thoroughly clean the sealing surfaces.

9   Fit a new gasket onto the thermostat. Make sure it is evenly fitted all the way around.

10   Install the thermostat and housing, positioning the jiggle pin at the highest point.

11   Tighten the housing fasteners to the torque listed in this Chapter's Specifications and reinstall the remaining components in the reverse order of removal.

12   Refill the cooling system (see Chapter 1), run the engine and check for leaks and proper operation.

4   Engine cooling fan(s) - check and replacement

✳✳ WARNING 1:

To avoid possible injury, keep clear of the fan blades, as they may start turning at any time!

✳✳ WARNING 2:

Make sure power to the hybrid system is turned Off before performing any work on this vehicle. Also, on models equipped with the Smart Key system, place the key in a secure spot at least 20 feet away from the work area.

CHECK

1   On these models the engine cooling fan is controlled by the Powertrain Control Module (PCM) through the inputs it receives from the engine coolant temperature (ECT) sensor. Refer to Chapter 6 for ETC sensor information. To test an inoperative fan motor (one that doesn't come on when the engine gets hot or when the air conditioner is on), first check the fuses and/or fusible links (see Chapter 12). The relay that operates the fan is identified in the engine compartment fuse and relay box. Refer to Chapter 12 for information and testing this relay. Always test this relay and the fuses before proceeding with further tests.

2   Disconnect the electrical connector at the motor and use fused jumper wires to connect the fan directly to a 12-volt battery. If the fan still does not work, replace the fan motor.

✳✳ WARNING:

Do not allow the test lead terminals to contact each other or any metallic part of the vehicle.

3   If the motor tested OK in the previous test but is still inoperative, then the fault lies in the relays, fuse, wiring or PCM.

REPLACEMENT

▸ **Refer to illustration 4.24**

✳✳ WARNING:

Wait until the engine is completely cool before beginning this procedure.

2001 through 2003 models

4   Have the refrigerant evacuated from the air conditioning system

4.21 Radiator support fasteners (not all are visible in this photo)

4.24 Location of the lower shroud bolts; it's easiest to raise the vehicle for access to these fasteners

by an air conditioning technician.

5 Refer to Chapter 6 and disconnect the cable from the negative terminal of the auxiliary 12-volt battery. Be sure to perform the initialization procedure when reconnecting it.

6 Refer to Chapter 1 and drain some of the coolant from the cooling system.

7 Remove the radiator support (see illustration 4.21).

8 Disconnect both refrigerant hoses from the bottom of the condenser.

9 Disconnect both coolant hoses from the radiator.

10 Raise the front of the vehicle and support it securely on jackstands.

11 Remove the two bolts, then lift the cooling fan assembly away from the radiator/condenser module. When it's free, drop it down and out the bottom of the engine compartment.

12 Installation is the reverse of removal. Replace the O-rings on the air conditioning lines that were disconnected.

13 Take the car back to the repair shop and have the air conditioning system recharged.

2004 and later models

♦ Refer to illustration 4.21

14 Refer to Chapter 6 and disconnect the cable from the negative

terminal of the auxiliary 12-volt battery. Be sure to perform the initialization procedure when reconnecting it.

15 Refer to Chapter 1 and drain the engine coolant and the transaxle/inverter/converter coolant.

16 Remove the radiator cover (see illustration 3.5). Also remove the plastic lower engine covers.

17 Refer to Chapter 11 and remove the front bumper cover.

18 Label and disconnect the interfering hoses including the main radiator hoses and the inverter reservoir hose.

19 Disconnect the wiring from the fan motors and the horn.

20 Remove the interfering inverter and cooler brackets.

21 Remove the radiator support (see illustration).

22 Remove all five bolts from the radiator support and disconnect the hood latch cable from it.

23 Disconnect the fan motor wiring harness from the retaining clips.

24 Remove the four bolts from the fan motor frame (see illustration).

25 Lift out the fan motor assembly.

26 Installation is the reverse of removal. Replace the O-rings on the air conditioning lines that were disconnected.

27 Take the car back to the repair shop and have the air conditioning system recharged.

---

5 Radiator - removal and installation

♦ Refer to illustration 5.12

❋❋ WARNING 1:

Do not start this procedure until the engine is completely cool.

❋❋ WARNING 2:

Make sure power to the hybrid system is turned Off before performing any work on this vehicle. Also, on models equipped with the Smart Key system, place the key in a secure spot at least 20 feet away from the work area.

➥Note: The radiator is part of the radiator/condenser module on 2001 through 2003 models.

2001 THROUGH 2003 MODELS

1   Have the refrigerant evacuated from the air conditioning system by a repair shop.

2   Refer to Chapter 6 and disconnect the cable from the negative terminal of the auxiliary 12-volt battery. Be sure to perform the initialization procedure when reconnecting it.

3   Remove the engine cooling fan assembly (see Section 4).

4   Refer to Chapter 11 and remove the front bumper. Remove the radiator reservoir hose.

5   Disconnect both air conditioning refrigerant lines from the condenser.

6   Remove the upper radiator support bar.

7   Raise the vehicle and support it securely on jackstands.

8   Pull the radiator/condenser rearward and out of its lower support. Lower it down and out the bottom of the engine compartment.

2004 AND LATER MODELS

9   Refer to Chapter 6 and disconnect the cable from the negative terminal of the auxiliary 12-volt battery. Be sure to perform the initialization procedure when reconnecting it.

10 Remove the engine cooling fan assembly (see Section 4).

11 Remove each of the four radiator corner support brackets.

12 Disconnect the wiring from the temperature sensor and remove the radiator from the vehicle (see illustration).

ALL MODELS

13 With the radiator removed, it can be inspected for leaks, damage and internal blockage. If in need of repairs, have a professional radiator shop or dealer service department perform the work, as special techniques are required.

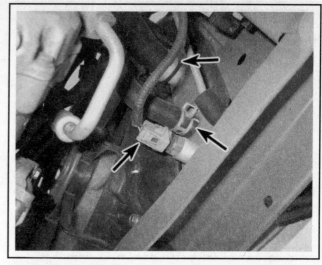

5.12 These hoses, as well as the wiring harness, must be disconnected for radiator removal

14 Bugs and dirt can be cleaned from the radiator with compressed air and a soft brush. Don't bend the cooling fins as this is done.

✳✳ WARNING:

Wear eye protection when using compressed air.

15 Installation is the reverse of the removal procedure. Be sure the rubber mounts are in place on the bottom of the radiator.

16 After installation, fill the cooling system with the proper mixture of antifreeze and water. Refer to Chapter 1 if necessary.

17 Start the engine and check for leaks. Allow the engine to reach normal operating temperature, indicated by both radiator hoses becoming hot. Recheck the coolant level and add more if required.

6   Water pump - check

✳✳ WARNING:

Make sure power to the hybrid system is turned Off before performing any work on this vehicle. Also, on models equipped with the Smart Key system, place the key in a secure spot at least 20 feet away from the work area.

1   A failure in the water pump can cause serious engine damage due to overheating.

2   With the engine running and warmed to normal operating temperature, squeeze the right-side radiator hose. If the water pump is working properly, a pressure surge should be felt as the hose is released.

✳✳ WARNING:

Keep hands away from fan blades!

3   Water pumps are equipped with weep or vent holes. If a failure occurs in the pump seal, coolant will leak from this hole. In most cases it will be necessary to use a flashlight to find the hole on the water pump by looking through the space behind the pulley just below the water pump shaft.

4   If the water pump shaft bearings fail there may be a howling sound at the front of the engine while it is running. Bearing wear can be felt if the water pump pulley is rocked up and down. Do not mistake drivebelt slippage, which causes a squealing sound, for water pump failure. Spray automotive drivebelt dressing on the belt to eliminate the belt as a possible cause of the noise.

7 Water pump - removal and installation

▶ Refer to illustration 7.5

❊❊ WARNING 1:

Do not start this procedure until the engine is completely cool.

❊❊ WARNING 2:

Make sure power to the hybrid system is turned Off before performing any work on this vehicle. Also, on models equipped with the Smart Key system, place the key in a secure spot at least 20 feet away from the work area.

1   Refer to Chapter 6 and disconnect the cable from the negative terminal of the auxiliary 12-volt battery. Be sure to perform the initialization procedure when reconnecting it.

2   Referring to Chapter 1, drain the cooling system and remove the engine drivebelt (see Chapter 1).

3   On 2004 and later models, support the right-end of the engine with a floor jack (be sure to place a block of wood on the jack head to protect the oil pan). Remove the right-side engine mount and bracket from the engine.

4   Place a screwdriver through one of the holes in the pulley to prevent it from turning, then remove the three pulley bolts. Remove the pulley.

5   Remove the fasteners retaining the water pump to the engine block and remove the water pump (see illustration). Note the length and the position of the bolts as they were originally installed before removing them.

7.5 The water pump is located adjacent to the thermostat housing

6   Thoroughly clean all sealing surfaces. Replace the gasket with a new one.

7   Install the fasteners in their original positions and tighten them to the torque listed in this Chapter's Specifications.

8   Install the remaining parts in the reverse order of removal. Refill the cooling system (see Chapter 1), run the engine and check for leaks and proper operation.

8 Coolant temperature sensor - replacement

On these vehicles the Engine Coolant Temperature (ECT) sensor provides information to the PCM for engine management and also for the temperature gauge on the instrument panel. Refer to Chapter 6 for the ECT sensor replacement procedure.

9 Blower motor - removal and installation

❊❊ WARNING 1:

These models are equipped with a Supplemental Restraint System (SRS), more commonly known as airbags. Always disable the airbag system before working in the vicinity of any airbag system component to avoid the possibility of accidental deployment of the airbag(s), which could cause personal injury (see Chapter 12).

❊❊ WARNING 2:

Make sure power to the hybrid system is turned Off before performing any work on this vehicle. Also, on models equipped with the Smart Key system, place the key in a secure spot at least 20 feet away from the work area.

1   The blower unit is located in the passenger compartment under the glove box area.

2   If the blower doesn't work, check the fuse and all connections in the circuit for looseness and corrosion.

2001 THROUGH 2003 MODELS

3   Refer to Chapter 11 and remove the glove compartment door.

4   Disconnect the electrical wiring from the blower.

5   Use a knife to cut out the glove compartment reinforcement bar. It will have to be replaced with a new brace (Toyota part number 55558-47010) during installation.

6   Remove the two bolts securing the PCM and slide it out.

7 Remove the four fasteners and remove the blower assembly.
8 Remove the cabin air filter (see Chapter 1).
9 Remove the single screw and the blower motor controller at the lower left corner of the assembly.
10 Remove the blower case by removing the four case screws and the two upper clips.
11 Disconnect the wiring from the motor, then remove the three motor mounting screws and lift off the motor.
12 Installation is the reverse of removal.

2004 AND LATER MODELS

13 Refer to Chapter 11 and remove the entire lower instrument panel to expose the heater assembly/blower.

→Note: This is a difficult and time-consuming job. Make sure you have enough time and the necessary equipment at hand before starting.

10 Heater core - removal and installation

✳✳ WARNING 1:

These models are equipped with a Supplemental Restraint System (SRS), more commonly known as airbags. Always disable the airbag system before working in the vicinity of any airbag system component to avoid the possibility of accidental deployment of the airbag(s), which could cause personal injury (see Chapter 12).

✳✳ WARNING 2:

Wait until the engine is completely cool before beginning this procedure.

✳✳ WARNING 3:

Make sure power to the hybrid system is turned Off before performing any work on this vehicle. Also, on models equipped with the Smart Key system, place the key in a secure spot at least 20 feet away from the work area.

→Note: This procedure requires the removal of the instrument panel, and the cross-cowl support tube and steering column. This involves disconnecting numerous electrical connectors and there is the potential for breakage of delicate plastic tabs on various components. This is a difficult job for the average home mechanic. Make sure you have enough time and the necessary equipment at hand before starting.

1 Have the air conditioning system evacuated by a service facility with the proper equipment.
2 Refer to Chapter 6 and disconnect the cable from the negative terminal of the auxiliary 12-volt battery. Be sure to perform the initialization procedure when reconnecting it.

2001 THROUGH 2003 MODELS

3 Remove the wiper arms (see Chapter 12)
4 Remove the rubber cowl top weatherstrip.

14 Remove the three interfering computers.
15 Remove the upper air duct from the blower.
16 There are 10 connectors that must be disconnected. Carefully disconnect and label them one at a time. Each must be properly connected at reassembly to avoid having to remove the instrument panel to correct a problem. Unclip the wiring harnesses and lay them out of the way.
17 There are three screws and one nut securing the blower unit. Remove these fasteners and lift the blower assembly out.
18 Remove the air inlet servo.
19 Remove the two screws and the motor control.
20 Remove the five screws securing the blower motor cover, then lift off the cover.
21 Detach the wiring harness from the blower motor.
22 Remove the blower motor with the fan attached
23 Installation is the reverse of removal. Recheck all of the connections before installing the instrument panel.

5 Remove the two screws, then lift out the two louvered cowl top covers.
6 Refer to Chapter 12 and remove the wiper motor.
7 Remove the ABS relay wiring block.
8 Remove the wiper motor wiring harness.
9 Unbolt and remove the outer front cowl top panel.
10 Refer to Chapter 1 and drain the engine coolant.
11 Disconnect the two air conditioning lines near the firewall. This requires a special tool to release the lock; once the lock has been taken off, you will be able to pull the lines apart using your hands.

→Note: Don't try to use a screwdriver to separate the lines. This could damage them.

12 Disconnect the two coolant hoses from the lines at the firewall.
13 Refer to Chapter 11 and remove the entire instrument panel assembly along with its lower brace.
14 Remove the blower unit (see Section 9).
15 Remove the defroster duct.
16 Remove the lower air duct.
17 Disconnect the connectors, then remove the two nuts and lift out the air conditioning unit.
18 Once the air conditioning assembly is on a workbench, remove the lower air ducts, the thermistor and the expansion valve.
19 Remove the electric heaters, the drain hose and the aspirator and hose.
20 Remove the cover from the heater coolant tubes.
21 Remove the clamps from the heater coolant tubes and slide out the heater core.
22 Installation is the reverse of removal. Refill the cooling system (see Chapter 1). Check for leaks and proper system operation. Return the car to the service facility to have the air conditioning system charged and leak-tested.

2004 AND LATER MODELS

23 Refer to Chapter 1 and drain the engine coolant.
24 Disconnect the two air conditioning lines near the firewall. This requires a special tool to release the lock; once the lock has been taken

off, you will be able to pull the lines apart using your hands.

➡**Note: Don't try to use a screwdriver to separate the lines. This could damage them.**

25 Disconnect the two coolant hoses from the lines at the firewall.

26 Refer to Chapter 11 and remove the entire instrument panel assembly.

27 Fold back the floor carpet to expose the floor air duct. Detach the clips and remove the floor duct.

28 Remove the upper air ducts from the assembly.

29 Remove the transmission control computer and the powertrain control module. Remove the network gateway computer.

30 Remove the instrument panel brace.

31 Remove the air conditioning amplifier assembly

32 Refer to Chapter 10 and remove the steering column.

33 Disconnect and label each of the various wiring connectors interfering with air conditioning module removal.

34 Remove all seven bolts and two nuts that secure the instrument panel brace and the air conditioner. Lift the entire assembly from the car with the help of an assistant.

35 Disconnect the wiring harness from the unit.

36 Remove the bolt, screws and the clamps, then separate the brace from the air conditioner.

37 Remove the two screws, then separate the blower assembly from the air conditioner assembly.

38 Remove the lower air nozzle.

39 Remove or simply disconnect any interfering components, then detach the evaporator temperature sensor.

40 Remove the cover from the heater tube cover.

41 Remove the four tube clamps, then slide the heater core from the case.

42 Installation is the reverse of removal. Refill the cooling system (see Chapter 1). Return the car to the service facility to have the air conditioning system charged and leak-tested.

11 Heater and air conditioning control assembly - removal and installation

❋❋ WARNING:

These models are equipped with a Supplemental Restraint System (SRS), more commonly known as airbags. Always disable the airbag system before working in the vicinity of any airbag system component to avoid the possibility of accidental deployment of the airbag(s), which could cause personal injury (see Chapter 12).

1 Refer to Chapter 6 and disconnect the cable from the negative terminal of the auxiliary 12-volt battery. Be sure to perform the initialization procedure when reconnecting it.

2001 THROUGH 2003 MODELS

2 Refer to Chapter 11 and pry off the panel below the heater control panel. Use a plastic trim tool or a screwdriver with the tip wrapped with electrical tape.

3 Use the same screwdriver or trim tool to pry off the hazard warning switch assembly. Disconnect the wiring after sliding it back.

4 Remove the fasteners securing the heater control panel. There are

two screws below it and two nuts behind the hazard warning switch.

5 Using the same screwdriver, pry off the heater control panel at the top. There are four clips at the top edge and two near the middle. Disconnect the wiring as you pull it free.

6 Remove the five knobs and remove the nuts beneath them.

7 Remove the display and radio assembly.

8 Remove the AC amplifier after removing all 12 mounting screws.

9 Release the lock and slide out the flat harness.

10 Use a screwdriver to remove all the bulbs.

11 Remove the screws then remove the cluster module circuit board from the case.

12 Installation is the reverse of removal.

13 Run the engine and check for proper functioning of the heater and air conditioning.

2004 AND LATER MODELS

14 These models use the center multi-function display to operate the climate control system. Any problems with this system should be referred to a dealer or other qualified service center.

12 Air conditioning and heating system - check and maintenance

AIR CONDITIONING SYSTEM

❋❋ WARNING 1:

The air conditioning system is under high pressure. Do not loosen any hose fittings or remove any components until the system has been discharged. Air conditioning refrigerant should be properly discharged into an EPA-approved recovery/recycling unit by a dealer service department or an automotive air conditioning repair facility. Always wear eye protection when disconnecting air conditioning system fittings.

❋❋ WARNING 2:

Make sure power to the hybrid system is turned Off before performing any work on this vehicle. Also, on models equipped with the Smart Key system, place the key in a secure spot at least 20 feet away from the work area.

1 The following maintenance checks should be performed on a regular basis to ensure that the air conditioner continues to operate at peak efficiency:

  a) *Inspect the condition of the drivebelt on 2001 through 2003 models. If it is worn or deteriorated, replace it (see Chapter 1).*

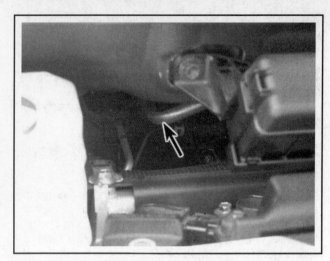

12.9 The large evaporator pipe should feel cool to the touch; the smaller line to the left should be warm (or even hot)

12.10 Check the temperature of the output air in the center register with a thermometer - it should be 35-40 degrees below the ambient air temperature

b) *Inspect the system hoses. Look for cracks, bubbles, hardening and deterioration. Inspect the hoses and all fittings for oil bubbles or seepage. If there is any evidence of wear, damage or leakage, replace the hose(s).*

c) *Inspect the condenser fins for leaves, bugs and any other foreign material that may have embedded itself in the fins. Use a "fin comb" or compressed air to remove debris from the condenser.*

d) *Make sure the system has the correct refrigerant charge.*

2   It's a good idea to operate the system for about ten minutes at least once a month. This is particularly important during the winter months because long term non-use can cause hardening, and subsequent failure, of the seals.

3   Leaks in the air conditioning system are best spotted when the system is brought up to operating temperature and pressure, by running the engine with the air conditioning ON for five minutes. Shut the engine off and inspect the air conditioning hoses and connections. Traces of oil usually indicate refrigerant leaks.

4   Because of the complexity of the air conditioning system and the special equipment required to effectively work on it, accurate troubleshooting of the system should be left to a professional technician.

5   If the air conditioning system doesn't operate at all, check the fuse panel and the air conditioning relay, located in the fuse/relay box in the engine compartment.

6   The most common cause of poor cooling is simply a low system refrigerant charge. If a noticeable drop in cool air output occurs, the following quick check will help you determine if the refrigerant level is low. For more complete information on the air conditioning system, refer to the Haynes Automotive Heating and Air Conditioning Manual.

Checking the refrigerant charge

▶ **Refer to illustration 12.9, 12.10 and 12.11**

7   Warm the engine up to normal operating temperature.

8   Place the air conditioning temperature selector at the coldest setting and put the blower at the highest setting. Open the doors (to make sure the air conditioning system doesn't cycle off as soon as it cools the passenger compartment).

9   With the compressor operating, feel the large pipe exiting from the evaporator at the firewall (see illustration).

10   The large evaporator outlet pipe should feel cold. If the evaporator outlet is warm or moderately warm, the system needs a charge. Insert

a thermometer in the center air distribution duct while operating the air conditioning system (see illustration) - the temperature of the output air should be 35 to 40 degrees F below the ambient air temperature (down to approximately 40 degrees F). If the ambient (outside) air temperature is very high, say 110 degrees F, the duct air temperature may be as high as 60 degrees F, but generally the air conditioning is 35 to 40 degrees F cooler than the ambient air. If the air isn't as cold as it used to be, the system probably needs a charge.

11   Observe the sight glass in the right front corner of the engine compartment (see illustration). If there are bubbles visible when the system is operating, the refrigerant charge is low. If there are no bubbles then the system may have too much refrigerant or none at all. No bubbles is also the correct condition when the system is properly charged. When the system is turned off the sight glass should become foamy, then go clear. Further inspection or testing of the system is beyond the scope of the home mechanic and should be left to a professional. Before any components are replaced, the refrigerant should be discharged and recovered by a licensed air conditioning technician first. After your repairs, the shop can recharge your system, giving you credit for the amount they removed originally.

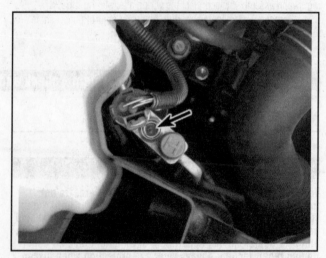

12.11 Check the sight glass to get a basic idea of the refrigerant charge

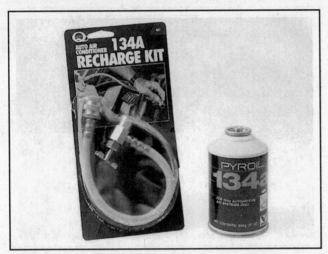

12.12 A charging kit is available at most auto parts stores - it must say R-134a and so must the cans of refrigerant you buy

12.15 Add R-134a refrigerant to the low-side port only (it's located below and in front of the coolant reservoir for the inverter/converter) - the procedure will go faster if you wrap the can with a warm wet towel to prevent icing (2004 and later model shown)

Adding refrigerant

▶ Refer to illustrations 12.12 and 12.15

> ✳✳ **CAUTION:**
>
> All models covered by this manual use environmentally friendly R-134a refrigerant. When replacing entire components, additional refrigerant oil should be added equal to the amount that is removed with the component being replaced. Be sure to read the can before adding any oil to the system, to make sure it is compatible with an R-134a system.

12 Buy an automotive charging kit at an auto parts store. A charging kit includes a can of R-134a refrigerant, a tap valve and a short section of hose that can be attached between the tap valve and the system low side service valve (see illustration).

13 Connect the charging kit by following the manufacturer's instructions.

14 Back off the valve handle on the charging kit and screw the kit onto the refrigerant can, making sure first that the O-ring or rubber seal inside the threaded portion of the kit is in place.

> ✳✳ **WARNING:**
>
> Wear protective eyewear when dealing with pressurized refrigerant cans.

15 Remove the dust cap from the low-side charging port and attach the quick-connect fitting on the kit hose (see illustration).

> ✳✳ **WARNING:**
>
> DO NOT hook the charging kit hose to the system high side! The fittings on the charging kit are designed to fit only on the low side of the system. The high side fitting usually has a pressure switch adjacent to it.

16 Warm the engine to normal operating temperature and turn on the air conditioner. Keep the charging kit hose away from the fan and other moving parts.

17 Turn the valve handle on the kit until the stem pierces the can, then back the handle out to release the refrigerant. You should be able to hear the rush of gas. Add refrigerant to the low side of the system until both the outlet and the evaporator inlet pipe feel about the same temperature.

> ✳✳ **CAUTION:**
>
> Don't add more than one can of refrigerant to the system. If more refrigerant than that is required, the system should be evacuated and leak tested.

18 If you have an accurate thermometer, you can place it in the center air conditioning duct inside the vehicle to monitor the air temperature. A charged system that is working properly should output air down to approximately 40 degrees F.

19 When the can is empty, turn the valve handle to the closed position and release the connection from the low-side port. Reinstall the dust cap.

20 Remove the charging kit from the can and store the kit for future use with the piercing valve in the UP position, to prevent inadvertently piercing the can on the next use.

HEATING SYSTEMS

▶ Refer to illustration 12.25

21 If the air coming out of the heater vents never becomes hot, the problem could stem from any of the following causes:

a) *The thermostat is stuck open, preventing the engine coolant from warming up enough to carry heat to the heater core. Replace the thermostat (see Section 3).*

b) *A heater hose is blocked, preventing the flow of coolant through the heater core. Feel both heater hoses at the firewall. They should be hot. If one of them is cold, there is an obstruction in one of the hoses or in the heater core, or the heater control valve is shut. Detach the hoses and back flush the heater core with a water hose. If the heater core is clear but circulation is impeded, remove the two hoses and flush them out with a water hose.*

12.25 The drain hose from the heater/air-conditioning unit (arrow) should be kept clear to allow drainage of condensation - shown here from underneath

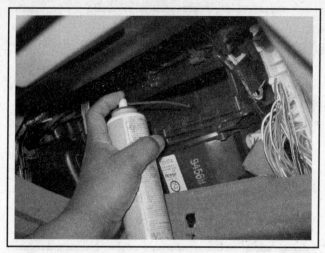

12.29 Remove the cabin air filter, then insert the disinfectant spray nozzle - be sure to support the nozzle so it doesn't get tangled in the blower

c) If flushing fails to remove the blockage from the heater core, the core must be replaced. (see Section 10).

22 If the blower motor speed does not correspond to the setting selected on the blower switch, the problem could be a bad fuse, circuit, switch, blower motor resistor or motor (see Section 9).

23 If there isn't any air coming out of the vents:

a) Turn the system ON and activate the fan control. Place your ear at the heating/air conditioning register (vent) and listen. Most motors are audible. Can you hear the motor running?

b) If you can't, the blower motor itself is probably bad (see Section 9).

24 If the carpet under the heater core is damp, or if antifreeze vapor or steam is coming through the vents, the heater core is leaking. Remove it (see Section 10) and install a new unit (most radiator shops will not repair a leaking heater core).

25 Inspect the drain hose from the heater/air conditioning assembly at the right side of the firewall, making sure it is not clogged (see illustration).

ELIMINATING AIR-CONDITIONING ODORS

▶ **Refer to illustration 12.29**

26 Unpleasant odors that often develop in air-conditioning systems are caused by the growth of a fungus, usually on the surface of the evaporator core. The warm, humid environment there is a perfect breeding ground for mildew to develop. The evaporator core has been factory-treated with an anti-bacterial coating to reduce this, but climactic conditions can still cause odors to develop.

27 Dealerships have a lengthy and often expensive process for eliminating the fungus by opening up the evaporator case and using a powerful disinfectant and rinse on the core until the fungus is gone. You can service your own system at home, but it takes something much stronger than basic household germ-killers or deodorizers.

28 Aerosol disinfectants for automotive air-conditioning systems are available in most auto parts stores, but remember when shopping for them that the most effective treatments are also the most expensive. The basic procedure for using these sprays is to start by running the system in the RECIRC mode for ten minutes with the blower on its highest speed. Use the highest heat mode to dry out the system.

29 The disinfectant can usually comes with a long spray hose. Remove the cabin air filter, point the nozzle inside the hole and to the left towards the evaporator core, and spray according to the manufacturer's recommendations (see illustration). Follow the manufacturer's recommendations for the length of spray and waiting time between applications.

30 Once the evaporator has been cleaned, the best way to prevent the mildew from coming back again is to make sure your evaporator housing drain tube is clear (see illustration 12.25) and to run the defrost cycle briefly to dry the evaporator out after a long drive with the air conditioning on.

13 Air conditioning receiver-drier - removal and installation

▶ **Refer to illustration 13.3**

✳✳ WARNING 1:

The air conditioning system is under high pressure. Do not loosen any hose fittings or remove any components until the system has been discharged. Air conditioning refrigerant should be properly discharged into an EPA-approved recovery/recycling unit by a dealer service department or an automotive air conditioning repair facility. Always wear eye protection when disconnecting air conditioning system fittings.

✳✳ WARNING 2:

Make sure power to the hybrid system is turned Off before performing any work on this vehicle. Also, on models equipped with the Smart Key system, place the key in a secure spot at least 20 feet away from the work area.

1   Have the refrigerant discharged and recovered by an air conditioning technician.

2   The receiver-drier is mounted on the end of the condenser, which is adjacent to the radiator. Refer to Section 15 and remove the condenser from the vehicle.

3   Using an Allen wrench, remove the large plug from the receiver-drier (see illustration). Use needle-nose pliers to grip and remove the filter-drier element inside the receiver.

4   Installation is the reverse of removal. Install a new filter-drier element and lubricate the plug's O-ring with refrigerant oil.

5   Have the system evacuated, charged and leak tested by the shop that discharged it. If the receiver-drier or condenser was replaced, have them add new refrigeration oil to the system. Use only refrigerant oil compatible with R-134a refrigerant.

13.3 After the system has been discharged, remove the plug at the bottom of the receiver-drier

14 Air conditioning compressor - removal and installation

▶ **Refer to illustration 14.10**

❊❊ WARNING 1:

The air conditioning system is under high pressure. Do not loosen any hose fittings or remove any components until the system has been discharged. Air conditioning refrigerant should be properly discharged into an EPA-approved recovery/recycling unit by a dealer service department or an automotive air conditioning repair facility. Always wear eye protection when disconnecting air conditioning system fittings.

❊❊ WARNING 2:

Make sure power to the hybrid system is turned Off before performing any work on this vehicle. Also, on models equipped with the Smart Key system, place the key in a secure spot at least 20 feet away from the work area.

❊❊ CAUTION:

The receiver-drier element should be replaced whenever a new compressor is installed (see Section 13).

14.10 2004 and later models use a unique electrically powered air conditioning compressor; it is not belt driven

1   Have the refrigerant discharged by an automotive air conditioning technician.

2   Refer to Chapter 6 and disconnect the cable from the negative terminal of the auxiliary 12-volt battery. Be sure to perform the initialization procedure when reconnecting it.

2001 THROUGH 2003 MODELS

3   Raise the front of the vehicle and support it securely on jackstands. Remove the engine lower cover.

4   Remove the drivebelt from the compressor (see Chapter 1).

5   Detach the wiring connector and disconnect the refrigerant lines.

6   Unbolt the compressor and lift it from the vehicle.

7   If a new or rebuilt compressor is being installed, follow the directions supplied with the compressor regarding the proper level of oil prior to installation.

8   Installation is the reverse of removal. Replace any O-rings with new ones specifically made for R-134a refrigerant and lubricate them with the same oil.

9   Have the system evacuated, recharged and leak tested by the shop that discharged it.

2004 AND LATER MODELS

❊❊ WARNING:

Wear heavy rubber safety gloves while performing the following procedure (see Chapter 5). There is high voltage near that could be fatal.

10 Disconnect the refrigerant lines from the compressor (see illustration). Cap the ends of the lines to prevent contamination.

❊❊ WARNING:

Refer to Chapter 5 and remove the safety plug.

11 Release the green lock tab and disconnect the compressor wiring harness. Detach the three clamps and free the wiring harness.

12 Unbolt the compressor and remove it from the vehicle.

13 Installation is the reverse of removal. Replace any O-rings with new ones specifically made for R-134a refrigerant and lubricate them with the same oil.

14 Have the system evacuated, recharged and leak tested by the shop that discharged it.

15 Air conditioning condenser - removal and installation

♦ Refer to illustration 15.4

❊❊ WARNING 1:

The air conditioning system is under high pressure. Do not loosen any hose fittings or remove any components until the system has been discharged. Air conditioning refrigerant should be properly discharged into an EPA-approved recovery/recycling unit by a dealer service department or an automotive air conditioning repair facility. Always wear eye protection when disconnecting air conditioning system fittings.

❊❊ WARNING 2:

These models are equipped with a Supplemental Restraint System (SRS), more commonly known as airbags. Always disable the airbag system before working in the vicinity of any airbag system component to avoid the possibility of accidental deployment of the airbag(s), which could cause personal injury (see Chapter 12).

❊❊ WARNING 3:

Wait until the engine is completely cool before beginning this procedure.

❊❊ WARNING 4:

Make sure power to the hybrid system is turned Off before performing any work on this vehicle. Also, on models equipped with the Smart Key system, place the key in a secure spot at least 20 feet away from the work area.

➡Note: This procedure only applies to 2004 and later models. Refer to Section 5 for earlier models (the condenser is a part of the radiator assembly on 2001 through 2003 vehicles).

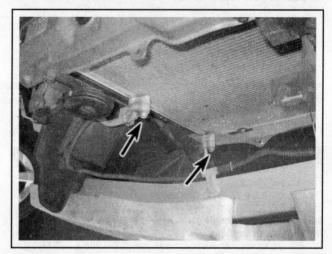

15.4 The condenser fittings are easily accessible after the front bumper cover and grille have been removed

1 Have the refrigerant discharged and recovered by an air conditioning technician.

2 Remove the fender inner covers and the front bumper cover (see Chapter 11).

3 Remove the interfering inverter bracket.

4 Disconnect both air conditioning refrigerant lines from the condenser (see illustration). Cap the ends to avoid contamination.

5 Remove both upper radiator support brackets.

6 Remove the two bolts from the bottom of the condenser and the two angle spacers from the top.

7 Carefully lift out the condenser.

8 Installation is the reverse of removal.

9 Have the system evacuated, charged and leak tested by the shop that discharged it.

16 Inverter/converter and transaxle cooling system pump - removal and installation

✳✳ WARNING 1:

Make sure power to the hybrid system is turned Off before performing any work on this vehicle. Also, on models equipped with the Smart Key system, place the key in a secure spot at least 20 feet away from the work area.

✳✳ WARNING 2:

Wait until the engine and transaxle/inverter/converter are completely cool before beginning this procedure.

1 Drain the inverter/converter/transaxle coolant (see Chapter 1).

2001 THROUGH 2003 MODELS

2 Refer to Chapter 6 and disconnect the cable from the negative terminal of the auxiliary 12-volt battery.
3 Refer to Chapter 11 and remove the front bumper cover.
4 Remove the left headlight (see Chapter 12).
5 Disconnect the wiring from the pump.
6 Place rags beneath the water pump.

7 Disconnect the two hoses from the pump, then unbolt the pump and remove it.
8 Installation is the reverse of removal. Refill the system with coolant (see Chapter 1).

2004 AND LATER MODELS

9 Refer to Chapter 6 and disconnect the cable from the negative terminal of the auxiliary 12-volt battery. Be sure to perform the initialization procedure when reconnecting it.
10 Refer to Chapter 11 and remove both front wheel well liners
11 Raise the vehicle and support it securely on jackstands. Remove the three engine lower covers.
12 Remove the cover from the front spoiler (see Chapter 11). Also remove the front bumper cover.
13 Remove the front bumper energy-absorbing mechanism.
14 Remove the left headlight housing (see Chapter 12).
15 Place a drain pan or rags under the pump.
16 Remove the coolant valve.
17 Disconnect the inverter cooler hose and remove the coolant pump. Detach the wiring.
18 Installation is the reverse of removal. Refill the system with coolant (see Chapter 1).

17 Heat storage tank and pump - removal and installation

▸ Refer to illustration 17.4

✳✳ WARNING 1:

The storage tank may be very hot even if the vehicle has not been driven for days. Handle it with caution.

✳✳ WARNING 2:

Make sure power to the hybrid system is turned Off before performing any work on this vehicle. Also, on models equipped with the Smart Key system, place the key in a secure spot at least 20 feet away from the work area.

➡Note: This system is only used on 2004 and later models.

COOLANT HEAT STORAGE TANK

1 Refer to Chapter 6 and disconnect the cable from the negative terminal of the auxiliary 12-volt battery. Be sure to perform the initialization procedure when reconnecting it.

17.4 The coolant storage tank may be very hot even after the rest of the cooling system has cooled, so be very careful to avoid burns - its water pump is located directly below it

2   Release the fasteners and lift off the cover from the top of the radiator.

3   Raise the vehicle and support it securely on jackstands. Remove both engine lower covers.

4   Refer to Chapter 11 and remove the front bumper cover and the left inner wheel well liner. Disconnect the electrical connector for the heat storage tank (see illustration).

❈❈ WARNING:

Read all of the labels on the tank, and wait until the heat storage tank cools down before proceeding

5   After the coolant in the tank has cooled, drain the tank (see Chapter 1, Section 22).

6   Disconnect the hoses from the storage tank.

7   Detach the wiring connectors.

8   Support the tank to avoid bending the bracket, then remove the nut and the four bolts securing it.

9   Separate the two hooks and lift the tank from the vehicle.

10   Installation is the reverse of removal. Be sure to refill the cooling system through the reservoir and bleed out any trapped air.

HEATED COOLANT PUMP

11   Refer to Chapter 6 and disconnect the cable from the negative terminal of the auxiliary 12-volt battery. Be sure to perform the initialization procedure when reconnecting it.

12   Release the fasteners and lift off the cover from the top of the radiator.

13   Loosen the nuts securing the left front wheel, then raise the vehicle and support it securely on jackstands.

14   Remove the left engine lower cover.

15   Refer to Chapter 11 and remove the left inner wheel well liner.

16   Clamp-off the hoses to the pump. Place a large pan under the water pump and disconnect both hoses from it.

17   Disconnect the wiring from the pump.

18   Remove the bolt and detach the pump.

19   Installation is the reverse of removal. Be sure to refill the cooling system through the reservoir and bleed out any trapped air.

18   Heating system coolant pump - removal and installation

❈❈ WARNING 1:

Make sure power to the hybrid system is turned Off before performing any work on this vehicle. Also, on models equipped with the Smart Key system, place the key in a secure spot at least 20 feet away from the work area.

❈❈ WARNING 2:

Wait until the engine and transaxle/inverter/converter are completely cool before beginning this procedure.

1   Drain the engine coolant from the radiator (see Chapter 1).

2001 THROUGH 2003 MODELS

2   Refer to Chapter 5 and remove the inverter/converter assembly.

3   Disconnect the wiring harness from the pump.

4   Disconnect the hoses from the pump.

5   Remove the refrigerant line support bracket.

6   Remove the coolant pump.

7   Installation is the reverse of removal. Be sure to refill the cooling system through the reservoir and bleed out any trapped air (see Chapter 1).

2004 AND LATER MODELS

8   Detach the clamp and the upper wiring harness from the coolant pump.

9   Place rags under the pump to catch spillage.

10   Disconnect the accessible coolant hose.

11   Disconnect the wiring from the pump.

12   Unbolt the pump and disconnect the lower hose.

13   Installation is the reverse of removal. Be sure to refill the cooling system through the reservoir and bleed out any trapped air (see Chapter 1).

Specifications

General

Radiator cap pressure rating	10.7 to 14.9 psi
Thermostat rating	176 to 183 degrees F
Refrigerant type	R-134a
Refrigerant capacity	
2001 through 2003 models	16 to 20 ounces
2004 and later models	14 to 18 ounces

Torque specifications

Thermostat housing bolts	96 in-lbs
Water pump bolts	96 in-lbs

Notes

Section

Reference to other Chapters

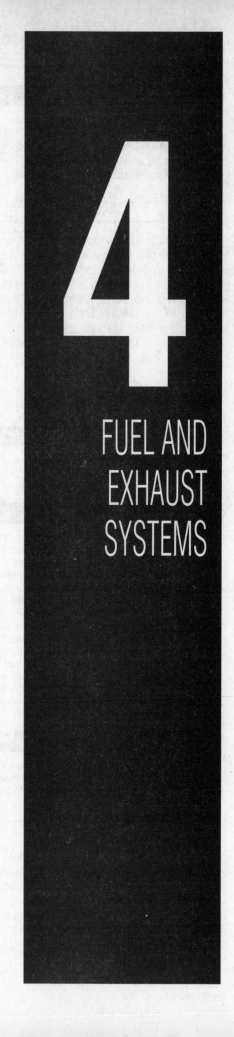

4

**FUEL AND
EXHAUST
SYSTEMS**

1 General information

The fuel system consists of a fuel tank, an electric fuel pump (located on the fuel tank), an SFI/fuel pump relay, fuel injectors, an air filter assembly and a throttle body unit. All models covered by this manual are equipped with a multi port fuel injection system.

MULTI PORT FUEL INJECTION SYSTEM

Multi port fuel injection uses timed impulses to sequentially inject the fuel directly into the intake port of each cylinder. The injectors are controlled by the Powertrain Control Module (PCM). The PCM monitors various engine parameters and delivers the exact amount of fuel, in the correct sequence, into the intake ports. The throttle body serves only to control the amount of air passing into the system. Because each cylinder is equipped with an injector mounted immediately adjacent to the intake valve, excellent control of the fuel/air mixture ratio is possible.

FUEL PUMP AND LINES

Fuel is delivered from the fuel tank to the fuel injection system through a metal line running along the bottom of the vehicle by an electric fuel pump on the fuel tank. Excessive fuel pressure is bled-off directly into the tank. The system does not use a return fuel line from the engine to the fuel tank.

EXHAUST SYSTEM

The exhaust system includes an exhaust manifold, a catalytic converter, an exhaust pipe and a muffler. The catalytic converter is an emission control device added to the exhaust system to reduce pollutants. A three-way (reduction) catalyst is used to reduce hydrocarbons (HC), carbon monoxide (CO) and oxides of nitrogen (NOx). Refer to Chapter 6 for more information regarding the catalytic converter.

2 Fuel pressure relief procedure

▶ **Refer to illustration 2.3**

✳✳ WARNING 1:

Gasoline is extremely flammable, so take extra precautions when you work on any part of the fuel system. Don't smoke or allow open flames or bare light bulbs near the work area, and don't work in a garage where a gas-type appliance (such as a water heater or a clothes dryer) is present. Since gasoline is carcinogenic, wear fuel-resistant gloves when there's a possibility of being exposed to fuel, and, if you spill any fuel on your skin, rinse it off immediately with soap and water. Mop up any spills immediately and do not store fuel-soaked rags where they could ignite. The fuel system is under constant pressure, so, if any fuel lines are to be disconnected, the fuel pressure in the system must be relieved first. When you perform any kind of work on the fuel system, wear safety glasses and have a Class B type fire extinguisher on hand.

✳✳ WARNING 2:

Make sure power to the hybrid system is turned Off before performing any work on this vehicle. Also, on models equipped with the Smart Key system, place the key in a secure spot at least 20 feet away from the work area.

1 Before servicing any fuel system component, you must relieve the fuel pressure to minimize the risk of fire or personal injury.

2 Remove the fuel filler cap - this will relieve any pressure built up in the tank.

3 Remove the rear seat cushion (see Chapter 11), then remove the access cover and unplug the fuel pump electrical connector. The fuel pump cover is sealed with a butyl rubber covering that requires a putty knife or chisel to scrape it loose (see illustration).

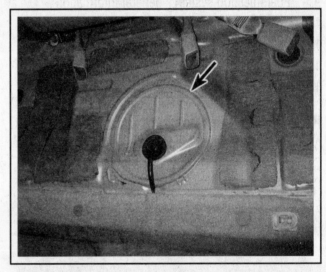

2.3 The sealant around the fuel pump access cover will have to be scraped away prior to removal

4 Operate the vehicle to initiate the starting of the engine - the engine will stall.

➡**Note: Depress the brake pedal and, if necessary, turn on the air conditioner to get the engine to start.**

5 The fuel system is now depressurized.

➡**Note: Place a rag around the fuel line before removing any hose clamp or fitting to prevent any residual fuel from spilling onto the engine.**

6 Before working on the fuel system, see Chapter 6 and disconnect the cable from the negative terminal of the auxiliary 12-volt battery. Be sure to perform the initialization procedure when reconnecting it.

3 Fuel pump/fuel pressure - check

▶ Refer to illustration 3.2a, 3.2b and 3.4

✳✳ WARNING 1:

Gasoline is extremely flammable, so take extra precautions when you work on any part of the fuel system. See the Warning in Section 2.

✳✳ WARNING 2:

Make sure power to the hybrid system is turned Off before performing any work on this vehicle. Also, on models equipped with the Smart Key system, place the key in a secure spot at least 20 feet away from the work area.

➡Note: In order to perform the fuel pressure test, you will need to obtain a fuel pressure gauge capable of measuring high fuel pressure and the proper adapter set for the specific fuel injection system.

1 Check that there is adequate fuel in the fuel tank.

2 Relieve the fuel system pressure (see Section 2). Remove the fuel line from the fuel rail and from where this line attaches to a steel line near the master cylinder. A simple special tool is used to separate the quick-connect fittings (see Section 4). The fuel pressure test hose temporarily replaces this factory hose (see illustrations). Make sure the clamps are tight on the hoses.

3 Operate the vehicle to initiate the starting of the engine.

➡Note: Depress the brake pedal and, if necessary, turn on the air conditioner to get the engine to start.

Note the reading on the gauge, comparing your reading to the value listed in this Chapter's Specifications, then turn off the engine. After five minutes it should not drop below the minimum "hold pressure" listed in this Chapter's Specifications.

4 Disconnect the wiring to the fuel pump. Using fused jumper wires, connect a 12-volt battery to the fuel pump wiring connector with the positive lead to the #3 terminal and the negative lead to the #7 terminal (see illustration). Check the fuel pressure.

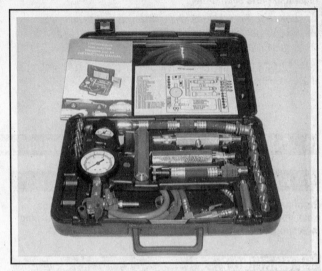

3.2a This fuel pressure testing kit contains all the necessary fittings and adapters, along with the fuel pressure gauge, to test most automotive systems

✳✳ CAUTION:

Only run the fuel pump in this mode for a maximum of ten seconds. Any longer can damage it.

5 If the fuel pressure is not within specifications, check the following:

   a) If the pressure is higher than specified, replace the fuel tank (see Section 6).

   b) If the pressure is lower than specified, the fuel filter could be clogged, the fuel line from the fuel rail to the fuel tank could be restricted, the fuel injectors could be leaking, or the fuel pressure regulator and/or the fuel pump could be defective (this is probably the most likely cause).

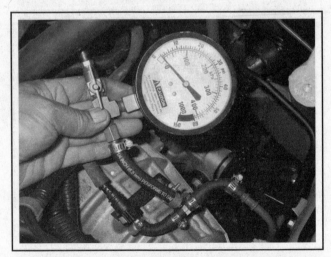

3.2b Attach the fuel pressure gauge with fuel hose and clamps between the fuel rail and the fuel supply line; turn the ignition ON and check the fuel pressure

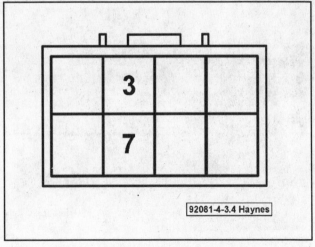

92081-4-3.4 Haynes

3.4 Fuel pump terminals 3 and 7

➡Note: The fuel filter is part of the fuel pump assembly. Check with your local auto parts store or dealer parts department regarding parts availability.

   c) *After disconnecting the jumper wires, connect an ohmmeter across terminals #3 and #7. The resistance should be as listed in this Chapter's Specifications.*

6   After the testing is done, relieve the fuel pressure (see Section 2) and remove the fuel pressure gauge.

4   Fuel lines and fittings - general information and replacement

✻✻ WARNING 1:

Gasoline is extremely flammable, so take extra precautions when you work on any part of the fuel system. See the Warning in Section 2.

✻✻ WARNING 2:

Make sure power to the hybrid system is turned Off before performing any work on this vehicle. Also, on models equipped with the Smart Key system, place the key in a secure spot at least 20 feet away from the work area.

1   Always relieve the fuel pressure before servicing fuel lines or fittings (see Section 2).

2   The fuel line extends from the fuel tank to the engine compartment. The line is secured to the underbody with clip and screw assemblies. This line must be occasionally inspected for leaks, kinks and dents.

3   If evidence of dirt is found in the system or fuel filter during disassembly, the line should be disconnected and blown out.

STEEL TUBING

4   If replacement of a fuel line or emission line is called for, use welded steel tubing meeting the manufacturer's specifications or its equivalent.

FUEL PUMP ELECTRICAL CIRCUIT CHECK

7   If the pump does not turn on (makes no sound) when the engine is supposed to be operating, check the SFI fuse located in the engine compartment fuse center. If the fuse is blown, replace the fuse and see if the pump works. If the pump now works, check for a short in the circuit between the EFI main relay and the fuel pump. Also check the EFI relay.

8   If the relays are good and the fuel pump does not operate, check the wiring from the underhood fuse/relay box to the fuel pump.

5   Don't use copper or aluminum tubing to replace steel tubing. These materials cannot withstand normal vehicle vibration.

6   Because fuel lines used on fuel-injected vehicles are under high pressure, they require special consideration.

7   Some fuel lines have threaded fittings with O-rings. Any time the fittings are loosened to service or replace components:

   a) *Use a back-up wrench to hold the stationary part of the fitting while loosening and tightening the fittings.*
   b) *Check all O-rings for cuts, cracks and deterioration. Replace any that appear hardened, worn or damaged.*
   c) *If the lines are replaced, always use original equipment parts, or parts that meet the original equipment standards specified in this Section.*

FLEXIBLE HOSE

✻✻ WARNING:

Use only original equipment replacement hoses or their equivalent. Others may fail from the high pressures of this system.

8   Don't route fuel hose within four inches of any part of the exhaust system or within ten inches of the catalytic converter. Metal lines and rubber hoses must never be allowed to chafe against the frame. A mini-

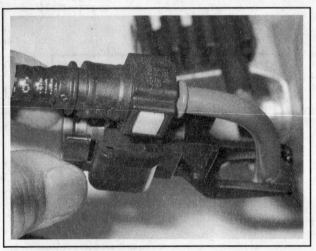

4.12a Some fuel line fittings have a cover over the joint; remove the cover, then push the button on each side to disconnect the fitting

4.12b Push this simple special tool into the fuel connection, push the line toward the tool, then pull the line back to separate the fuel line connection

mum of 1/4-inch clearance must be maintained around a line or hose to prevent contact with the frame.

9 Some models may be equipped with nylon fuel line and quick-connect fittings at the fuel filter and/or fuel pump. The quick-connect fittings cannot be serviced separately. Do not attempt to service these types of fuel lines in the event the retainer tabs or the line becomes damaged. Replace the entire fuel line as an assembly.

REPLACEMENT

▶ **Refer to illustrations 4.12a and 4.12b**

10 In the event of any fuel line damage (metal or flexible lines) it is necessary to replace the damaged lines with factory replacement parts. Others may fail from the high pressures of this system.

11 Relieve the fuel pressure.

12 Remove all fasteners attaching the lines to the vehicle body. On fuel lines so equipped, detach the clamp(s) that attach the fuel hoses to the metal lines, then pull the hose off the fitting. Twisting the hoses back and forth will allow them to separate more easily. To separate quick-connect fittings, hold the connector with one hand and depress the retaining tab(s) with the other hand, then separate the connector from the pipe (see illustration). Some fittings require the use of a dedicated, yet simple tool (see illustration).

13 Installation is the reverse of removal, making sure to use new O-rings. On plastic quick-connect fittings, align the retainer locking pawls with the connector grooves. Push the connector onto the pipe until both retaining pawls lock with a clicking sound, then reinstall the covers.

5 Fuel pump module - removal and installation

✳✳ WARNING 1:

Gasoline is extremely flammable, so take extra precautions when you work on any part of the fuel system. See the Warning in Section 2.

✳✳ WARNING 2:

Make sure power to the hybrid system is turned Off before performing any work on this vehicle. Also, on models equipped with the Smart Key system, place the key in a secure spot at least 20 feet away from the work area.

This assembly contains the fuel pump, the fuel level sensor and the pressure regulator. At the time of writing, the fuel pump module was not available as a separate component. If a problem arises with the fuel pump or any of the other components of the fuel pump module, the entire fuel tank assembly must be replaced as a unit.

➡**Note: Check with a dealer parts department or auto parts store to see if separate components have become available before assuming the fuel tank must be replaced.**

6 Fuel tank - removal and installation

▶ **Refer to illustration 6.10**

✳✳ WARNING 1:

Gasoline is extremely flammable, so take extra precautions when you work on any part of the fuel system. See the Warning in Section 2.

✳✳ WARNING 2:

Make sure power to the hybrid system is turned Off before performing any work on this vehicle. Also, on models equipped with the Smart Key system, place the key in a secure spot at least 20 feet away from the work area.

✳✳ CAUTION:

The fuel tank used on most of these models contains a rubber bladder that is used to lessen the amount of vapors in the tank.

Be careful to avoid damaging this bladder. Do not let anyone attempt to repair these tanks. If the tank is damaged it must be replaced.

1 Remove the fuel filler cap to relieve fuel tank pressure. Relieve the fuel system pressure (see Section 2).

2 Refer to Chapter 6 and disconnect the cable from the negative terminal of the auxiliary 12-volt battery. Be sure to perform the initialization procedure when reconnecting it.

3 Siphon or pump the fuel into an approved container using a siphoning kit or hand-operated pump (available at most auto parts stores).

✳✳ WARNING:

Do not start the siphoning action by mouth!

4 Raise the vehicle and support it securely on jackstands.

5 Remove the floor brace that is under the exhaust pipe. Disconnect

the oxygen sensor (on some models it will be necessary to remove the center instrument panel cover for access to the connector). Remove the front exhaust pipe.

6   Remove the rear seat cushion (see Chapter 11).

7   Remove the fuel system access cover in the floor. Disconnect the wiring as you lift it.

8   Refer to Section 4 and disconnect all lines that interfere with fuel tank removal.

➡Note: Be sure to plug the hoses to prevent leakage and contamination of the fuel system.

9   Support the fuel tank with a floor jack. Place a sturdy plank between the jack head and the fuel tank to protect the tank. Loosen the clamp and disconnect the fuel fill pipe from the tank inlet pipe.

10 Remove the bolts from the fuel tank retaining straps and set the straps aside (see illustration).

11 Lower the tank and disconnect the fuel inlet pipe.

12 Remove the tank from the vehicle.

13 Installation is the reverse of removal.

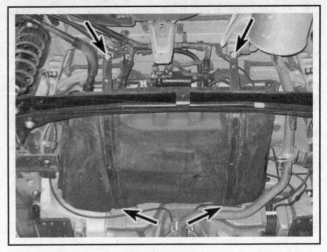

6.10 Fuel tank strap bolt locations

7   Fuel tank cleaning and repair - general information

1   The fuel tank installed in the vehicles covered by this manual is not repairable. If it becomes damaged, it must be replaced.

2   Cleaning the fuel tank (due to fuel contamination) should be performed by a professional with the proper training to carry out this critical and potentially dangerous work. Even after cleaning and flushing, explosive fumes may remain inside the fuel tank.

3   If the fuel tank is removed from the vehicle, it should not be placed in an area where sparks or open flames could ignite the fumes coming out of the tank. Be especially careful inside a garage where a

gas-type appliance is located.

4   2004 and later fuel tanks are equipped with rubber bladders that serve to reduce the amount of vapor in the system.

✳✳ CAUTION:

Do not let anyone attempt to repair these tanks. If the tank is damaged it must be replaced.

8   Air filter housing - removal and installation

◆ **Refer to illustrations 8.1 and 8.3**

✳✳ WARNING:

Make sure power to the hybrid system is turned Off before performing any work on this vehicle. Also, on models equipped with the Smart Key system, place the key in a secure spot at least 20 feet away from the work area.

1   Disconnect the air intake hose and breather hose from the housing cover (see illustration).

8.1 Disconnect the intake tube from the air filter housing - it need not be removed from the vehicle

2   Disconnect the wiring from the MAF sensor. Also unclip the sensor from the retainer on the air filter housing.

3   Loosen the hose clamp holding the filter housing to the throttle body. Remove the bolts and remove the air filter housing from the engine compartment (see illustration).

4   Installation is the reverse of removal.

8.3 The air filter housing is secured with two bolts (A) and a hose clamp (B)

9 Fuel injection system - general information

1   All models are equipped with a multi port fuel injection system. The fuel injection system is composed of three basic subsystems: fuel system, air induction system and electronic engine control system.

FUEL SYSTEM

2   An electric fuel pump located in the fuel tank supplies fuel under constant pressure to the fuel rail, which distributes fuel evenly to all injectors. From the fuel rail, fuel is injected into the intake ports, just above the intake valves, by electronic fuel injectors. The amount of fuel supplied by the injectors is precisely controlled by an electronic Powertrain Control Module (PCM). The fuel pump module, which includes the fuel pressure regulator and fuel filter, is located in the fuel tank.

AIR INDUCTION SYSTEM

3   The air induction system consists of the air filter housing and the throttle body. The throttle plate inside the throttle body is controlled by the driver via the PCM. As the throttle plate opens, additional air is drawn into the cylinders. The information provided by the various sensors allows the PCM to determine the exact amount of fuel to be injected by the injectors during the various operating conditions.

ELECTRONIC ENGINE CONTROL SYSTEM

4   The electronic engine control system controls the fuel injection, ignition and emissions systems by means of a Powertrain Control Module (PCM), which employs a microprocessor. The PCM receives signals from a number of information sensors, which monitor such variables as intake air temperature, throttle angle, coolant temperature, engine rpm, engine load, vehicle speed and exhaust oxygen content. These signals help the PCM determine the injection duration necessary for the optimum air/fuel ratio. The sensors and their corresponding PCM-controlled relays, are located throughout the engine compartment. For further information regarding the PCM and its relationship to the fuel injection and ignition systems, see Chapter 6.

10 Fuel injection system - check

♦ **Refer to illustrations 10.7 and 10.8**

⚠ WARNING:

Make sure power to the hybrid system is turned Off before performing any work on this vehicle. Also, on models equipped with the Smart Key system, place the key in a secure spot at least 20 feet away from the work area.

➡**Note: The following procedure is based on the assumption that the fuel pump is working and the fuel pressure is adequate (see Section 3).**

1   Check the ground wire connections for tightness. Check all wiring and electrical connectors that are related to the system. Loose electrical connectors and poor grounds can cause many problems that resemble more serious malfunctions.

2   Check to see that the battery is fully charged, as the control unit and sensors depend on an accurate supply voltage in order to properly meter the fuel.

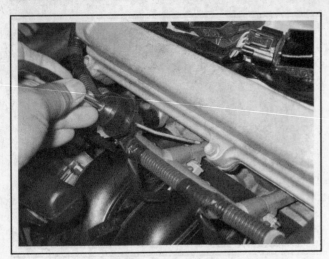

10.7 Use a stethoscope to determine if the injectors are working properly - they should make a steady clicking sound that rises and falls with engine speed changes

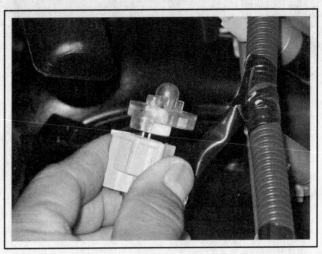

10.8 Install the "noid" light into the fuel injector electrical connector and check to see that it blinks when the engine is running

3   Check the air filter element - a dirty or partially blocked filter will severely impede performance and economy (see Chapter 1).

4   Check the fuses. If a blown fuse is found, replace it and see if it blows again. If it does, search for a grounded wire in the fuel injection system wiring harness.

5   Check the air intake duct and the intake manifold for leaks, which will result in an excessively lean mixture. Also check the condition of the vacuum hoses connected to the intake manifold.

6   Remove the air intake duct from the throttle body and check for dirt, carbon, varnish, or other residue in the throttle body, particularly around the throttle plate. If it's dirty, see Chapter 6 and troubleshoot the PCV system for the cause of excessive varnish buildup.

7   With the engine running, place a stethoscope against each injector, one at a time, and listen for a clicking sound, indicating operation (see illustration).

➡Note: An assistant would be helpful here.

If you don't have an automotive stethoscope you can use a long screwdriver; just place the tip of the screwdriver against the injector body and press your ear against the handle.

8   If there is a problem with an injector, purchase a special injector test light (noid light) and install it into the injector electrical connector (see illustration). Start the engine and make sure that each injector connector flashes the noid light. This will test for the proper voltage signal to the injector.

9   With the engine OFF and the fuel injector electrical connectors disconnected, measure the resistance of each injector. Compare your measurement with the value listed in this Chapter's Specifications. If the injector resistance is excessive or an open or short circuit is indicated, replace the injector (see Section 12).

10   Additional fuel injection control system component checks can be found in Chapter 6.

11 Throttle body - cleaning, removal and installation

▸ Refer to illustrations 11.1, 11.5 and 11.7

❋❋ WARNING:

Make sure power to the hybrid system is turned Off before performing any work on this vehicle. Also, on models equipped with the Smart Key system, place the key in a secure spot at least 20 feet away from the work area.

CLEANING

1   To clean the throttle body, first remove the air filter housing (see Section 8). Use carburetor cleaner to clean the throttle body, especially if idling problems occur (see illustration).

REMOVAL AND INSTALLATION

❋❋ WARNING:

Wait until the engine is completely cool before beginning this procedure.

2   On 2004 and later models detach the six clips and remove the radiator top cover.

3   Refer to Section 8 and remove the air filter housing.

4   Clamp off the coolant hoses to the throttle body.

5   Disconnect the throttle position sensor and the control motor wiring connectors (see illustration).

6   Disconnect the PCV, vapor and coolant hoses. Be prepared for a little coolant spillage.

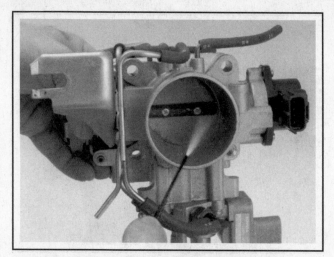

11.1 With the engine off, use aerosol carburetor cleaner, a toothbrush and a rag to clean the throttle body - open the throttle plate so you can see behind it (make sure the cleaner is safe for use with catalytic converters and oxygen sensors) (typical)

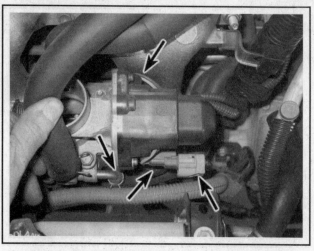

11.5 Disconnect the electrical connectors and coolant hoses from the throttle body

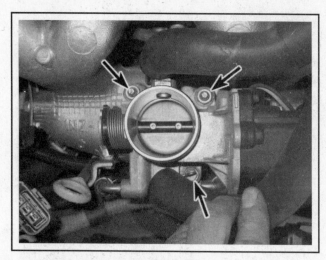

11.7 Throttle body mounting fasteners

7   Unscrew the throttle body fasteners (see illustration) and remove the throttle body along with the bracket, if equipped.

8   Using a soft brush and carburetor cleaner, thoroughly clean the throttle body casting, then blow out all passages with compressed air.

❋❋ CAUTION:

Do not clean the throttle position sensor with anything. Just wipe it off carefully with a clean, soft cloth.

9   Installation of the throttle body is the reverse of removal. Be sure to use a new gasket.

10 Tighten the throttle body mounting bolts/nuts to the torque listed in this Chapter's Specifications.

11 Check the coolant level, adding as necessary (see Chapter 1).

12 Fuel rail and injectors - removal and installation

▶ Refer to illustrations 12.6, 12.7a and 12.7b

❋❋ WARNING 1:

Gasoline is extremely flammable, so take extra precautions when you work on any part of the fuel system. See the Warning in Section 2.

❋❋ WARNING 2:

Make sure power to the hybrid system is turned Off before performing any work on this vehicle. Also, on models equipped with the Smart Key system, place the key in a secure spot at least 20 feet away from the work area.

1   Relieve the fuel pressure (see Section 2).

2   Refer to Chapter 6 and disconnect the cable from the negative terminal of the auxiliary 12-volt battery. Be sure to perform the initialization procedure when reconnecting it.

3   Remove the air filter housing (see Section 8).

4   Disconnect the electrical connectors from the fuel injectors. Open the wiring harness clamps and position the wiring harness aside.

5   Disconnect the fuel line leading to the fuel rail (see Section 4 for fuel line disconnect procedures).

6   Remove the fuel rail mounting bolts and carefully withdraw the fuel rail and injectors from the cylinder head (see illustration). Remove the spacers from the cylinder head.

7   Remove the injectors from the fuel rail (see illustration). Replace the O-ring and grommet on each injector (see illustration).

8   Remove the insulators in the cylinder head and replace them with new ones.

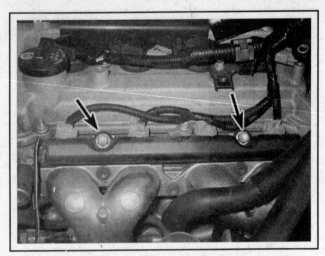

12.6 Location of the fuel rail mounting bolts

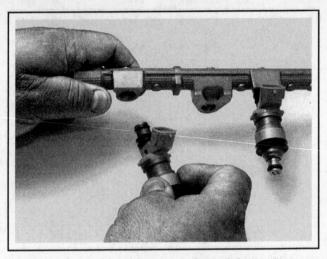

12.7a Twist and pull the injector to remove it from the fuel rail

9   Lubricate the O-rings with clean engine oil and install the fuel injectors onto the fuel rail. Make sure the spacers are in place and install the fuel rail/injector assembly onto the cylinder head. Install the fuel rail mounting bolts and tighten the bolts to the torque listed in this Chapter's Specifications.

10 The remainder of installation is the reverse of removal.

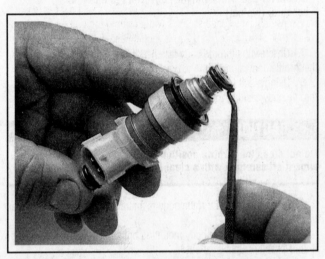

12.7b If you plan to reinstall the old injectors, remove and discard the O-rings and grommets and replace them with new ones

13 Exhaust system servicing - general information

♦ Refer to illustration 13.1

✷✷ WARNING 1:

Inspection and repair of exhaust system components should be done only after the system components have cooled completely.

✷✷ WARNING 2:

Make sure power to the hybrid system is turned Off before performing any work on this vehicle. Also, on models equipped with the Smart Key system, place the key in a secure spot at least 20 feet away from the work area.

1   The exhaust system consists of the exhaust manifold, catalytic converter, the muffler, the tailpipe and all connecting pipes, brackets, hangers and clamps. The exhaust system is attached to the body with mounting brackets and rubber hangers (see illustration). If any of these parts are damaged or deteriorated, excessive noise and vibration will be transmitted to the body.

2   Conducting regular inspections of the exhaust system will keep it safe and quiet. Look for any damaged or bent parts, open seams, holes, loose connections, excessive corrosion or other defects that could allow exhaust fumes to enter the vehicle. Deteriorated exhaust system components should not be repaired - they should be replaced with new parts.

3   If the exhaust system components are extremely corroded or rusted together, they will probably have to be cut from the exhaust sys-

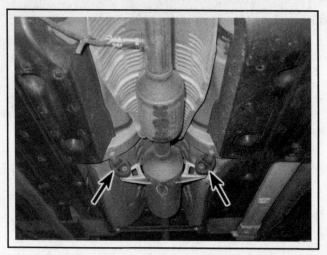

13.1 Check all rubber hangers for damage or deterioration

tem. The convenient way to accomplish this is to have a muffler repair shop remove the corroded sections with a cutting torch. If, however, you want to save money by doing it yourself and you don't have an oxy/acetylene welding outfit with a cutting torch, simply cut off the old components with a hacksaw. If you have compressed air, special pneumatic cutting chisels can also be used. If you do decide to tackle the job at home, be sure to wear eye protection to protect your eyes from metal chips and work gloves to protect your hands.

4 Here are some simple guidelines to apply when repairing the exhaust system:

a) *Work from the back to the front when removing exhaust system components.*

b) *Apply penetrating oil to the exhaust system component fasteners to make them easier to remove.*

c) *Use new gaskets, hangers and clamps when installing exhaust system components.*

d) *Apply anti-seize compound to the threads of all exhaust system fasteners during reassembly.*

e) *Be sure to allow sufficient clearance between newly installed parts and all points on the underbody to avoid overheating the floor pan and possibly damaging the interior carpet and insulation. Pay particularly close attention to the catalytic converter and its heat shield.*

✳✳ WARNING:

The catalytic converter operates at very high temperatures and takes a long time to cool. Wait until it's completely cool before attempting to remove the converter. Failure to do so could result in serious burns.

Specifications

Fuel system

Fuel pressure	44 to 50 psi
Fuel system hold pressure (engine Off, after five minutes)	21 psi minimum
Fuel injector resistance (at 68-degrees F)	13.4 to 14.2 ohms (approximately)
Fuel pump resistance (at 68 degrees F)	0.2 to 3.0 ohms (approximately)

Torque specifications   Ft-lbs (unless otherwise indicated)

Intake manifold mounting bolts	22
Fuel rail mounting bolts	168 in-lbs
Throttle body mounting bolts/nuts	15

Notes

Section

Reference to other Chapters

5

HYBRID
SYSTEMS

1 General information

▶ Refer to illustrations 1.1 and 1.8

HYBRID SYSTEM

Toyota uses two hybrid systems on the models covered in this manual. The Toyota Hybrid System (THS) is used on 2001 through 2003 models. This was refined and termed THS-II on 2004 and later models (see illustration)

The Toyota hybrid systems use computer controls and a mechanical power-splitting transaxle to mix the most efficient traits of two power sources - a modified internal combustion engine and electric motors. By using these power-providers in combination only when each is at its highest efficiency, very high fuel-mileage is realized. The main components of the hybrid system are:

a) *The internal combustion engine*
b) *Two electric motors that can also function as generators*
c) *An electrical inverter/converter*
d) *A high voltage battery*
e) *Computers*
f) *A mechanical, continuously variable power-splitting transaxle*

INTERNAL COMBUSTION ENGINE

The engine used in the Prius is of conventional design but with a major modification: It uses an altered camshaft that converts it to an Atkinson-Miller cycle engine rather than an Otto cycle engine. The engine only operates in a narrow rpm range and produces low power, but it is very fuel-efficient. It is connected to the transaxle along with the two motor/generators.

MOTOR/GENERATOR #1

This is the smaller of the two motor/generators. The computer uses

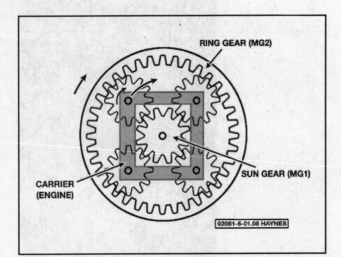

1.8 The heart of the transaxle is this very simple planetary gear set; the outer ring gear is connected to the motor/generator #2, the center sun gear is connected to motor/generator #1 and the carrier/planet gears are connected to the engine

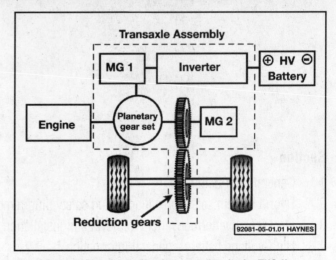

1.1 A simplified chart of basic power flow in the THS-II system used on 2004 and later models; note that the transaxle assembly includes motor/generators #1 and #2 as well as the inverter/converter

this unit to control the operation of the transaxle, allowing it to work in a continuously variable mode, i.e., there are no gear changes - simply a smooth increase in vehicle speed as it accelerates. It does this by changing its resistance and thereby changing its speed. Motor/generator #1 also acts as the starter for the engine. When it is not starting the engine it is either charging the high voltage battery or supplying power to motor/generator #2.

The motor/generator #1 is an integral component of the transaxle assembly. Its replacement is beyond the scope of this manual.

MOTOR/GENERATOR #2

This unit supplies power to the vehicle, either by itself (at low speeds) or with the engine (when high power is needed). It also operates as a generator for battery charging when the vehicle is braking. Energy that would normally be lost in the braking process is thereby converted to electrical power.

The motor/generator #2 is an integral component of the transaxle assembly. Its replacement is beyond the scope of this manual.

ELECTRICAL INVERTER/CONVERTER

This electrical device is mounted on the transaxle along with the motor/generators. Its job is to change the alternating current produced by the motor/generators into the direct current used by the high and low-voltage batteries and vice versa. On 2004 and later models, the inverter provides 202 volts of alternating current to power the air conditioning compressor.

HIGH VOLTAGE BATTERY

This large battery is used by the system to provide power to the motor/generators. It is charged by motor/generator #1 and (during braking) motor/generator #2. 2001 through 2003 models batteries are made up of 38 nickel-metal hydride modules and produce 274 volts. 2004 and later models with the THS-II system have 28 modules and put out 202 volts. The THS-II system increases the battery's 202 volts to 500 volts by using a boost converter system. The high-voltage battery has its own blower system for cooling.

A conventional automotive 12-volt battery is also used to provide power for all of the components that normally use it. Refer to Chapter 6 for more information on the 12-volt battery.

COMPUTERS

There are several separate computers that work together to operate the hybrid system. Simply stated, their main function is to coordinate and seamlessly blend all the other components' functions so that the result is the greatest possible fuel efficiency and good performance. In addition to a main engine-control computer there is also a computer specifically for the brake system and another for the high-voltage hybrid control system.

POWER-SPLITTING TRANSAXLE

This simple planetary gearbox is connected to the motor/generators, the engine and the wheels of the vehicle. Because of its design, the computer can use it to give or take power from all of these components simultaneously (see illustration). The motor/generators can receive power (operating as generators) or apply power (operating as motors). Likewise the engine can receive power (when it is started) or apply it. The wheels of the vehicle generally receive power to drive the vehicle, but under "regenerative" braking the transaxle uses braking power to spin the motor/generator #2 thereby charging the battery. See Chapter 7 for more information on the transaxle assembly.

---

2   Hybrid system safety precautions and safety plug removal

▶ **Refer to illustrations 2.3, 2.5, 2.8, 2.11 and 2.15**

❋❋ WARNING:

These vehicles use high voltage! Failure to follow these precautions can result in vehicle damage or destruction, personal injury or death!

1   Always perform the following procedures any time you are working near any hybrid system components, high-voltage components or orange-colored wiring.

2   On models so equipped, remove the ignition key from the ignition.

3   If the vehicle is a 2004 or later model with the Smart Key system, turn the system OFF. The switch is on the lower section of the instrument panel (see illustration). Also move the Smart Key at least 20 feet away from the vehicle and locate it so that another person won't find it and carry it near the vehicle.

4   Refer to Chapter 6 and disconnect the cable from the negative terminal of the auxiliary 12-volt battery. Be sure to perform the initialization procedure when reconnecting it (also described in Chapter 6).

2001 THROUGH 2003 MODELS

5   Open the luggage compartment lid. Put on undamaged insulating rubber lineman's safety gloves (minimum Class 0) (see illustration). These gloves are available from electricians' supply stores and directly from Toyota.

6   Grasp the safety plug and pull it to the rear of the vehicle. Removing this plug will disconnect the high voltage battery from the rest of the vehicle. Put the plug somewhere secure so that another person can't find and install it.

7   Cover the plug opening with vinyl electrical tape and proceed to Step 13.

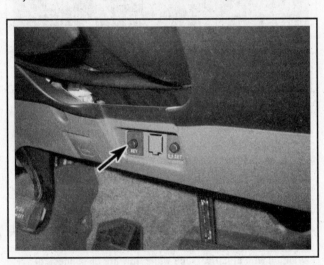

2.3 Before working on models with the Smart Key system, turn the system Off by depressing this button, and be sure to store the Smart Key at least 20 feet away from the vehicle

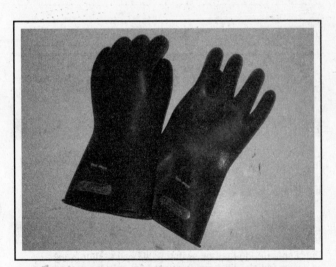

2.5 Insulating rubber gloves are mandatory when working near any of the high voltage components; the early THS system puts out 274 volts and the THS-II system generates 500 volts - easily enough to cause a fatal injury

2.8 Remove the rear floor box to access the high-voltage battery safety plug

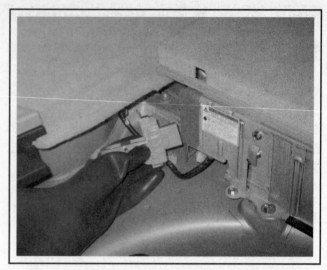

2.11 Removing the safety plug disconnects the high voltage battery from the rest of the vehicle for safety; put it in your pocket immediately or somewhere else secure - someone else may unknowingly reinstall it while you're working on the car

2004 AND LATER MODELS

8   Raise the rear hatch. Turn the two rear knobs and then lift out the rear floorboard. Remove the rear floor box (see illustration). Also remove the trim panel on the left side of the luggage compartment.

9   Put on undamaged insulating rubber lineman's safety gloves (minimum Class 0) (see illustration 2.5). These gloves are available from electricians' supply stores and directly from Toyota.

10 Pull the release lever upward then swing it down (towards the left side of the vehicle).

11 Grasp the safety plug and pull it out of the battery (see illustration). Removing this plug will disconnect the high voltage battery from the rest of the vehicle. Put the plug somewhere secure so that another person can't find and install it.

12 Cover the plug opening with vinyl electrical tape and proceed to Step 13.

ALL MODELS

13 Wait for at least five minutes after disconnecting the safety plug before working near any high-voltage sources on the vehicle.

WARNING:

There will still be high voltage in the system even after removing the safety plug! The voltage will decrease gradually but will take at least five minutes to be considered safe. Even then, insulating gloves must be worn.

CAUTION:

Don't operate the ignition switch (2003 and earlier models) or power switch (2004 and later models) with the safety plug removed. The hybrid control ECU could be damaged.

14 Always use insulated tools. Don't use tools with damaged insulation.

15 Cover disconnected high-voltage terminals with vinyl electrical tape immediately (see illustration).

16 Wear insulating rubber lineman's safety gloves (minimum Class 0) when working near high voltage.

17 If the vehicle becomes flooded, contact your local Toyota dealer for instructions on how to proceed. In an emergency, follow the above Steps and then remove all four fuses from the engine compartment before trying to move the car.

18 The best rule of thumb is to not get near any high-voltage components or orange-colored wiring.

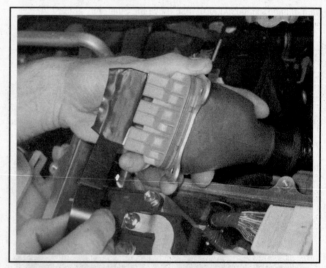

2.15 All disconnected high-voltage terminals must be wrapped with electrical tape while they are disconnected; you can tell the high voltage wire harnesses easily - they are bright orange to warn you not to be careless when working near them

3 Electrical inverter/converter - removal and installation

❋❋ WARNING 1:

Refer to Section 2 and follow all safety precautions before working on this system.

❋❋ WARNING 2:

Wait until the vehicle is completely cool before beginning this procedure.

2001 THROUGH 2003 MODELS

1 Refer to Chapter 6 and disconnect the cable from the negative terminal of the auxiliary 12-volt battery. Be sure to perform the initialization procedure when reconnecting it.

2 Remove the high-voltage safety plug (see Section 2). Be sure to wait at least five minutes before proceeding. Drain the coolant from the inverter/converter/transaxle cooling system (see Chapter 1).

3 Disconnect the battery cable from the inverter/converter. Cover it with vinyl electrical tape.

4 Remove the four small Torx-head screws from the cover.

5 Remove the two larger Torx-head screws from the circuit breaker sensor and connector cover.

6 Use a voltmeter to test for voltage between each pair of the three terminals and also between each terminal and a good ground. The meter must read approximately zero volts everywhere. If not, wait for the system to discharge further. When all points read zero volts, proceed.

7 Remove the six bolts and disconnect the three cables for motor/generator #2.

8 Remove the three bolts and the cable from motor/generator #1. You will remove the cable along with the inverter/converter later.

9 Remove the bolt and the ground cable.

10 Place rags around the inverter/converter to catch coolant. Disconnect the three coolant hoses from the assembly.

11 Remove the four mounting bolts and lift off the inverter/converter assembly.

12 Installation is the reverse of removal. Be sure to refill the cooling system (see Chapter 1).

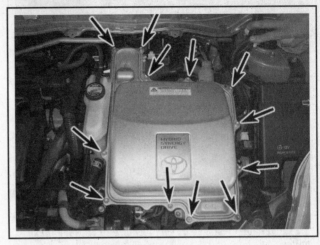

3.19 Inverter/converter cover bolts

2004 AND LATER MODELS

▶ **Refer to illustrations 3.19, 3.20a, 3.20b, 3.21a, 3.21b, 3.22, 3.23, 3.24, 3.25, 3.27, 3.28, 3.30a and 3.30b**

13 Refer to Chapter 6 and disconnect the cable from the negative terminal of the auxiliary 12-volt battery. Be sure to perform the initialization procedure when reconnecting it.

14 Remove the high-voltage safety plug (see Section 2). Be sure to wait at least five minutes before proceeding.

15 Drain the coolant from the inverter/converter/transaxle cooling system (see Chapter 1).

16 Refer to Chapter 12 and remove the windshield wiper motor assembly.

17 Remove the outer front cowl top panel.

18 Remove the radiator upper cover (see Chapter 1, illustration 11.3).

19 Remove the bolts and lift off the inverter/converter cover (see illustration).

20 Wear insulating rubber lineman's safety gloves (minimum Class 0) and use a voltmeter to test the voltage of the high-voltage DC cable. It must be near zero to safely continue (see illustrations).

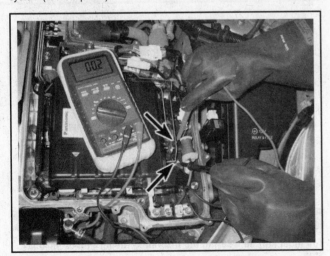

3.20a Wear insulating gloves when verifying that there is little or no voltage present between these terminals . . .

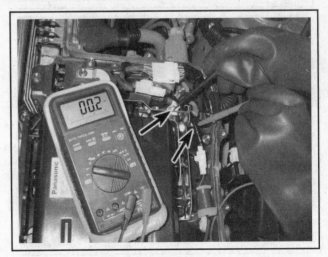

3.20b . . . as well as these terminals

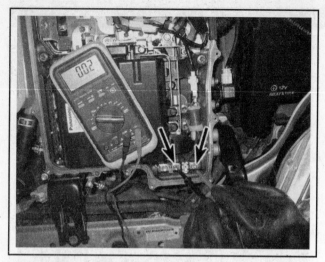

3.21a Voltage must also be very low or zero between these points . . .

3.21b . . . and these normally high-voltage terminals

3.22 There are three cooling hoses that must be disconnected after coolant has been drained from the system; don't drain any coolant from the engine cooling system

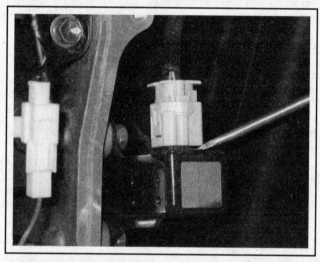

3.23 Pry back the outer portion of the electrical connector to unlock it, then disconnect it from circuit breaker

3.24 Unplug these two electrical connectors and detach the frame cables from the inverter/converter

21 Also test the voltage between each pair of cables (three readings) (see illustrations). All must be near zero to safely continue.

22 Disconnect the three coolant hoses from the inverter/converter (see illustration).

23 Pull back the lock on the number one circuit breaker sensor, then disconnect it (see illustration).

24 Wear insulating rubber gloves and disconnect the frame cables (see illustration). Wrap the exposed terminals with vinyl electrical tape.

25 Disconnect the wiring for the air conditioning compressor inverter (see illustration). There is a small lock that must be lifted in order to release the connector.

❋❋ WARNING:

You must still be wearing the insulating rubber gloves for this Step.

3.25 The locking tab must be released before the high-voltage harnesses can be disconnected

3.27 Remove these bolts and disconnect the harness for motor/generator #2

26 Label and disconnect the six other smaller wiring connections at the inverter/converter assembly.

27 Wear the rubber insulating gloves and remove the five bolts that connect the motor/generator #2 cable (see illustration). Pull the cable free. Cover the terminals with vinyl electrical tape.

28 Perform the same procedure with the motor/generator #1 cable (see illustration).

29 Disconnect the air conditioning wiring from its bracket.

30 Remove the three inverter/converter mounting bolts and lift the assembly out (see illustrations).

31 Installation is the reverse of removal. Be sure to refill the inverter/converter/transaxle cooling system (see Chapter 1).

3.28 There are also five bolts that secure the #1 power cable

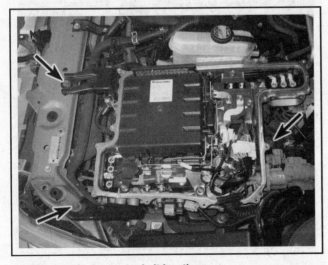

3.30a Inverter/converter bolt locations

3.30b Lift the inverter/converter assembly carefully to avoid damaging it and other nearby components

4 High-voltage battery - general information

▶ Refer to illustration 4.1

Due to the extreme danger, the high-voltage battery must only be replaced by a factory-trained technician who has completed hybrid vehicle servicing courses. Do not attempt to remove this battery (see illustration). Additionally, refer to Section 2 and remove the safety plug whenever working near this battery or near any part of the high-voltage system (as evidenced by the orange wiring harnesses).

4.1 The high-voltage battery is located behind the rear seat backs and under the floorboard. Warning: Do not attempt to remove this battery!

5 Battery cooling blower - removal and installation

✳ WARNING:

Refer to Section 2 and follow all safety precautions before working on this system.

1 Refer to Chapter 6 and disconnect the cable from the negative terminal of the auxiliary 12-volt battery. Be sure to perform the initialization procedure when reconnecting it.

2 Remove the high-voltage safety plug (see Section 2). Be sure to wait at least five minutes before proceeding.

2001 THROUGH 2003 MODELS

3 Refer to Chapter 11 and remove the rear seat.

4 Remove the luggage compartment trim panel.

5 Disconnect and remove all five vent ducts. Lay them out in order to avoid confusion later.

6 Disconnect the blower wiring.

7 Unbolt the blower and lift it out. Installation is the reverse of removal.

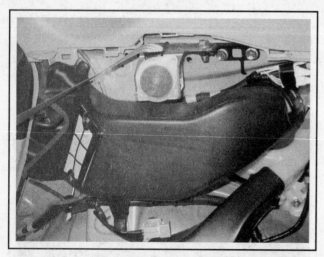

5.14 The intake duct with its filter is the upper one - the lower is the discharge duct

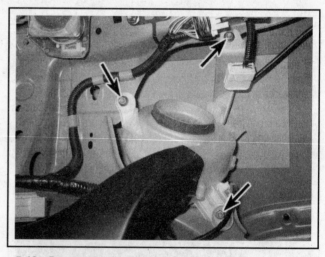

5.16a Remove the three blower housing nuts . . .

2004 AND LATER MODELS

▶ **Refer to illustrations 5.14, 5.16a and 5.16b**

8   Release the clips and remove the rear hatch sill molding.
9   Remove the luggage cover if you haven't already done so.
10 Refer to Chapter 11 and remove the rear seat cushion.
11 Remove the luggage tie-down strikers from the rear floorboard. Remove the five clips and lift out the floorboard.
12 Remove the lower bolt from each side of the rear seat back frames. Disconnect the joints, then remove the rear side seat back frames.
13 Remove the right side trim panel. This requires removal of the luggage tie-down striker, two bolts and eight clips.
14 Disconnect the blower relay wiring, remove the two clips and remove the inner quarter vent duct. Slide it towards the battery to remove it (see illustration).
15 Unclip the three retainers and remove the inner vent duct.
16 Remove the three blower mounting nuts and pull the blower loose (see illustrations). Disconnect the wiring and lift the blower free.
17 Installation is the reverse of removal.

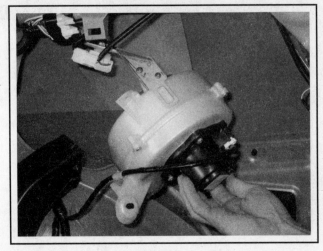

5.16b . . . then lift the blower free and disconnecting the wiring

Specifications

General

Motor/generator system voltage	
2001 through 2003 THS models	273.6 volts
2004 and later THS-II models	500 volts

High-voltage battery

Number of modules	
2001 through 2003 THS models	38 nickel-metal hydride
2004 and later THS-II models	28 nickel-metal hydride
Battery voltage	
2001 through 2003 THS models	273.6 volts
2004 and later THS-II models	201.6 volts

Torque specifications   Ft-lbs (unless otherwise indicated)

Inverter/converter assembly mounting bolts	
2001 through 2003 THS models	15
2004 and later THS-II models	16

Notes

6

EMISSIONS AND ENGINE ELECTRICAL/ CONTROL SYSTEMS

1 General information

◆ Refer to illustrations 1.9a and 1.9b

The engine electrical system includes all ignition components. Because of their engine-related functions, these components are discussed separately from chassis electrical devices such as the lights, the instruments, etc. (which are included in Chapter 12).

Always observe the following precautions when working on the electrical systems:

a) *Be extremely careful when servicing engine electrical components. They are easily damaged if checked, connected or handled improperly.*

b) *Don't disconnect the battery cables while the engine is running.*

c) *Maintain correct polarity when connecting a battery cable from another vehicle during jump-starting.*

d) *Always disconnect the negative cable first and hook it up last or the battery may be shorted by the tool being used to loosen the cable clamps.*

It's also a good idea to review the safety-related information regarding the engine electrical systems located in the *Safety first!* Section near the front of this manual before beginning any operation included in this Chapter.

To prevent pollution of the atmosphere from incompletely burned and evaporating gases, and to maintain good driveability and fuel economy, a number of emission control systems are incorporated. They include the:

On-Board Diagnostic (OBD) II system
Electronic Fuel Injection (EFI) system
Evaporative Emissions Control (EVAP) system
Positive Crankcase Ventilation (PCV) system
Catalytic converter

The Sections in this Chapter include general descriptions, checking procedures within the scope of the home mechanic and component replacement procedures (when possible) for each of the systems listed above.

Before assuming that an emissions control system is malfunctioning, check the fuel and ignition systems carefully. The diagnosis of some emission control devices requires specialized tools, equipment and training. If checking and servicing become too difficult or if a procedure is beyond your ability, consult a dealer service department or other repair shop. Remember, the most frequent cause of emissions problems is simply a loose or broken wire or vacuum hose, so always check the hose and wiring connections first.

This doesn't mean, however, that emissions control systems are particularly difficult to maintain and repair. You can quickly and easily perform many checks and do most of the regular maintenance at home with common tune-up and hand tools.

➡**Note: Because of a Federally mandated warranty that covers the emissions control system components, check with your dealer about warranty coverage before working on any emissions-related systems. Once the warranty has expired, you may wish to perform some of the component checks and/or replacement procedures in this Chapter to save money.**

Pay close attention to any special precautions outlined in this Chapter. It should be noted that the illustrations of the various systems may not exactly match the system installed on your vehicle because of changes made by the manufacturer during production or from year-to-year.

A Vehicle Emissions Control Information (VECI) label is attached to the bottom of the hood (see illustration). This label contains important emissions specifications and adjustment information. Also under the hood, the Vacuum Hose Routing Diagram (see illustration), provides a vacuum hose schematic with emissions components identified. When servicing the engine or emissions systems, the VECI label and the vacuum hose routing diagram in your particular vehicle should always be checked for up-to-date information.

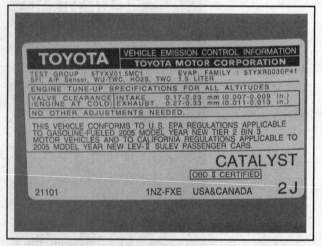

1.9a The Vehicle Emission Control Information (VECI) label contains such essential information as the types of emission control systems installed on the engine and certain tune-up specifications

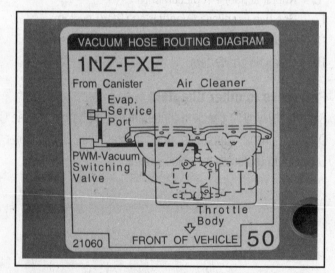

1.9b Vacuum hose routing diagram for a 2005 model

2   Battery (12-volt) - emergency jump starting

Refer to the Booster battery (jump) starting procedure at the front of this manual.

3   Battery (12-volt) - check and replacement

✳✳ WARNING 1:

Hydrogen gas is produced by the battery, so keep open flames and lighted cigarettes away from it at all times. Always wear eye protection when working around a battery. Rinse off spilled electrolyte immediately with large amounts of water.

✳✳ WARNING 2:

Make sure power to the hybrid system is turned Off before performing any work on this vehicle. Also, on models equipped with the Smart Key system, place the key in a secure spot at least 20 feet away from the work area.

CHECK

▶ Refer to illustrations 3.2 and 3.3

1   The battery's surface charge must be removed before accurate voltage measurements can be made. Turn On the high beams for ten seconds, then turn them Off, and let the vehicle stand for two minutes. Remove the battery from the vehicle (see Steps 4 through 10).

2   Check the battery state of charge. Visually inspect the indicator eye (if it has one) on the top of the battery, if the indicator eye is clear, charge the battery as described in Chapter 1. Next perform an open voltage circuit test using a digital voltmeter (see illustration). With the engine and all accessories Off, connect the negative probe of the voltmeter to the negative terminal of the battery and the positive probe to the positive terminal of the battery. The battery voltage should be 12.6 volts or more. If the battery is less than the specified voltage, charge the battery before proceeding to the next test. Do not proceed with the battery load test unless the battery charge is correct. If it's a non-maintenance-free battery, remove the caps from the battery and verify

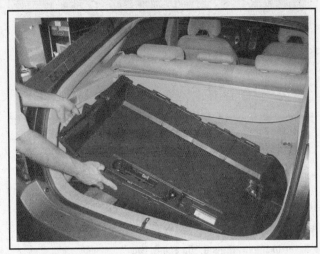

3.6 Lift out the storage box

that there is sufficient electrolyte. If it is low, add distilled water.

3   Perform a battery load test. An accurate check of the battery condition can only be performed with a load tester (available at most auto parts stores). This test evaluates the ability of the battery to operate the starter and other accessories during periods of heavy amperage draw (load). Connect a battery load-testing tool onto the terminals (see illustration). Load test the battery according to the tool manufacturer's instructions. Maintain the load on the battery for 15 seconds or less and observe that the battery voltage does not drop below 9.6 volts. If the battery condition is weak or defective, the tool will indicate this condition immediately.

➡Note: Cold temperatures will cause the minimum voltage reading to drop slightly. Follow the chart given in the tool manufacturer's instructions to compensate for cold climates. Minimum load voltage for freezing temperatures (32-degrees F) should be approximately 9.1 volts.

REPLACEMENT

2001 through 2003 models

4   Open the luggage compartment. The battery is under a cover on the left side.

5   Push in the centers of the three plastic rivets that secure the battery lid. Pull the rivet bodies out, then remove the cover.

2004 and later models

▶ Refer to illustrations 3.6, 3.7, 3.8 and 3.9

6   Open the rear hatch, turn the two knobs and lift the rear cargo area cover. Lift out the luggage storage box (see illustration).

7   The battery is under a cover on the right side. Remove the battery cover (see illustration).

8   Disconnect the power supply connector and remove the module

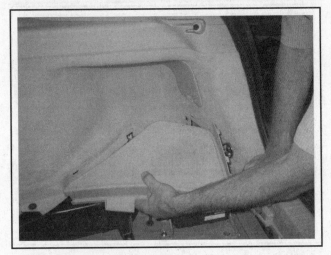

3.7 The battery is located under this cover on the right side of the vehicle (2004 and later models)

3.8 The battery has power supply modules attached to it that must be removed

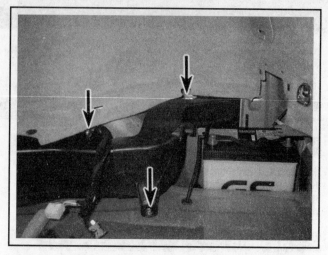

3.9 The battery cooling duct interferes with battery removal

from the side of the battery (see illustration).

9   Disconnect the wiring harness from the plastic duct, then remove the three fasteners from the duct (see illustration). Remove the duct.

All models

▶ **Refer to illustrations 3.10a and 3.10b**

10   Disconnect the cable from the negative battery terminal first (see illustration). Loosen the positive battery cable clamp, remove the battery hold-down clamp (see illustration), then lift the hold-down clamp, fuse box and battery terminal from the battery.

11   Remove the battery and place it on a workbench.

➥**Note: Battery handling tools are available at most auto parts stores for a reasonable price. They make it easier to remove and carry the battery.**

12   While the battery is removed, inspect the tray, retainer brackets and related fasteners for corrosion or damage.

13   If corrosion is evident, remove the battery tray and use a baking soda/water solution to clean the corroded area to prevent further oxidation. Repaint the area as necessary using rust resistant paint.

14   Clean and service the battery and cables (see Chapter 1).

15   If you are replacing the battery, make sure you purchase one that

is identical to yours, with the same dimensions, amperage rating, cold cranking amps rating, etc. Make sure it is fully charged prior to installation in the vehicle.

16   Installation is the reverse of removal. Connect the positive cable first and the negative cable last.

17   After connecting the cables to the battery, apply a light coating of battery terminal corrosion inhibitor to the connections to help prevent corrosion.

2004 AND LATER MODELS - INITIALIZATION PROCEDURE

18   The power window system needs to be set up any time the battery is disconnected on these vehicles.

19   Turn the ignition ON.

20   Put the driver's window half way up.

21   Close the window completely and continue holding the switch for at least a full second.

22   Make sure that the UP and DOWN operations work properly. If they don't, you'll have to disconnect and the reconnect the battery again and start all over.

3.10a Negative battery cable

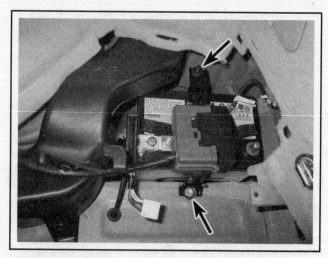

3.10b The battery hold-down bracket (with attached fuse box) and fasteners

4 Battery cables - replacement

❋❋ **WARNING:**

Make sure power to the hybrid system is turned Off before performing any work on this vehicle. Also, on models equipped with the Smart Key system, place the key in a secure spot at least 20 feet away from the work area.

1 Periodically inspect each battery cable for damage, cracked or burned insulation and corrosion. Poor battery cable connections can cause starting problems and decreased engine performance.

2 Check the cable-to-terminal connections at the ends of the cables for cracks, loose wire strands and corrosion. The presence of white, fluffy deposits under the insulation at the cable terminal connection is a sign that the cable is corroded and should be replaced. Check the terminals for distortion, missing mounting bolts and corrosion.

3 When removing the cables, always disconnect the negative cable first and hook it up last or the battery may be shorted by the tool used to loosen the cable clamps. Even if only the positive cable is being replaced, be sure to disconnect the negative cable from the battery first (see Chapter 1 for further information regarding battery cable removal).

4 Disconnect the old cables from the battery, then trace each of them to their opposite ends and detach them from the terminals. Note the routing of each cable to ensure correct installation.

5 If you are replacing either or both of the old cables, take them with you when buying new cables. It is vitally important that you replace the cables with identical parts. Cables have characteristics that make them easy to identify: positive cables are usually red, larger in cross-section and have a larger diameter battery post clamp; ground cables are usually black, smaller in cross-section and have a slightly smaller diameter clamp for the negative post.

6 Clean the threads of the solenoid or ground connection with a wire brush to remove rust and corrosion. Apply a light coat of battery terminal corrosion inhibitor, or petroleum jelly, to the threads to prevent future corrosion.

7 Attach the cable to the solenoid or ground connection and tighten the mounting nut/bolt securely.

8 Before connecting a new cable to the battery, make sure that it reaches the battery post without having to be stretched.

9 Connect the positive cable first, followed by the negative cable.

5 Ignition system - general information and precautions

1 All models are equipped with a distributorless ignition system. The ignition system consists of the battery, ignition coils, spark plugs, camshaft position sensor, crankshaft position sensor and the Engine Control Module (ECM). The ECM controls the ignition timing and spark advance characteristics for the engine. The ignition timing is not adjustable. The intake camshaft timing is also controlled by the ECM.

2 The crankshaft position sensor and camshaft position sensor generate pulses that are input to the Engine Control Module. The ECM determines piston position and engine speed from these two sensors. The ECM calculates injector sequence and ignition timing from the piston position. Refer to Chapter 6 for testing and replacement procedures for the crankshaft position sensor and camshaft position sensor.

3 These models utilize an individual ignition coil for each cylinder. The unit is positioned directly over each spark plug. The ECM fires each coil sequentially in the firing order sequence.

4 The ECM controls the ignition system by opening and closing the primary ignition coil control circuit. The computerized ignition system provides complete control of the ignition timing by determining the optimum timing in response to engine speed, coolant temperature, throttle position and engine load. These parameters are relayed to the ECM by the camshaft position sensor, crankshaft position sensor, throttle position sensor, coolant temperature sensor and manifold absolute pressure sensor or mass airflow sensor

5 The ignition system is also integrated with a knock sensor. The system uses a knock sensor in conjunction with the ECM to control spark timing. The knock sensor system allows the engine to use maximum spark advance without spark knock, which improves driveability and fuel economy.

6 When working on the ignition system, take the following precautions:

  a) *Do not keep the ignition switch on for more than 10 seconds if the engine will not start.*

  b) *Always connect a tachometer in accordance with the manufacturer's instructions. Some tachometers may be incompatible with this ignition system. Consult the tachometer manufacturer's consultant before buying a tachometer for use with this vehicle.*

  c) *Never allow the ignition coil terminals to touch ground. Grounding the coil could result in damage to the igniter and/or the ignition coil.*

  d) *Do not disconnect the battery when the engine is running.*

  e) *Make sure the igniter is properly grounded.*

6 Ignition system - check

❋❋ **WARNING 1:**

Because of the high voltage generated by the ignition system, extreme care should be taken whenever an operation is performed involving ignition components.

❋❋ **WARNING 2:**

Make sure power to the hybrid system is turned Off before performing any work on this vehicle. Also, on models equipped with the Smart Key system, place the key in a secure spot at least 20 feet away from the work area.

1   If a malfunction occurs and the engine won't start, do not immediately assume that the ignition system is causing the problem. First, check the following items:

a) *Make sure the battery cable clamps, where they connect to the battery, are clean and tight.*
b) *Test the condition of the battery (see Section 3). If it does not pass all the tests, replace it with a new battery.*
c) *Check the ignition system wiring and connections.*
d) *Check the related fuses inside the fuse box (see Chapter 12). If they're burned, determine the cause and repair the circuit.*

2   Because the engine on these models cannot be started with the starter motor, the usual ignition system checks do not apply.

3   Remove the spark plugs (see Chapter 1) and check for fouling, wear and damage.

7   Ignition coils - replacement

▶ **Refer to illustration 7.3**

✳ WARNING:

Make sure power to the hybrid system is turned Off before performing any work on this vehicle. Also, on models equipped with the Smart Key system, place the key in a secure spot at least 20 feet away from the work area.

➡**Note: Toyota does not publish primary or secondary resistance specifications for the ignition coil units used on these models. The only way to check them is to substitute a known good unit. But this option isn't feasible for a home mechanic because you can't return electrical components to a parts department once you have purchased them. If you have already eliminated all other possible causes of an ignition malfunction, a defective ignition coil/igniter unit is the likely cause of the problem, but the only way to verify this is to substitute a known good unit. If a particular coil is suspect, visually inspect it with a magnifying glass for cracks. Use an ohmmeter to see if its resistance varies substantially from the others.**

1   Refer to Section 3 and disconnect the cable from the negative terminal of the auxiliary 12-volt battery. Be sure to perform the initialization procedure when reconnecting it.

2   On 2001 through 2003 models refer to Chapter 4 and remove the air cleaner assembly. On 2004 and later models remove the interfering

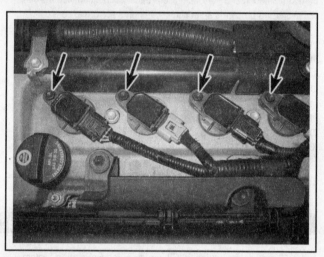

7.3 The four ignition coils are accessible on top of the valve cover; each one is secured by a single bolt

engine compartment relay block.

3   Disconnect the electrical connector(s) from the coil(s), then remove the mounting bolt(s) (see illustration).

4   Carefully withdraw each coil from the cylinder head.

5   Installation is the reverse of removal.

8   On Board Diagnostic (OBD) system and trouble codes

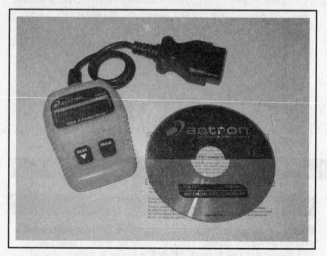

8.1 Simple code readers are an economical way to extract trouble codes when the CHECK ENGINE light comes on

SCAN TOOL INFORMATION

▶ **Refer to illustrations 8.1 and 8.2**

1   Hand-held scanners are handy for analyzing the engine management systems used on late-model vehicles. Because extracting the Diagnostic Trouble Codes (DTCs) from an engine management system is now the first step in troubleshooting many computer-controlled systems and components, even the most basic generic code readers are capable of accessing a computer's DTCs (see illustration). More powerful scan tools can also perform many of the diagnostics once associated with expensive factory scan tools. If you're planning to obtain a generic scan tool for your vehicle, make sure that it's compatible with OBD-II systems. If you don't plan to purchase a code reader or scan tool and don't have access to one, you can have the codes extracted by a dealer service department or by an independent repair shop.

2   With the advent of the Federally mandated emission control system known as On-Board Diagnostics-II (OBD-II), specially designed

scanners were developed. Several tool manufacturers have released OBD-II scan tools for the home mechanic (see illustration).

➡Note: An aftermarket generic scanner should work with any model covered by this manual. Before purchasing a generic scan tool, verify that it will work properly with the OBD-II system you want to scan. If necessary, of course, you can always have the codes extracted by a dealer service department or an independent repair shop with a professional scan tool. Some auto parts stores even provide this service.

OBD-II SYSTEM GENERAL DESCRIPTION

3   All vehicles covered by this manual are equipped with the OBD-II system. This system consists of the on-board computer, known as the Engine Control Module (ECM), and information sensors that monitor various functions of the engine and send a constant stream of data to the ECM during engine operation. Unlike earlier on-board diagnostics systems, the OBD-II system doesn't just monitor everything, store Diagnostic Trouble Codes (DTCs) and illuminate a Check Engine light or Malfunction Indicator Light (MIL) when there's a problem. (This warning light was referred to as the "Check Engine" light prior to OBD-II, and many do-it-yourselfers and professional technicians still use this term. However, its name was changed to "Malfunction Indicator Light," or simply "MIL," as part of the Society of Automotive Engineers' standard terminology that was introduced in 1996 to encourage all manufacturers to use the same terms when referring to the same components. So in this manual we will refer to this warning light as the Malfunction Indicator Light, or MIL.)

4   The ECM is the "brain" of the electronically controlled OBD-II system. It receives data from a number of information sensors and switches. Based on the data that it receives from the sensors, the ECM constantly alters engine operating conditions to optimize driveability, performance, emissions and fuel economy. It does so by turning on and off and by controlling various output actuators such as relays, solenoids, valves and other devices. The ECM can only be accessed with an OBD-II scan tool plugged into the 16-pin Data Link Connector (DLC).

5   If your vehicle is still under warranty, virtually every fuel, ignition and emission control component in the OBD-II system is covered by a Federally mandated emissions warranty that is longer than the warranty covering the rest of the vehicle. Vehicles sold in California and in some other states have even longer emissions warranties than other states. Read your owner's manual for the terms of the warranty protecting the emission-control systems on your vehicle. It isn't a good idea to "do-it-yourself" at home while the vehicle emission systems are still under warranty because owner-induced damage to the ECM, the sensors and/or the control devices might VOID this warranty. So as long as the emission systems are still under warranty, take the vehicle to a dealer service department if there's a problem.

INFORMATION SENSORS

6   **Oxygen sensor (O2S)** - The O2S generates a voltage signal that varies with the difference between the oxygen content of the exhaust and the oxygen in the surrounding air.

7   **Crankshaft Position (CKP) sensor** - The crankshaft sensor provides information on crankshaft position and the engine speed signal to the ECM.

8   **Camshaft Position (CMP) sensor** - The camshaft sensor produces a signal that the ECM uses to identify number 1 cylinder and to time the sequential fuel injection.

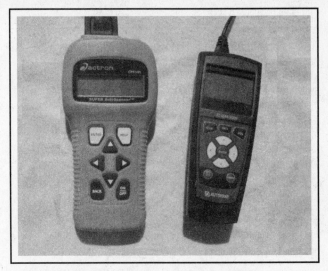

8.2 **Scanners like these from Actron and AutoXray are powerful diagnostic aids - they can tell you just about anything that you want to know about your engine management system**

9   **Air/Fuel Sensor** - Some vehicles are equipped with an air/fuel ratio sensor mounted upstream of the catalytic converter. These sensors work similar to the O2 sensors.

10   **Engine Coolant Temperature (ECT) sensor** - The coolant temperature (ECT) sensor monitors engine coolant temperature and sends the ECM a voltage signal that affects ECM control of the fuel mixture, ignition timing, and EGR operation.

11   **Mass Airflow Meter (MAF)** - The MAF sensor measures the mass of the intake air by detecting volume and weight of the air from samples passing over the hot wire element.

12   **Vehicle Speed Sensor (VSS)** - The vehicle speed sensors provide information to the ECM to indicate vehicle speed. They are a part of the anti-skid system.

13   **Throttle position sensor (TPS)** - This sensor gives the ECM information about the angle of the throttle blade. It cannot be replaced independently on these models; If defective, the entire throttle body must be replaced.

14   **Vapor pressure sensor** - The vapor pressure sensor is part of the evaporative emission control system and is used to monitor vapor pressure in the EVAP system at the fuel tank. The ECM uses this information to turn on and off the vacuum switching valves (VSV) of the evaporative emission system.

15   **Accelerator pedal position sensor** - These vehicles do not have a throttle cable, but rather a "drive-by-wire" system with an electronically- controlled throttle body. This sensor informs the ECM of the driver's pedal input, which is compared to the operation of the throttle body to check for malfunctions. On most models, there are two of these sensors.

16   **Knock sensor** - The knock sensor is a "piezoelectric" crystal that oscillates in proportion to engine vibration. The oscillation of the piezoelectric crystal produces a voltage output that is monitored by the ECM, which retards the ignition timing when the oscillation exceeds a certain threshold. When detonation occurs, engine vibration increases, and the oscillation of the knock sensor exceeds a design threshold. If allowed to continue, the engine could be damaged. The knock sensor is located below the intake manifold. You have to remove the intake manifold to access the knock sensor.

OUTPUT ACTUATORS

17 **EFI main relay** - The EFI main relay activates power to the fuel pump relay (circuit opening relay). It is activated by the ignition switch and supplies battery power to the ECM and the EFI system when the switch is in the Start or Run position. Refer to Chapter 4 or your owner's manual for more information on relay location.

18 **Fuel injectors** - The ECM opens the fuel injectors individually in firing order sequence. The ECM also controls the time the injector is open, called the "pulse width." The pulse width of the injector (measured in milliseconds) determines the amount of fuel delivered. For more information on the fuel delivery system and the fuel injectors, including injector replacement, refer to Chapter 4.

19 **EVAP vacuum switching valve (VSV)** - The EVAP vacuum switching valve is a solenoid valve, operated by the ECM to purge the fuel vapor canister and route fuel vapor to the intake manifold for combustion. This valve is also called the purge control valve.

OBTAINING TROUBLE CODES

♦ **Refer to illustration 8.21**

20 The ECM will illuminate the CHECK ENGINE light (also called the Malfunction Indicator Light) on the dash if it recognizes a component fault for two consecutive drive cycles. It will continue to set the light until the ECM does not detect any malfunction for three or more consecutive drive cycles.

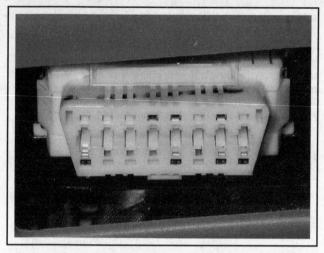

8.21 The 16-pin Data Link Connector (DLC) is located under the left side of the dash

21 The diagnostic codes for the OBD-II system can be extracted from the ECM by plugging a generic OBD-II scan tool (see illustrations 8.1 and 8.2) into the ECM's data link connector (see illustration), which is located under the left end of the dash.

22 Plug the scan tool into the 16-pin data link connector (DLC), and then follow the instructions included with the scan tool to extract all the diagnostic codes.

DIAGNOSTIC TROUBLE CODES

P0 - generic codes

➡**Note: The following list of OBD II trouble codes is a generic list applicable to all models equipped with an OBD II system, although not all codes apply to all models.**

Trouble code	Code identification
P0010	Intake camshaft position actuator circuit open (bank 1)
P0011	"A" Camshaft position - timing - over-advanced (bank 1)
P0012	"A" Camshaft position - timing over-retarded (bank 1)
P0016	Crankshaft position/camshaft position, bank 1, sensor A - correlation
P0031	HO2S heater control circuit low (bank 1, sensor 1)
P0032	HO2S heater control circuit high (bank 1, sensor 1)
P0037	HO2S heater control circuit low (bank 1, sensor 2)
P0038	HO2S heater control circuit high (bank 1, sensor 2)
P0100	Mass air flow or volume air flow circuit malfunction
P0101	Mass air flow or volume air flow circuit, range or performance problem

Trouble code	Code identification
P0102	Mass air flow or volume air flow circuit, low input
P0103	Mass air flow or volume air flow circuit, high input
P0110	Intake air temperature circuit malfunction
P0112	Intake air temperature circuit, low input
P0113	Intake air temperature circuit, high input
P0115	Engine coolant temperature circuit
P0116	Engine coolant temperature circuit range/performance problem
P0117	Engine coolant temperature circuit, low input
P0118	Engine coolant temperature circuit, high input
P0120	Throttle position or pedal position sensor/switch circuit malfunction
P0121	Throttle position or pedal position sensor/switch circuit, range or performance problem
P0122	Throttle position or pedal position sensor/switch circuit, low input
P0123	Throttle position or pedal position sensor/switch circuit, high input
P0125	Insufficient coolant temperature for closed loop fuel control
P0128	Coolant thermostat (coolant temperature below thermostat regulating temperature)
P0136	O2 sensor circuit malfunction (bank 1, sensor 2)
P0137	O2 sensor circuit, low voltage (bank 1, sensor 2)
P0138	O2 sensor circuit, high voltage (bank 1, sensor 2)
P0141	O2 sensor heater circuit malfunction (bank 1, sensor 2)
P0171	System too lean (bank 1)
P0172	System too rich (bank 1)
P0220	Throttle position or pedal position sensor/switch B circuit malfunction
P0222	Throttle position or pedal position sensor/switch B circuit, low input
P0223	Throttle position or pedal position sensor/switch B circuit, high input
P0300	Random/multiple cylinder misfire detected
P0301	Cylinder no. 1 misfire detected
P0302	Cylinder no. 2 misfire detected

P0 - generic codes (continued)

➡Note: The following list of OBD II trouble codes is a generic list applicable to all models equipped with an OBD II system, although not all codes apply to all models.

Trouble code	Code identification
P0303	Cylinder no. 3 misfire detected
P0304	Cylinder no. 4 misfire detected
P0325	Knock sensor no. 1 circuit malfunction (bank 1 or single sensor)
P0327	Knock sensor no. 1 circuit, low input (bank 1 or single sensor)
P0328	Knock sensor no. 1 circuit, high input (bank 1 or single sensor)
P0335	Crankshaft position sensor A circuit malfunction
P0340	Camshaft position sensor "A", circuit malfunction (bank 1)
P0341	Camshaft position sensor "A", circuit - range or performance problem
P0351	Ignition coil A primary or secondary circuit malfunction
P0352	Ignition coil B primary or secondary circuit malfunction
P0353	Ignition coil C primary or secondary circuit malfunction
P0354	Ignition coil D primary or secondary circuit malfunction
P0420	Catalyst system efficiency below threshold (bank 1)
P043E	Evaporative emission control system reference orifice clog
P043F	Same as P043E
P0440	Catalyst system efficiency low
P0441	Evaporative emission control system, incorrect purge flow
P0442	Evaporative emission system leak
P0446	Evaporative emission control system, vent control circuit malfunction
P0450	Evaporative emission control system, pressure sensor malfunction
P0451	Evaporative emission control system, pressure sensor range or performance problem
P0452	Evaporative emission control system, pressure sensor low input
P0453	Evaporative emission control system, pressure sensor high input
P0455	Evaporative emission (EVAP) control system leak detected (no purge flow or large leak)
P0456	Evaporative emission (EVAP) control system leak detected (very small leak)

Trouble code	Code identification
P0500	Vehicle speed sensor malfunction
P0505	Idle control system malfunction
P0560	System voltage malfunction
P0604	Internal control module, random access memory (RAM) error
P0606	ECM processor fault
P0607	Control module performance
P0657	Actuator supply voltage – circuit open
P0658	Actuator supply voltage – circuit low
P0659	Actuator supply voltage – circuit high
P0660	Intake manifold tuning valve control circuit (bank 1)
P0661	Intake manifold tuning valve control circuit low (bank 1)
P0662	Intake manifold tuning valve control circuit high (bank 1)
P0663	Intake manifold tuning valve control circuit (bank 2)
P0664	Intake manifold tuning valve control circuit low (bank 2)
P0665	Intake manifold tuning valve control circuit high (bank 2)
P0666	ECM/TCM internal temperature sensor – circuit malfunction
P0667	ECM/TCM internal temperature sensor – circuit range/performance

P1, P2 and P3 manufacturer controlled codes

Trouble code	Code identification
P1115	Coolant Temperature Sensor Circuit for Coolant Heat Storage System
P1116	Coolant Temperature Sensor Circuit Stack for Coolant Heat Storage
P1117	Coolant Temperature Sensor Circuit Low for Coolant Heat Storage
P1118	Coolant Temperature Sensor Circuit High for Coolant Heat Storage
P1120	Coolant Flow Control Valve Position Sensor Circuit
P1121	Coolant Flow Control Valve Position Sensor Circuit Stuck
P1122	Coolant Flow Control Valve Position Sensor Circuit Low

P1, P2 and P3 manufacturer controlled codes (continued)

Trouble code	Code identification
P1123	Coolant Flow Control Valve Position Sensor Circuit High
P1150	Coolant path clog of coolant heat storage system
P1151	Coolant heat storage tank
P1450	Fuel Tank Pressure Sensor
P1451	Fuel Tank Pressure Sensor range/performance
P1452	Fuel Tank Pressure Sensor low input
P1453	Fuel Tank Pressure Sensor high input
P1455	Vapor reducing fuel tank system malfunction
P2102	Throttle actuator control motor circuit low
P2103	Throttle actuator control motor circuit high
P2111	Throttle actuator control system - stuck open
P2112	Throttle actuator control system - stuck closed
P2118	Throttle actuator control motor current range/performance
P2119	Throttle actuator control throttle body range/performance
P2135	Throttle/Pedal Position sensor/Switch A/B Voltage correlation
P2195	Oxygen (A/F) sensor signal stuck lean (Bank 1, Sensor 1)
P2196	Oxygen (A/F) sensor signal stuck rich (Bank 1, Sensor 1)
P2237	Oxygen (A/F) sensor pumping current circuit/open (Bank 1, Sensor 1)
P2238	Oxygen (A/F) sensor pumping current circuit low (Bank 1, Sensor 1)
P2239	Oxygen (A/F) sensor pumping current circuit high (Bank 1, Sensor 1)
P2252	Oxygen (A/F) sensor reference ground circuit low (Bank 1, Sensor 1)
P2253	Oxygen (A/F) sensor reference ground circuit high (Bank 1, Sensor 1)
P2401	Evaporative Emission leak detection pump stuck OFF
P2402	Evaporative Emission leak detection pump stuck ON
P2419	Evaporative Emission pressure switching valve stuck ON
P2420	Evaporative Emission pressure switching valve stuck OFF

Trouble code	Code identification
P2601	Coolant pump control circuit range/performance
P2610	ECM/PCM internal engine off timer performance
P2A00	A/F sensor circuit slow response (Bank 1, Sensor 1)
P3190	Poor engine power
P3191	Engine does not start
P3193	Fuel run out

Hybrid Control System Codes - 2001 through 2003 models

Trouble code	Code identification
B2799	Immobilizer malfunction
C2692	Regenerative brake check
C2693	Regenerative brake check
P1120	Accelerator Pedal Position sensor circuit malfunction
P1520	Stop light switch (cruise control system) malfunction
P1566	Cruise control system malfunction
P1600	BATT malfunction
P1780	Park/Neutral Position switch system malfunction
P3000	HV battery malfunction
P3001	HV battery ECU malfunction
P3004	Power cable malfunction
P3100	HV ECU malfunction
P3101	Engine system malfunction
P3105	Battery ECU communication circuit malfunction
P3106	ECM communication circuit malfunction
P3107	Airbag ECU communication circuit malfunction
P3108	A/C amplifier communication circuit malfunction
P3109	Brake ECU communication circuit malfunction

Hybrid Control System Codes - 2001 through 2003 models (continued)

Trouble code	Code identification
P3110	IGCT relay malfunction
P3115	System main relay malfunction
P3120	HV Transaxle malfunction
P3125	Converter & inverter assembly malfunction
P3130	Inverter cooling system malfunction
P3135	Circuit breaker sensor malfunction
P3140	Interlock malfunction
P3145	Vehicle Speed Sensor circuit malfunction

Hybrid Control System Codes - 2004 and later models

Trouble code	Code identification
P0336-137	Crankshaft Position sensor "A" circuit range/performance
P0336-600	Crankshaft Position sensor "A" circuit high input
P0340-532	Camshaft Position sensor "A" circuit
P0353-601	Camshaft Position sensor "A" circuit high input
P0560-117	System voltage
P0630-804	VIN not programmed or mismatch-ECM/PCM
P0705-571	Transmission Range sensor circuit
P0705-572	Transmission Range sensor circuit
P0705-573	Transmission Range sensor circuit
P0705-574	Transmission Range sensor circuit
P0705-575	Transmission Range sensor circuit
P0705-576	Transmission Range sensor circuit
P0705-577	Transmission Range sensor circuit
P0705-578	Transmission Range sensor circuit
P0705-595	Transmission Range sensor circuit

Trouble code	Code identification
P0705-596	Transmission Range sensor circuit
P0851-579	Park/Neutral switch input circuit low
P0852-580	Park/Neutral switch input circuit high
P0A0F-238	Engine failed to start
P0A0F-533	Engine failed to start
P0A0F-534	Engine failed to start
P0A10-263	DC/DC converter status circuit high input
P0A10-592	DC/DC converter status circuit high input
P0A1D-134	Hybrid Powertrain Control Module
P0A1D-135	Hybrid Powertrain Control Module
P0A1D-139	Hybrid Powertrain Control Module
P0A1D-140	Hybrid Powertrain Control Module
P0A1D-141	Hybrid Powertrain Control Module
P0A1D-142	Hybrid Powertrain Control Module
P0A1D-143	Hybrid Powertrain Control Module
P0A1D-144	Hybrid Powertrain Control Module
P0A1D-145	Hybrid Powertrain Control Module
P0A1D-148	Hybrid Powertrain Control Module
P0A1D-149	Hybrid Powertrain Control Module
P0A1D-150	Hybrid Powertrain Control Module
P0A1D-151	Hybrid Powertrain Control Module
P0A1D-152	Hybrid Powertrain Control Module
P0A1D-155	Hybrid Powertrain Control Module
P0A1D-156	Hybrid Powertrain Control Module
P0A1D-158	Hybrid Powertrain Control Module
P0A1D-159	Hybrid Powertrain Control Module
P0A1D-160	Hybrid Powertrain Control Module

Hybrid Control System Codes - 2004 and later models (continued)

Trouble code	Code identification
P0A1D-163	Hybrid Powertrain Control Module
P0A1D-164	Hybrid Powertrain Control Module
P0A1D-165	Hybrid Powertrain Control Module
P0A1D-166	Hybrid Powertrain Control Module
P0A1D-167	Hybrid Powertrain Control Module
P0A1D-168	Hybrid Powertrain Control Module
P0A1D-177	Hybrid Powertrain Control Module
P0A1D-178	Hybrid Powertrain Control Module
P0A1D-180	Hybrid Powertrain Control Module
P0A1D-181	Hybrid Powertrain Control Module
P0A1D-182	Hybrid Powertrain Control Module
P0A1D-183	Hybrid Powertrain Control Module
P0A1D-184	Hybrid Powertrain Control Module
P0A1D-185	Hybrid Powertrain Control Module
P0A1D-186	Hybrid Powertrain Control Module
P0A1D-187	Hybrid Powertrain Control Module
P0A1D-188	Hybrid Powertrain Control Module
P0A1D-189	Hybrid Powertrain Control Module
P0A1D-192	Hybrid Powertrain Control Module
P0A1D-193	Hybrid Powertrain Control Module
P0A1D-195	Hybrid Powertrain Control Module
P0A1D-196	Hybrid Powertrain Control Module
P0A1D-197	Hybrid Powertrain Control Module
P0A1D-198	Hybrid Powertrain Control Module
P0A1D-199	Hybrid Powertrain Control Module
P0A1D-200	Hybrid Powertrain Control Module

Trouble code	Code identification
P0A1D-390	Hybrid Powertrain Control Module
P0A1D-392	Hybrid Powertrain Control Module
P0A1D-393	Hybrid Powertrain Control Module
P0A1D-511	Hybrid Powertrain Control Module
P0A1D-512	Hybrid Powertrain Control Module
P0A1D-564	Hybrid Powertrain Control Module
P0A1D-565	Hybrid Powertrain Control Module
P0A1D-567	Hybrid Powertrain Control Module
P0A1D-568	Hybrid Powertrain Control Module
P0A1D-569	Hybrid Powertrain Control Module
P0A1D-570	Hybrid Powertrain Control Module
P0A1D-615	Hybrid Powertrain Control Module
P0A1F-123	Battery Energy Control Module
P0A1F-129	Battery Energy Control Module
P0A1F-593	Battery Energy Control Module
P0A2B-248	Drive motor "A" Temperature Sensor circuit range/performance
P0A2B-250	Drive motor "A" Temperature Sensor circuit range/performance
P0A2C-247	Drive motor "A" Temperature Sensor circuit low
P0A2D-249	Drive motor "A" Temperature Sensor circuit high
P0A37-258	Generator Temperature sensor circuit range/performance
P0A37-260	Generator Temperature sensor circuit range/performance
P0A38-257	Generator Temperature sensor circuit low
P0A39-259	Generator Temperature sensor circuit high
P0A3D-243	Drive motor "A" Position sensor circuit
P0A40-500	Drive motor "A" Position sensor circuit range/performance
P0A41-245	Drive motor "A" Position sensor circuit low
P0A4B-253	Generator position sensor circuit

Hybrid Control System Codes - 2004 and later models (continued)

Trouble code	Code identification
P0A4C-513	Generator position sensor circuit range/performance
P0A4D-255	Generator position sensor circuit low
P0A51-174	Drive motor "A" current sensor circuit
P0A60-288	Drive motor "A" Phase V current
P0A60-189	Drive motor "A" Phase V current
P0A60-290	Drive motor "A" Phase V current
P0A60-292	Drive motor "A" Phase V current
P0A60-294	Drive motor "A" Phase V current
P0A60-501	Drive motor "A" Phase V current
P0A63-296	Drive motor "A" Phase W current
P0A63-297	Drive motor "A" Phase W current
P0A63-298	Drive motor "A" Phase W current
P0A63-300	Drive motor "A" Phase W current
P0A63-302	Drive motor "A" Phase W current
P0A63-502	Drive motor "A" Phase W current
P0A72-326	Generator Phase V current
P0A72-327	Generator Phase V current
P0A72-328	Generator Phase V current
P0A72-330	Generator Phase V current
P0A72-333	Generator Phase V current
P0A72-515	Generator Phase V current
P0A75-334	Generator Phase W current
P0A75-335	Generator Phase W current
P0A75-336	Generator Phase W current
P0A75-338	Generator Phase W current
P0A75-341	Generator Phase W current

Trouble code	Code identification
P0A75-516	Generator Phase W current
P0A78-255	Drive motor "A" inverter performance
P0A78-256	Drive motor "A" inverter performance
P0A78-272	Drive motor "A" inverter performance
P0A78-278	Drive motor "A" inverter performance
P0A78-279	Drive motor "A" inverter performance
P0A78-280	Drive motor "A" inverter performance
P0A78-282	Drive motor "A" inverter performance
P0A78-283	Drive motor "A" inverter performance
P0A78-284	Drive motor "A" inverter performance
P0A78-285	Drive motor "A" inverter performance
P0A78-286	Drive motor "A" inverter performance
P0A78-287	Drive motor "A" inverter performance
P0A78-304	Drive motor "A" inverter performance
P0A78-305	Drive motor "A" inverter performance
P0A78-306	Drive motor "A" inverter performance
P0A78-308	Drive motor "A" inverter performance
P0A78-503	Drive motor "A" inverter performance
P0A78-504	Drive motor "A" inverter performance
P0A78-505	Drive motor "A" inverter performance
P0A78-506	Drive motor "A" inverter performance
P0A78-507	Drive motor "A" inverter performance
P0A78-508	Drive motor "A" inverter performance
P0A78-510	Drive motor "A" inverter performance
P0A78-523	Drive motor "A" inverter performance
P0A78-586	Drive motor "A" inverter performance
P0A7A-309	Generator inverter performance

Hybrid Control System Codes - 2004 and later models (continued)

Trouble code	Code identification
P0A7A-321	Generator inverter performance
P0A7A-322	Generator inverter performance
P0A7A-323	Generator inverter performance
P0A7A-324	Generator inverter performance
P0A7A-325	Generator inverter performance
P0A7A-342	Generator inverter performance
P0A7A-343	Generator inverter performance
P0A7A-344	Generator inverter performance
P0A7A-517	Generator inverter performance
P0A7A-518	Generator inverter performance
P0A7A-519	Generator inverter performance
P0A7A-520	Generator inverter performance
P0A7A-522	Generator inverter performance
P0A90-239	Drive motor "A" performance
P0A90-240	Drive motor "A" performance
P0A90-241	Drive motor "A" performance
P0A90-242	Drive motor "A" performance
P0A90-251	Drive motor "A" performance
P0A90-509	Drive motor "A" performance
P0A90-302	Drive motor "A" performance
P0A90-304	Drive motor "A" performance
P0A90-305	Drive motor "A" performance
P0A92-261	Hybrid generator performance
P0A92-521	Hybrid generator performance
P0A92-606	Hybrid generator performance
P0A92-607	Hybrid generator performance

Trouble code	Code identification
P0A93-346	Inverter cooling system performance
P0A93-347	Inverter cooling system performance
P0A94-442	DC/DC converter performance
P0A94-545	DC/DC converter performance
P0A94-546	DC/DC converter performance
P0A94-547	DC/DC converter performance
P0A94-548	DC/DC converter performance
P0A94-549	DC/DC converter performance
P0A94-550	DC/DC converter performance
P0A94-551	DC/DC converter performance
P0A94-552	DC/DC converter performance
P0A94-553	DC/DC converter performance
P0A94-554	DC/DC converter performance
P0A94-555	DC/DC converter performance
P0A94-556	DC/DC converter performance
P0A94-557	DC/DC converter performance
P0A94-558	DC/DC converter performance
P0A94-559	DC/DC converter performance
P0A94-560	DC/DC converter performance
P0A94-561	DC/DC converter performance
P0A94-583	DC/DC converter performance
P0A94-584	DC/DC converter performance
P0A94-585	DC/DC converter performance
P0A94-587	DC/DC converter performance
P0A94-588	DC/DC converter performance
P0A94-589	DC/DC converter performance
P0A94-590	DC/DC converter performance

Hybrid Control System Codes - 2004 and later models (continued)

Trouble code	Code identification
P0AA1-231	Hybrid battery positive contactor circuit stuck closed
P0AA1-233	Hybrid battery positive contactor circuit stuck closed
P0AA4-232	Hybrid battery negative contactor circuit stuck closed
P0AA6-526	Hybrid battery voltage system isolation fault
P0AA6-611	Hybrid battery voltage system isolation fault
P0AA6-612	Hybrid battery voltage system isolation fault
P0AA6-613	Hybrid battery voltage system isolation fault
P0AA6-614	Hybrid battery voltage system isolation fault
P0ADB-227	Hybrid battery positive contactor control circuit low
P0ADC-226	Hybrid battery positive contactor control circuit high
P0ADF-229	Hybrid battery negative contactor control circuit low
P0AE0-228	Hybrid battery negative contactor control circuit high
P0AE6-225	Hybrid battery precharge contractor control circuit low
P0AE7-224	Hybrid battery precharge contractor control circuit high
P0AEE-276	Motor inverter Temperature sensor "A" circuit range/performance
P0AEE-277	Motor inverter Temperature sensor "A" circuit range/performance
P0AEF-275	Drive motor inverter Temperature sensor "A" circuit low
P0AF0-274	Drive motor inverter Temperature sensor "A" circuit high
P2120-111	Throttle/Pedal Position sensor/switch "D" circuit
P2121-106	Throttle/Pedal Position sensor/switch "D" circuit range/performance
P2121-114	Throttle/Pedal Position sensor/switch "D" circuit range/performance
P2122-104	Throttle/Pedal Position sensor/switch "D" circuit low input
P2123-105	Throttle/Pedal Position sensor/switch "D" circuit high input
P2125-112	Throttle/Pedal Position sensor/switch "E" circuit
P2126-109	Throttle/Pedal Position sensor/switch "E" circuit range/performance
P2127-107	Throttle/Pedal Position sensor/switch "E" circuit low input

Trouble code	Code identification
P2128-108	Throttle/Pedal Position sensor/switch "E" circuit high input
P2138-110	Throttle/Pedal Position sensor/switch "D" / "E" voltage correlation
P3000-123	HV battery malfunction
P3000-125	HV battery malfunction
P3000-388	HV battery malfunction
P3000-389	HV battery malfunction
P3000-603	HV battery malfunction
P3004-131	Power cable malfunction
P3004-132	Power cable malfunction
P3004-133	Power cable malfunction
P3102-524	Transmission control ECU malfunction
P3102-525	Transmission control ECU malfunction
P3102-581	Transmission control ECU malfunction
P3102-582	Transmission control ECU malfunction
P3102-597	Transmission control ECU malfunction
P3102-598	Transmission control ECU malfunction
P3102-599	Transmission control ECU malfunction
P3107-213	Airbag ECU communication circuit malfunction
P3107-214	Airbag ECU communication circuit malfunction
P3107-215	Airbag ECU communication circuit malfunction
P3108-535	A/C amplifier communication circuit malfunction
P3108-536	A/C amplifier communication circuit malfunction
P3108-537	A/C amplifier communication circuit malfunction
P3108-538	A/C amplifier communication circuit malfunction
P3108-594	A/C amplifier communication circuit malfunction
P3110-223	IGCT relay malfunction
P3110-827	HV main relay malfunction

Hybrid Control System Codes - 2004 and later models (continued)

Trouble code	Code identification
P3137-348	Collision sensor low input
P3138-349	Collision sensor high input
P3221-314	Generator inverter Temperature sensor circuit range/performance
P3221-315	Generator inverter Temperature sensor circuit range/performance
P3222-313	Generator inverter Temperature sensor circuit high/low
P3223-312	Generator inverter Temperature sensor circuit high
P3226-562	DC/DC Boost converter temperature sensor
P3226-563	DC/DC Boost converter temperature sensor
U0100-211	Lost communication with ECM/PCM "A"
U0100-212	Lost communication with ECM/PCM "A"
U0100-530	Lost communication with ECM/PCM "A"
U0111-208	Lost communication with battery energy control module "A"
U0111-531	Lost communication with battery energy control module "A"
U0129-220	Lost communication with Brake system control module
U0129-222	Lost communication with Brake system control module
U0129-528	Lost communication with Brake system control module
U0129-529	Lost communication with Brake system control module
U0131-433	Lost communication with Power steering control module
U0131-434	Lost communication with Power steering control module
U0146-435	Lost communication with Gateway "A"

9 Engine Control Module (ECM) - removal and installation

❋❋ WARNING 1:

The models covered by this manual are equipped with Supplemental Restraint systems (SRS), more commonly known as airbags. Always disable the airbag system before working in the vicinity of any airbag system component to avoid the possibility of accidental deployment of the airbag, which could cause personal injury (see Chapter 12).

❋❋ **WARNING 2:**

Make sure power to the hybrid system is turned Off before performing any work on this vehicle. Also, on models equipped with the Smart Key system, place the key in a secure spot at least 20 feet away from the work area.

❋❋ **CAUTION:**

To avoid electrostatic discharge damage to the ECM, handle the ECM only by its case. Do not touch the electrical terminals during removal and installation. If available, ground yourself to the vehicle with an anti-static ground strap, available at computer supply stores.

1   The ECM is located inside the passenger compartment behind the glove box.
2   Refer to Section 3 and disconnect the cable from the negative terminal of the auxiliary 12-volt battery. Be sure to perform the initialization procedure when reconnecting it.

2001 THROUGH 2003 MODELS

3   Refer to Chapter 11 and remove the glove compartment door.
4   Unplug the four electrical connectors from the ECM.

❋❋ **CAUTION:**

The ignition switch must be turned OFF when pulling out or plugging in the electrical connectors to prevent damage to the ECM.

5   Remove the retaining bolts from the ECM bracket.
6   Carefully remove the ECM.
➡ **Note:** Avoid any static electricity damage to the computer by grounding yourself to the body before touching the ECM and using a special anti-static pad to store the ECM on once it is removed.

7   Installation is the reverse of removal.

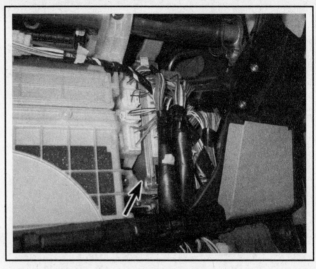

9.11 The ECM is located behind the right side of the instrument panel

2004 AND LATER MODELS

▶ **Refer to illustration 9.11**

8   Refer to Chapter 11 and remove the entire section of the instrument panel that interferes with access to the ECM.
➡ **Note: This is a difficult and time-consuming job, make sure you have the proper tools and plenty of time before starting.**
9   Remove the right heater duct.
10 Disconnect the eight wiring plugs from the ECM.
11 Unbolt the ECM brackets from the body of the vehicle and carefully remove the ECM (see illustration).
➡ **Note: Avoid any static electricity damage to the computer by grounding yourself to the body before touching the ECM and using a special anti-static pad to store the ECM on once it is removed.**
12 Remove the brackets from the ECM. Make marks to indicate positions of the brackets for reassembly.
13 Installation is the reverse of removal.

10 Accelerator pedal position sensor - replacement

▶ **Refer to illustration 10.2**

❋❋ **WARNING 1:**

The models covered by this manual are equipped with Supplemental Restraint systems (SRS), more commonly known as airbags. Always disable the airbag system before working in the vicinity of any airbag system component to avoid the possibility of accidental deployment of the airbag, which could cause personal injury (see Chapter 12).

❋❋ **WARNING 2:**

Make sure power to the hybrid system is turned Off before performing any work on this vehicle. Also, on models equipped with the Smart Key system, place the key in a secure spot at least 20 feet away from the work area.

1   Refer to Section 3 and disconnect the cable from the negative terminal of the auxiliary 12-volt battery. Be sure to perform the initialization procedure when reconnecting it.

2 Disconnect the wiring from the top of the accelerator pedal assembly (see illustration).

3 Remove the two bolts and carefully lift out the assembly.

4 Installation is the reverse of removal.

10.2 Unplug the wiring harness from the top of the accelerator pedal position sensor

11 Mass Airflow (MAF) sensor - replacement

▶ Refer to illustration 11.3

✳✳ WARNING:

Make sure power to the hybrid system is turned Off before performing any work on this vehicle. Also, on models equipped with the Smart Key system, place the key in a secure spot at least 20 feet away from the work area.

1 The Mass Airflow (MAF) sensor is located on the air filter housing, directly above the throttle body. The sensor measures the molecular mass (weight) of air entering the engine. This voltage signal is measured by the ECM, which converts this signal into a digital waveform, calculates the fuel injector pulse width (duration) and turns the injectors on and off accordingly. A problem in the MAF sensor circuit will set a diagnostic trouble code (see Section 2).

2 Make sure the ignition key is in the OFF position or the Power switch is turned OFF. Refer to Section 3 and disconnect the cable from the negative terminal of the auxiliary 12-volt battery. Be sure to perform the initialization procedure when reconnecting it.

3 Disconnect the electrical connector from the MAF sensor (see illustration).

4 Remove the two screws and remove the MAF sensor and O-ring from the air filter housing.

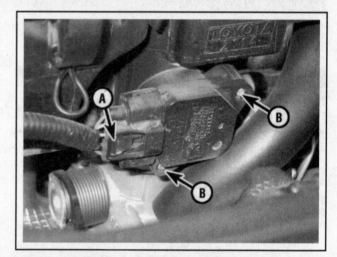

11.3 Depress the tab (A) and disconnect the electrical connector, then remove the screws (B) and pull the MAF sensor from the air filter housing

5 Installation is the reverse of removal. Be sure to install a new O-ring.

12 Engine Coolant Temperature (ECT) sensor - replacement

▶ Refer to illustration 12.4

✳✳ WARNING 1:

Wait until the engine has cooled completely before beginning this procedure.

✳✳ WARNING 2:

Make sure power to the hybrid system is turned Off before performing any work on this vehicle. Also, on models equipped with the Smart Key system, place the key in a secure spot at least 20 feet away from the work area.

1 The Engine Coolant Temperature (ECT) sensor is a thermistor

(a resistor that varies the value of its resistance in accordance with temperature changes). The change in the resistance values will directly affect the voltage signal from the sensor to the ECM. As the sensor temperature DECREASES, the resistance values will INCREASE. As the sensor temperature INCREASES, the resistance values will DECREASE. A problem in any of the ECT sensor circuits will set a diagnostic trouble code.

2   Make sure the ignition key is in the OFF position. Drain the engine coolant and the transaxle/inverter/converter coolant (see Chapter 1).

3   Refer to Chapter 5 and remove the inverter/converter assembly

4   Disconnect the wiring from the sensor and remove it along with the gasket (see illustration).

5   Installation is the reverse of removal. Be sure to replace the gasket.

6   Refill the cooling systems (see Chapter 1).

12.4 The engine coolant temperature sensor is located at the left end of the engine

13   Crankshaft Position (CKP) sensor - replacement

▶ Refer to illustration 13.5

1   The Crankshaft Position (CKP) sensor determines the timing for the fuel injection and ignition on each cylinder. It is located at the bottom of the timing chain cover. A problem in the crankshaft sensor circuit will set a diagnostic trouble code (see Section 8).

2   Refer to Section 3 and disconnect the cable from the negative terminal of the auxiliary 12-volt battery. Be sure to perform the initialization procedure when reconnecting it.

3   Loosen the right front wheel lug nuts. Raise the vehicle and support it securely on jackstands. Remove the wheel.

4   Working under the vehicle, remove the bottom cover from the right side of the engine compartment (see Chapter 11).

5   Disconnect the wiring from the sensor (see illustration).

6   Remove the bolt and detach the sensor.

7   Installation is the reverse of removal. Tighten the wheel lug nuts to the torque listed in the Chapter 1 Specifications.

13.5 The crankshaft position sensor is mounted adjacent to the crankshaft pulley

14   Camshaft Position (CMP) sensor - replacement

▶ Refer to illustration 14.3

❊❊ WARNING 1:

Wait until the engine has cooled completely before beginning this procedure.

❊❊ WARNING 2:

Make sure power to the hybrid system is turned Off before performing any work on this vehicle. Also, on models equipped

with the Smart Key system, place the key in a secure spot at least 20 feet away from the work area.

1   The camshaft position sensor determines the position of the cylinder for sequential fuel injection signals to each cylinder. The camshaft sensor is mounted on the transaxle end of the engine. A problem in the camshaft sensor circuit will set a diagnostic trouble code (see Section 8).

2   Refer to Chapter 5 and remove the inverter/converter assembly.

3   Disconnect the harness connector, remove the mounting bolt and

remove the camshaft sensor from the cylinder head (see illustration).

4 Installation is the reverse of the removal. Use a new O-ring, lightly coated with engine oil.

5 Refill the cooling systems (see Chapter 1).

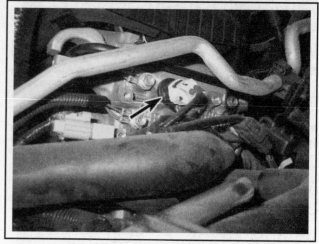

14.3 View of the camshaft position sensor with the inverter/converter assembly removed

15 Oxygen sensor and air/fuel sensor - general information and replacement

GENERAL INFORMATION

▶ **Refer to illustration 15.2**

1 All vehicles covered by this manual have On-Board Diagnostics II (OBD-II) engine management systems, which means that they have the ability to verify the accuracy of the basic feedback loop between the oxygen sensor and the ECM. They accomplish this by using an oxygen sensor or air/fuel sensor ahead of the catalytic converter and an oxygen sensor behind the catalytic converter. By sampling the exhaust gas before and after the catalytic converter, the ECM can determine the efficiency of the converter and can even predict when it will fail.

2 The primary (upstream) oxygen sensor is located in the exhaust manifold and the secondary (downstream) oxygen sensor is located behind the catalytic converter (see illustration). The downstream sensor on all models is a heated oxygen sensor. The upstream sensor is an air/fuel sensor.

3 Don't confuse oxygen sensors and air/fuel sensors. They're similar in appearance, but they operate differently and have different operating characteristics. Like an oxygen sensor, the air/fuel sensor provides a variable voltage output to the ECM that's proportional to the air/fuel mixture ratio in the exhaust stream. The air/fuel sensor doesn't "switch" back and forth like an oxygen sensor at the 14.7 to 1 stoichiometric threshold. Instead, it alters an ECM-controlled voltage between 3.3 volts (at the positive ECM terminal for the air/fuel sensor) and 3.0 volts (at the negative ECM terminal for the air/fuel sensor) in direct proportion to the amount of oxygen in the exhaust. As the air/fuel mixture in the exhaust becomes leaner, the air/fuel sensor voltage increases (within its operating range of 3.0 to 3.3 volts). Like an oxygen sensor, the air/fuel sensor doesn't operate correctly until it's warmed up. Also, like an oxygen sensor, the air/fuel sensor has a heating element that enables it to warm up quickly.

4 Special care must be taken whenever a sensor is serviced.

a) *Oxygen sensors and air/fuel sensors have a permanently attached*

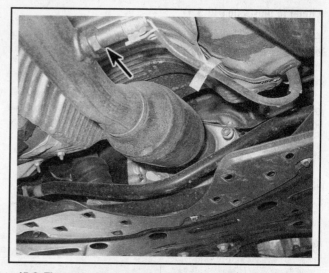

15.2 The secondary oxygen sensor is located to the rear of the catalytic converter

pigtail and electrical connector, which should not be removed from the sensor. Damage or removal of the pigtail or electrical connector can adversely affect operation of the sensor.

b) *Grease, dirt and other contaminants should be kept away from the electrical connector and the louvered end of the sensor.*

c) *Do not use cleaning solvents of any kind on an oxygen sensor or air/fuel ratio sensor.*

d) *Do not drop or roughly handle an oxygen sensor or air/fuel ratio sensor.*

e) *The silicone boot must be installed in the correct position to prevent the boot from being melted and to allow the sensor to operate properly.*

REPLACEMENT

✳✳ WARNING:

Make sure power to the hybrid system is turned Off before performing any work on this vehicle. Also, on models equipped with the Smart Key system, place the key in a secure spot at least 20 feet away from the work area.

➡Note: Because it is installed in the exhaust manifold or pipe, which contracts when cool, the oxygen sensor may be very difficult to loosen when the engine is cold. Rather than risk damage to the sensor (assuming you are planning to reuse it in another manifold or pipe), start and run the engine for a minute or two, then shut it off. Be careful not to burn yourself during the following procedure.

5   Refer to Section 3 and disconnect the cable from the negative terminal of the auxiliary 12-volt battery. Be sure to perform the initialization procedure when reconnecting it.

6   If you're replacing the downstream sensor, raise the vehicle and secure it on jackstands. Access the oxygen sensor harness and unplug the electrical connector. 2004 and later models use a sensor harness that runs through the floorboard. You will have to remove the lower instrument panel (see Chapter 11) for access and pull back the carpet.

7   The upstream sensor can be replaced without raising the vehicle. On most models it will be necessary to remove engine compartment components to gain access. Unplug the sensor electrical connector. If access is severely limited, the wires can be cut and repaired when the new sensor is installed.

8   Unscrew the sensor from the exhaust manifold or exhaust pipe.

➡Note: The best tool for removing an oxygen sensor is a special slotted socket, especially if you're planning to reuse a sensor. If you don't have this tool, and you plan to reuse the sensor, be extremely careful when unscrewing the sensor.

9   Apply anti-seize compound to the threads of the sensor to facilitate future removal. The threads of new sensors should already be coated with this compound, but if you're planning to reuse an old sensor, re-coat the threads. Install the sensor and tighten it securely.

10 Reconnect the electrical connector of the pigtail lead to the main wiring harness.

11 Lower the vehicle (if it was raised), test drive the car and verify that no trouble codes have been set.

16 Knock sensor - replacement

♦ Refer to illustration 16.3

✳✳ WARNING 1:

Wait for the engine to cool completely before performing this procedure.

✳✳ WARNING 2:

Make sure power to the hybrid system is turned Off before performing any work on this vehicle. Also, on models equipped with the Smart Key system, place the key in a secure spot at least 20 feet away from the work area.

1   The knock control system is designed to reduce spark knock during periods of heavy detonation. This allows the engine to use optimal spark advance to improve driveability. The knock sensor detects abnormal vibration in the engine and produces a voltage output that increases with the severity of the knock. The voltage signal is monitored by the ECM, which retards ignition timing until the detonation ceases. The knock sensor is located on the front of the engine, directly below the cylinder head (facing toward the front of the engine compartment).

2   Remove the intake manifold (see Chapter 2A).

3   Disconnect the electrical connector and remove the knock sensor (see illustration).

4   If you're going to reuse the old sensor, coat the threads with thread sealant. New sensors are pre-coated with thread sealant, do

16.3 The knock sensor (A) is located above the oil pressure sensor (B) and behind the intake manifold

not apply any additional sealant or the operation of the sensor may be affected.

5   Install the knock sensor and tighten it to 15 ft-lbs. Don't overtighten the sensor or damage may occur.

6   The remainder of installation is the reverse of removal.

7   Refill the cooling system and check for leaks.

17 Positive Crankcase Ventilation (PCV) system

♦ **Refer to illustration 17.1**

1   The Positive Crankcase Ventilation (PCV) system reduces hydrocarbon emissions by scavenging crankcase vapors. It does this by circulating fresh air from the air cleaner through the crankcase, where it mixes with blow-by gases and is then rerouted through a PCV valve to the intake manifold (see illustration).

2   The main components of the PCV system are the PCV valve, a blow-by filter and the vacuum hoses connecting these two components with the engine.

3   To maintain idle quality, the PCV valve restricts the flow when the intake manifold vacuum is high. If abnormal operating conditions (such as piston ring problems) arise, the system is designed to allow excessive amounts of blow-by gases to flow back through the crankcase vent tube into the air cleaner to be consumed by normal combustion.

4   Checking and replacement of the PCV valve is covered in Chapter 1.

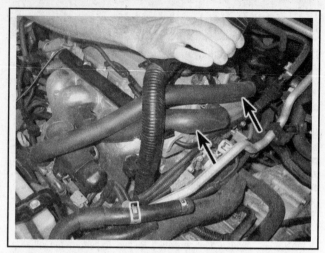

17.1 The PCV hoses are under the wiring harness - they look like very large diameter hoses at first glance (that's insulation)

18 Evaporative emissions control (EVAP) system

GENERAL DESCRIPTION

1   The fuel evaporative emissions control (EVAP) system absorbs fuel vapors and, during engine operation, releases them into the engine intake where they mix with the incoming air-fuel mixture. The charcoal canister is mounted above the fuel tank and under the vehicle.

2   When the engine is not operating, fuel vapors are transferred from the fuel tank, throttle body and intake manifold to the charcoal canister where they are stored. When the engine is running, the fuel vapors are purged from the canister by the purge control valve. The gasses are consumed in the normal combustion process. The electronic purge control valve is directly controlled by the ECM.

3   The fuel filler cap is fitted with a two-way valve as a safety device. The valve vents fuel vapors to the atmosphere if the EVAP system fails.

4   The EVAP system also incorporates a vapor pressure sensor. This sensor detects abnormal vapor pressure in the system. The vapor pressure sensor is mounted on top of the fuel tank.

5   After the engine has been running and warmed up to a pre-set temperature, the vacuum switching valve (VSV) opens. The vacuum switching valve (purge control valve) allows intake manifold vacuum to draw the fuel vapors from the canister to the intake manifold, where they are mixed with intake air before being burned with the air/fuel mixture inside the combustion chambers.

6   The fuel tank vapor pressure sensor monitors changes in pressure inside the tank and, when the pressure exceeds a preset threshold,

opens a vacuum switching valve (VSV), which allows a purge port in the canister to admit fuel tank vapors into the canister.

REPLACEMENT

❊❊ WARNING:

Make sure power to the hybrid system is turned Off before performing any work on this vehicle. Also, on models equipped with the Smart Key system, place the key in a secure spot at least 20 feet away from the work area.

Charcoal canister

7   Refer to Section 3 and disconnect the cable from the negative terminal of the auxiliary 12-volt battery. Be sure to perform the initialization procedure when reconnecting it.

8   Refer to Chapter 4 and lower the fuel tank enough to access the canister above it.

9   Unplug all electrical connectors and clearly label and disconnect the vent hoses to the charcoal canister, remove the bolts and separate the canister from the vehicle.

10 Installation is the reverse of removal.

19 Catalytic converters

➥**Note 1: Because of a Federally mandated extended warranty which covers emissions-related components such as the catalytic converter, check with a dealer service department before replacing the converter at your own expense.**

➥**Note 2: The front catalytic converter is incorporated into the exhaust manifold. Refer to Chapter 2A for the exhaust manifold replacement procedure.**

GENERAL DESCRIPTION

1   The catalytic converter is an emission control device added to the exhaust system to reduce pollutants from the exhaust gas stream. There are two types of converters. The conventional oxidation catalyst reduces the levels of hydrocarbon (HC) and carbon monoxide (CO). The three-way catalyst lowers the levels of oxides of nitrogen (NOx) as well as hydrocarbons (HC) and carbon monoxide (CO). These models are equipped with three-way catalytic converters (see illustration 15.2).

CHECK

2   The test equipment for a catalytic converter is expensive and highly sophisticated. If you suspect that the converter on your vehicle is malfunctioning, take it to a dealer or authorized emissions inspection facility for diagnosis and repair.

3   Whenever the vehicle is raised for servicing of underbody components, check the converter for leaks, corrosion, dents and other damage. Check the welds/flange bolts that attach the front and rear ends of the converter to the exhaust system. If damage is discovered, the converter should be replaced.

4   Although catalytic converters don't break too often, they can become plugged. The easiest way to check for a restricted converter is to use a vacuum gauge to diagnose the effect of a blocked exhaust on intake vacuum.

   a) Connect a vacuum gauge to an intake manifold vacuum source (see Chapter 2B).

   b) Warm the engine to operating temperature, place the transaxle in Park (automatic) and apply the parking brake.

   c) Note and record the vacuum reading at idle.

   d) Quickly open the throttle to near full throttle and release it shut. Note and record the vacuum reading.

   e) Perform the test three more times, recording the reading after each test.

   f) If the reading after the fourth test is more than one in-Hg lower than the reading recorded at idle, the exhaust system may be restricted (the catalytic converter could be plugged or an exhaust pipe or muffler could be restricted).

REPLACEMENT

❋❋ WARNING:

Make sure power to the hybrid system is turned Off before performing any work on this vehicle. Also, on models equipped with the Smart Key system, place the key in a secure spot at least 20 feet away from the work area.

5   Be sure to spray the nuts on the exhaust flange studs before removing them from the catalytic converter.

6   Remove the nuts and separate the catalytic converter from the exhaust manifold.

7   Installation is the reverse of removal.

Notes

Section

Reference to other Chapters

7

TRANSAXLE

1   General information

♦ **Refer to illustration 1.1**

The transaxle used in these vehicles is very small and simple. It's called a continuously variable planetary type - also called a power-splitter (see illustration).

Continuously variable means that there are no components that shift to change the speed of the car or to provide reverse. Planetary refers to the arrangement of the power-transmitting parts. It is called a power splitting device because all of the functions of the transaxle are controlled by a computer that constantly makes adjustments to the relationships of all of its input sources to attain the highest overall efficiency.

Basically there is a "sun" gear driven by and driving a small motor/generator, "planet gears" driven by and driving the engine and an outer ring gear driven by and driving a large electric motor/generator.

The two electric motor/generators are mounted directly to the transaxle and are parts of it. The entire transaxle assembly is mounted on the engine as in a conventional layout. 2001 through 2003 models use the P-111 transaxle with manual shift cable linkage; 2004 and later models use a revised version termed the P-112 that uses electronic shift linkage. The transaxle is not connected directly to the engine's flywheel. Instead, a damper clutch is used to smooth power pulses from the engine.

Due to the fact that the automatic transaxle rarely needs service, this Chapter contains only those procedures related to general diagnosis, routine maintenance and removal and installation.

If the transaxle requires major repair work, it should be left to a

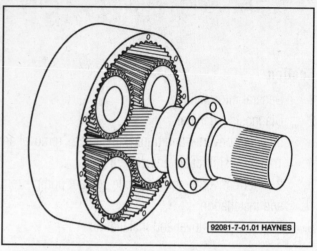

1.1 The unique and simple design of the transaxle makes the hybrid system possible - it is a continuously-variable transmission (CVT), meaning it has no gears that shift

dealer service department or other qualified repair shop. You can, however, remove and install the transaxle yourself and save the expense even if a shop does the repair work. Be sure a proper diagnosis has been made before removing the transaxle, however.

2   Diagnosis - general

⁕⁕⁕ WARNING:

Make sure power to the hybrid system is turned Off before performing any work on this vehicle. Also, on models equipped with the Smart Key system, place the key in a secure spot at least 20 feet away from the work area.

Transaxle malfunctions may be caused by the following general conditions:

a) *Mechanical breakage*
b) *Oil leakage*
c) *Coolant leakage*
d) *Malfunctions of the computer or its signal network*
e) *Malfunctions of either motor/generator*

Diagnosis of these problems should always begin with a check of the easily repaired items: fluid level and condition (see Chapter 1) and shift cable adjustment (on 2001 through 2003 models only). Next perform a road test to determine if the problem has been corrected or if more diagnosis is necessary. A dealer service department should do additional diagnosis if required.

PRELIMINARY CHECKS

1   Drive the vehicle to warm the transaxle to normal operating temperature.

2   Check the fluid level as described in Chapter 1:
a) *If the lubricant is low, add enough to bring it to the bottom of the sight plug opening, then check for external leaks (see below).*
b) *If the lubricant is too high, drain off the excess and then check the drained fluid for contamination by coolant (this is possible only on 2004 and later models). Contamination indicates a failure has occurred in the internal radiator walls that separate the coolant from the transaxle lubricant.*

3   Inspect the shift cable on 2001 through 2003 models (see Section 4). Make sure that it's properly adjusted and that it operates smoothly.

COOLANT LEAKS

4   2001 through 2003 models have a separate fluid cooler mounted in front of the conventional radiator. Later models use the lower section of the radiator to cool the transaxle lubricant. Both of these areas are the most common sources of leaks because they are the most prone to damage by road debris. Check the surfaces carefully with a bright light. These coolers also cool the inverter/converter assembly.

5   Check each coolant hose along its entire length, especially at the ends. Make sure that the hose clamps are tight and not damaged.

6   Check the electric coolant pump for signs of leakage. It can be replaced if it's defective.

7   The coolant reservoir itself can be cracked. Check beneath it for signs of coolant drips.

8   The transaxle and motor/generator cases can have a crack into a coolant jacket. Check the case for signs of impact or other damage.

LUBRICANT LEAKS

9   Identify the fluid. Make sure it's lubricant and not engine oil or brake fluid.

10 Carefully inspect the suspected area. Pay particular attention to gasket surfaces and O-rings. A mirror is often helpful for finding leaks in areas that are hard to see.

11 If the leak still can't be found, clean the suspected areas with a degreaser or solvent, then dry it.

12 Drive the vehicle for several miles and inspect it again. Parking the car over a clean sheet of cardboard may be helpful if it is a slow leak.

3   Transaxle and inverter/converter cooler - removal and installation

✳ WARNING 1:

Wait until the engine and transaxle are completely cool before beginning this procedure.

✳ WARNING 2:

Make sure power to the hybrid system is turned Off before performing any work on this vehicle. Also, on models equipped with the Smart Key system, place the key in a secure spot at least 20 feet away from the work area.

➡Note: This procedure applies only to 2001 through 2003 models with a separate cooler. Later models use part of the engine radiator as a cooler. Refer to Chapter 3 for information on the radiator/condenser assembly.

1   Raise the vehicle and support it securely on jackstands. Refer to Chapter 11 and remove the front bumper cover.

2   Place a drain pan under the inverter/converter cooler, disconnect both hoses and drain the contents into the pan.

3   Disconnect the wiring from both temperature sensors

4   Remove the mounting nuts and lift the cooler out the bottom of the vehicle.

5   Installation is the reverse of removal. Be sure to follow the refilling and bleeding instructions in Chapter 1.

4   Transaxle shift cable adjustment

✳ WARNING:

Make sure power to the hybrid system is turned Off before performing any work on this vehicle. Also, on models equipped with the Smart Key system, place the key in a secure spot at least 20 feet away from the work area.

➡Note: This procedure applies only to 2001 through 2003 models with manual shift linkage. Later models use electronic shift control.

1   This adjustment is made at the steering column inside the vehicle.

2   Remove the three screws and lift off the lower steering column cover.

3   Remove the hood release handle from the lower instrument panel.

4   Open the shifter hole cover.

5   Remove the fasteners from the lower corners of the lower instrument panel.

6   Use a screwdriver with tape around the tip to release the upper clips. Pull the panel rearward.

7   Disconnect the wiring from the panel.

8   Remove the shifter hole cover, then remove the lower instrument panel.

9   Move the shifter into Park.

10 Loosen the cable adjusting nut.

11 Verify that the vehicle is still in Park by rocking it with the parking brake released. Make sure to block the wheels loosely first. Set the parking brake.

12 Push the lever to the Park side. Pull the rod at the end of the cable gently and then let it go. Keep holding the lever to the Park position.

13 Tighten the adjuster and release the lever.

14 Replace the removed panels.

5 Inverter/converter and transaxle coolant pump - removal and installation

✳✳ WARNING 1:

Wait until the engine and transaxle are completely cool before beginning this procedure.

✳✳ WARNING 2:

Make sure power to the hybrid system is turned Off before performing any work on this vehicle. Also, on models equipped with the Smart Key system, place the key in a secure spot at least 20 feet away from the work area.

2001 THROUGH 2003 MODELS

1 Raise the vehicle and support it securely on jackstands. Refer to Chapter 6 and disconnect the cable from the negative terminal of the auxiliary 12-volt battery. Be sure to perform the initialization procedure when reconnecting it.

2 Drain the inverter/converter and transaxle coolant (see Chapter 1).

3 Refer to Chapter 11 and remove the front bumper cover.

4 Remove the left headlight (see Chapter 12).

5 Disconnect the wiring from the pump.

6 Disconnect both hoses from the pump.

7 Unbolt and remove the pump.

8 Installation is the reverse of removal. Refer to Chapter 1 for refilling and bleeding instructions.

2004 AND LATER MODELS

▶ **Refer to illustration 5.16**

9 Refer to Chapter 6 and disconnect the cable from the negative terminal of the auxiliary 12-volt battery. Be sure to perform the initialization procedure when reconnecting it. Raise the vehicle and support it securely on jackstands.

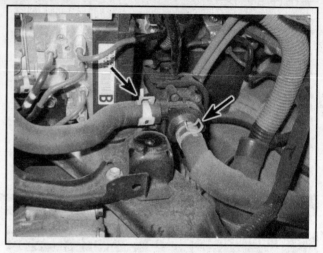

5.16 Use pliers to squeeze the hose clamps and slide them back on the hoses

10 Remove the front wheels as well as the front wheel inner liners.

11 Remove the center engine bottom cover.

12 Remove the front spoiler cover and the front bumper cover (see Chapter 11).

13 Remove the energy absorber for the front bumper.

14 Remove the left headlight assembly (see Chapter 12).

15 Drain the coolant from the inverter/converter and transaxle cooler (see Chapter 1).

16 Remove the bolt and nut and detach the coolant valve. Disconnect the two hoses from the pump (see illustration).

17 Unbolt the pump and lift it off, disconnecting the wiring as you do so.

18 Installation is the reverse of removal. Refer to Chapter 1 for refilling and bleeding instructions

6 Transaxle - removal and installation

✳✳ WARNING 1:

Wait until the engine and transaxle are completely cool before beginning this procedure.

✳✳ WARNING 2:

Make sure power to the hybrid system is turned Off before performing any work on this vehicle. Also, on models equipped with the Smart Key system, place the key in a secure spot at least 20 feet away from the work area.

2001 THROUGH 2003 MODELS

1 Refer to Chapter 2B and remove the transaxle along with the engine as a complete assembly.

2 Secure the engine/transaxle assembly solidly to the floor or a sturdy workbench,

3 Separate the transaxle by removing the eight mounting bolts.

4 Lift the transaxle off with the help of an assistant.

5 Installation is the reverse of removal. Tighten the transaxle bolts to the torque listed in this Chapter's Specifications. Refill the transaxle with the proper lubricant, and refill and bleed the inverter/converter/transaxle cooling system (see Chapter 1).

2004 AND LATER MODELS

▶ **Refer to illustrations 6.11 and 6.18**

6 Refer to Chapter 6 and disconnect the cable from the negative terminal of the auxiliary 12-volt battery. Be sure to perform the initialization procedure when reconnecting it.

7 Refer to Chapter 5 and remove the safety plug.

6.11 The large hex drain plug closer to the engine is for the transaxle coolant (A); the smaller one that requires an Allen wrench is for the lubricant (B)

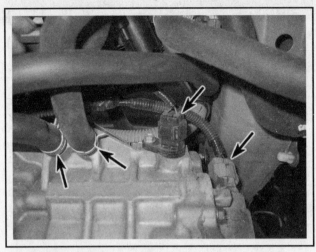

6.18 Make sure that all wiring harnesses and hoses are labeled, disconnected and secured out of the way before removing the transaxle

8   Loosen the wheel lug nuts and driveaxle/hub nuts. Raise the vehicle and support it securely on jackstands.

9   Remove the front wheels.

10 Remove both engine bottom covers.

11 Drain the coolant (see illustration).

12 Drain the transaxle lubricant (see Chapter 1).

13 Refer to Chapter 11 and remove the hood.

14 Refer to Chapter 12 and remove both front wiper arms.

15 Remove the outer cowl top front panel.

16 Refer to Chapter 5 and remove the inverter/converter assembly.

17 Refer to Chapter 4 and remove the air filter housing.

18 Label, then disconnect all interfering wiring and hoses (see illustration)

19 Remove the driveaxles (see Chapter 8).

20 Disconnect the exhaust pipe from the exhaust manifold.

21 Using an engine support fixture, securely support the engine from

above with chains attached to the front and rear of the cylinder head.

22 Support the transaxle from below, preferably using a floor jack equipped with a transmission adapter head. Remove the front suspension crossmember.

23 Disconnect engine mount #3 and allow the engine support to take the weight of the engine (see Chapter 2A, illustration 18.3a).

24 Remove the starter hole cover and the housing side cover.

25 Remove the six transaxle-to-engine mounting bolts and pull the transaxle from the engine.

26 Disconnect any remaining hoses and/or wiring.

27 Remove the #3 engine mount bracket.

28 Installation is the reverse of removal. Be sure to tighten the mounting bolts to the torque listed in this Chapter's Specifications.

29 Refill the transaxle with the proper lubricant, and refill and bleed the inverter/converter/transaxle cooling system (see Chapter 1).

Specifications

Transaxle

Fluid type	See Chapter 1

Torque specifications

	Ft-lbs
Transaxle-to-engine bolts	24

Notes

Section

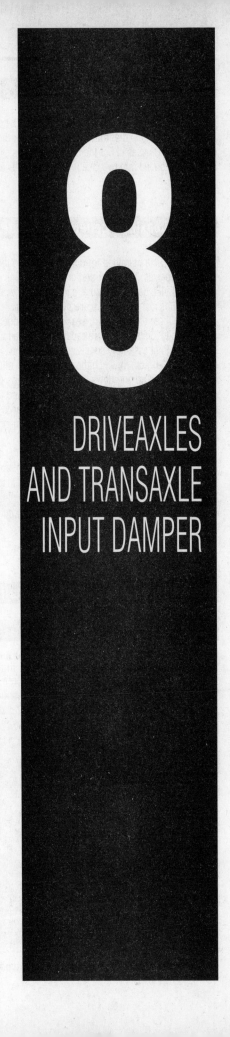

8

DRIVEAXLES
AND TRANSAXLE
INPUT DAMPER

1 General information

The information in this Chapter deals with the components from the rear of the engine to the front wheels, except for the transaxle, which is dealt with in Chapter 7. For the purposes of this Chapter, these components are grouped into two categories: driveaxles and flywheel damper.

Since nearly all the procedures covered in this Chapter involve working under the vehicle, make sure it's securely supported on sturdy jackstands or a hoist.

2 Driveaxles - general information and inspection

1 Power is transmitted from the transaxle to the wheels through a pair of driveaxles. The inner end of each driveaxle is splined into the differential side gears. The outer ends of the driveaxles are splined to the axle hubs and locked in place by a large nut.

2 The inner ends of the driveaxles are equipped with sliding constant velocity joints, which are capable of both angular and axial motion. Each inner joint assembly consists of a tripod bearing and a joint housing (outer race) in which the joint is free to slide in and out as the driveaxle moves up and down with the wheel. The joints can be disassembled and cleaned in the event of a boot failure (see Section 4), but if any parts are damaged, the joints must be replaced as a unit. When buying parts for a driveaxle, or a complete replacement driveaxle assembly, make sure you get the right components.

3 The outer CV joints consist of ball bearings running between an inner race and an outer cage, and are capable of angular but not axial movement. The outer joints should be cleaned, inspected and repacked, but they cannot be disassembled. If an outer joint is damaged, it must be replaced along with the axleshaft (the outer joint and axleshaft are sold as a single component).

4 The boots should be inspected periodically for damage and leaking lubricant. Torn CV joint boots must be replaced immediately or the joints can be damaged. Boot replacement involves removal of the driveaxle (see Section 3).

➡Note: Some auto parts stores carry split-type replacement boots, which can be installed without removing the driveaxle from the vehicle. This is a convenient alternative; however, the driveaxle should be removed and the CV joint disassembled and cleaned to ensure the joint is free from contaminants such as moisture and dirt which will accelerate CV joint wear.

The most common symptom of worn or damaged CV joints, besides lubricant leaks, is a clicking noise in turns, a clunk when accelerating after coasting and vibration at highway speeds. To check for wear in the CV joints and driveaxle shafts, grasp each axle (one at a time) and rotate it in both directions while holding the CV joint housings, feeling for play indicating worn splines or sloppy CV joints. Also check the driveaxle shafts for cracks, dents and distortion.

3 Driveaxle - removal and installation

✳✳ **WARNING:**

Make sure power to the hybrid system is turned Off before performing any work on this vehicle. Also, on models equipped with the Smart Key system, place the key in a secure spot at least 20 feet away from the work area.

3.4 Use a center punch to unstake the driveaxle nut

✳✳ **CAUTION:**

The manufacturer states that a new driveaxle/hub nut must be installed whenever it is removed.

REMOVAL

▶ **Refer to illustrations 3.4, 3.5, 3.6, 3.9 and 3.10**

1 Refer to Chapter 6 and disconnect the cable from the negative terminal of the auxiliary 12-volt battery. Be sure to perform the initialization procedure when reconnecting it.

2 Set the parking brake.

3 Loosen the front wheel lug nuts, raise the vehicle and support it securely on jackstands. Remove the wheel.

4 Unstake the driveaxle/hub nut (see illustration). On 2004 and later models, disconnect the left speed sensor.

5 Remove the driveaxle/hub nut. To prevent the hub from turning, wedge a prybar between two of the wheel studs and allow the prybar to rest against the ground or the floor pan of the vehicle (see illustration).

6 To loosen the driveaxle from the hub splines, tap the end of the driveaxle with a soft-faced hammer or a hammer and a brass punch (see illustration).

3.5 You will need a large breaker bar to loosen the driveaxle/hub nut - use a prybar to keep the wheel from turning

➡ **Note: Don't attempt to push the end of the driveaxle through the hub yet. Applying force to the end of the driveaxle, beyond just breaking it loose from the hub, can damage the driveaxle or transaxle. If the driveaxle is stuck in the hub splines and won't move, it may be necessary to remove the brake disc (see Chapter 9) and push it from the hub with a two-jaw puller after Step 8 is performed.**

7   Remove the engine splash shields (see Chapter 1). Place a drain pan underneath the transaxle to catch any lubricant that may spill out when the driveaxle is removed.

8   Disconnect the tie-rod end from the steering knuckle (see Chapter 10). Remove the three nuts and bolt securing the balljoint to the control arm, then pry the control arm down to separate the components (see Chapter 10).

9   Pull out on the steering knuckle and detach the driveaxle from the hub (see illustration). Don't let the driveaxle hang by the inner CV joint after the outer end has been detached from the steering knuckle, as the inner joint could become damaged. Support the outer end of the driveaxle with a piece of wire, if necessary.

3.6 Use a hammer and punch to sharply strike the end of the driveaxle - it should move noticeably (don't push it in too far though, only until it's loose)

10 Carefully pry the inner CV joint out of the transaxle (see illustration).

11 If necessary, refer to Section 5 for the driveaxle oil seal replacement procedure.

INSTALLATION

12 Installation is the reverse of the removal procedure, but with the following additional points:

   a) *Push the driveaxle sharply in to seat the retaining ring on the inner CV joint in the groove in the differential side gear.*
   b) *Tighten the new driveaxle/hub nut to the torque listed in this Chapter's Specifications, then stake the collar of the nut into the groove in the driveaxle.*
   c) *Tighten the lug nuts to the torque listed in the Chapter 1 Specifications.*
   d) *Check the transaxle lubricant and add, if necessary, to bring it to the proper level (see Chapter 1).*

3.9 Pull the steering knuckle out and slide the end of the driveaxle out of the hub

3.10 Use a prybar to carefully pull the inner driveaxle end out of the transaxle

4 Driveaxle boot replacement

→Note: If the CV joint boots must be replaced, explore all options before beginning the job. Complete rebuilt driveaxles are available on an exchange basis, which eliminates much time and work. Whichever route you choose to take, check on the cost and availability of parts before disassembling the vehicle.

1 Remove the driveaxle (see Section 3).

DISASSEMBLY

▶ Refer to illustrations 4.3, 4.4, 4.5 and 4.6

2 Mount the driveaxle in a vise with wood lined jaws (to prevent damage to the axleshaft). Check the CV joint for excessive play in the radial direction, which indicates worn parts. Check for smooth operation throughout the full range of motion for each CV joint. If a boot is torn, disassemble the joint, clean the components and inspect for damage due to loss of lubrication and possible contamination by foreign matter.

3 Cut the boot claps with side-cutters, then remove and discard them (see illustration).

4 Using a screwdriver, carefully pry up on the edge of the outer boot and push it away from the CV joint. Old and worn boots can be cut off. Pull the inner CV joint boot back from the housing and slide the housing from the tripod (see illustration).

5 Remove the tripod joint snap-ring with a pair of snap-ring pliers (see illustration).

6 Mark the tripod and axleshaft to ensure that they are reassembled properly (see illustration).

7 Remove the tripod joint from the driveaxle, then remove the inner stop-ring from its groove on the shaft.

8 If you haven't already cut them off, remove both boots. If you're working on a right-side driveaxle, you'll also have to cut off the clamp for the dynamic damper and slide the damper off.

→Note: Before removing the damper, measure its distance from the end of the driveaxle - when reassembling, it must be returned to the same spot.

4.3 Cut off the old boot clamps and discard them

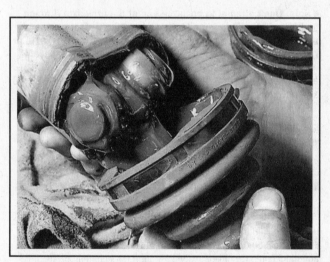

4.4 Remove the boot from the inner CV joint and slide the tripod from the joint housing

4.5 Remove the snap-ring with a pair of snap-ring pliers

4.6 Mark the relationship of the tripod bearing assembly to the axleshaft

4.10a Wrap the splined area of the axleshaft with tape to prevent damage to the boots when removing or installing them

CHECK

9   Thoroughly clean all components, including the outer CV joint assembly, with solvent until the old CV joint grease is completely removed. Inspect the bearing surfaces of the inner tripods and housings for cracks, pitting, scoring and other signs of wear. It's very difficult to inspect the bearing surfaces of the inner and outer races of the outer CV joint, but you can at least check the surfaces of the ball bearings themselves. If they're in good shape, the races probably are too; if they're not, neither are the races. If the inner CV joint is worn, you can buy a new inner CV joint and install it on the old axleshaft; if the outer CV joint is worn, you'll have to purchase a new outer CV joint and axleshaft (they're sold preassembled).

REASSEMBLY

▶ Refer to illustrations 4.10a, 4.10b, 4.10c, 4.10d, 4.11, 4.12a and 4.12b

10   Wrap the splines on the inner end of the axleshaft with electrical or duct tape to protect the boots from the sharp edges of the splines (see illustration). Slide the clamps and boots onto the axleshaft, outer

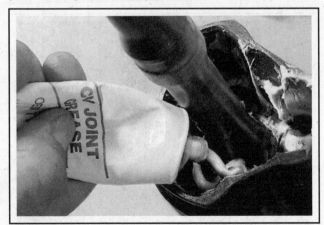

4.10d Install the boot and clamps onto the axleshaft, then insert the tripod into the housing, followed by the rest of the grease

4.10b Install the tripod with the recessed portion of the splines facing the axleshaft, then install a new snap-ring

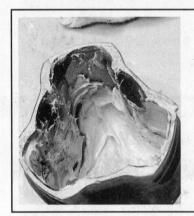

4.10c Put the grease at the bottom of the CV joint housing

boot first, then place the tripod on the shaft and install a new snap-ring.

➡Note: If you removed the dynamic damper, be sure to install it in its original location with the measurement you recorded earlier.

Apply grease to the tripod assembly and inside the housing. Insert the tripod into the housing and pack the remainder of the grease around the tripod (see illustrations). If you're repacking the outer joint, be sure to work the entire tube of CV joint grease (included with the boot kit) into the bearing assembly.

11   Slide the boots into place, making sure the ends of both boots seat in their respective grooves in the axleshaft. Check the length of the driveaxle and make sure it is within the tolerances listed in this Chapter's Specifications (see illustration).

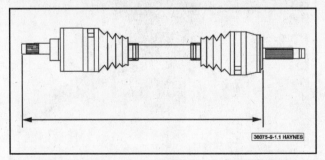

36075-8-1.1 HAYNES

4.11 Before tightening the boot clamps, adjust the length of the driveaxle to the dimension listed in this Chapter's Specifications

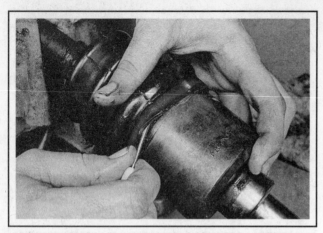

4.12a Equalize the pressure inside the boot by inserting a small, dull screwdriver between the boot and the outer race

4.12b You'll need a special boot clamp installation tool like this to tighten the new clamps; follow the instructions provided by the tool manufacturer

12 Equalize the pressure in the boot and tighten the boot clamps (see illustrations). The driveaxle is now ready for installation (see Section 3).

5   Driveaxle oil seals - replacement

▶ **Refer to illustrations 5.4 and 5.6**

❊❊ WARNING:

Make sure power to the hybrid system is turned Off before performing any work on this vehicle. Also, on models equipped with the Smart Key system, place the key in a secure spot at least 20 feet away from the work area.

1 Fluid leaks frequently occur due to wear of the driveaxle oil seals. Replacement of these seals is relatively easy, since the repairs can usually be performed without removing the transaxle from the vehicle.

2 The driveaxle oil seals are located in either side of the transaxle, where the driveaxle inner CV joint is splined into the differential. If leak-age at the seal is suspected, raise the vehicle and support it securely on jackstands. If the seal is leaking, fluid will be found on the side of the transaxle.

3 Remove the driveaxle (see Section 3).

4 Using a screwdriver or prybar, carefully pry the oil seal out of the transaxle bore (see illustration).

5 If the oil seal cannot be removed with a screwdriver or prybar, a special oil seal removal tool (available at auto parts stores) will be required.

6 Using a seal driver or a large deep socket as a drift, install the new oil seal. Drive it into the bore squarely and make sure that it is completely seated (see illustration). Lubricate the lip of the new seal with multi-purpose grease.

7 Install the driveaxle assembly (see Section 3). Be careful not to damage the lip of the new seal.

5.4 Carefully pry out the old driveaxle seal with a prybar, screwdriver or a special seal removal tool; make sure you don't gouge or nick the surface of the seal bore

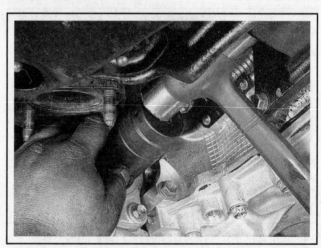

5.6 Drive in the new driveaxle seal with a large socket or a special seal installer

6   Transaxle input damper - removal and installation

REMOVAL

1   The transaxle input damper is bolted to the rear of the flywheel much like a clutch. It's purpose is to smooth the power pulses from the engine.

2   The transaxle must be separated from the engine in order to access the input damper (see Chapter 7)

3   Mark the damper assembly and the flywheel with paint so they can be assembled in the same position.

4   Hold the opposite end of the crankshaft with a suitable tool such as a chain or strap wrench, then evenly loosen the six damper mounting bolts a little at a time until they can be removed.

5   Lift off the damper assembly and inspect it thoroughly for damage and wear.

INSTALLATION

6   Position the damper on the flywheel using an alignment tool. A clutch alignment tool of the correct size may be used. Make sure the damper is facing the proper direction and the match marks are aligned.

7   Tighten the bolts finger-tight.

8   Center the damper by ensuring the alignment tool is through the splined hub and into the recess in the crankshaft. Wiggle the tool to make sure it is centered. Tighten the bolts a little at a time, working in a criss-cross pattern. After all the bolts are snug, tighten them to the torque listed in this Chapter's Specifications.

9   Remove the alignment tool. Visually verify that the damper is centered with the bore of the crankshaft.

Specifications

Driveaxles

Driveaxle length	
2001 through 2003 models	
Left driveaxle	22.63 to 23.03 inches
Right driveaxle	32.75 to 33.15 inches
2004 and later models	
Left driveaxle	22.22 inches
Right driveaxle	33.32 inches

Torque specifications
Ft-lbs (unless otherwise indicated)

Driveaxle/hub nut	159 ft-lbs
Flywheel bolts	See Chapter 2A
Transaxle input damper bolts	
2001 through 2003 models	144 in-lbs
2004 and later models	15
Wheel lug nuts	See Chapter 1

Notes

Section

Reference to other Chapters

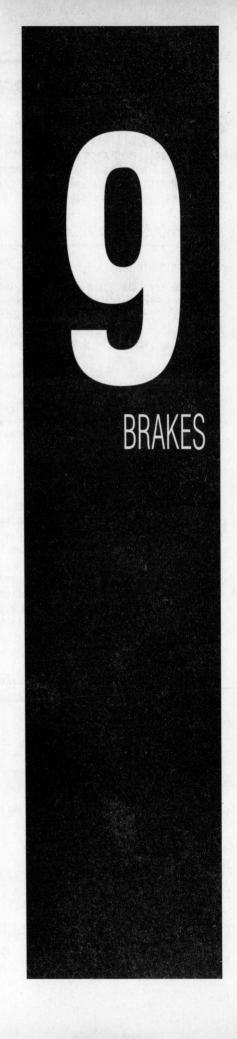

9

BRAKES

The vehicles covered by this manual are equipped with hydraulically operated front and rear brake systems. The front brakes are disc type and the rear brakes are drum type. Both the front and rear brakes are self-adjusting. The disc brakes automatically compensate for pad wear while the drum brakes incorporate an adjustment mechanism that is activated as the parking brake is applied.

2001 THROUGH 2003 MODELS

System description

The Anti-lock Brake System (ABS) is designed to maintain vehicle steerabilty, directional stability and optimum deceleration under severe braking conditions and on most road surfaces. It does so by monitoring the rotational speed of each wheel and controlling the brake line pressure to each wheel during braking. This prevents the wheels from locking up.

The ABS system is primarily designed to prevent wheel lockup during heavy braking, but the information provided by the wheel speed sensors of the ABS system is shared with another system that uses the data to control vehicle handling. EBD (Electronic Brakeforce Distribution) varies the front-to-rear and side-to-side braking balance under different vehicle loads and skidding conditions.

Hydraulic system

The hydraulic system consists of the master cylinder, the brake actuator assembly, the lines and the calipers/wheel cylinders. Basically, when the driver's foot presses on the brake pedal, hydraulic pressure is created in the master cylinder. This pressure is then transmitted to the brake actuator, which supplies the proper pressures to the individual wheels. A computer instructs the actuator as to which wheels need increased or reduced pressure according to information from wheel speed sensors and other inputs. This provides an anti-lock brake system as well as an electronic brake force distribution system that changes braking when loads are being carried, for example. A proportioning valve provides brake balance between the front and rear brakes.

Power brake booster

A separate hydraulic power brake booster is used to provide pedal-force assistance and better feel. An electric motor supplies power to the unit. 2004 and later models have power assist designed into the system.

2004 AND LATER MODELS

System description

The brake system used on these later models is unique in that all functions are performed electronically with the aid of a "skid control" computer. The major components are:

Pedal stroke sensor - This senses the amount of effort the driver is putting into the brake pedal and sends this information to the skid control ECU.

Steering angle sensor - This sensor gives information to the skid control ECU regarding the angle of the steering wheel.

Skid control ECU - This computer calculates which wheel should receive how much braking pressure. It functions as a brake controller, a skid control system and an anti-lock brake system all in one unit.

Pedal stroke simulator - This device creates a pedal stroke when the brakes are applied in proportion to the force on the brake pedal.

Master cylinder - The master cylinder creates hydraulic pressure for the brake actuator, which then applies pressure to the calipers and wheel cylinders. In the event of a brake actuator failure, the master cylinder will apply pressure directly to the calipers and wheel cylinders.

Wheel cylinder pressure sensors - There are sensors at all of the wheels that inform the skid control ECU of how much pressure they are receiving.

Wheel speed sensors - These sensors tell the skid control ECU the speeds of all four wheels so it can make corrections to prevent brake lock-up and skids.

Brake actuator - This device creates the pressure used to actuate the brake system.

Yaw and deceleration sensor - This sensor detects sideways forces and also deceleration. The skid control ECU uses this information to vary the pressure sent to each wheel's brake.

ALL MODELS

Parking brake

The parking brake pedal operates the rear brakes only, through cable actuation.

Service

After completing any operation involving disassembly of any part of the brake system, always test-drive the vehicle to check for proper braking performance before resuming normal driving. When testing the brakes, perform the tests on a clean, dry, flat surface. Conditions other than these can lead to inaccurate test results.

Test the brakes at various speeds with both light and heavy pedal pressure. The vehicle should stop evenly without pulling to one side or the other.

Tires, vehicle load and wheel alignment are factors that also affect braking performance.

2 Disc brake pads - replacement

♦ Refer to illustrations 2.5 and 2.6a through 2.6p

✳✳ WARNING 1:

Disc brake pads must be replaced on both front wheels at the same time - never replace the pads on only one wheel. Also, the dust created by the brake system is harmful to your health. Never blow it out with compressed air and don't inhale any of it. An approved filtering mask should be worn when working on the brakes. Do not, under any circumstances, use petroleum-based solvents to clean brake parts. Use brake system cleaner only!

✳✳ WARNING 2:

Make sure power to the hybrid system is turned Off before performing any work on this vehicle. Also, on models equipped with the Smart Key system, place the key in a secure spot at least 20 feet away from the work area.

➥Note: The manufacturer recommends replacing the pad shims and wear-indicators whenever the pads are replaced.

1   Remove the cap from the brake fluid reservoir.

2   Loosen the wheel lug nuts, raise the front of the vehicle and support it securely on jackstands. Block the wheels at the rear end.

3   Remove the wheels. Work on one brake assembly at a time, using the assembled brake for reference if necessary.

4   Inspect the brake disc carefully as outlined in Section 3. If machining is necessary, follow the information in that Section to remove the disc, at which time the pads can be removed as well.

5   Push the piston back into its bore to provide room for the new brake pads. A C-clamp can be used to accomplish this (see illustration). As the piston is depressed to the bottom of the caliper bore, the fluid in the master cylinder will rise. Make sure that it doesn't overflow. If necessary, siphon off some of the fluid.

6   Follow the accompanying photos, beginning with illustration 2.6a. Be sure to stay in order and read the caption under each illustration.

2.5 Before removing the caliper, be sure to depress the piston into its bore with a large C-clamp to make room for the new, thicker pads

2.6a Always wash the brakes with brake cleaner before disassembling anything

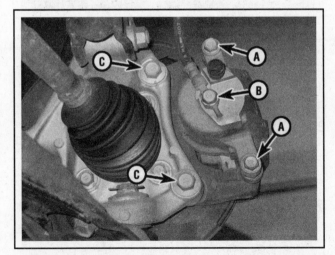

2.6b Brake caliper mounting details

A   *Caliper mounting bolts*
B   *Brake hose banjo bolt (do not remove)*
C   *Caliper mounting bracket bolts*

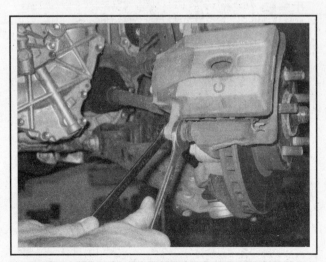

2.6c Remove the caliper lower mounting bolt. Hold the caliper pin with an open-end wrench while unscrewing the bolt

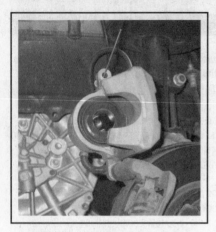

2.6d Swing the caliper up and secure it with a bent piece of coat hanger or some wire - don't let it hang by the hose. Also, make sure the upper slide pin boot doesn't get distorted

2.6e Remove the inner pad . . .

2.6f . . . and the outer pad

7   When reinstalling the caliper, be sure to tighten the mounting bolts to the torque listed in this Chapter's Specifications. After the job has been completed, firmly depress the brake pedal a few times to bring the pads into contact with the disc. Check the level of the brake fluid, adding some if necessary. Tighten the wheel lug nuts to the torque listed in the Chapter 1 Specifications. Check the operation of the brakes carefully before placing the vehicle into normal service.

2.6g Lift out the support springs

2.6h After cleaning, lubricate the caliper pin with brake grease, then reinstall it

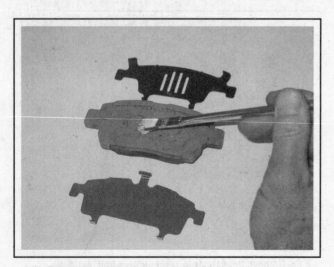

2.6i Coat the backs of the new pads with a thin layer of brake grease

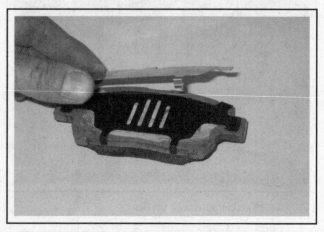

2.6j Clean the shims and install them on the new pads

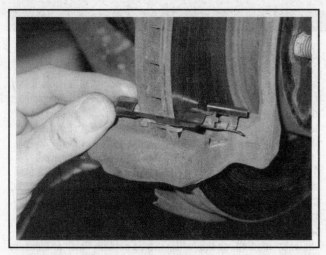

2.6k Install the pad support springs

2.6l Make sure that the pad surfaces are perfectly clean before installing the inner pad . . .

2.6m . . . and the outer pad

2.6n Compress the piston to the bottom of its bore with a large C-clamp

2.6o Swing the caliper down into place

2.6p . . . then install the lower mounting bolt and tighten it to the torque listed in this Chapter's Specifications

3 Brake disc - inspection, removal and installation

▸ Refer to illustrations 3.3, 3.4a, 3.4b, 3.5a and 3.5b

✳✳ WARNING:

Make sure power to the hybrid system is turned Off before performing any work on this vehicle. Also, on models equipped with the Smart Key system, place the key in a secure spot at least 20 feet away from the work area.

INSPECTION

1 Loosen the wheel lug nuts, raise the vehicle and support it securely on jackstands. Remove the wheel and install the lug nuts to hold the disc in place.

2 Remove the brake caliper by referring to illustration 2.6b. DO NOT disconnect the brake hose. After removing the caliper bolts (see illustration 2.6c), suspend the caliper out of the way with a piece of wire (see illustration 2.6d). Remove the caliper mounting bracket bolts and detach the bracket.

3 Visually inspect the disc surface for score marks and other damage. Light scratches and shallow grooves are normal after use and may not always be detrimental to brake operation, but deep scoring requires disc removal and refinishing by an automotive machine shop. Be sure to check both sides of the disc (see illustration). If pulsating has been noticed during application of the brakes, suspect disc runout.

4 To check disc runout, place a dial indicator at a point about 1/2-inch from the outer edge of the disc (see illustration). Set the indicator to zero and turn the disc. The indicator reading should not exceed the specified allowable runout limit. If it does, the disc should be refinished by an automotive machine shop.

➡Note: The discs should be resurfaced regardless of the dial indicator reading, as this will impart a smooth finish and ensure a perfectly flat surface, eliminating any brake pedal pulsation or other undesirable symptoms related to questionable discs. At the very least, if you elect not to have the discs resurfaced, remove the glaze from the surface with sandpaper or emery cloth using a swirling motion (see illustration).

3.3 The brake pads on this vehicle were obviously neglected, as they wore down completely and cut deep grooves into the disc - wear this severe means the disc must be replaced

3.4a Use a dial indicator to check disc runout; if the reading exceeds the allowable runout limit, the disc will have to be machined or replaced

3.4b Using a swirling motion, remove the glaze from the disc surface with sandpaper or emery cloth

3.5a The minimum wear dimension is cast into the rear of the disc (typical)

3.5b Use a micrometer to measure the disc thickness

5   It's absolutely critical that the disc not be machined to a thickness under the specified minimum allowable refinish thickness. The minimum wear (or discard) thickness is cast into the inside of the disc (see illustration). The disc thickness can be checked with a micrometer (see illustration).

REMOVAL

6   Make match marks on the disc and one of the wheel studs so it can be reinstalled in the same position. Remove the lug nuts that were put on to hold the disc in place and slide the disc from the hub.

INSTALLATION

7   Place the disc in position over the threaded studs.

8   Install the caliper mounting bracket, tightening the bolts to the torque listed in this Chapter's Specifications.

9   Install the caliper, tightening the bolts to the torque listed in this Chapter's Specifications. Bleeding won't be necessary since the brake hose was not disconnected from the caliper.

10   Install the wheel and lug nuts. Lower the vehicle and tighten the lug nuts to the torque listed in the Chapter 1 Specifications. Depress the brake pedal a few times to bring the brake pads into contact with the disc. Check the operation of the brakes carefully before driving the vehicle.

4   Drum brake shoes - replacement

♦ Refer to illustrations 4.4a through 4.4cc and 4.5

❊❊ WARNING 1:

Drum brake shoes must be replaced on both wheels at the same time - never replace the shoes on only one wheel. Also, the dust created by the brake system is harmful to your health. Never blow it out with compressed air and don't inhale any of it. An approved filtering mask should be worn when working on the brakes. Do not, under any circumstances, use petroleum-based solvents to clean brake parts. Use brake system cleaner only!

❊❊ WARNING 2:

Make sure power to the hybrid system is turned Off before performing any work on this vehicle. Also, on models equipped with the Smart Key system, place the key in a secure spot at least 20 feet away from the work area.

❊❊ CAUTION:

Whenever the brake shoes are replaced, the return and hold-down springs should also be replaced. Due to the continuous heating/cooling cycle the springs are subjected to, they lose ten-

sion over a period of time and may allow the shoes to drag on the drum and wear at a much faster rate than normal.

1   Loosen the wheel lug nuts, raise the rear of the vehicle and support it securely on jackstands. Block the front wheels to keep the vehicle from rolling.

2   Release the parking brake.

3   Remove the wheel.

➡Note: All four rear brake shoes must be replaced at the same time, but to avoid mixing up parts, work on the brake assembly for only one side at a time.

4   Follow the accompanying illustrations for the brake shoe replacement procedure (see illustrations). Be sure to stay in order and read the caption under each illustration.

➡Note: If the brake drum cannot be easily removed, make sure the parking brake is completely released. If the drum still cannot be pulled off, the brake shoes will have to be retracted. This is done by first removing the plug from the backing plate. With the plug removed, push the lever off the adjuster star wheel with a narrow screwdriver while turning the adjuster wheel with another screwdriver, moving the shoes away from the drum. The drum should now come off.

4.4a Mark the relationship of the drum to the axle with paint; if the drum is stuck to the hub, it can be pushed off with two bolts threaded through its holes

4.4b Before removing anything, clean the brakes with brake cleaner and allow it to dry (position a drain pan under the brake to catch the fluid and residue); DON'T USE COMPRESSED AIR TO BLOW OFF BRAKE DUST!

4.4c Unhook the spring from a brake shoe; use a pair of locking pliers to stretch the spring and pull the end out of the hole in the shoe

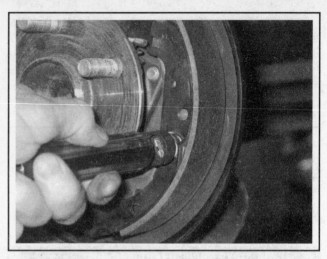

4.4d Depress the hold-down spring and turn the retainer 90-degrees, then release it; a pair of pliers will work, but an inexpensive special removal tool makes the job easier

4.4e Pull the trailing shoe from the backing plate . . .

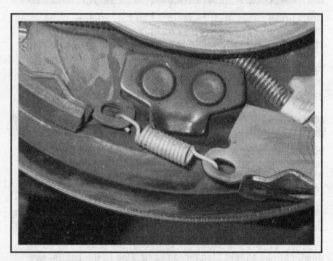

4.4f . . . and unhook the anchor spring from the end of the shoe

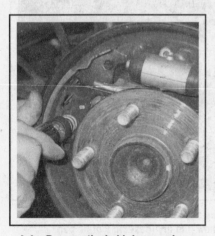

4.4g Remove the hold-down spring from the leading shoe

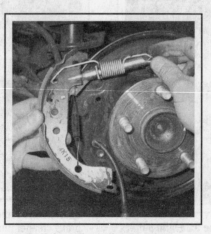

4.4h Unhook the spring from the shoe and slide the adjuster off

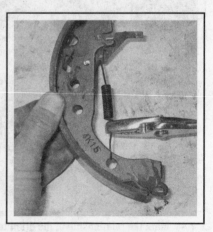

4.4i Release the adjuster lever spring . . .

4.4j . . . and remove the adjuster lever

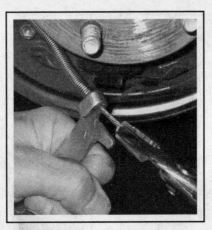

4.4k Detach the parking brake cable from the lever

4.4l Use a screwdriver to spread the retainer, then detach the parking brake lever from the shoe

4.4m Apply a small amount of brake grease to the points where the shoes contact the backing plate

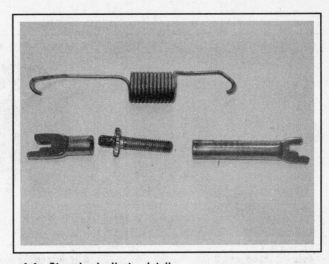

4.4n Star wheel adjuster details

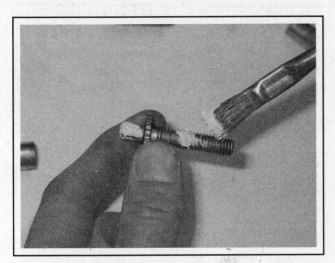

4.4o Apply a small amount of grease to both ends of the star wheel adjuster

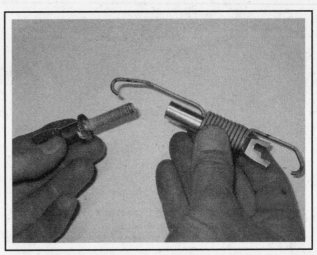

4.4p Assemble the adjuster; be sure to keep everything clean from this point on

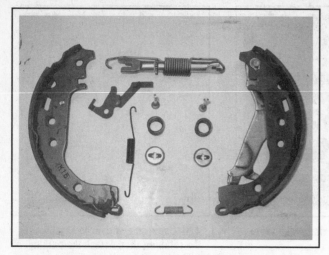

4.4q Layout of the drum brake components

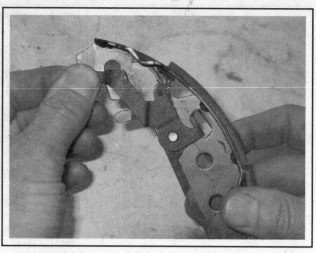

4.4r Assemble the adjuster lever to the new leading shoe . . .

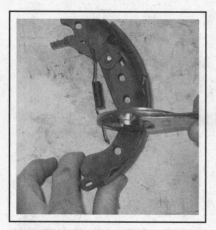

4.4s . . . then install the return spring

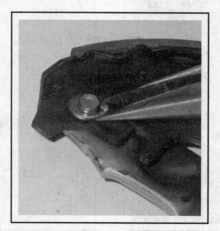

4.4t Attach the parking brake lever to the trailing shoe and crimp the new retainer to the pivot pin

4.4u Attach the parking brake cable to the lever

4.4v Install the trailing shoe, then secure it to the backing plate with the hold-down spring and retainer . . .

4.4w . . . then install the lower return spring

4.4x Put the leading shoe into position and connect the lower return spring to it . . .

4.4y . . . then install the adjuster mechanism

4.4z Make sure that the adjuster properly engages the trailing shoe and parking brake lever

4.4aa Attach the upper return spring to the trailing shoe

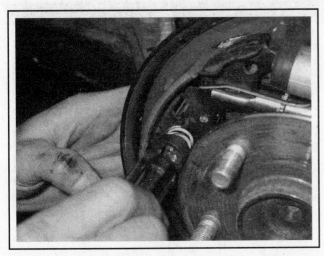

4.4bb Install the front shoe hold-down spring and retainer

4.4cc The brake assembly is now ready for adjustment to ensure a close fit to the drum

5   Before reinstalling the drum, it should be checked for cracks, score marks, deep scratches and hard spots, which will appear as small discolored areas. If the hard spots cannot be removed with fine emery cloth or if any of the other conditions listed above exist, the drum must be taken to an automotive machine shop to have it resurfaced. There is a maximum drum diameter cast into each drum. Be sure to avoid exceeding this dimension when having it machined (see illustration).

→Note: Professionals recommend resurfacing the drums each time a brake job is done. Resurfacing will eliminate the possibility of out-of-round drums. If the drums are worn so much that they can't be resurfaced without exceeding the maximum allowable diameter (stamped into the drum), then new ones will be required. At the very least, if you elect not to have the drums resurfaced, remove the glaze from the surface with emery cloth using a swirling motion.

6   Install the brake drum on the axle flange. Pump the brake several times, then turn the adjuster star wheel using a screwdriver inserted through the hole in the backing plate until the shoes slightly drag on the drums as the drums are turned. Now, back off the adjuster until the shoes don't drag on the drums. Install the plug in the brake backing plate.

7   Install the wheel and lug nuts, then lower the vehicle. Tighten the lug nuts to the torque listed in the Chapter 1 Specifications.

8   Make a number of forward and reverse stops and operate the

4.5 The maximum drum diameter is cast into the rear drums (typical)

parking brake to adjust the brakes until satisfactory pedal action is obtained.

9   Check the operation of the brakes carefully before driving the vehicle.

5   Brake hoses and lines - inspection

⁕⁕ WARNING:

Make sure power to the hybrid system is turned Off before performing any work on this vehicle. Also, on models equipped with the Smart Key system, place the key in a secure spot at least 20 feet away from the work area.

1   About every six months, with the vehicle raised and supported securely on jackstands, the rubber hoses which connect the steel brake lines with the front and rear brake assemblies should be inspected for cracks, chafing of the outer cover, leaks, blisters and other damage. These are important and vulnerable parts of the brake system and inspection should be complete. A light and mirror will be helpful for a thorough check. If a hose exhibits any of the above conditions, replace it with a new one.

2   We do not recommend that you attempt to replace brake lines yourself, as the brake bleeding procedure is very complex and requires a special scan tool (see Section 6).

6   Brake hydraulic system - bleeding

Any time a component of the hydraulic brake system is disconnected or damaged, air will enter the system. On conventional vehicles, this air can be removed through a bleeding process after the repair is completed. However, the vehicles covered in this manual have complex braking systems that require special equipment and training to accomplish a complete and safe removal of all air. For this reason we do not recommend that you attempt to replace any components that are part of the hydraulic system. These items include:

a) *Master cylinder*
b) *Rear wheel cylinders*
c) *Front calipers*
d) *Brake lines and hoses*
e) *Hydraulic control unit*
f) *Hydraulic brake booster (2001 through 2003 models)*

7 Parking brake - adjustment

❋❋ WARNING:

Make sure power to the hybrid system is turned Off before performing any work on this vehicle. Also, on models equipped with the Smart Key system, place the key in a secure spot at least 20 feet away from the work area.

1 The parking brake pedal, when properly adjusted, should travel the specified number of clicks when a moderate force is applied (refer to the value listed in the Specifications in this Chapter). If it travels fewer than the minimum number of clicks, there's a chance the parking brake might not be releasing completely and might be dragging on the drum. If the pedal can be pushed in more than the maximum number of clicks, the parking brake may not hold adequately on an incline, allowing the car to roll.

2 The rear brake shoes must be properly adjusted in order for the system to work correctly. Make sure their self-adjusting mechanism is operating as designed before proceeding.

2001 THROUGH 2003 MODELS

3 Remove the left front door threshold plate, the cowl side trim (kick) panel and the two lower trim panels that interfere with access to the parking brake cable adjustment mechanism.

4 Loosen the lock nut on the cable end and turn the adjusting nut until the pedal travel is satisfactory. Tighten the lock nut.

5 Replace the panels that were removed.

2004 AND LATER MODELS

▶ **Refer to illustration 7.8**

6 Remove the rear console container (see Chapter 11).

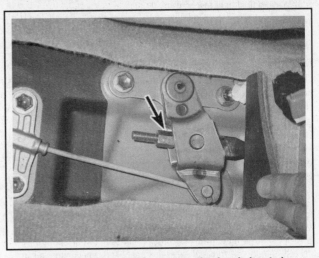

7.8 The parking brake adjustment mechanism is located under the console (2004 and later models)

7 Pull back the rubber cover from the cable adjusting nuts and loosen the rear lock nut.

8 Adjust the front nut (see illustration) to obtain the correct number of clicks when using the parking brake pedal (see this Chapter's Specifications).

9 Reinstall the console.

ALL MODELS

10 Make sure that the brake shoes do not drag when the parking brake pedal is released. Also check the operation of the parking brake warning lamp.

8 Brake pedal - adjustment

▶ **Refer to illustration 8.1**

❋❋ WARNING:

Make sure power to the hybrid system is turned Off before performing any work on this vehicle. Also, on models equipped with the Smart Key system, place the key in a secure spot at least 20 feet away from the work area.

2001 THROUGH 2003 MODELS

Pedal height

1 The height of the brake pedal is the distance the pedal sits off the asphalt insulator under the carpet (see illustration). If the pedal height is not within Specifications, it must be adjusted.

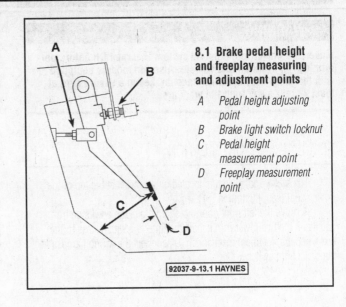

8.1 Brake pedal height and freeplay measuring and adjustment points

A *Pedal height adjusting point*
B *Brake light switch locknut*
C *Pedal height measurement point*
D *Freeplay measurement point*

92037-9-13.1 HAYNES

2 Remove the left front door threshold plate, the cowl side trim panel and the two lower trim panels that interfere with access to the brake pedal adjustment mechanism.

3 Remove the brake light switch (see Section 9).

4 Loosen the locknut at the clevis.

5 Turn the pushrod to obtain the correct pedal height (refer to the distance listed in this Chapter's Specifications).

6 Install the brake light switch and adjust it so that it operates when the pedal is depressed 0.20 to 0.60-inch.

7 Replace the panels that were removed.

Pedal freeplay

8 The freeplay is the pedal slack, or the distance the pedal can be depressed before it begins to have any effect on the brake system (see illustration 8.1). Before checking brake pedal freeplay, depress the brake pedal a minimum of 40 times (with the key off).

9 If the pedal freeplay is not within the specified range, check the adjustment of the brake light switch (see Section 9).

10 If the brake light switch is properly adjusted, troubleshoot the brake system for the cause of excessive freeplay (suspect either air in the hydraulic system [see Section 6], or excessive clearance between the rear brake shoes and the brake drums [see Section 4]).

Brake pedal reserve distance

11 With the parking brake released and the engine running, depress the pedal with normal braking effort and have an assistant measure the distance from the center of the pedal pad to the asphalt sheet under the carpet. If the distance is less than specified, check for excessive clearance between the rear brake shoes and the brake drums (see Section 4).

2004 AND LATER MODELS

Pedal height

12 The height of the brake pedal is the distance the pedal sits off the asphalt insulator under the carpet (see illustration 8.1). If the pedal height is not within Specifications, it must be adjusted.

13 Remove the left front door threshold plate, the cowl side trim panel and the two lower trim panels that interfere with access to the brake pedal adjustment mechanism.

14 Install the brake light switch and adjust it so that it operates when the pedal is depressed 0.20 to 0.60-inch.

15 Further adjustments of the pedal height involves adjustment of the pedal stroke sensor. This is an operation that involves factory scan tools and must be left to a dealer service department or other properly equipped repair shop.

16 Reinstall the panels removed.

Pedal freeplay

17 The freeplay is the pedal slack, or the distance the pedal can be depressed before it begins to have any effect on the brake system (see illustration 8.1). Before checking brake pedal freeplay, depress the brake pedal several times (with the engine off).

18 If the pedal freeplay is not within the specified range, check the adjustment of the brake light switch (see Section 9).

19 If the brake light switch is properly adjusted, troubleshoot the brake system for the cause of excessive freeplay (suspect either air in the hydraulic system [see Section 6], or excessive clearance between the rear brake shoes and the brake drums [see Section 4]).

Brake pedal reserve distance

20 With the parking brake released and the engine running, depress the pedal with normal braking effort and have an assistant measure the distance from the center of the pedal pad to the asphalt sheet under the carpet. If the distance is less than specified, check for excessive clearance between the rear brake shoes and the brake drums (see Section 4).

9 Brake light switch - removal, installation and adjustment

✳✳ WARNING:

Make sure power to the hybrid system is turned Off before performing any work on this vehicle. Also, on models equipped with the Smart Key system, place the key in a secure spot at least 20 feet away from the work area.

REMOVAL AND INSTALLATION

1 The brake light switch is located on a bracket at the top of the brake pedal (see illustration 8.1).

2 Remove the left front door threshold plate, the cowl side trim panel and the two lower trim panels that interfere with access to the brake pedal adjustment mechanism. Disconnect the wiring harness at the brake light switch.

3 Loosen the locknut and unscrew the switch from the pedal bracket.

4 Installation is the reverse of removal.

ADJUSTMENT

5 Check and, if necessary, adjust brake pedal height (see Section 8).

6 Loosen the switch locknut; adjust the switch so that the clearance between the switch body and the pedal is as listed in this Chapter's Specifications. (If you're unable to measure this distance, adjust the plunger so that it lightly contacts the pedal stop.) Tighten the locknut.

7 Plug the electrical connector into the switch and reconnect the battery. Make sure the brake lights come on when the brake pedal is depressed and go off when the pedal is released. If not, repeat the adjustment procedure until the brake lights function properly.

Specifications

General

Brake fluid type	See Chapter 1
Brake pedal height	
2001 through 2003 models	5-1/16 to 5-1/2 inches
2004 and later models	5-7/16 to 5-13/16 inches
Brake pedal freeplay	
2001 through 2003 models	1/16 to 1/4 inch
2004 and later models	1/32 to 3/16 inch
Brake pedal minimum reserve distance	
2001 through 2003 models	3-3/8 inches
2004 and later models	4-1/8 inches
Parking brake pedal travel	
2001 through 2003 models	5 to 8 clicks
2004 and later models	6 to 9 clicks
Brake light switch clearance (between the switch body and pedal)	0.020 to 0.094-inch

Disc brakes

Minimum brake pad thickness	See Chapter 1
Front disc thickness	
Standard	0.866 inches
Minimum*	0.787 inches
Disc runout limit	0.002 inch
Parking brake shoe minimum thickness	1/32 inch

Drum brakes

Brake shoe minimum lining thickness	See Chapter 1
Drum inside diameter	
Standard	7.874 inches
Maximum*	7.913 inches

* Note: If different specifications are cast into the disc or drum, they supersede information printed here.

Torque specifications — Ft-lbs (unless otherwise indicated)

Caliper mounting bolts	25
Caliper mounting bracket bolts	80
Wheel lug nuts	See Chapter 1

Notes

Section

10

SUSPENSION AND STEERING SYSTEMS

1 General information

▸ **Refer to illustrations 1.1 and 1.2**

The front suspension (see illustration) is a MacPherson strut design. The upper end of each strut/coil spring assembly is attached to the vehicle's body strut support. The lower end of the strut assembly is connected to the upper end of the steering knuckle. The steering knuckle is attached to a balljoint mounted on the outer end of the suspension control arm. A stabilizer bar reduces body roll.

The rear suspension (see illustration) utilizes shock absorber/coil spring assemblies. The upper end of each assembly is attached to the vehicle body. The lower ends are attached to a beam axle. The axle is connected to the chassis by bolts through pivot bushings.

The rack-and-pinion steering gear is located behind the engine/transaxle assembly and actuates the tie-rods, which are attached to the steering knuckles. The inner ends of the tie-rods are protected by rubber boots, which should be inspected periodically for secure attachment, tears and leaking lubricant.

The power assist system consists of an electric motor mounted low on the steering rack on 2001 through 2003 models and on the steering shaft on 2004 and later models.

The steering wheel operates the steering shaft, which actuates the steering gear through universal joints. Looseness in the steering can be caused by wear in the steering shaft universal joints, the steering gear, the tie-rod ends and loose retaining bolts.

PRECAUTIONS

❊❊ **WARNING:**

Make sure power to the hybrid system is turned Off before performing any work on this vehicle. Also, on models equipped with the Smart Key system, place the key in a secure spot at least 20 feet away from the work area.

Frequently, when working on the suspension or steering system components, you may come across fasteners that seem impossible to loosen. These fasteners on the underside of the vehicle are continually subjected to water, road grime, mud, etc., and can become rusted or "frozen," making them extremely difficult to remove. In order to unscrew these stubborn fasteners without damaging them (or other components), be sure to use lots of penetrating oil and allow it to soak in for a while. Using a wire brush to clean exposed threads will also ease removal of the nut or bolt and prevent damage to the threads. Sometimes a sharp blow with a hammer and punch will break the bond between a nut and bolt threads, but care must be taken to prevent the punch from slipping off the fastener and ruining the threads. Heating the stuck fastener and surrounding area with a torch sometimes helps too, but isn't recommended because of the obvious dangers associated with fire. Long

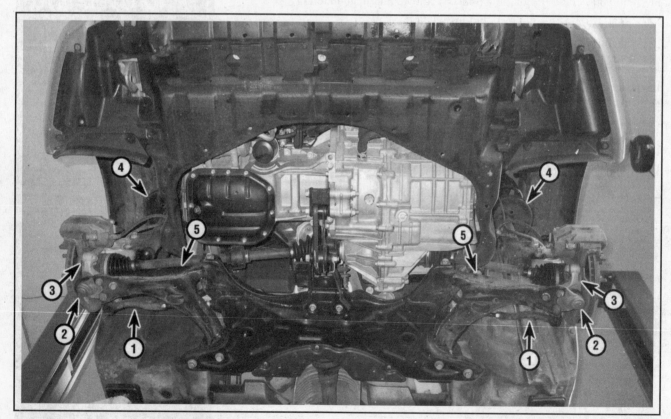

1.1 Front suspension and steering components

1	Tie-rod end	3	Steering knuckle	5	Control arm
2	Ball joint	4	Strut and spring assembly		

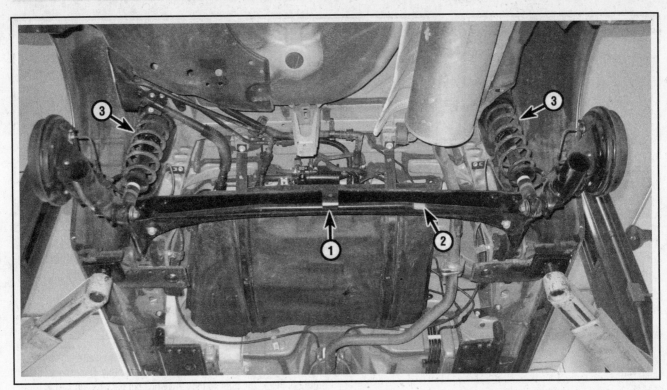

1.2 Rear suspension components

1	*Rear axle*	2	*Stabilizer bar (inside axle)*	3	*Shock absorber/coil spring assembly*

breaker bars and extension, or "cheater," pipes will increase leverage, but never use an extension pipe on a ratchet - the ratcheting mechanism could be damaged. Sometimes tightening the nut or bolt first will help to break it loose. Fasteners that require drastic measures to remove should always be replaced with new ones.

Since most of the procedures dealt with in this Chapter involve jacking up the vehicle and working underneath it, a good pair of jackstands will be needed. A hydraulic floor jack is the preferred type of jack to lift the vehicle, and it can also be used to support certain components during various operations.

✳✳ WARNING:

Never, under any circumstances, rely on a jack to support the vehicle while working on it. Whenever any of the suspension or steering fasteners are loosened or removed they must be inspected and, if necessary, replaced with new ones of the same part number or of original equipment quality and design. Torque specifications must be followed for proper reassembly and component retention. Never attempt to heat or straighten any suspension or steering components. Instead, replace any bent or damaged part with a new one.

2 Strut assembly (front) - removal, inspection and installation

✳✳ WARNING:

Make sure power to the hybrid system is turned Off before performing any work on this vehicle. Also, on models equipped with the Smart Key system, place the key in a secure spot at least 20 feet away from the work area.

REMOVAL

▶ Refer to illustrations 2.5a, 2.5b and 2.7

1 Refer to Chapter 12 and remove the wiper motor and link assembly.

2 Loosen the wheel lug nuts, raise the vehicle and support it securely on jackstands. Remove the wheel.

3 Unbolt the brake hose bracket from the strut. Also detach the speed sensor wiring harness from the strut by removing the clamp bracket bolt. Refer to Section 4 and disconnect the stabilizer link from the strut.

4 Disconnect the stabilizer bar links and allow the stabilizer bar to hang loosely.

5 Mark the relationship of the strut to the steering knuckle.

➡Note: Also mark the positions of the bolts, as special camber adjusting bolts may have been fitted at some point (see illustration).

Remove the strut-to-knuckle nuts and knock the bolts out with a hammer and punch (see illustration).

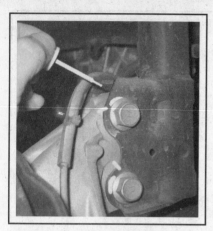

2.5a Mark the steering knuckle position with paint before removing it

2.5b Remove the nuts, then tap the bolts out from the lower portion of the strut where it attaches to the steering knuckle

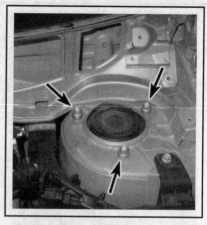

2.7 Strut upper mounting nuts - don't try to remove the center nut (under the plastic cover) at this time

6   Separate the strut from the steering knuckle. Be careful not to overextend the inner CV joint. Also, don't let the steering knuckle fall outward and strain the brake hose.

7   Support the strut and spring assembly (an assistant would be helpful here) and remove the three strut-to-body nuts (see illustration). Remove the assembly out from the fenderwell.

INSPECTION

8   Check the strut body for leaking fluid, dents, cracks and other obvious damage that would warrant repair or replacement.

9   Check the coil spring for chips or cracks in the spring coating (this will cause premature spring failure due to corrosion). Inspect the spring seat for cuts, hardness and general deterioration.

10   If any undesirable conditions exist, proceed to the strut disassembly procedure (see Section 3).

INSTALLATION

11   Guide the strut assembly up into the fenderwell and insert the upper mounting studs through the holes in the body. Once the studs protrude, install the nuts so the strut won't fall back through. This is most easily accomplished with the help of an assistant, as the strut is quite heavy and awkward.

12   Slide the steering knuckle into the strut flange and insert the two bolts. Install the nuts, align the previously made match-marks and tighten them to the torque listed in this Chapter's Specifications.

13   Connect the brake hose bracket to the strut and tighten the bolt securely. Also install the speed sensor wiring harness bracket.

14   Install the wheel and lug nuts, then lower the vehicle and tighten the lug nuts to the torque listed in the Chapter 1 Specifications.

15   Tighten the upper mounting nuts to the torque listed in this Chapter's Specifications.

16   Drive the vehicle to an alignment shop to have the front-end alignment checked, and if necessary, adjusted.

3   Strut or shock absorber/coil spring assembly - replacement

➡Note: The photo sequence in this procedure shows assembly and disassembly of a front strut; assembly and disassembly of a rear shock absorber/coil assembly is similar but slightly different.

1   If the struts or coil springs exhibit the telltale signs of wear (leaking fluid, loss of damping capability, chipped, sagging or cracked coil springs) explore all options before beginning any work. The strut/shock absorber assemblies are not serviceable and must be replaced if a problem develops. However, strut assemblies complete with springs may be available on an exchange basis, which eliminates much time and work.

Whichever route you choose to take, check on the cost and availability of parts before disassembling your vehicle.

✳✳ WARNING:

Disassembling a strut is potentially dangerous and utmost attention must be directed to the job, or serious injury may result. Use only a high-quality spring compressor and carefully follow the manufacturer's instructions furnished with the tool. After removing the coil spring from the strut assembly, set it aside in a safe, isolated area.

3.3 Install the spring compressor in accordance with the manufacturer's instructions and compress the spring until all force is relieved from the upper spring seat

3.4 Remove the damper shaft nut

DISASSEMBLY

♦ **Refer to illustrations 3.3, 3.4, 3.5, 3.6 and 3.7**

2 Remove the strut assembly following the procedure described in Section 2 (front), or if you're working on a rear shock absorber/coil spring assembly, Section 10. Mount the assembly in a vise. Line the vise jaws with wood or rags to prevent damage to the unit and don't tighten the vise excessively.

3 Following the tool manufacturer's instructions, install the spring compressor (which can be obtained at most auto parts stores or equipment yards on a daily rental basis) on the spring and compress it sufficiently to relieve all pressure from the upper spring seat (front) (see illustration) or spring bracket (rear). This can be verified by wiggling the spring.

4 Mark the positions of the upper and lower spring seats and suspension support to each other. Loosen the damper shaft nut with a socket (see illustration).

5 Remove the nut and suspension support (front) (see illustration) or nut and spring bracket (rear). Inspect the bearing in the suspension support for smooth operation. If it doesn't turn smoothly, replace the suspension support. Check the rubber portion of the suspension sup-

port for cracking and general deterioration. If there is any separation of the rubber, replace it.

6 Lift the spring seat and upper insulator from the damper shaft (see illustration). Check the rubber spring seat for cracking and hardness, replacing it if necessary.

7 Carefully lift the compressed spring from the assembly (see illustration) and set it in a safe place.

✳✳ WARNING:

Never place your head near the end of the spring!

8 Slide the rubber bumper off the damper shaft.

9 Check the lower insulator (if equipped) for wear, cracking and hardness and replace it if necessary.

REASSEMBLY

♦ **Refer to illustrations 3.11 and 3.12**

10 If the lower insulator is being replaced, set it into position with the dropped portion seated in the lowest part of the seat. Extend the damper rod to its full length and install the rubber bumper.

3.5 Lift the suspension support off the damper shaft

3.6 Remove the spring seat from the damper shaft

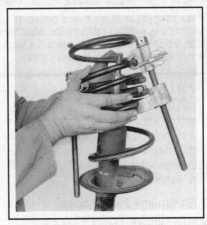

3.7 Remove the compressed spring assembly - keep the ends of the spring pointed away from your body

3.11 When installing the spring, make sure the end fits into the recessed portion of the lower seat

3.12 The flats on the damper shaft must match up with the flats in the spring seat

11 Carefully place the coil spring onto the lower insulator, with the end of the spring resting in the lowest part of the insulator (see illustration).

12 Install the upper insulator and spring seat, making sure that the flats in the hole in the seat match up with the flats on the damper shaft (see illustration).

13 Install the dust seal and suspension support to the damper shaft. Make sure all of the marks made in Step 4 are in alignment.

14 Install a new nut and tighten it to the torque listed in this Chapter's Specifications.

✳✳ CAUTION:

The manufacturer states that a new damper shaft nut must be installed.

15 Install the strut assembly following the procedure outlined in Section 2 (front), or the rear shock absorber/coil spring as described in Section 10.

4   Stabilizer bar and bushings (front) - removal and installation

✳✳ WARNING:

Make sure power to the hybrid system is turned Off before performing any work on this vehicle. Also, on models equipped with the Smart Key system, place the key in a secure spot at least 20 feet away from the work area.

REMOVAL

1 Loosen the front wheel lug nuts. Raise the front of the vehicle and support it securely on jackstands. Apply the parking brake and block the rear wheels to keep the vehicle from rolling off the stands. Remove the front wheels.

2001 through 2003 models

▶ Refer to illustrations 4.2 and 4.8

2 Detach the stabilizer bar links from the bar (see illustration). If the ballstud turns with the nut, use an Allen wrench to hold the stud.

4.2 Stabilizer bar link nuts

3 Remove the engine bottom cover.

4 Disconnect the tie-rod ends from the steering knuckles (see Section 15).

5 Disconnect the control arms from the balljoints (see Section 5).

6 Paint match marks, loosen the pinch bolt, then disconnect the steering shaft at the slide joint (see Section 17).

7 Support the subframe with two floor jacks.

8 Disconnect the engine torque strut from the suspension crossmember (see illustration).

9 Remove the four crossmember mounting bolts, then use the jacks to carefully lower the crossmember.

10 Remove the stabilizer bar bracket bolts and detach the stabilizer bar from the crossmember.

2004 and later models

11 Disconnect both stabilizer bar links (see illustration 4.2). If the ballstud turns with the nut, use an Allen wrench to hold the stud.

12 Refer to Section 17 and remove the steering gear.

13 Slide the stabilizer bar out the right side of the vehicle.

All models

14 While the stabilizer bar is off the vehicle, slide off the bushings and inspect them. If they're cracked, worn or deteriorated, replace them. It's also a good idea to inspect the stabilizer bar links.

15 Clean the bushing area of the stabilizer bar with a stiff wire brush to remove any rust or dirt.

INSTALLATION

16 Lubricate the inside and outside of the new bushing with vegetable oil (used in cooking) to simplify reassembly.

❋❋ CAUTION:

Don't use petroleum or mineral-based lubricants or brake fluid - they will lead to deterioration of the bushings.

17 Installation is the reverse of removal. Tighten all fasteners to the torque values listed in this Chapter's Specifications.

➡**Note: When installing the subframe on 2001 through 2003 models, use a rod of the same diameter as the four subframe-to-chassis bolts to align each side until that side's bolts can be inserted one at a time. Do not tighten any of the four bolts until all have been installed finger tight, then tighten them to the Specifications in this Chapter.**

4.8 Remove the bolt that attaches the torque strut to the crossmember

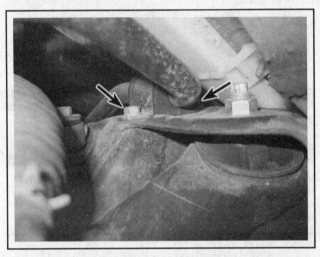

4.13 View of the stabilizer bar clamp fasteners - make sure to inspect the rubber bushings after you've removed the bar

18 Install the wheel and lug nuts, lower the vehicle and tighten the lug nuts to the torque listed in the Chapter 1 Specifications.

19 It's a good idea to have the front wheel alignment checked, and if necessary, adjusted after this job has been performed.

5 Control arm - removal, inspection and installation

❋❋ WARNING:

Make sure power to the hybrid system is turned Off before performing any work on this vehicle. Also, on models equipped with the Smart Key system, place the key in a secure spot at least 20 feet away from the work area.

REMOVAL

▶ Refer to illustration 5.4

1 Loosen the wheel lug nuts on the side to be disassembled.

2 Apply the parking brake, raise the front of the vehicle, support it securely on jackstands and remove the wheel.

3   Separate the balljoint from the control arm (see Section 6).

4   Remove the bolts that attach the control arm to the subframe (see illustration).

➡**Note: On 2004 and later models, the subframe assembly may need to be lowered for easier access to the control arm rear mounting bolt and nut.**

5   Remove the control arm.

INSPECTION

6   Check the control arm for distortion and the bushings for wear, replacing parts as necessary. Do not attempt to straighten a bent control arm.

INSTALLATION

7   Installation is the reverse of removal. Tighten all of the fasteners to the torque values listed in this Chapter's Specifications, but don't tighten the front pivot bolt until the outer end of the control arm has been raised with a floor jack to simulate normal ride height.

8   Install the wheel and lug nuts, lower the vehicle and tighten the

5.4 Remove the control arm mounting bolts

lug nuts to the torque listed in the Chapter 1 Specifications.

9   It's a good idea to have the front wheel alignment checked, and if necessary, adjusted after this job has been performed.

6   Balljoint - replacement

▸ **Refer to illustrations 6.2 and 6.4**

❄❄ **WARNING:**

Make sure power to the hybrid system is turned Off before performing any work on this vehicle. Also, on models equipped with the Smart Key system, place the key in a secure spot at least 20 feet away from the work area.

1   Loosen the wheel lug nuts, raise the vehicle and support it securely on jackstands. Remove the wheel.

2   Remove the cotter pin from the balljoint stud and loosen the nut (but don't remove it yet) (see illustration).

3   Separate the balljoint from the steering knuckle with a picklefork-

type balljoint separator. Remove the balljoint stud nut. The clearance between the balljoint stud and the CV joint is very tight. To remove the stud nut, you'll have to alternately back off the nut a turn or two, pull down the stud, turn the nut another turn or two, etc. until the nut is off.

4   Remove the bolt and nuts securing the balljoint to the control arm (see illustration), then separate the balljoint from the control arm with a prybar.

5   To install the balljoint, insert the balljoint stud through the hole in the steering knuckle and install the nut, but don't tighten it yet. Don't push the balljoint stud all the way up into and through the hole; instead, thread the nut onto the stud as soon as the stud protrudes through the hole, then turn the nut to draw the stud up through the hole.

6   Attach the balljoint to the control arm and install the bolt and

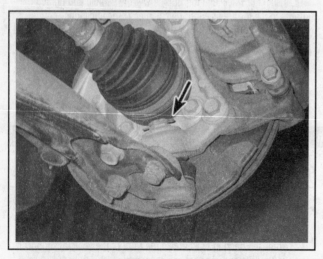

6.2 Remove the cotter pin from the lower balljoint and back the nut off a few threads

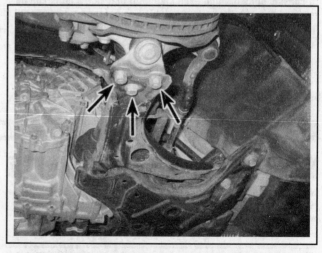

6.4 The lower control arm is secured to the balljoint with three fasteners

nuts, tightening them to the torque listed in this Chapter's Specifications.

7   Tighten the balljoint stud nut to the torque listed in this Chapter's Specifications and install a new cotter pin. If the cotter pin hole doesn't line up with the slots on the nut, tighten the nut additionally until it does line up - don't loosen the nut to insert the cotter pin.

8   Install the wheel and lug nuts. Lower the vehicle and tighten the lug nuts to the torque listed in the Chapter 1 Specifications.

7   Steering knuckle and hub - removal and installation

⁂ WARNING 1:

Dust created by the brake system is harmful to your health. Never blow it out with compressed air and don't inhale any of it. Do not, under any circumstances, use petroleum-based solvents to clean brake parts. Use brake system cleaner only.

⁂ WARNING 2:

Make sure power to the hybrid system is turned Off before performing any work on this vehicle. Also, on models equipped with the Smart Key system, place the key in a secure spot at least 20 feet away from the work area.

REMOVAL

▶ **Refer to illustration 7.3**

1   Loosen the wheel lug nuts and the driveaxle/hub nut. Raise the vehicle and support it securely on jackstands, then remove the wheel.

2   Remove the brake caliper (don't disconnect the hose) and the brake disc (see Chapter 9), then disconnect the brake hose from the strut. Hang the caliper from the coil spring with a piece of wire - don't let it hang by the brake hose.

3   Remove the wheel speed sensor (see illustration).

4   Mark the relationship of the strut to the steering knuckle (see illustration 2.5a). Loosen, but don't remove the strut-to-steering knuckle nuts and bolts (see Section 2).

5   Separate the tie-rod end from the steering knuckle arm (see Section 15).

6   Remove the balljoint-to-lower arm bolt and nuts.

7   Remove the driveaxle/hub nut and push the driveaxle from the hub as described in Chapter 8. Support the end of the driveaxle with a piece of wire.

8   Since the axle is out in this case, you can use a balljoint removal tool or a small puller to remove the balljoint from the steering knuckle.

➡**Note: If you're removing the steering knuckle to replace the hub bearings, and the balljoint is in good condition, the balljoint can remain attached.**

9   The strut-to-knuckle bolts can now be removed.

10 Separate the steering knuckle from the strut.

INSTALLATION

11 If you removed the balljoint from the old knuckle, and are planning to use it with the new knuckle, connect the balljoint to the knuckle and tighten the balljoint stud nut to the torque listed in this Chapter's Specifications. Install a new cotter pin.

12 Guide the knuckle and hub assembly into position, inserting the driveaxle into the hub.

13 Push the knuckle into the strut flange and install the bolts and nuts, but don't tighten them yet.

14 Attach the balljoint to the control arm, but don't tighten the bolt and nuts yet.

15 Attach the tie-rod to the steering knuckle arm (see Section 15). Tighten the strut bolt nuts, the balljoint-to-control arm bolt and nuts and the tie-rod nut to the torque listed in this Chapter's Specifications.

16 Place the brake disc on the hub and install the caliper as outlined in Chapter 9.

17 Install the driveaxle/hub nut and tighten it to the torque listed in the Chapter 8 Specifications.

18 Install the wheel and lug nuts. Lower the vehicle and tighten the lug nuts to the torque listed in the Chapter 1 Specifications.

19 It's a good idea to have the front wheel alignment checked, and if necessary, adjusted after this job has been performed.

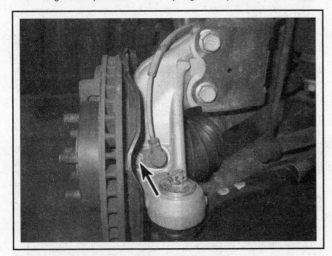

7.3 Remove the wheel speed sensor mounting bolt, then remove the sensor from the steering knuckle

8   Hub and bearing assembly (front) - removal and installation

Due to the special tools and expertise required to press the hub and bearing from the steering knuckle, this job should be left to a professional shop. However, the steering knuckle and hub may be removed and the assembly taken to an automotive machine shop or other qualified repair facility equipped with the necessary tools. See Section 7 for the steering knuckle and hub removal procedure.

9 Stabilizer bar and bushings (rear) - removal and installation

♦ Refer to illustration 9.2

⁕⁕ WARNING:

Make sure power to the hybrid system is turned Off before performing any work on this vehicle. Also, on models equipped with the Smart Key system, place the key in a secure spot at least 20 feet away from the work area.

1 Loosen the rear wheel lug nuts. Raise the rear of the vehicle and place it securely on jackstands.
2 Remove the stabilizer bar-to-axle beam bolts/nuts (see illustration).
3 On 2004 and later models, remove the damper from the center of the stabilizer bar.
4 Installation is the reverse of the removal procedure. When reinstalling the bar to the axle beam, look for a distinctive mark on the bar at one side. When properly installed, this mark will be on the right side of the vehicle.
5 Tighten the bolts/nuts to the Specifications listed in this Chapter.

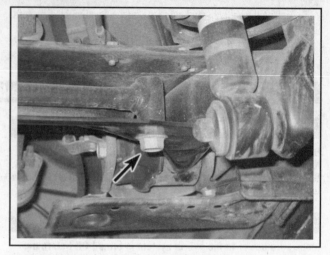

9.2 Remove the fasteners securing the ends of the stabilizer bar

10 Shock absorber/coil spring assembly (rear) - removal, inspection and installation

⁕⁕ WARNING 1:

This procedure involves working around the high-voltage battery, failure to follow the precautions outlined in Chapter 5, Section 2 can result in vehicle damage or destruction, personal injury or death!

⁕⁕ WARNING 2:

Make sure power to the hybrid system is turned Off before performing any work on this vehicle. Also, on models equipped with the Smart Key system, place the key in a secure spot at least 20 feet away from the work area.

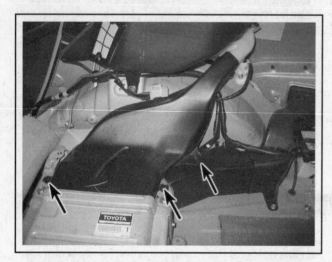

10.10 Remove the push-pin fasteners, then remove the duct

➡Note: Shock absorber/coil spring assemblies should only be replaced in pairs.

REMOVAL

1 Remove the safety plug from the high-voltage battery (see Chapter 5, Section 2).
2 Raise the rear of the vehicle and support it securely on jackstands. Remove the rear wheels.

2003 and earlier models

3 Refer to Chapter 11 and remove the rear seat.
4 Disconnect the speed sensor wire from the axle only if it interferes with shock removal.
5 Put jacks (with wood blocks on top) under the rear of each end of the rear axle to support it.
6 Remove the upper three fasteners from the shock absorber.
7 Remove the nut and washers from the lower mounts and guide the shocks out.

2004 and later models

♦ Refer to illustrations 10.10, 10.11, 10.13a, 10.13b and 10.14

8 Remove the rear seat back framework (see Chapter 11).
9 Remove the right side trim panel. This requires removal of the luggage tie-down striker, two bolts and eight clips.
10 Unclip the three retainers and remove the battery cooling duct (see illustration).
11 Remove the high-voltage battery reinforcement (see illustration).
12 Put a jack (with a wood block on top) under the center of the rear axle to support it.

13 Remove the upper three fasteners from the shock absorber (see illustrations).

14 Remove the nut and washers from the lower mounts and guide the shocks out (see illustration).

All models

INSPECTION

15 Follow the inspection procedures described in Section 3. If you determine that the shock absorber assembly must be disassembled for replacement of the shock body or the coil spring, refer to Section 3.

INSTALLATION

16 Maneuver the assembly up into the fenderwell, install the lower mount onto the stud and guide the upper mounting studs into the holes in the body. Install the bolt from below, tightening it to the torque listed in this Chapter's Specifications.

17 Install the lower washer and nut. Raise the axle beam with the floor jack to simulate normal ride height, then tighten the nut to the torque listed in this Chapter's Specifications.

18 Install the upper mounting nuts and tighten them to the torque listed in this Chapter's Specifications.

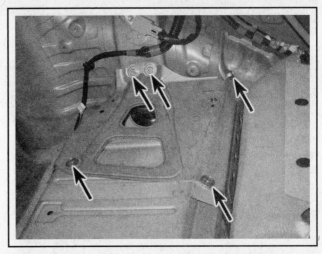

10.11 Remove the fasteners securing the high-voltage battery reinforcement, to access the left side shock upper mounting fasteners

19 The remainder of installation is the reverse of removal.

20 Install the wheel and lug nuts. Lower the vehicle and tighten the lug nuts to the torque listed in the Chapter 1 Specifications.

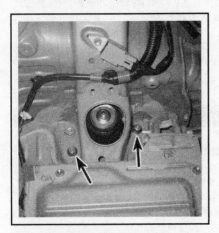

10.13a Remove the two upper mounting bolts . . .

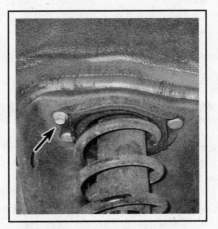

10.13b . . . then remove the one remaining fastener from inside the wheel opening

10.14 Remove the nut and washers from the lower mount

11 Hub and bearing assembly (rear) - removal and installation

❋❋ WARNING:

Dust created by the brake system is harmful to your health. Never blow it out with compressed air and don't inhale any of it. Do not, under any circumstances, use petroleum-based solvents to clean brake parts. Use brake system cleaner only.

❋❋ WARNING:

Make sure power to the hybrid system is turned Off before performing any work on this vehicle. Also, on models equipped with the Smart Key system, place the key in a secure spot at least 20 feet away from the work area.

REMOVAL

◆ Refer to illustration 11.4

1 Loosen the wheel lug nuts, raise the vehicle and support it securely on jackstands. Remove the wheel.

2 Remove the brake drum (see Chapter 9). Disconnect the wheel speed sensor.

3 Remove the adjusting lever, the brake shoe adjuster and its spring.

4 Remove the four hub-to-axle beam bolts, accessed from behind the brake backing plate (see illustration).

5   Remove the hub and bearing assembly from its seat, maneuvering it out through the brake assembly.

6   If the hub exhibits looseness or excessive runout, the hub and bearing assembly must be replaced as a unit.

INSTALLATION

7   Position the hub and bearing assembly on the axle carrier and align the holes in the backing plate. After all four bolts have been installed, tighten them to the torque listed in this Chapter's Specifications.

8   Install the brake drum (and ABS sensor if equipped) and the wheel. Lower the vehicle and tighten the lug nuts to the torque listed in the Chapter 1 Specifications.

11.4 Rear hub bolt locations

12 Rear axle beam - removal and installation

Removal of the rear axle assembly involves disconnecting the brake lines at each rear wheel where they are attached to the rear axle. Because of the problems associated with the brake bleeding process on these vehicles, we recommend that the brake lines not be disconnected, and therefore that the rear axle not be removed by the home mechanic.

13 Steering system - general information

All models are equipped with rack-and-pinion steering. The steering gear operates the steering knuckles via tie-rods. The inner ends of the tie-rods are protected by rubber boots that should be inspected periodically for secure attachment, tears and leaking lubricant.

The power assist system is made up of an electric motor mounted to the steering gear on 2001 through 2003 models and higher on the steering shaft on later models.

The steering wheel operates the steering shaft, which actuates the steering gear through universal joints. Looseness in the steering can be caused by wear in the steering shaft universal joints, the steering gear, the tie-rod ends, or loose retaining bolts.

14 Steering wheel - removal and installation

❊❊ WARNING 1:

These models are equipped with airbags. Always disable the airbag system before working in the vicinity of any airbag system component to avoid the possibility of accidental deployment of the airbag(s), which could cause personal injury (see Chapter 12).

❊❊ WARNING 2:

Make sure power to the hybrid system is turned Off before performing any work on this vehicle. Also, on models equipped with the Smart Key system, place the key in a secure spot at least 20 feet away from the work area.

REMOVAL

▶ **Refer to illustrations 14.2, 14.3, 14.4a, 14.4b, 14.4c, 14.5, 14.6 and 14.7**

1   Refer to Chapter 6 and disconnect the cable from the negative terminal of the auxiliary 12-volt battery. Be sure to perform the initialization procedure when reconnecting it.

2   On 2004 and later models, remove the two steering wheel covers (see illustration).

3   Turn the steering wheel so the wheels are pointing straight ahead, then loosen the Torx screws that attach the airbag module to the steering wheel (see illustration). Loosen each screw until the groove in the

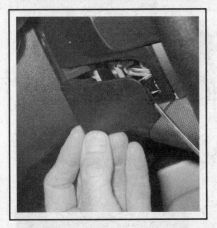

14.2 Use a screwdriver to pry the plastic covers from the sides of the steering wheel

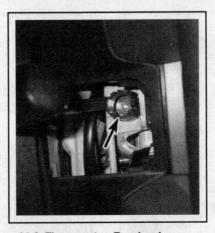

14.3 There are two Torx-head screws under the covers that must be removed

14.4a Carefully pull the assembly from the steering wheel . . .

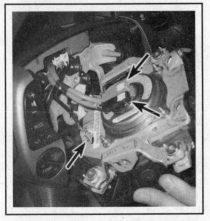

14.4b . . . turn it over to expose the wiring connections . . .

14.4c . . . use a small screwdriver to pry up the locks (center part)

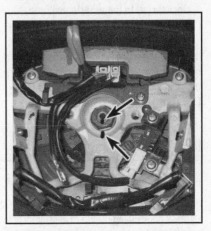

14.5 Mark the relationship of the steering wheel to the shaft with paint; it must be installed exactly as removed

circumference of the screw catches on the screw case.

4   Pull the airbag module off the steering wheel and disconnect the module electrical connectors (see illustrations). To disconnect the connectors, use a small screwdriver to pry up the locks (center part) (see

14.6 Use the proper puller to remove the steering wheel from the shaft

illustration), then disconnect the connectors. Set the airbag module in a safe, isolated area.

✸✸ WARNING:

Carry the airbag module with the trim side facing away from you, and set the airbag module down with the trim side facing up. Don't place anything on top of the airbag module.

5   Mark the relationship of the steering shaft to the hub (if marks don't already exist or don't line up) to simplify installation and ensure steering wheel alignment, then remove the steering wheel retaining nut (see illustration).

6   Use a puller to disconnect the steering wheel from the shaft (see illustration).

✸✸ WARNING:

Do not hammer on the shaft or the puller in an attempt to loosen the wheel from the shaft. Also, don't allow the steering shaft to turn with the steering wheel removed. If the shaft turns, the airbag spiral cable will become uncentered, which may cause the wire inside to break when the vehicle is returned to service.

14.7 Close-up of one of the three claws that retain the clockspring to the steering column

14.8 When the clockspring is centered, the mark will appear in this window

7   If it is necessary to remove the airbag clockspring, follow the clockspring wiring harness and unplug the electrical connector, then disengage the three claws and detach it from the combination switch (see illustration).

INSTALLATION

▶ **Refer to illustration 14.8**

8   Make sure that the front wheels are pointing straight ahead. Depress the lock tab or hub of the spiral cable and turn the spiral cable counterclockwise by hand until it stops (don't apply too much force). Rotate the cable clockwise about 2-1/2 turns and align the two pointers that are visible in the clear window on the left side of the column (see illustration).

9   To install the wheel, align the mark on the steering wheel hub with the mark on the shaft and slip the wheel onto the shaft. Install the nut and tighten it to the torque listed in this Chapter's Specifications.

10   Plug in the cruise control connector.

11   Plug in the electrical connectors for the airbag module and press down the locking tab.

12   Make sure the airbag module electrical connector is positioned correctly and that the wires don't interfere with anything, then install the airbag module and tighten the retaining screws to the torque listed in this Chapter's Specifications.

13   Connect the negative battery cable. Be sure to perform the initialization procedure when reconnecting it (see Chapter 6).

15 Tie-rod ends - removal and installation

REMOVAL

▶ **Refer to illustrations 15.2, 15.3a, 15.3b and 15.4**

✳✳ WARNING:

Make sure power to the hybrid system is turned Off before performing any work on this vehicle. Also, on models equipped with the Smart Key system, place the key in a secure spot at least 20 feet away from the work area.

1   Loosen the wheel lug nuts. Raise the front of the vehicle, support it securely on jackstands, block the rear wheels and set the parking brake. Remove the front wheel.

2   Remove the cotter pin and loosen the nut on the tie-rod end stud (see illustration).

3   Hold the tie-rod with a pair of locking pliers or wrench and loosen the jam nut enough to mark the position of the tie-rod end in relation to the threads (see illustrations).

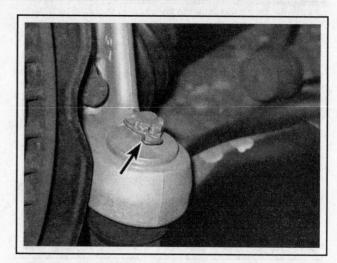

15.2 Remove the cotter pin from the tie-rod stud

15.3a Hold the tie-rod with a wrench on its flats while loosening the lock-nut

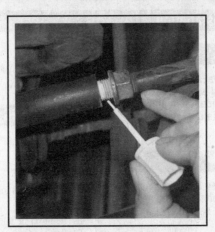

15.3b Mark the position of the tie-rod end with a dab of paint before removing it

15.4 Use a special puller to avoid damage to the components

4   Disconnect the tie-rod from the steering knuckle arm with a puller (see illustration). Remove the nut and detach the tie-rod.

5   Unscrew the tie-rod end from the tie-rod.

INSTALLATION

6   Thread the tie-rod end on to the marked position and insert the tie-rod stud into the steering knuckle arm. Tighten the jam nut securely.

7   Install the castle nut on the stud and tighten it to the torque listed in this Chapter's Specifications. Install a new cotter pin. If the hole for the cotter pin doesn't line up with one of the slots in the nut, turn the nut an additional amount until it does.

8   Install the wheel and lug nuts. Lower the vehicle and tighten the lug nuts to the torque listed in the Chapter 1 Specifications.

9   Have the alignment checked and, if necessary, adjusted.

16 Steering gear boots - replacement

▶ Refer to illustration 16.3

✳✳ WARNING:

Make sure power to the hybrid system is turned Off before performing any work on this vehicle. Also, on models equipped with the Smart Key system, place the key in a secure spot at least 20 feet away from the work area.

1   Loosen the lug nuts, raise the vehicle and support it securely on jackstands. Remove the wheel.

2   Remove the tie-rod end and jam nut (see Section 15).

3   Remove the outer steering gear boot clamp with a pair of pliers. Cut off the inner boot clamp with a pair of diagonal cutters (see illustration). Slide off the boot.

4   Before installing the new boot, wrap the threads and serrations on the end of the steering rod with a layer of tape so the small end of the new boot isn't damaged.

5   Slide the new boot into position on the steering gear until it seats in the groove in the steering rod, then install new clamps.

6   Remove the tape and install the tie-rod end (see Section 15).

7   Install the wheel and lug nuts. Lower the vehicle and tighten the lug nuts to the torque listed in the Chapter 1 Specifications.

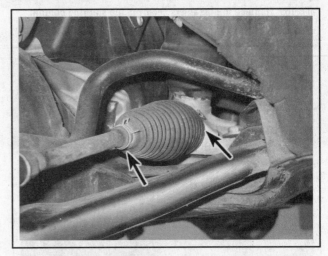

16.3 Steering gear boot clamps are on each end of the boot

17 Steering gear - removal and installation

✳✳ WARNING 1:

These models are equipped with airbags. Always disable the airbag system before working in the vicinity of any airbag system component to avoid the possibility of accidental deployment of the airbag(s), which could cause personal injury (see Chapter 12).

✳✳ WARNING 2:

Make sure power to the hybrid system is turned Off before performing any work on this vehicle. Also, on models equipped with the Smart Key system, place the key in a secure spot at least 20 feet away from the work area.

1 Refer to Chapter 6 and disconnect the cable from the negative terminal of the auxiliary 12-volt battery. Be sure to perform the initialization procedure when reconnecting it.

2 Aim the front wheels straight ahead.

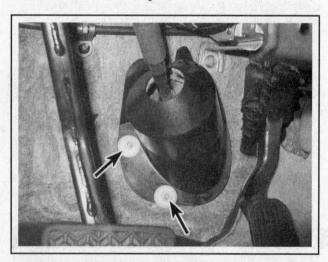

17.16a Remove the fasteners securing the steering column cover, then slide the cover up

17.16b Paint match marks on the steering shaft and joint

3 Pass the seat belt through the steering wheel and click it into its latch (this is to prevent the steering wheel from turning while the steering gear is removed, which could damage the airbag clockspring).

✳✳ WARNING:

Do not allow the steering wheel to turn while the steering gear is removed.

4 Raise the vehicle and support it securely on jackstands. Remove the front wheels.

5 Remove the engine bottom covers.

6 Refer to Section 15 and disconnect the tie-rod ends from the steering knuckles.

2001 THROUGH 2003 MODELS

7 Disconnect the stabilizer bar from the end links.

8 Disconnect the lower control arms from the balljoints.

9 Disconnect the wiring and the EMPS bracket.

10 Make match marks on the steering shaft joint, remove the bolt and disconnect the intermediate steering shaft from the control valve shaft.

11 Disconnect the engine torque rod from the crossmember (see illustration 4.8).

12 Place a floor jack (with a block of wood on top) under the crossmember, remove the crossmember mounting bolts, then carefully lower the crossmember assembly.

13 Remove the stabilizer bar.

14 Unbolt the steering gear from the crossmember and lift it off.

2004 AND LATER MODELS

▶ **Refer to illustrations 17.16a, 17.16b and 17.17**

15 Remove both stabilizer bar links (see illustration 4.2), then

17.17 Steering gear mounting bolt locations (not all fasteners visible in photo)

remove the fasteners securing the stabilizer bar brackets.

16 Slide the steering column cover up and paint match marks on the steering shaft and joint (see illustrations), then disconnect the intermediate shaft.

17 Remove the four steering gear mounting bolts and slide the gear out the driver's side of the vehicle (see illustration).

ALL MODELS

18 Installation is the reverse of removal, noting the following points:

a) *Tighten all steering and suspension fasteners to the torque listed in this Chapter's Specifications.*

b) *Install the wheels and lug nuts. Lower the vehicle and tighten the lug nuts to the torque listed in the Chapter 1 Specifications.*

18 Wheel studs - replacement

✳✳ WARNING:

Make sure power to the hybrid system is turned Off before performing any work on this vehicle. Also, on models equipped with the Smart Key system, place the key in a secure spot at least 20 feet away from the work area.

➡**Note: This procedure applies to both the front and rear wheel studs.**

1 Loosen the wheel lug nuts, raise the vehicle and support it securely on jackstands. Remove the wheel.

2 Remove the brake disc or drum (see Chapter 9).

3 Install a lug nut part way onto the stud being replaced. Push the stud out of the hub flange with a press tool.

4 Insert the new stud into the hub flange from the back side and install some flat washers and a lug nut on the stud.

5 Tighten the lug nut until the stud is seated in the flange.

6 Reinstall the brake drum or disc. Install the wheel and lug nuts. Lower the vehicle and tighten the lug nuts to the torque listed in the Chapter 1 Specifications.

19 Wheels and tires - general information

▶ **Refer to illustration 19.1**

1 All vehicles covered by this manual are equipped with metric-sized steel belted radial tires (see illustration). Use of other size or type of tires may affect the ride and handling of the vehicle. Don't mix different types of tires, such as radials and bias belted on the same vehicle, as handling may be seriously affected. It's recommended that tires be replaced in pairs on the same axle, but if only one tire is being replaced, be sure it's the same size, structure and tread design as the other.

2 Because tire pressure has a substantial effect on handling and wear, the pressure on all tires should be checked at least once a month or before any extended trips (see Chapter 1).

3 Wheels must be replaced if they are bent, dented, leak air, have elongated bolt holes, are heavily rusted, out of vertical symmetry or if the lug nuts won't stay tight. Wheel repairs that use welding or peening are not recommended.

4 Tire and wheel balance is important in the overall handling, braking and performance of the vehicle. Unbalanced wheels can adversely affect handling and ride characteristics as well as tire life. Whenever a tire is installed on a wheel, the tire and wheel should be balanced by a shop with the proper equipment.

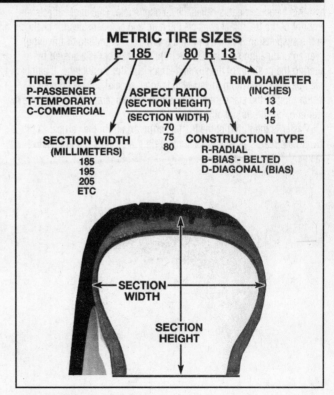

19.1 Metric tire size code

20 Wheel alignment - general information

▶ **Refer to illustration 20.1**

A wheel alignment refers to the adjustments made to the wheels so they are in proper angular relationship to the suspension and the ground. Wheels that are out of proper alignment not only affect vehicle control, but also increase tire wear. The alignment angles normally measured are camber, caster and toe-in (see illustration). Toe-in and camber are the only adjustable angles on the front. Caster should be measured to check for bent or worn suspension parts. Camber and toe-in should be measured on the rear to check for a bent axle.

Getting the proper wheel alignment is a very exacting process, one in which complicated and expensive machines are necessary to perform the job properly. Because of this, you should have a technician with the proper equipment perform these tasks. We will, however, use this space to give you a basic idea of what is involved with a wheel alignment so you can better understand the process and deal intelligently with the shop that does the work.

Toe-in is the turning in of the wheels. The purpose of a toe specification is to ensure parallel rolling of the wheels. In a vehicle with zero toe-in, the distance between the front edges of the wheels will be the same as the distance between the rear edges of the wheels. The actual amount of toe-in is normally only a fraction of an inch. On the front end, toe-in is controlled by the tie-rod end position on the tie-rod. On the rear end, it's not adjustable. Incorrect toe-in will cause the tires to wear improperly by making them scrub against the road surface.

Camber is the tilting of the wheels from vertical when viewed from one end of the vehicle. When the wheels tilt out at the top, the camber is said to be positive (+). When the wheels tilt in at the top the camber is negative (-). The amount of tilt is measured in degrees from vertical and this measurement is called the camber angle. This angle affects the amount of tire tread that contacts the road and compensates for changes in the suspension geometry when the vehicle is cornering or traveling over an undulating surface. On the front end, camber is adjusted by altering the position of the steering knuckle in the strut flange. If camber can't be adjusted within the specified range, special adjuster bolts, which replace the standard strut-to-knuckle bolts, are available. On the rear end, camber is not adjustable.

Caster is the tilting of the front steering axis from the vertical. A tilt toward the rear is positive caster and a tilt toward the front is negative caster.

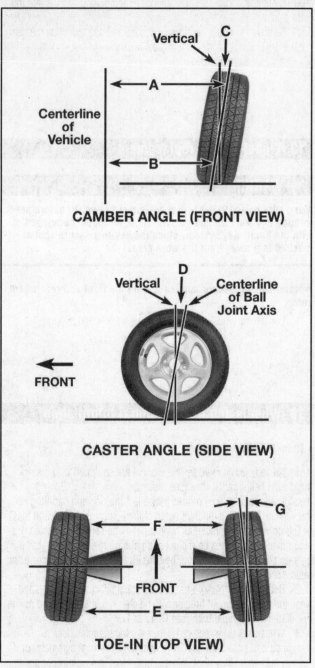

CAMBER ANGLE (FRONT VIEW)

CASTER ANGLE (SIDE VIEW)

TOE-IN (TOP VIEW)

20.1 Camber, caster and toe-in angles

A minus B = C (degrees camber)
D = degrees caster
E minus F = toe-in (measured in inches)
G = toe-in (expressed in degrees)

Specifications

Torque specifications	Ft-lbs (unless otherwise indicated)

Front suspension

Balljoints	
Balljoint-to-control arm bolt/nuts	
2003 and earlier models	105
2004 and later models	66
Balljoint-to-steering knuckle nut	
2003 and earlier models	76
2005 and later models	52
Control arm-to-crossmember bolts	101
Stabilizer bar	
Bracket-to-crossmember bolts	168 in-lbs
Link nuts	55
Struts	
Strut-to-steering knuckle bolts/nuts	113
Strut upper mounting nuts	29
Damper shaft nut	34
Subframe crossmember bolts	
Front bolts	83
Rear bolts	116
Torque rod bolt/nut	83

Rear suspension

Hub and bearing assembly-to-rear axle carrier bolts	
2003 and earlier models	38
2004 and later models	45
Stabilizer bar-to-axle bolts	110
Shock absorber/coil spring assembly	
Lower mounting nut	59
Upper mounting nuts/bolt	59
Damper shaft nut	41

Steering

Airbag module Torx screws	78 in-lbs
Steering gear-to-crossmember bolts	
2003 and earlier models	61
2004 and later models	43
Steering wheel nut	37
Tie-rod end-to-steering knuckle nut	36
U-joint-to-pinion shaft pinch bolt	26

Notes

Section

11

BODY

1 General information

The models covered by this manual feature a unibody construction, using a floor pan with front and rear frame side rails which support the body components, front and rear suspension systems and other mechanical components. Certain components are particularly vulnerable to accident damage and can be unbolted and repaired or replaced.

Among these parts are the body moldings, bumpers, hood and trunk lid/liftgate and all glass.

Only general body maintenance practices and body panel repair procedures within the scope of the do-it-yourselfer are included in this Chapter.

2 Body - maintenance

1 The condition of your vehicle's body is very important, because the resale value depends a great deal on it. It's much more difficult to repair a neglected or damaged body than it is to repair mechanical components. The hidden areas of the body, such as the wheel wells, the frame and the engine compartment, are equally important, although they don't require as frequent attention as the rest of the body.

2 Once a year, or every 12,000 miles, it's a good idea to have the underside of the body steam cleaned. All traces of dirt and oil will be removed and the area can then be inspected carefully for rust, damaged brake lines, frayed electrical wires, damaged cables and other problems. The front suspension components should be greased after completion of this job.

3 At the same time, clean the engine and the engine compartment with a steam cleaner or water-soluble degreaser.

4 The wheel wells should be given close attention, since undercoating can peel away and stones and dirt thrown up by the tires can cause the paint to chip and flake, allowing rust to set in. If rust is found, clean down to the bare metal and apply an anti-rust paint.

5 The body should be washed about once a week. Wet the vehicle thoroughly to soften the dirt, and then wash it down with a soft sponge and plenty of clean soapy water. If the surplus dirt is not washed off very carefully, it can wear down the paint.

6 Spots of tar or asphalt thrown up from the road should be removed with a cloth soaked in solvent.

7 Once every six months, wax the body and chrome trim. If chrome cleaner is used to remove rust from any of the vehicle's plated parts, remember that the cleaner also removes part of the chrome, so use it sparingly.

3 Vinyl trim - maintenance

Don't clean vinyl trim with detergents, caustic soap or petroleum-based cleaners. Plain soap and water works just fine, with a soft brush to clean dirt that may be ingrained. Wash the vinyl as frequently as the rest of the vehicle.

After cleaning, application of a high quality rubber and vinyl protectant will help prevent oxidation and cracks. The protectant can also be applied to weather-stripping, vacuum lines and rubber hoses, which often fail as a result of chemical degradation, and to the tires.

4 Upholstery and carpets - maintenance

1 Every three months remove the carpets or mats and clean the interior of the vehicle (more frequently if necessary). Vacuum the upholstery and carpets to remove loose dirt and dust.

2 Leather upholstery requires special care. Stains should be removed with warm water and a very mild soap solution. Use a clean, damp cloth to remove the soap, then wipe again with a dry cloth. Never use alcohol, gasoline, nail polish remover or thinner to clean leather upholstery.

3 After cleaning, regularly treat leather upholstery with a leather wax. Never use car wax on leather upholstery.

4 In areas where the interior of the vehicle is subject to bright sunlight, cover leather seats with a sheet if the vehicle is to be left out for any length of time.

5 Body repair - minor damage

▶ **See photo sequence**

REPAIR OF MINOR SCRATCHES

1 If the scratch is superficial and does not penetrate to the metal of the body, repair is very simple. Lightly rub the scratched area with a fine rubbing compound to remove loose paint and built-up wax. Rinse the area with clean water.

2 Apply touch-up paint to the scratch, using a small brush. Continue to apply thin layers of paint until the surface of the paint in the scratch is level with the surrounding paint. Allow the new paint at least two weeks to harden, and then blend it into the surrounding paint by rubbing with a very fine rubbing compound. Finally, apply a coat of wax to the scratch area.

3 If the scratch has penetrated the paint and exposed the metal of the body, causing the metal to rust, a different repair technique is

required. Remove all loose rust from the bottom of the scratch with a pocket knife, then apply rust inhibiting paint to prevent the formation of rust in the future. Using a rubber or nylon applicator, coat the scratched area with glaze-type filler. If required, the filler can be mixed with thinner to provide a very thin paste, which is ideal for filling narrow scratches. Before the glaze filler in the scratch hardens, wrap a piece of smooth cotton cloth around the tip of a finger. Dip the cloth in thinner and then quickly wipe it along the surface of the scratch. This will ensure that the surface of the filler is slightly hollow. The scratch can now be painted over as described earlier in this section.

REPAIR OF DENTS

4   When repairing dents, the first job is to pull the dent out until the affected area is as close as possible to its original shape. There is no point in trying to restore the original shape completely as the metal in the damaged area will have stretched on impact and cannot be restored to its original contours. It is better to bring the level of the dent up to a point that is about 1/8-inch below the level of the surrounding metal. In cases where the dent is very shallow, it is not worth trying to pull it out at all.

5   If the back side of the dent is accessible, it can be hammered out gently from behind using a soft-face hammer. While doing this, hold a block of wood firmly against the opposite side of the metal to absorb the hammer blows and prevent the metal from being stretched.

6   If the dent is in a section of the body which has double layers, or some other factor makes it inaccessible from behind, a different technique is required. Drill several small holes through the metal inside the damaged area, particularly in the deeper sections. Screw long, self-tapping screws into the holes just enough for them to get a good grip in the metal. Now the dent can be pulled out by pulling on the protruding heads of the screws with locking pliers.

7   The next stage of repair is the removal of paint from the damaged area and from an inch or so of the surrounding metal. This is done with a wire brush or sanding disk in a drill motor, although it can be done just as effectively by hand with sandpaper. To complete the preparation for filling, score the surface of the bare metal with a screwdriver or the tang of a file, or drill small holes in the affected area. This will provide a good grip for the filler material. To complete the repair, see the subsection on filling and painting later in this Section.

REPAIR OF RUST HOLES OR GASHES

8   Remove all paint from the affected area and from an inch or so of the surrounding metal using a sanding disk or wire brush mounted in a drill motor. If these are not available, a few sheets of sandpaper will do the job just as effectively.

9   With the paint removed, you will be able to determine the severity of the corrosion and decide whether to replace the whole panel, if possible, or repair the affected area. New body panels are not as expensive as most people think and it is often quicker to install a new panel than to repair large areas of rust.

10   Remove all trim pieces from the affected area except those which will act as a guide to the original shape of the damaged body, such as headlight shells, etc. Using metal snips or a hacksaw blade, remove all loose metal and any other metal that is badly affected by rust. Hammer the edges of the hole in to create a slight depression for the filler material.

11   Wire brush the affected area to remove the powdery rust from the surface of the metal. If the back of the rusted area is accessible, treat it with rust inhibiting paint.

12   Before filling is done, block the hole in some way. This can be done with sheet metal riveted or screwed into place, or by stuffing the hole with wire mesh.

13   Once the hole is blocked off, the affected area can be filled and painted. See the following subsection on filling and painting.

FILLING AND PAINTING

14   Many types of body fillers are available, but generally speaking, body repair kits which contain filler paste and a tube of resin hardener are best for this type of repair work. A wide, flexible plastic or nylon applicator will be necessary for imparting a smooth and contoured finish to the surface of the filler material. Mix up a small amount of filler on a clean piece of wood or cardboard (use the hardener sparingly). Follow the manufacturer's instructions on the package, otherwise the filler will set incorrectly.

15   Using the applicator, apply the filler paste to the prepared area. Draw the applicator across the surface of the filler to achieve the desired contour and to level the filler surface. As soon as a contour that approximates the original one is achieved, stop working the paste. If you continue, the paste will begin to stick to the applicator. Continue to add thin layers of paste at 20-minute intervals until the level of the filler is just above the surrounding metal.

16   Once the filler has hardened, the excess can be removed with a body file. From then on, progressively finer grades of sandpaper should be used, starting with a 180-grit paper and finishing with 600-grit wet-or-dry paper. Always wrap the sandpaper around a flat rubber or wooden block, otherwise the surface of the filler will not be completely flat. During the sanding of the filler surface, the wet-or-dry paper should be periodically rinsed in water. This will ensure that a very smooth finish is produced in the final stage.

17   At this point, the repair area should be surrounded by a ring of bare metal, which in turn should be encircled by the finely feathered edge of good paint. Rinse the repair area with clean water until all of the dust produced by the sanding operation is gone.

18   Spray the entire area with a light coat of primer. This will reveal any imperfections in the surface of the filler. Repair the imperfections with fresh filler paste or glaze filler and once more smooth the surface with sandpaper. Repeat this spray-and-repair procedure until you are satisfied that the surface of the filler and the feathered edge of the paint are perfect. Rinse the area with clean water and allow it to dry completely.

19   The repair area is now ready for painting. Spray painting must be carried out in a warm, dry, windless and dust free atmosphere. These conditions can be created if you have access to a large indoor work area, but if you are forced to work in the open, you will have to pick the day very carefully. If you are working indoors, dousing the floor in the work area with water will help settle the dust that would otherwise be in the air. If the repair area is confined to one body panel, mask off the surrounding panels. This will help minimize the effects of a slight mismatch in paint color. Trim pieces such as chrome strips, door handles, etc., will also need to be masked off or removed. Use masking tape and several thickness of newspaper for the masking operations.

20   Before spraying, shake the paint can thoroughly, then spray a test area until the spray painting technique is mastered. Cover the repair area with a thick coat of primer. The thickness should be built up using several thin layers of primer rather than one thick one. Using 600-grit wet-or-dry sandpaper, rub down the surface of the primer until it is very smooth. While doing this, the work area should be thoroughly rinsed with water and the wet-or-dry sandpaper periodically rinsed as well. Allow the primer to dry before spraying additional coats.

These photos illustrate a method of repairing simple dents. They are intended to supplement Body repair - minor damage in this Chapter and should not be used as the sole instructions for body repair on these vehicles.

1 If you can't access the backside of the body panel to hammer out the dent, pull it out with a slide-hammer-type dent puller. In the deepest portion of the dent or along the crease line, drill or punch hole(s) at least one inch apart . . .

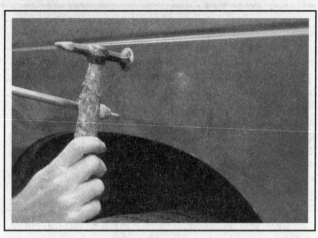

2 . . . then screw the slide-hammer into the hole and operate it. Tap with a hammer near the edge of the dent to help 'pop' the metal back to its original shape. When you're finished, the dent area should be close to its original contour and about 1/8-inch below the surface of the surrounding metal

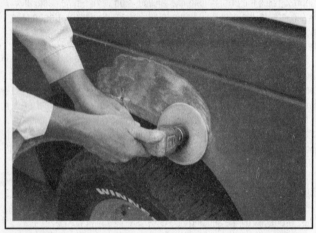

3 Using coarse-grit sandpaper, remove the paint down to the bare metal. Hand sanding works fine, but the disc sander shown here makes the job faster. Use finer (about 320-grit) sandpaper to feather-edge the paint at least one inch around the dent area

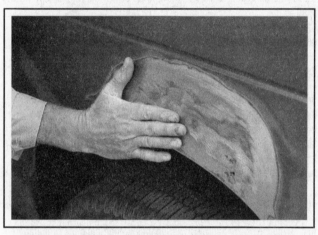

4 When the paint is removed, touch will probably be more helpful than sight for telling if the metal is straight. Hammer down the high spots or raise the low spots as necessary. Clean the repair area with wax/silicone remover

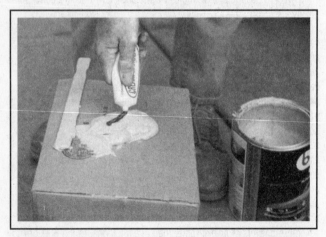

5 Following label instructions, mix up a batch of plastic filler and hardener. The ratio of filler to hardener is critical, and, if you mix it incorrectly, it will either not cure properly or cure too quickly (you won't have time to file and sand it into shape)

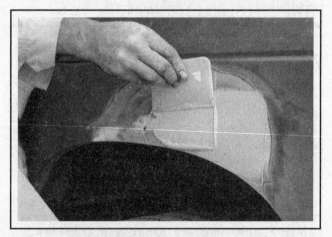

6 Working quickly so the filler doesn't harden, use a plastic applicator to press the body filler firmly into the metal, assuring it bonds completely. Work the filler until it matches the original contour and is slightly above the surrounding metal

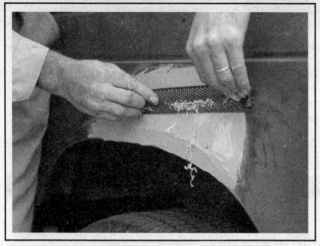

7 Let the filler harden until you can just dent it with your fingernail. Use a body file or Surform tool (shown here) to rough-shape the filler

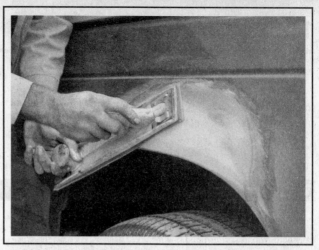

8 Use coarse-grit sandpaper and a sanding board or block to work the filler down until it's smooth and even. Work down to finer grits of sandpaper - always using a board or block - ending up with 360 or 400 grit

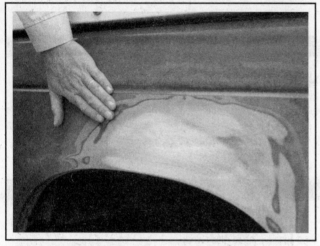

9 You shouldn't be able to feel any ridge at the transition from the filler to the bare metal or from the bare metal to the old paint. As soon as the repair is flat and uniform, remove the dust and mask off the adjacent panels or trim pieces

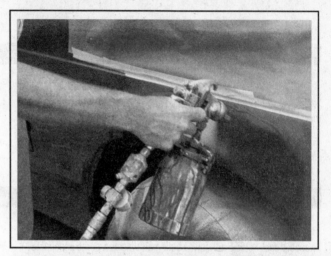

10 Apply several layers of primer to the area. Don't spray the primer on too heavy, so it sags or runs, and make sure each coat is dry before you spray on the next one. A professional-type spray gun is being used here, but aerosol spray primer is available inexpensively from auto parts stores

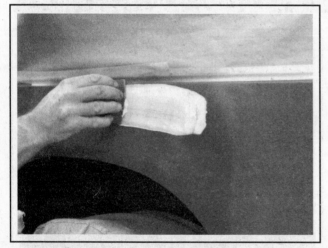

11 The primer will help reveal imperfections or scratches. Fill these with glazing compound. Follow the label instructions and sand it with 360 or 400-grit sandpaper until it's smooth. Repeat the glazing, sanding and respraying until the primer reveals a perfectly smooth surface

12 Finish sand the primer with very fine sandpaper (400 or 600-grit) to remove the primer overspray. Clean the area with water and allow it to dry. Use a tack rag to remove any dust, then apply the finish coat. Don't attempt to rub out or wax the repair area until the paint has dried completely (at least two weeks)

21 Spray on the top coat, again building up the thickness by using several thin layers of paint. Begin spraying in the center of the repair area and then, using a circular motion, work out until the whole repair area and about two inches of the surrounding original paint is covered.

Remove all masking material 10 to 15 minutes after spraying on the final coat of paint. Allow the new paint at least two weeks to harden, then use a very fine rubbing compound to blend the edges of the new paint into the existing paint. Finally, apply a coat of wax.

6 Body repair - major damage

1 Major damage must be repaired by an auto body shop specifically equipped to perform unibody repairs. These shops have the specialized equipment required to do the job properly.

2 If the damage is extensive, the body must be checked for proper alignment or the vehicle's handling characteristics may be adversely affected and other components may wear at an accelerated rate.

3 Due to the fact that all of the major body components (hood, fenders, etc.) are separate and replaceable units, any seriously damaged components should be replaced rather than repaired. Sometimes the components can be found in a wrecking yard that specializes in used vehicle components, often at considerable savings over the cost of new parts.

7 Hinges and locks - maintenance

Once every 3000 miles, or every three months, the hinges and latch assemblies on the doors, hood and trunk should be given a few drops of light oil or lock lubricant. The door latch strikers should also

be lubricated with a thin coat of grease to reduce wear and ensure free movement. Lubricate the door and trunk locks with spray-on graphite lubricant.

8 Windshield and fixed glass - replacement

Replacement of the windshield and fixed glass requires the use of special fast-setting adhesive/caulk materials and some specialized

tools. It is recommended that these operations be left to a dealer or a shop specializing in glass work.

9 Hood - removal, installation and adjustment

✳✳ WARNING:

Make sure power to the hybrid system is turned Off before performing any work on this vehicle. Also, on models equipped with the Smart Key system, place the key in a secure spot at least 20 feet away from the work area.

➡Note: The hood is heavy and awkward to remove and install - at least two people should perform this procedure.

REMOVAL AND INSTALLATION

▶ Refer to illustrations 9.1 and 9.5

1 Make marks around the hinge plate to ensure proper alignment during installation (see illustration).

2 Use blankets or pads to cover the cowl area of the body and fenders. This will protect the body and paint as the hood is lifted off.

3 Disconnect the windshield washer hose.

9.1 Mark the exact position of the hood hinges before removing the bolts

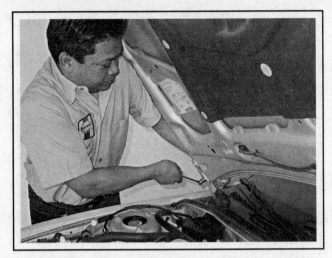

9.5 Support the hood with your shoulder while removing the hood bolts

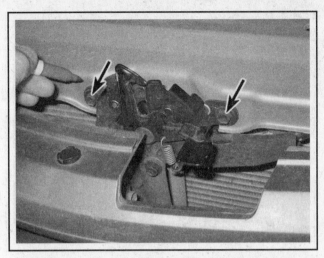

9.10 Draw a line around the hood latch and mounting bolts, then loosen the bolts to adjust the hood latch horizontally or vertically

4   Have an assistant support one side of the hood while you support the other. Simultaneously remove the hinge-to-hood bolts (see illustration).

5   Lift off the hood.

6   Installation is the reverse of removal.

ADJUSTMENT

▶ **Refer to illustrations 9.10 and 9.11**

7   Fore-and-aft and side-to-side adjustment of the hood is done by moving the hinge plate slot after loosening the bolts.

8   Scribe a line around the entire hinge plate so you can judge the amount of movement.

9   Loosen the bolts or nuts and move the hood into correct alignment. Move it only a little at a time. Tighten the hinge bolts and carefully lower the hood to check the position.

10 If necessary after installation, the entire hood latch assembly can be adjusted up-and-down as well as from side-to-side on the radiator support so the hood closes securely, flush with the fenders. To make the adjustment, scribe a line around the hood latch mounting bolts to provide a reference point, then loosen them and reposition the latch assembly, as necessary (see illustration). Following adjustment, retighten the mounting bolts.

11 Finally, adjust the hood bumpers on the radiator support so the

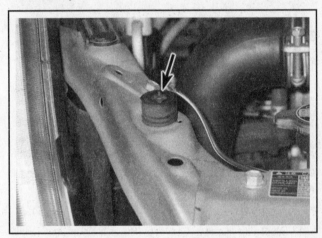

9.11 To adjust the vertical height of the leading edge of the hood so that it's flush with the fenders, turn each edge cushion clockwise to lower the hood or counter-clockwise to raise the hood

hood, when closed, is flush with the fenders (see illustration).

12 The hood latch assembly, as well as the hinges, should be periodically lubricated with white, lithium-base grease to prevent binding and wear.

10 Rear trunk lid/liftgate - removal, installation and adjustment

2001 THROUGH 2003 MODELS

1   Open the trunk lid and cover the edges of the trunk compartment with pads or cloths to protect the painted surfaces when the lid is removed.

2   Follow the wiring harness into the trunk lid and mark and disconnect all electrical connectors.

3   Make alignment marks around the hinge mounting bolts.

4   While an assistant supports the trunk lid, remove the lid-to-hinge bolts on both sides and lift it off.

5   Installation is the reverse of removal.

➥**Note: When reinstalling the trunk lid, align the lid-to-hinge bolts with the marks made during removal.**

6   After installation, close the trunk lid and make sure it's in proper alignment with the surrounding panels.

7   Forward-and-backward and side-to-side adjustments are made by loosening the hinge-to-lid bolts and gently moving the trunk lid into correct alignment.

8   To adjust the trunk lid so it is flush with the body when closed, loosen the mounting bolts and move the lock and striker.

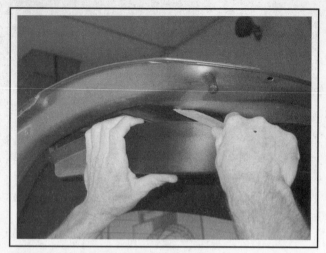

10.10 Using a trim removal tool, carefully pry out the clips and remove the trim panel from the liftgate

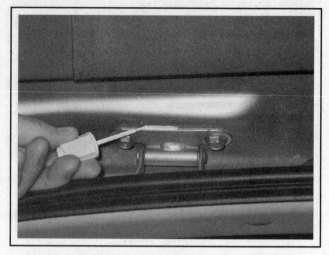

10.12 Liftgate alignment is critical so be sure to mark the hinge positions before disassembly

2004 AND LATER MODELS

▶ **Refer to illustrations 10.10, 10.12 and 10.13**

9   Open the liftgate and cover the edges of the liftgate compartment with pads or cloths to protect the painted surfaces when the liftgate is removed.

10 Remove the liftgate interior trim panels (see illustration).

11 All electrical connectors for the license plate lamp, the wiper motor and the television camera must be labeled, then disconnected. Make sure that the harnesses are free so that the hatch can be lifted off with no interference.

12 Make alignment marks around the hinge mounting bolts (see illustration).

13 Support the liftgate with a stick or have an assistant hold it while you use a small screwdriver to disconnect the support struts from the hatch (see illustration).

14 While an assistant supports the liftgate, remove the liftgate-to-hinge bolts on both sides and lift it off.

15 Installation is the reverse of removal.

➡**Note: When reinstalling the liftgate, align the liftgate-to-hinge bolts with the marks made during removal.**

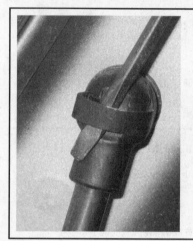

10.13 Pry these clips out to release the tailgate support struts

16 After installation, close the liftgate and make sure it's in proper alignment with the surrounding panels. Check that all of the wiring is correctly connected and secured.

17 Forward-and-backward and side-to-side adjustments are made by loosening the hinge-to-liftgate bolts and gently moving the liftgate into correct alignment.

11 Door trim panel - removal and installation

❊❊ **WARNING:**

The models covered by this manual are equipped with Supplemental Restraint systems (SRS), more commonly known as airbags. Always disarm the airbag system before working in the vicinity of any airbag system component to avoid the possibility of accidental deployment of the airbag, which could cause personal injury (see Chapter 12).

❊❊ **CAUTION:**

Wear gloves when working inside the door openings to protect against cuts from sharp metal edges.

FRONT AND REAR DOORS

▶ **Refer to illustrations 11.2, 11.3, 11.5, 11.6 and 11.7**

1   Refer to Chapter 6 and disconnect the cable from the negative terminal of the auxiliary 12-volt battery. Be sure to perform the initialization procedure when reconnecting it.

2   Remove the set-screw to remove the bezel around the inside door handle (see illustration).

3   Remove the door pull handle set screw (see illustration).

4   On 2003 and earlier models, remove the push-pin fastener at the outer edge of the door trim panel.

11.2 Carefully pry off the cover then remove the set screw

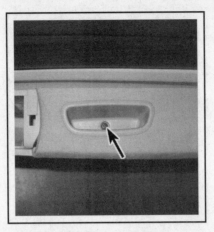

11.3 Remove the screw in the bottom of the handle

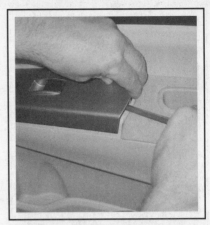

11.5 Pry the switch plate up and then disconnect the wiring

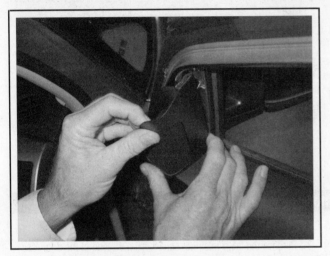

11.6 Carefully pry off the mirror trimplate

11.7 Lift the panel from the door - if you feel resistance, stop and locate the problem

5   Using a trim removal tool, pry up the window switch plate and disconnect the electrical connectors (see illustration).

6   Using a trim removal tool, pry out the outside mirror trim plate (see illustration).

7   Carefully pry the panel out until the clips disengage (see illustration). Work slowly and carefully around the outer edge of the trim panel until it's free. Unplug any wiring harness connectors and remove the panel.

8   For access to the door outside handle or the door window regulator inside the door, raise the window fully, then carefully peel back the plastic watershield.

9   Installation is the reverse of removal.

12 Door - removal, installation and adjustment

▶ **Refer to illustrations 12.3, 12.5 and 12.6**

REMOVAL AND INSTALLATION

1   Remove the door trim panel (see Section 11). Disconnect any electrical connectors and push them through the door opening so they won't interfere with removal.

2   Position a jack or jackstands under the door or have an assistant on hand to support the door when the hinge bolts are removed.

➡**Note: If a jack or stand is used, place a rag between it and the door to protect the door's paint.**

3   Remove the door stop strut bolt (see illustration).

4   Draw a mark around the hinges to aid in alignment.

5   Remove the hinge-to-door bolts and carefully detach the door (see illustration). Installation is the reverse of removal.

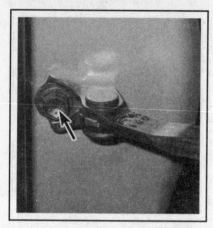

12.3 Remove the door stop strut bolt

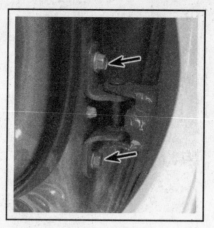

12.5 Remove the hinge-to-door bolts

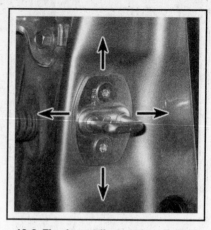

12.6 The door striker can be adjusted for correct latching of the door

ADJUSTMENT

6   Following installation, make sure the door is aligned properly. Adjust it if necessary as follows:

a) Up-and-down and forward-and-backward adjustments are made by loosening the hinge-to-body bolts and moving the door, as necessary. A special offset tool may be required to reach some of the bolts.

b) In-and-out and up-and-down adjustments are made by loosening the door side hinge bolts and moving the door, as necessary. A special offset tool may be required to reach some of the bolts.

c) The door lock striker can also be adjusted both up-and-down and sideways to provide a positive engagement with the locking mechanism. This is done by loosening the screws and moving the striker, as necessary (see illustration).

13   Door latch, lock cylinder and handles - removal and installation

1   Remove the door trim panel and the plastic watershield (see Section 11).

DOOR LATCH

▶ **Refer to illustration 13.3**

2   Working through the access holes in the door, reach inside the door and disconnect the control links from the latch.

3   Remove the latch retaining screws from the end of the door (see illustration).

4   Detach the door latch and (if equipped) the door lock solenoid.

5   Installation is the reverse of removal.

LOCK CYLINDER AND OUTSIDE HANDLE

▶ **Refer to illustrations 13.7 and 13.8**

6   Working through the access holes in the door, disconnect the control rods from the lock cylinder and outside handle.

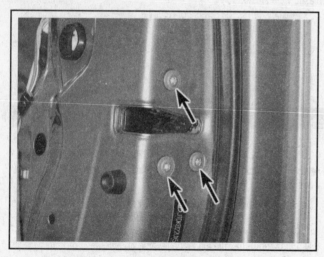

13.3 These three screws retain the latch assembly

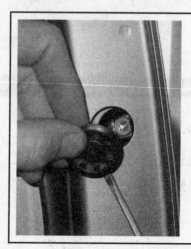

13.7 The outer door handle and the lock are accessible through a hole in the inner door frame

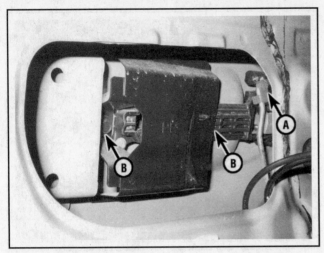

13.8 Disconnect the control rod (A), then remove the two bolts securing the handle cover (B)

13.13 Carefully pry the assembly off with a screwdriver

7   Loosen the screw and pull the lock cover and lock cylinder from the outside of the door (see illustration).

8   To remove the outside handle, disconnect the control rod and remove the two handle cover mounting screws inside the door (see illustration). After removing the handle cover, remove the one remaining fastener securing the door handle.

9   If the outside handle assembly is to be replaced, disconnect the rod and door operating cable from the handle assembly and transfer them to the new handle.

10   Use a screwdriver to pry the retaining clip off, or remove the lock cylinder retaining bolt, and remove the lock cylinder from the handle.

11   Installation is the reverse of removal.

INSIDE HANDLE

▶ **Refer to illustration 13.13**

12   Remove the retaining screw.

13   Pull the handle free, disconnect the cables from the inside handle control and remove the handle from the door (see illustration).

14   Installation is the reverse of removal.

14 Door window glass - removal and installation

▶ **Refer to illustrations 14.2 and 14.4, 14.5**

1   Remove the door trim panel and the plastic watershield (see Section 11).

2   Lower the window glass. Remove the door access plate from the door frame (see illustration).

3   Carefully pry the inner weatherstrip out of the door window opening.

4   Place a rag inside the door panel to help prevent scratching the glass, then remove the two glass mounting bolts (see illustration).

5   Remove the glass by pulling the rear up while lowering the front. The window regulators can be removed after removing their mounting bolts (see illustration).

6   Installation is the reverse of the removal procedure.

14.2 Remove the fasteners securing the door access plate to the door frame

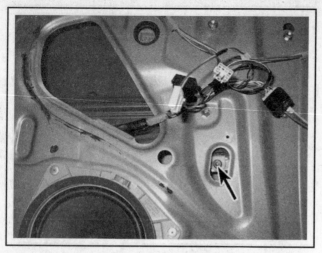

14.4 Remove the two glass mounting bolts (one bolt not visible in photo)

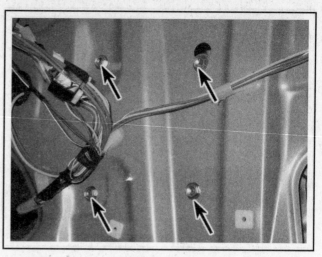

14.5 Window regulator mounting bolts

15 Bumper covers - removal and installation

✳✳ WARNING 1:

The models covered by this manual are equipped with Supplemental Restraint systems (SRS), more commonly known as airbags. Always disable the airbag system before working in the vicinity of any airbag system component to avoid the possibility of accidental deployment of the airbag, which could cause personal injury (see Chapter 12).

✳✳ WARNING 2:

Make sure power to the hybrid system is turned Off before performing any work on this vehicle. Also, on models equipped with the Smart Key system, place the key in a secure spot at least 20 feet away from the work area.

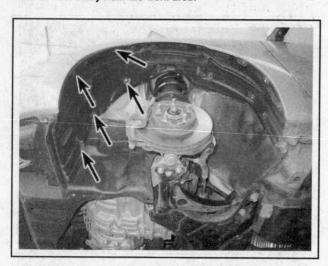

15.7a Remove the fasteners at the front of the inner fender liner

FRONT BUMPER COVER

1   Apply the parking brake, raise the front of the vehicle and support it securely on jackstands.

2   Refer to Chapter 6 and disconnect the cable from the negative terminal of the auxiliary 12-volt battery. Be sure to perform the initialization procedure when reconnecting it.

2001 through 2003 models

3   Remove the engine bottom covers and the lower chin spoiler if necessary for access. Disconnect the wiring from the side maker lamps.

4   Detach the screws and/or pushpins securing the top, bottom, sides and top of the bumper cover.

➡Note 1: Use a small screwdriver to pop the center button up on the plastic fasteners, but do not try to remove the center buttons. They stay in the ferrules.

➡Note 2: Don't try to remove the cover until all fasteners have been located and removed.

5   If the bumper beam itself is to be replaced, remove the nuts and pull the beam off its mounts.

6   Installation is the reverse of removal. Make sure the tabs on the back of the bumper cover fit into the corresponding clips on the body before attaching the bolts and screws.

2004 and later models

▶ Refer to illustrations 15.7a, 15.7b, 15.8, 15.10a, 15.10b and 15.13

7   Remove the four screws from the front of the inner fender liners so they can be pulled away from the bumper cover (see illustration). Remove the bolts at each corner of the bumper cover (see illustration).

8   Remove the engine bottom cover (see illustration).

9   Remove the front chin spoiler.

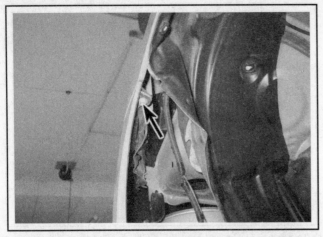

15.7b With the inner fender liner pulled back, remove the fasteners at the coner of the bumper cover

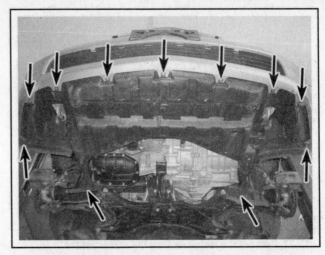

15.8 The bumper cover is attached to the lower engine cover

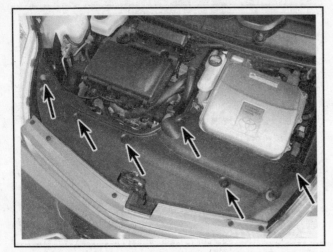

15.10a The grille protector by these fasteners

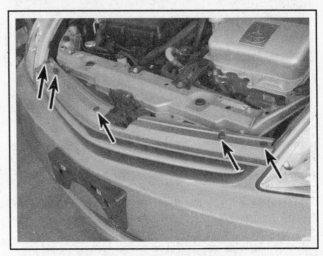

15.10b Bumper cover upper mounting fasteners

10 Remove the upper grille protector (see illustration), then remove the bumper cover upper fasteners (see illustration).

11 Detach the two clips at each upper end of the grille by holding the upper part of the bumper cover while pulling up on the lower bumper.

12 Use a screwdriver to detach the 8 claw-type clips at the upper part of each end of the bumper cover. Make sure to tape the screwdriver to avoid paint damage.

13 Pull up on the lower part of the bumper cover while holding the upper part tightly (see illustration). This will release the remaining retainers.

14 Disconnect the fog lamp wiring as you lift the bumper cover off.

REAR BUMPER COVER

2001 through 2003 models

15 Refer to Chapter 6 and remove the auxiliary 12-volt battery.

16 Remove the luggage compartment floor components and the left and right side covers.

17 Remove the cover plate from the rear of the luggage compartment.

18 On most models it is necessary to remove the housing for the right warning reflector in order to get access to all of the fasteners for the bumper cover.

19 Remove the two screws from the bottom of the rear bumper cover.

20 Working inside the luggage compartment, remove the nuts from the bumper cover studs.

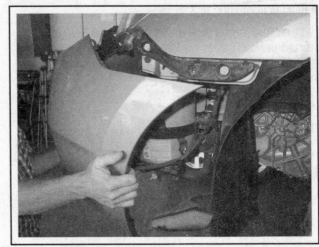

15.13 Plastic clips hold the bumper cover to the vehicle's structure

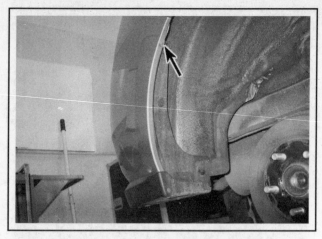

15.23 Remove the fasteners from the corners of the bumper cover

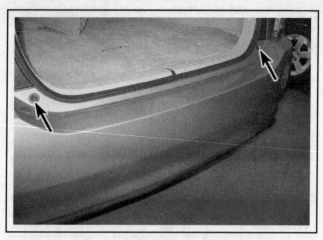

15.24 Remove the fasteners securing the upper part of the bumper

21 Lift the cover carefully from the rear of the vehicle.

22 Installation is the reverse of removal.

2004 and later models

▶ Refer to illustrations 15.23, 15.24 and 15.25

23 Remove the screws from the corners of the bumper cover (see illustration). Remove the single nut from the bottom of the right side of the bumper.

24 Remove the two stoppers from the upper part of the bumper cover (see illustration).

25 Remove the fasteners securing the bottom portion of the bumper cover (see illustration).

26 Wrap the end of a screwdriver with tape and use it to release the five claw retainers at each upper end of the bumper cover.

27 There are two claws at the upper center part of the bumper cover that retain it. Hold the upper part of the bumper cover tightly and pull rearward and upward to release the claws.

28 Installation is the reverse of removal.

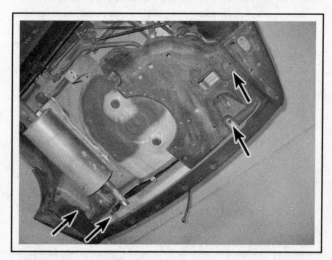

15.25 Remove the fasteners at each end of the bottom portion of the bumper cover

16 Outside mirror - removal and installation

▶ Refer to illustration 16.2

1 Detach the mirror cover by using a small screwdriver to pry the retainers free from the door (see illustration 11.6).

2 Unplug the electrical connector, then remove the three retaining nuts and detach the mirror (see illustration).

3 Installation is the reverse of removal.

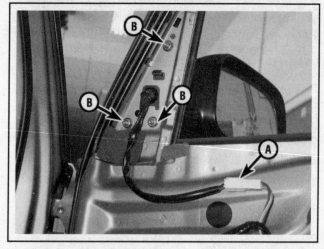

16.2 Unplug the electrical connector (A), then remove the three retaining nuts (B)

17 Seats - removal and installation

⁂ WARNING:

These models are equipped with airbags. Always disable the airbag system before working in the vicinity of any airbag system component to avoid the possibility of accidental deployment of the airbag(s), which could cause personal injury (see Chapter 12).

FRONT SEATS

1   Refer to Chapter 6 and disconnect the cable from the negative terminal of the auxiliary 12-volt battery. Be sure to perform the initialization procedure when reconnecting it.

2001 through 2003 models

2   Pry off the seat track covers and remove the retaining bolts, unplug all electrical connectors and lift the seats from the vehicle.
3   Installation is the reverse of removal.

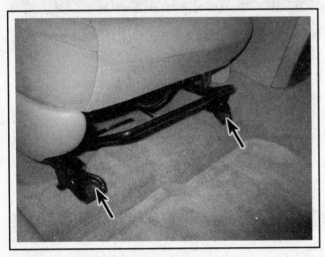

17.6 Front seat forward bolt locations

2004 and later models

▶ Refer to illustrations 17.6 and 17.7

4   Use a screwdriver to pry outward on the seat track covers until they pop off.
5   Remove the headrests.
6   Slide the seats all the way to the rear and remove the front bolts (see illustration).
7   Slide the seat to the front and remove the rear bolts (see illustration).
8   Disconnect the wiring as you lift the seats out.
9   Installation is the reverse of removal.

REAR SEATS

2001 through 2003 models

10 Lift the front of the cushion up, then pull it out toward the front of the vehicle.
11 Remove the seat back retaining bolts at the floor, then lift up on the back to release the seat back from the body.
12 Installation is the reverse of removal.

2004 and later models

▶ Refer to illustrations 17.13, 17.15 and 17.19

13 There is a lower seat cushion hook near the center of each of the two rear seating areas. Carefully feel under the seat cushion until you locate one, then pull it upwards to release it. Repeat for the other hook (see illustration).
14 Press the center rear of the cushion down then forward to release it. Lift the seat cushion out.
15 Open the floorboard at the left front area adjacent to the back of the left rear seat (see illustration).
16 Tilt the left seat forward.
17 Unbolt the left seat back and lift it out,
18 Unbolt and disconnect the back seat's outer seat belt floor anchor.
19 Tilt the right seat forward. Unclip the retainer (see illustration).
20 Unbolt the right seat back and lift it out.

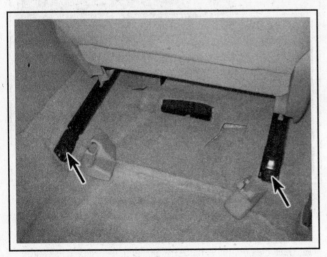

17.7 Front seat rearward bolt locations

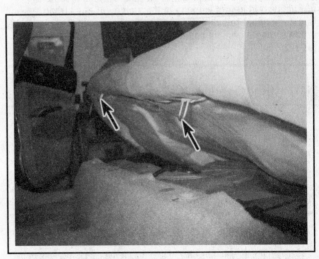

17.13 Pull up on the front of the rear seat cushion to release these hooks

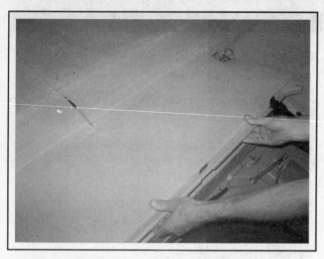

17.15 Lift up the panel at the back of the rear seat

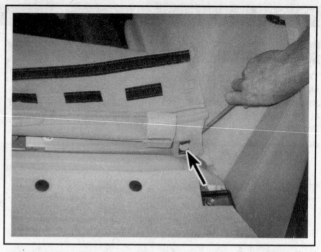

17.19 Remove this clip with a special tool or a screwdriver

18 Instrument cluster bezel - removal and installation

✳✳ WARNING:

These models are equipped with airbags. Always disable the airbag system before working in the vicinity of any airbag system component to avoid the possibility of accidental deployment of the airbag(s), which could cause personal injury (see Chapter 12).

➡Note: This procedure applies only to 2001 through 2003

models. Later models use a multi-display assembly that is discussed in Chapter 12.

1   Refer to Chapter 6 and disconnect the cable from the negative terminal of the auxiliary 12-volt battery. Be sure to perform the initialization procedure when reconnecting it.

2   Remove the two screws at the bottom of the cluster bezel, behind the center compartment door, then wrap a screwdriver with tape and use it to pry out the cluster bezel.

3   Installation is the reverse of the removal procedure.

19 Glove box - removal and installation

✳✳ WARNING:

These models are equipped with airbags. Always disable the airbag system before working in the vicinity of any airbag system component to avoid the possibility of accidental deployment of the airbag(s), which could cause personal injury (see Chapter 12).

2001 THROUGH 2003 MODELS

1   Open the glove box door and turn the stoppers a quarter turn, then pull them out.
2   Remove the two screws and lift off the door.
3   Installation is the reverse of removal.

2004 AND LATER MODELS

▸ **Refer to illustration 19.4**

4   Open the glove compartment and unclip the check rod (see illustration).
5   Push inward on the sides of the box to release it.

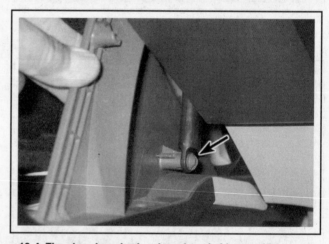

19.4 The glove box check rod can be pried loose with a screwdriver

6   Open the door to the horizontal position, then slide it rearward and out.
7   Installation is the reverse of removal.

20 Steering column covers - removal and installation

❋❋ WARNING:

These models are equipped with airbags. Always disable the airbag system before working in the vicinity of any airbag system component to avoid the possibility of accidental deployment of the airbag(s), which could cause personal injury (see Chapter 12).

2001 THROUGH 2003 MODELS

1   Remove the three screws and pull the lower column cover off.
2   Remove the single screw and detach the upper cover.
3   Installation is the reverse of the removal procedure.

2004 AND LATER MODELS

▸ Refer to illustration 20.4

4   Remove the two screws and separate the tilt lever bracket from the lower column cover. Turn the steering wheel to get access to the two upper screws and remove them (see illustration).
5   Remove the three screws from the bottom of the covers.

20.4 The upper steering column cover screws are only visible when the steering wheel is rotated (steering wheel removed for clarity)

6   Release the four clips as you pull the column covers off.
7   Installation is the reverse of removal.

21 Center console - removal and installation

❋❋ WARNING:

These models are equipped with airbags. Always disable the airbag system before working in the vicinity of any airbag system component to avoid the possibility of accidental deployment of the airbag(s), which could cause personal injury (see Chapter 12).

1   Refer to Chapter 6 and disconnect the cable from the negative terminal of the auxiliary 12-volt battery. Be sure to perform the initialization procedure when reconnecting it.

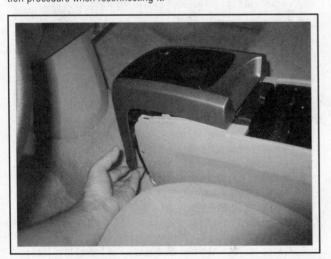

21.4 Pull the top of the console assembly upwards

2001 THROUGH 2003 MODELS

2   Remove the three bolts and lift off the console box.
3   Installation is the reverse of the removal procedure.

2004 AND LATER MODELS

▸ Refer to illustrations 21.4, 21.10a, 21.10b

4   Pull the top of the console assembly upwards while releasing the two clips at the bottom front (see illustration).
5   Disconnect the four clips that are around the upper section and lift it free.

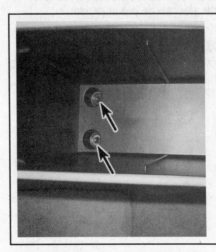

21.10a Remove the two bolts from the inside the console box

6   Remove the four screws that secure the front cup holder assembly.

7   Remove the console box pocket and the carpet liner.

8   Grasp the rear panel of the console box and pull it rearward and upward to release the six clips.

9   Remove the four screws and the rear cup holder.

10   Remove the two screws from the front sides of the console box and the two bolts from the inside rear (see illustration). Lift the console box out and disconnect the wiring (see illustration).

11   Installation is the reverse of removal.

21.10b Lift the console box out and disconnect the wiring

22 Instrument panel - removal and installation

✻✻ WARNING:

These models are equipped with airbags. Always disable the airbag system before working in the vicinity of any airbag system component to avoid the possibility of accidental deployment of the airbag(s), which could cause personal injury (see Chapter 12).

➡**Note 1: This is a difficult procedure for the home mechanic. There are many hidden fasteners, difficult angles to work in and many electrical connectors to tag and disconnect/connect. We recommend that this procedure be done only by an experienced do-it-yourselfer.**

➡**Note 2: During removal of the instrument panel, make careful notes of how each piece comes off, where it fits in relation to other pieces and what holds it in place. If you note how each part is installed before removing it, getting the instrument panel back together again will be much easier.**

➡**Note 3: It is not necessary, but it is suggested to remove both front seats to allow additional working space and lessen the chance of damage to the seats during this procedure.**

2001 THROUGH 2003 MODELS

1   Refer to Chapter 6 and disconnect the cable from the negative terminal of the auxiliary 12-volt battery.

2   Refer to Chapter 10 and remove the steering wheel.

3   Refer to Section 20 and remove the steering column covers.

4   Remove the two cowl side trim pieces.

5   Remove the front pillar moldings.

6   Remove the two mounting screws and the hood release handle.

7   Open the shifter hole cover.

8   Remove the fasteners from the lower corners of the lower instrument panel.

9   Use a screwdriver to carefully pry the panel off. Disconnect the wiring as you pull it free.

10   Refer to Chapter 12 and remove the combination switches, then remove the spiral cable from the steering column (see Chapter 10).

11   Refer to Section 19 and remove the glove compartment door.

12   Remove the panel that is immediately below the heater control knobs by first removing the pushpin retainers, then prying the panel out with a screwdriver wrapped with tape.

13   If there is a reinforcement bar behind the glove box opening, remove it at this time.

14   Disconnect the passenger airbag wiring.

15   Remove the two bolts and two nuts, then carefully lift out the passenger airbag.

16   Refer to Section 18 and remove the instrument cluster bezel.

17   Remove the sound system opening cover.

18   Carefully pry off the cluster panel, remove the three screws and disconnect the wiring as you lift out the combination meter.

19   Pry the defroster outlets from each upper end of the instrument panel.

20   Carefully pry out the air outlets below the defroster outlets.

21   Disconnect the shifter cable.

22   Remove the three bolts, disconnect the shift lever and remove the shift lever assembly.

23   Disconnect the column hole cover by releasing the three clips.

24   Remove the shift lock computer.

25   Paint match marks where the steering shaft u-joint attaches to the steering gear shaft. Remove the adjacent pinch bolt and loosen the steering shaft bolt that is located several inches higher.

26   Disconnect the steering column wiring.

27   Remove the two bolts and two nuts, then lift out the steering column.

28   Disconnect all remaining wiring from the instrument panel and release the wiring harness clips.

29   Remove the seven fasteners securing the instrument panel. There is one at each lower corner, two at the glove box lower rail, one at the glove box top and one in each defroster duct opening.

30   Have an assistant help you lift the instrument panel from the vehicle.

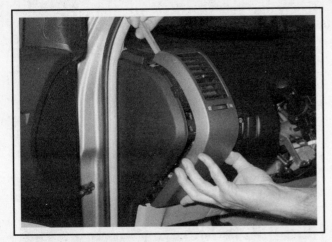

22.33 Pull off the left air register

22.34a There are two screws to be removed below the steering column

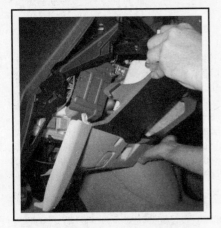

22.34b Pull the panel rearward . . .

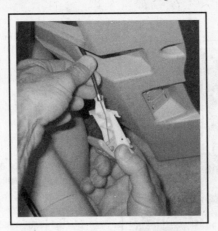

22.34c . . . then unclip the handle mechanism and disconnect the cable from the handle

22.35 Pull the upper panel free

31 Installation is the reverse of removal. Work methodically and make sure that all the wiring is connected and all the fasteners are installed before moving to subsequent steps in this procedure.

2004 AND LATER MODELS

▶ Refer to illustrations 22.33, 22.34a, 22.34b, 22.34c, 22.35, 22.36, 22.39, 22.47, 22.48, 22.50, 22.51, 22.55a and 22.55b

32 Refer to Chapter 6 and disconnect the cable from the negative terminal of the auxiliary 12-volt battery. Be sure to perform the initialization procedure when reconnecting it.

33 Use a screwdriver wrapped with tape to pry off the air register at the far left of the instrument panel. Pry first at the bottom and work your way to the top (see illustration).

34 Remove the two screws from below the steering column. Detach the clips on the panel, then pull the panel rearward. Disconnect the hood lock handle (see illustrations).

35 The flat panel above the steering wheel is retained in the same way with seven clips. Use the screwdriver to remove it, starting at the corners (see illustration).

36 Remove the air registers on each side of the center multi-display unit and on the far right side of the instrument panel (see illustration).

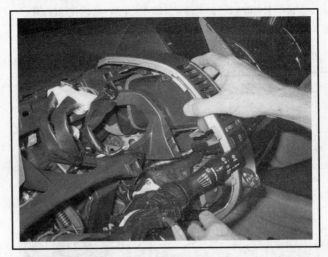

22.36 Pull the air register from the side of the steering column

37 Remove the multi-display unit (see Chapter 12).
38 Refer to Section 19 and remove the glove box.
39 Remove the panel cushion (see illustration).

22.39 Remove the panel cushion

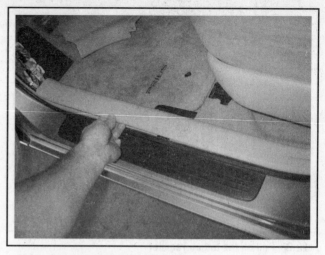

22.47 Pull off both threshold plates

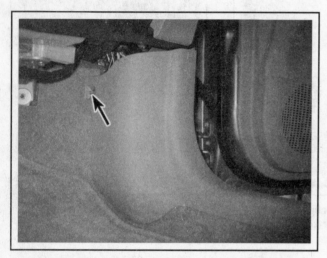

22.48 Remove the push-pin fastener then carefully pry off the kick panels

40 Remove the cluster panel end.

41 Pry out both of the instrument panel hole covers.

42 Carefully pry off the left and right windshield pillar moldings.

43 Refer to Chapter 10 and remove the steering wheel.

44 Refer to Section 20 and remove both steering column covers.

45 Refer to Chapter 12 and remove the combination switches, then the spiral cable from the steering column.

46 Refer to Chapter 12 and remove the radio.

47 Remove both front door threshold plates (see illustration).

48 Use the taped screwdriver to pry off both kick panels from under the sides of each end of the instrument panel (see illustration) after prying out the push-pins.

49 Refer to Section 21 and remove the center console.

50 The lower center instrument panel cover is retained by a pushpin retainer on the right side and six clips. Remove the pushpin and pry the cover off (see illustration).

51 Remove the upper glove box door (see illustration).

52 Disconnect the passenger airbag connector (see Chapter 12).

53 Unbolt the power steering computer and disconnect its wiring as you remove it.

54 Remove the lower shift lever assembly.

55 Disconnect all wiring from the instrument panel assembly, care-

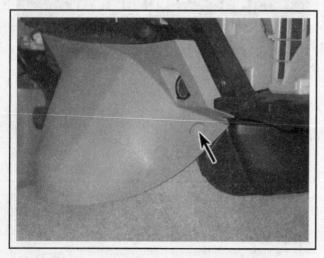

22.50 This cover is held in place by the large push-pin and some clips

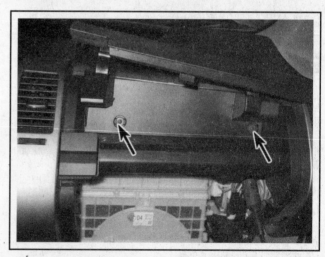

22.51 Remove the fasteners securing the glovebox door

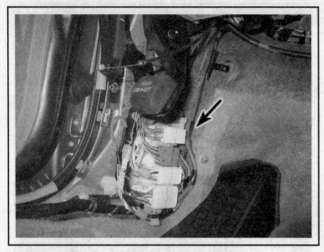

22.55a There are many wiring connections . . .

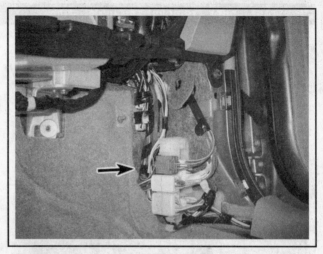

22.55b . . . be sure to label each one before you disconnect it to avoid problems later

fully labeling them as you do so (see illustrations).

56 Remove the two screws and six retaining bolts from the instrument panel.

57 Lift the instrument panel out of the vehicle with the aid of at least one assistant.

58 Installation is the reverse of removal. Work methodically and make sure that all wiring is connected and all fasteners installed before moving to subsequent steps in this procedure.

23 Radiator grille - removal and installation

1 Refer to Section 15 and remove the front bumper cover.

➡**Note: On some models it is possible to access the grille retaining clips with the front bumper cover in place. On these models, raise the vehicle and support it securely on jackstands, then reach behind the bumper cover to access the grille.**

2 Release the clips that retain the grille to the rear of the bumper cover.

3 Installation is the reverse of removal.

24 Cowl panels - removal and installation

▶ **Refer to illustration 24.5**

1 Mark the positions of the windshield wiper blades on the windshield with tape.

2 Remove the wiper arms (see Chapter 12).

3 Pull off the cowl-to-hood seal.

4 On 2003 and earlier models, remove the two screws from the cowl and lift up the two cowl pieces.

5 On 2004 and later models release the eight clips that secure each cowl piece and lift it off (see illustration).

6 Installation is the reverse of removal. Make sure to align the wiper blades with the marks made during removal.

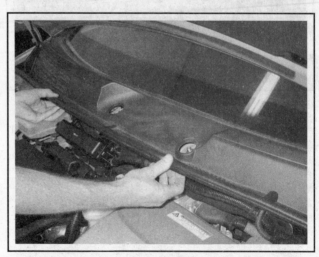

24.5 The plastic upper cowl is removed after first removing the wiper arms

25 Front fender - removal and installation

▶ **Refer to illustrations 25.3, 25.4, 25.5 and 25.6**

1   Raise the vehicle, support it securely on jackstands and remove the front wheels.

2   Refer to Section 15 and remove the front bumper cover.

3   Pull back the inner fender cover and remove the bolts behind it (see illustration).

4   Open the doors and remove the bolts accessible in the opening (see illustration).

5   Remove the fender bolts at the front that were covered by the bumper cover (see illustration)

6   Open the hood and remove the fender bolts along its top edge (see illustration)

7   With the help of an assistant, carefully remove the fender to avoid damaging painted surfaces.

8   Installation is the reverse of removal. Check the alignment of the fender to the hood and front edge of the door before final tightening of the fender fasteners.

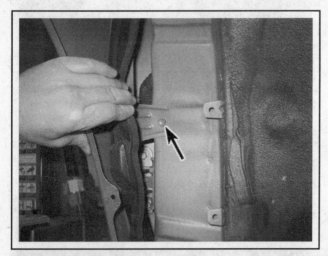

25.3 **Pull back the inner fender cover and remove the bolt**

25.4 **Remove the bolt that is accessible in the door opening**

25.5 **Remove the bolt at the front of the fender**

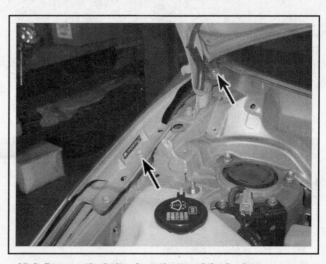

25.6 **Remove the bolts along the top of the fender**

Section

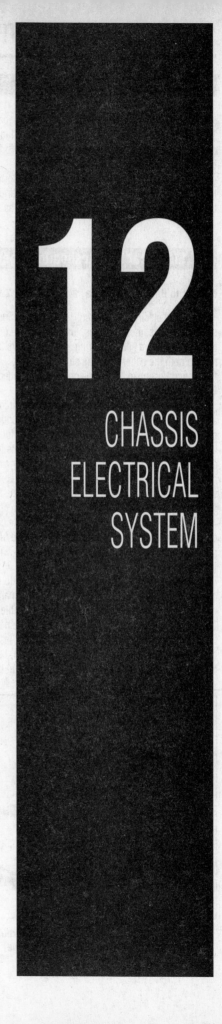

12

CHASSIS
ELECTRICAL
SYSTEM

1 General information

The chassis electrical system is a 12-volt, negative ground type. The hybrid power system is a separate high-voltage system that is not discussed in this Chapter. Information on the hybrid power system can be found in Chapter 5.

Power for the lights and all electrical accessories is supplied by a lead/acid-type battery that is charged by the hybrid system. It is not to be confused with the much larger high-voltage battery that is located nearby in the luggage compartment.

This Chapter covers repair and service procedures for the various electrical components. Information on the batteries can be found in Chapter 6.

It should be noted that when portions of the electrical system are serviced, the cable should be disconnected from the negative battery terminal to prevent electrical shorts and/or fires.

2 Electrical troubleshooting - general information

▶ **Refer to illustrations 2.5a, 2.5b, 2.6 and 2.9**

A typical electrical circuit consists of an electrical component, any switches, relays, motors, fuses, fusible links or circuit breakers related to that component and the wiring and connectors that link the component to both the battery and the chassis. To help you pinpoint an electrical circuit problem, wiring diagrams are included at the end of this Chapter.

Before tackling any troublesome electrical circuit, first study the appropriate wiring diagrams to get a complete understanding of what makes up that individual circuit. Trouble spots, for instance, can often be narrowed down by noting if other components related to the circuit are operating properly. If several components or circuits fail at one time, chances are the problem is in a fuse or ground connection, because several circuits are often routed through the same fuse and ground connections.

Electrical problems usually stem from simple causes, such as loose or corroded connections, a blown fuse, a melted fusible link or a failed relay. Visually inspect the condition of all fuses, wires and connections in a problem circuit before troubleshooting the circuit.

If test equipment and instruments are going to be utilized, use the diagrams to plan ahead of time where you will make the necessary connections in order to accurately pinpoint the trouble spot.

The basic tools needed for electrical troubleshooting include a circuit tester or voltmeter (a volt bulb with a set of test leads can also be used), a continuity tester, which includes a bulb, battery and set of test leads, and a jumper wire, preferably with a circuit breaker incorporated, which can be used to bypass electrical components (see illustrations). Before attempting to locate a problem with test instruments, use the wiring diagram(s) to decide where to make the connections.

VOLTAGE CHECKS

Voltage checks should be performed if a circuit is not functioning properly. Connect one lead of a circuit tester to either the negative battery terminal or a known good ground. Connect the other lead to a connector in the circuit being tested, preferably nearest to the battery or fuse (see illustration). If the bulb of the tester lights, voltage is present, which means that the part of the circuit between the connector and the battery is problem free. Continue checking the rest of the circuit in the same fashion. When you reach a point at which no voltage is present, the problem lies between that point and the last test point with voltage. Most of the time the problem can be traced to a loose connection.

FINDING A SHORT

One method of finding shorts in a live circuit is to remove the fuse and connect a test light in place of the fuse terminals (fabricate two jumper wires with small spade terminals, plug the jumper wires into the fuse box and connect the test light). There should be voltage present in the circuit. Move the suspected wiring harness from side-to-side while watching the test light. If the bulb goes off, there is a short to ground somewhere in that area, probably where the insulation has rubbed through.

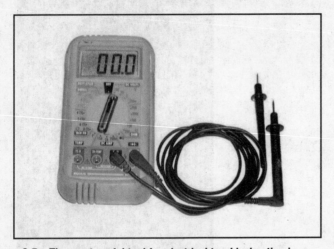

2.5a The most useful tool for electrical troubleshooting is a digital multimeter that can check voltage, amperage and continuity

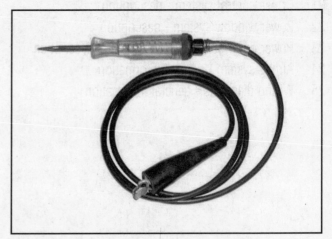

2.5b A simple test light is a very handy tool for testing voltage

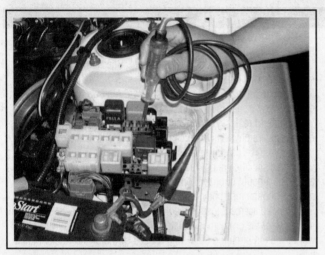

2.6 A basic test light's lead is clipped to a known good ground, then the pointed probe can test connectors, wires and electrical sockets - if the bulb lights, then the circuit being tested has battery voltage

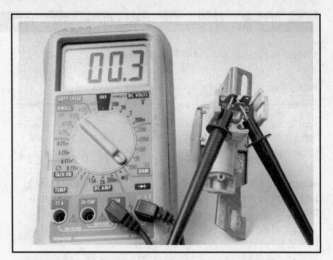

2.9 With a multimeter set to the ohms scale, resistance can be checked across two terminals - when checking for continuity, a high or infinity reading indicates lack of continuity

GROUND CHECK

Perform a ground test to check whether a component is properly grounded. Disconnect the battery and connect one lead of a continuity tester or multimeter (set to the ohms scale), to a known good ground. Connect the other lead to the wire or ground connection being tested. If the resistance is low (less than 5 ohms), the ground is good. If the bulb on a self-powered test light does not go on, the ground is not good.

CONTINUITY CHECK

A continuity check is done to determine if there are any breaks in a circuit - if it is passing electricity properly. With the circuit off (no power in the circuit), a self-powered continuity tester or multimeter can be used to check the circuit. Connect the test leads to both ends of the circuit (or to the "power" end and a good ground), and if the test light comes on the circuit is passing current properly (see illustration). If the resistance is low (less than 5 ohms), there is continuity; if the reading is 10,000 ohms or higher, there is a break somewhere in the circuit. The same procedure can be used to test a switch, by connecting the continuity tester to the switch terminals. With the switch turned On, the test light should come on (or low resistance should be indicated on a meter).

FINDING AN OPEN CIRCUIT

When diagnosing for possible open circuits, it is often difficult to locate them by sight because the connectors hide oxidation or terminal misalignment. Merely wiggling a connector on a sensor or in the wiring harness may correct the open circuit condition. Remember this when

an open circuit is indicated when troubleshooting a circuit. Intermittent problems may also be caused by oxidized or loose connections.

Electrical troubleshooting is simple if you keep in mind that all electrical circuits are basically electricity running from the battery, through the wires, switches, relays, fuses and fusible links to each electrical component (light bulb, motor, etc.) and to ground, from which it is passed back to the battery. Any electrical problem is an interruption in the flow of electricity to and from the battery.

CONNECTORS

Most electrical connections on these vehicles are made with multi-wire plastic connectors. The mating halves of many connectors are secured with locking clips molded into the plastic connector shells. The mating halves of large connectors, such as some of those under the instrument panel, are held together by a bolt through the center of the connector.

To separate a connector with locking clips, use a small screwdriver to pry the clips apart carefully, then separate the connector halves. Pull only on the shell; never pull on the wiring harness as you may damage the individual wires and terminals inside the connectors. Look at the connector closely before trying to separate the halves. Often the locking clips are engaged in a way that is not immediately clear. Additionally, many connectors have more than one set of clips.

Each pair of connector terminals has a male half and a female half. When you look at the end view of a connector in a diagram, be sure to understand whether the view shows the harness side or the component side of the connector. Connector halves are mirror images of each other, and a terminal shown on the right side end-view of one half will be on the left side end view of the other half.

3 Fuses and fusible links - general information

► **Refer to illustrations 3.1a, 3.1b and 3.3**

FUSES

The electrical circuits of these vehicles are protected by a combination of fuses, circuit breakers and fusible links. The fuse blocks are located under the instrument panel and in the engine compartment (see illustrations).

➡**Note: On 2003 and earlier models, the engine compartment fuse block is located on the right side of the engine compartment.**

Each of the fuses is designed to protect a specific circuit, and the various circuits are identified on the fuse panel cover.

Miniaturized fuses are employed in the fuse blocks. These compact fuses, with blade terminal design, allow fingertip removal and replace-ment. If an electrical component fails, always check the fuse first. The best way to check a fuse is with a test light. Check for power at the exposed terminal tips of each fuse. If power is present on one side of the fuse but not the other, the fuse is blown. A blown fuse can also be confirmed by visually inspecting it (see illustration).

Be sure to replace blown fuses with the correct type. Fuses of different ratings are physically interchangeable, but only fuses of the proper rating should be used. Replacing a fuse with one of a higher or lower value than specified is not recommended. Each electrical circuit needs a specific amount of protection. The amperage value of each fuse is molded into the fuse body.

If the replacement fuse immediately fails, don't replace it again until the cause of the problem is isolated and corrected. In most cases, this will be a short circuit in the wiring caused by a broken or deteriorated wire.

FUSIBLE LINKS

Some circuits are protected by fusible links. The links are used in circuits which are not ordinarily fused, such as the ignition circuit, or which carry high current.

Cartridge type fusible links are located in the engine compartment fuse box and are similar to a large fuse. After disconnecting the negative battery cable, simply unplug and replace it with a fusible link of the same amperage.

A wire-type fusible link, installed in the harness between the battery and the fuse/relay blocks, protects the entire chassis electrical system. It's located near the positive battery terminal. If the fusible link melts, the cause of the short must first be repaired, and then the fusible link must be replaced with a fusible link of the same gauge. Never substitute a regular wire for a fusible link.

To replace a wire-type fusible link, disconnect the cable from the negative terminal of the battery, cut the damaged link out and solder a new one in its place. Cover the exposed wires with shrink-wrap tubing or plenty of electrical tape.

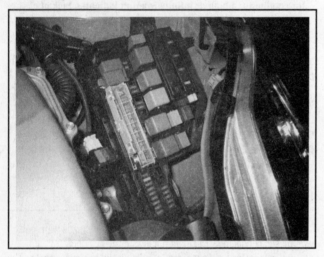

3.1a The exterior fuse box is under the hood - cover shown removed (2004 and later model shown)

3.1b Interior fuse box - instrument panel partially disassembled

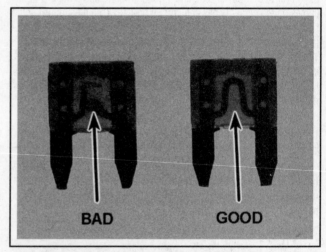

3.3 When a fuse blows, the element between the terminals melts

4   Circuit breakers - general information

Circuit breakers protect certain circuits, such as the power windows or heated seats. Depending on the vehicle's accessories, there may be one or two circuit breakers, located in the fuse/relay box in the engine compartment.

Because the circuit breakers reset automatically, an electrical overload in a circuit-breaker-protected system will cause the circuit to fail momentarily, and then come back on. If the circuit does not come back on, check it immediately.

For a basic check, pull the circuit breaker up out of its socket on the fuse panel, but just far enough to probe with a voltmeter. The breaker should still contact the sockets.

With the voltmeter negative lead on a good chassis ground, touch each end prong of the circuit breaker with the positive meter probe. There should be battery voltage at each end. If there is battery voltage only at one end, the circuit breaker must be replaced.

Some circuit breakers must be reset manually.

5   Relays - general information and testing

▶ **Refer to illustrations 5.3a, 5.3b and 5.6**

GENERAL INFORMATION

1   Several electrical accessories in the vehicle, such as the fuel injection system, horns, starter, and fog lamps use relays to transmit the electrical signal to the component. Relays use a low-current circuit (the control circuit) to open and close a high-current circuit (the power circuit). If the relay is defective, that component will not operate properly. Most relays are mounted in the engine compartment fuse/relay box. If a faulty relay is suspected, it can be removed and tested using the procedure below or by a dealer service department or a repair shop. Defective relays must be replaced as a unit. Identification of the circuit the relay controls is often marked on the top of the relay, but the decal or imprint inside the cover of the relay box should also indicate which circuits they control.

➡**Note: Some relays are an integral part of the interior fuse box. These include the starter relay, the IG1 relay, the defroster relay, the power window relay, the circuit-opening relay and the integration relay.**

TESTING

2   Refer to the wiring diagrams for the circuit to determine the proper connections for the relay you're testing. If you can't determine the correct connection from the wiring diagrams, however, you may be able to determine the test connections from the information that follows.

3   There are four basic types of relays used on these models (see illustrations). Some are normally open type and some normally closed, while others include a circuit of each type.

4   On most relays, two of the terminals are the relay control circuit (they connect to the relay coil which, when energized, closes the large

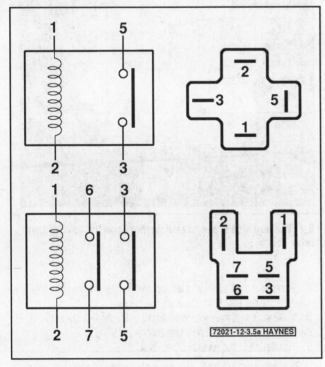

5.3a These two relays are typical normally open types; the upper one completes a single circuit (terminal 5 to terminal 3) when energized - the lower one completes two circuits (6 and 7, and 3 and 5) when energized

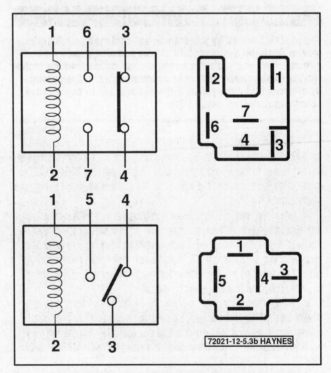

5.3b These relays are normally closed types, where current flows through one circuit until the relay is energized, which interrupts that circuit and completes the second circuit

contacts to complete the circuit). The other terminals are the power circuit (they are connected together within the relay when the control-circuit coil is energized).

5   Some relays may be marked as an aid to help you determine which terminals make up the control circuit and which make up the power circuit. If the relay is not marked, refer to the wiring diagrams at the end of this Chapter to determine the proper hook-ups for the relay you're testing.

6   To test a relay, connect an ohmmeter across the two terminals of the power circuit, continuity should not be indicated (see illustration). Now connect a fused jumper wire between one of the two control circuit terminals and the positive battery terminal. Connect another jumper wire between the other control circuit terminal and ground. When the connections are made, the relay should click and continuity should be indicated on the meter. On some relays, polarity may be critical, so, if the relay doesn't click, try swapping the jumper wires on the control circuit terminals.

7   If the relay fails the above test, replace it.

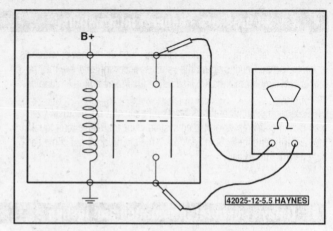

5.6 To test a typical four-terminal relay, connect an ohmmeter to the two terminals of the power circuit - the meter should indicate continuity with the relay energized and no continuity with the relay not energized

6   Turn signal and hazard flasher - check and replacement

▶ **Refer to illustration 6.1**

✳✳ WARNING:

The models covered by this manual are equipped with Supplemental Restraint Systems (SRS), more commonly known as airbags. Always disable the airbag system before working in the vicinity of any airbag system components to avoid the possibility of accidental deployment of the airbags, which could cause personal injury (see Section 24).

1   The turn signal and hazard flasher is a single combination unit, on 2003 and earlier models, it's located on the interior fuse/relay box at the left end of the instrument panel (see illustration). On 2004 and later models, it's located under the left end of the of the instrument panel (see illustration 3.1b).

2   When the flasher unit is functioning properly, a click can be heard during its operation. If the turn signals fail on one side or the other and the flasher unit does not make its characteristic clicking sound, or if a bulb on one side of the vehicle flashes much faster than normal but the bulb at the other end of the vehicle (on the same side) doesn't light at all, a faulty turn signal bulb may be indicated.

3   If both turn signals fail to blink, the problem may be due to a blown fuse, a faulty flasher unit, a defective switch or a loose or open connection. If a quick check of the fuse box indicates that the turn signal fuse has blown, check the wiring for a short before installing a new fuse.

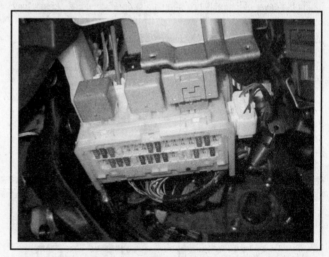

6.1 The turn signal and hazard flasher is on the interior fuse/relay box

4   To replace the flasher, disconnect the electrical connector and remove the flasher unit from the electrical center.

5   Make sure that the replacement unit is identical to the original. Compare the old one to the new one before installing it.

6   Installation is the reverse of removal.

7   Steering column switches - replacement

▸ **Refer to illustrations 7.4 and 7.6**

❋❋ WARNING:

The models covered by this manual are equipped with Supplemental Restraint Systems (SRS), more commonly known as airbags. Always disable the airbag system before working in the vicinity of any airbag system components to avoid the possibility of accidental deployment of the airbag(s), which could cause personal injury (see Section 24).

➡**Note: This procedure applies to 2004 and later models only.**

1   Refer to Chapter 6 and disconnect the cable from the negative terminal of the auxiliary 12-volt battery. Be sure to perform the initialization procedure when reconnecting it.

7.4 Depress the clip with a screwdriver and slide out the switch

2   Refer to Chapter 10 and remove the steering wheel.
3   Remove the steering column covers (see Chapter 11).
4   The steering column switches on these models consist of one combination switch that includes the switches on each side of the column, as well as the clockspring for the airbag system.

➡**Note: The wiper switch on the right side of the column can be removed independently by depressing its release tab with a screwdriver while pulling out on the switch (see illustration).**

5   Refer to Chapter 10, Section 14 and remove the airbag clockspring mechanism.
6   Pinch and compress the retaining spring at the top of the column (see illustration) and pull the combination switch up. Disconnect the wiring from the switch.
7   Installation is the reverse of removal.

7.6 Pinch these tabs using a pair of pliers and then lift off the combination switch assembly

8   Ignition switch and key lock cylinder (2003 and earlier models) - replacement

❋❋ WARNING:

The models covered by this manual are equipped with Supplemental Restraint Systems (SRS), more commonly known as airbags. Always disable the airbag system before working in the vicinity of any airbag system component to avoid the possibility of accidental deployment of the airbag(s), which could cause personal injury (see Section 24).

1   Refer to Chapter 6 and disconnect the cable from the negative terminal of the auxiliary 12-volt battery. Be sure to perform the initialization procedure when reconnecting it.
2   Remove the upper and lower steering column covers (see Chapter 11).

IGNITION SWITCH

3   Disconnect the electrical connector from the ignition switch (see illustration).
4   Remove the ignition switch retaining screws (see illustration) and remove the switch from the key lock cylinder housing.
5   Installation is the reverse of the removal.

KEY LOCK CYLINDER

▸ **Refer to illustrations 8.7a and 8.7b**

6   Place the ignition key in the ACC position.

8.7a To remove the key lock cylinder from the lock cylinder housing, put the lock cylinder in the ACC position, insert an awl or punch into this small hole in the housing, push it in until it depresses the lock cylinder retaining pin . . .

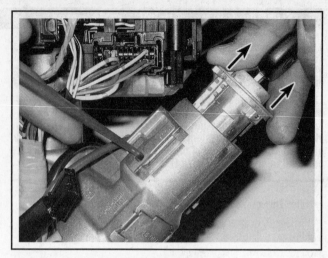

8.7b . . . and pull out the key lock cylinder

7   Use an awl or punch to depress the key lock cylinder retaining pin and remove the key lock cylinder from the housing (see illustrations).

8   To install the lock cylinder, depress the retaining pin and guide the lock cylinder into the housing until the retaining pin extends itself back into the locating hole in the housing.
9   The remainder of installation is the reverse of removal.

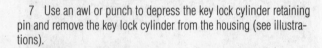

9   Instrument panel switches - replacement

✳✳ WARNING:

The models covered by this manual are equipped with Supplemental Restraint Systems (SRS), more commonly known as airbags. Always disable the airbag system before working in the vicinity of any airbag system components to avoid the possibility of accidental deployment of the airbag(s), which could cause personal injury (see Section 24).

HAZARD WARNING SWITCH

1   Refer to Chapter 6 and disconnect the cable from the negative terminal of the auxiliary 12-volt battery. Be sure to perform the initialization procedure when reconnecting it.

2001 through 2003 models

2   Use a screwdriver wrapped with tape to pry the ends of the hazard warning switch assembly out.

3   Disconnect the wiring as you lift it out.
4   Installation is the reverse of removal.

2004 and later models

5   The hazard warning switch is a part of the multi-display unit. Refer to Section 10 for information on its removal.
6   Remove the hazard warning switch from the multi-display unit.
7   Installation is the reverse of removal.

DEFOGGER SWITCH

8   The rear window defogger switch is located in the heating and air conditioning control panel.
9   Refer to Chapter 3 and remove the control panel, then pull the assembly out until you can disconnect the electrical connector at the rear of the switch. Depress the tab and remove the switch from the bezel.
10 Installation is the reverse of the removal procedure.

10 Combination meter/multi-display unit - removal and installation

✳✳ WARNING:

The models covered by this manual are equipped with Supplemental Restraint Systems (SRS), more commonly known as airbags. Always disable the airbag system before working in the vicinity of any airbag system component to avoid the possibility of accidental deployment of the airbag(s), which could cause personal injury (see Section 24).

10.6 Remove the screws from each side of the multi-display assembly (left side screw hidden)

1   Refer to Chapter 6 and disconnect the cable from the negative terminal of the auxiliary 12-volt battery. Be sure to perform the initialization procedure when reconnecting it.

2001 THROUGH 2003 MODELS

2   Refer to Chapter 11 and remove the instrument cluster bezel
3   Remove the three screws from the combination meter and lift it out, disconnecting the wiring as you do so.
4   Installation is the reverse of removal.

2004 AND LATER MODELS

▶ **Refer to illustration 10.6**

5   Use a screwdriver wrapped with tape to pry off the air registers on each side of the multi-display unit (see Chapter 11, Section 22).
6   Remove the screws from each side of the multi-display assembly and lift it off, disconnecting the wires as you do so (see illustration).
7   Installation is the reverse of removal.

11 Wiper motor - check and replacement

✳✳ WARNING:

Make sure power to the hybrid system is turned Off before performing any work on this vehicle. Also, on models equipped with the Smart Key system, place the key in a secure spot at least 20 feet away from the work area.

WIPER MOTOR CIRCUIT CHECK

➡**Note: Refer to the wiring diagrams for wire colors and locations in the following checks. When checking for voltage, probe a grounded volt test light to each terminal at a connector until it lights; this verifies voltage (power) at the terminal. If the following checks fail to locate the problem, have the system diagnosed by a dealer service department or other properly equipped repair facility.**

1   If the wipers work slowly, make sure the battery is in good condition and has a strong charge (see Chapter 5). If the battery is in good condition, remove the wiper motor (see below) and operate the wiper arms by hand. Check for binding linkage and pivots. Lubricate or repair the linkage or pivots as necessary. Reinstall the wiper motor. If the wipers still operate slowly, check for loose or corroded connections, especially the ground connection. If all connections look OK, replace the motor.

2   If the wipers fail to operate when activated, check the fuse in the driver's side interior fuse panel. If the fuse is OK, connect a jumper wire between the wiper motor's ground terminal and ground, then retest. If the motor works now, repair the ground connection. If the motor still doesn't work, turn the wiper switch to the HI position and check for voltage at the motor.
➡**Note: The cowl cover will have to be removed (see Chapter 11) to access the electrical connector.**

3   If there's voltage at the connector, remove the motor and check it off the vehicle with fused jumper wires from the battery. If the motor now works, check for binding linkage (see Step 1). If the motor still doesn't work, replace it. If there's no voltage to the motor, check for voltage at the wiper control relays. If there's voltage at the wiper control relays and no voltage at the wiper motor, have the switch tested. If the switch is OK, the wiper control relay is probably bad. See Section 5 for relay testing.
4   If the interval (delay) function is inoperative, check the continuity of all the wiring between the switch and wiper control module.
5   If the wipers stop at the position they're in when the switch is turned off (fail to park), check for voltage at the park feed wire of the wiper motor connector when the wiper switch is OFF but the ignition is ON. If no voltage is present, check for an open circuit between the wiper motor and the fuse panel.

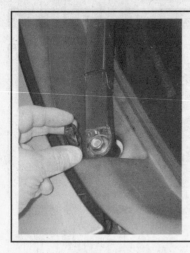

11.7a Pry the covers from the wiper arm pivots

REPLACEMENT

▶ Refer to illustrations 11.7a and 11.7b

6 Refer to Chapter 6 and disconnect the cable from the negative terminal of the auxiliary 12-volt battery. Be sure to perform the initialization procedure when reconnecting it.

7 Remove the covers over the wiper arm mounting nuts. Remove

11.7b After marking the relationship of the arms to the shafts, grasp the wiper arms and firmly lever them up and down to break them loose

the nuts, mark the relationship of the arms to the shafts, then lever off the wiper arms (see illustrations).

8 Remove the cowl rubber seal.

2001 through 2003 models

9 Remove the cowl cover (see Chapter 11).

10 Disconnect the wiper motor wiring harness. Remove the wiper assembly by first removing the five retaining bolts.

11 Remove the cover from the wiper motor.

12 Remove the nut from the wiper motor and link.

13 Paint match marks on the wiper motor shaft and the link.

14 Remove the three wiper motor bolts and separate it from the link assembly.

15 Installation is the reverse of removal.

2004 and later models

▶ Refer to illustrations 11.16, 11.17 and 11.20

16 Remove the cowl cover (see Chapter 11), then remove the wiper assembly cover (see illustration).

17 Disconnect the wiper motor wiring harness. Remove the wiper assembly by first removing the five retaining bolts (see illustration).

18 Use a screwdriver to pry the link arm from the wiper motor.

19 Remove the nut and washer from the crank arm.

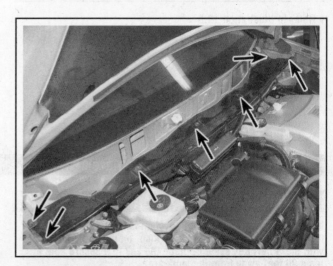

11.16 Remove the fasteners securing the wiper assembly cover

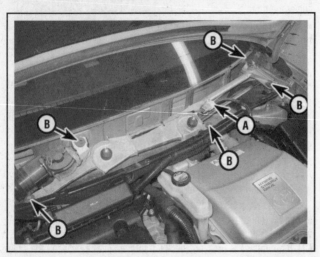

11.17 Disconnect the wiper motor wiring harness (A), then remove the mounting bolts (B)

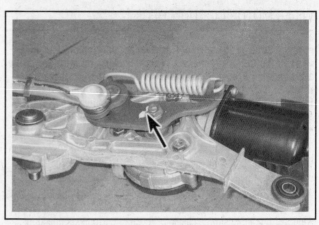

11.20 Be sure to paint match marks so the crank arm can be installed on the shaft in the same position

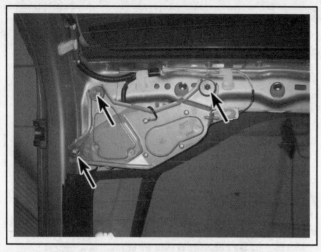

11.23 Remove the wiper motor mounting fasteners

20 Paint match marks on the crank arm and the motor shaft, then remove the crank arm (see illustration).

21 Remove the three wiper mounting bolts and separate the motor from the link assembly.

22 Installation is the reverse of removal.

Rear wiper motor

▶ **Refer to illustration 11.23**

23 Remove the tailgate trim panel for access to the rear wiper motor, then remove the wiper motor mounting fasteners (see illustration).

24 Remove the wiper arm assembly from the pivot stud. Make sure to mark the position of the blade on the glass prior to removal.

25 Disconnect the wiring harness from the motor and remove the wiper motor unit.

26 Installation is the reverse of removal.

---

12 Radio and speakers - removal and installation

❊❊ WARNING:

The models covered by this manual are equipped with Supplemental Restraint Systems (SRS), more commonly known as airbags. Always disable the airbag system before working in the vicinity of any airbag system components to avoid the possibility of accidental deployment of the airbag(s), which could cause personal injury (see Section 24).

1 Refer to Chapter 6 and disconnect the cable from the negative terminal of the auxiliary 12-volt battery. Be sure to perform the initialization procedure when reconnecting it.

RADIO

2001 through 2003 models

2 Use a screwdriver wrapped with tape to pry off the panel below the heater controls.

3 Pry out the hazard-warning switch and disconnect the wiring as you pull it out.

4 Remove the fasteners at the bottom of the center panel and beneath the hazard-warning switch.

5 Pry the center panel out and disconnect the wiring.

6 Remove the radio from the center panel.

7 Installation is the reverse of removal.

2004 and later models

▶ **Refer to illustrations 12.9, 12.12a, 12.12b and 12.12c**

8 Use a screwdriver wrapped with tape to pry off the air registers on each side of the multi-display unit (see Chapter 11, Section 22).

9 Remove the two screws at the bottom of the center panel that is directly beneath the radio (see illustration).

10 Pry off the center panel using the screwdriver wrapped with tape.

11 Refer to Section 10 and remove the multi-display unit.

12 Remove the four mounting screws and slide the radio out along with its bracket (see illustrations).

13 Separate the radio from its bracket.

14 Installation is the reverse of removal.

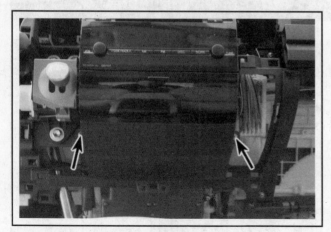

12.9 Center panel mounting fasteners

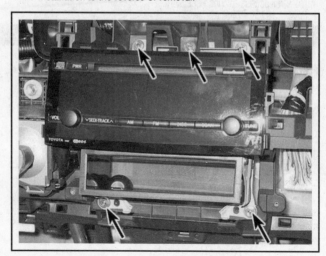

12.12a The radio is retained by five screws

12.12b Carefully pull the radio from the dash . . .

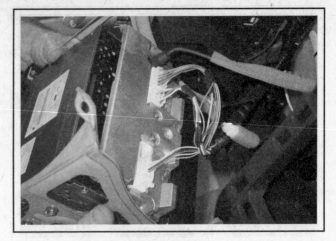

12.12c . . . then disconnect the wiring

DOOR SPEAKERS

▶ **Refer to illustration 12.16**

15 Remove the door trim panel (see Chapter 11).
16 Drill out the speaker mounting rivets (see illustration). Disconnect the electrical connector and remove the speaker from the vehicle.
17 Installation is the reverse of removal. The speakers can be mounted with rivets or with sheet metal screws if a rivet gun is not available.

2004 AND LATER MODELS

Upper instrument panel speaker

18 There is a small speaker in the center top of the instrument panel. Use a screwdriver wrapped with tape to pry up the speaker assembly.
19 Disconnect the wiring and remove the screws to disconnect the speaker from the grille.
20 Installation is the reverse of removal.

Upper door speakers

21 Refer to Chapter 11 and remove the cover panels for the outside mirrors for access to these speakers.

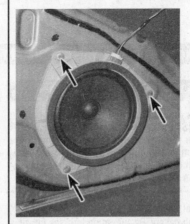

12.16 The speakers are retained with rivets on most models - drill them out and replace them with sheet metal screws if you don't have access to a rivet gun

22 Disconnect the speaker wiring and remove the speaker.
23 Installation is the reverse of removal.

Instrument panel lower center speakers

24 Remove the single screw and use a screwdriver wrapped with tape to pry off the lower center instrument panel cover.
25 Disconnect the speaker wiring and remove the speaker.
26 Installation is the reverse of removal.

13 Antenna - replacement

▶ **Refer to illustration 13.2**

1 The vehicles covered by this manual are equipped with a mast-type antenna attached to the roof.
2 If the antenna mast is damaged, it can be removed by turning it counterclockwise (see illustration). Wrap the antenna with tape for a good grip and it can be removed by hand.
3 The antenna cable runs from the radio up through the passenger-side windshield pillar under the headliner.
4 It's a difficult job for the home mechanic to remove all the panels and the headliner for access to the cables or replacement of the antenna mast base. This procedure is best left to a qualified shop.

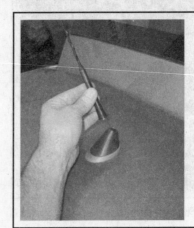

13.2 The antenna mast is easily separated from its base by turning it

14 Rear window defogger - check and repair

1   The rear window defogger consists of a number of horizontal elements baked onto the glass surface. If the defogger isn't working, first check the defogger relay and fuse in the interior fuse/relay box.

2   Small breaks in the element can be repaired without removing the rear window.

CHECK

▶ **Refer to illustrations 14.4, 14.5 and 14.7**

3   Turn the ignition switch and defogger system switches to the ON position. Using a voltmeter, place the positive probe against the defogger grid positive terminal and the negative probe against the ground terminal. If battery voltage is not indicated, check the defogger switch and related wiring. If voltage is indicated, but all or part of the defogger doesn't heat, proceed with the following tests.

4   When measuring voltage during the next two tests, wrap a piece of aluminum foil around the tip of the voltmeter positive probe and press the foil against the heating element with your finger (see illustration). Place the negative probe on the defogger grid ground terminal.

5   Check the voltage at the center of each heating element (see illustration). If the voltage is 5 or 6-volts, the element is okay (there is no break). If the voltage is 0-volts, the element is broken between the center of the element and the positive end. If the voltage is 10 to volts the element is broken between the center of the element and ground. Check each heating element.

6   Connect the negative lead to a good body ground. The reading should stay the same. If it doesn't, the ground connection is bad.

7   To find the break, place the voltmeter negative probe against the defogger ground terminal. Place the voltmeter positive probe with the foil strip against the heating element at the positive terminal end and slide it toward the negative terminal end. The point at which the voltmeter deflects from several volts to zero is the point at which the heating element is broken (see illustration).

14.4 When measuring the voltage at the rear window defogger grid, wrap a piece of aluminum foil around the positive probe of the voltmeter and press the foil against the wire with your finger

REPAIR

▶ **Refer to illustration 14.13**

8   Repair the break in the element using a repair kit specifically recommended for this purpose, available at most auto parts stores. Included in this kit is plastic conductive epoxy.

9   Prior to repairing a break, turn off the system and allow it to cool off for a few minutes.

10 Lightly buff the element area with fine steel wool, and then clean it thoroughly with rubbing alcohol.

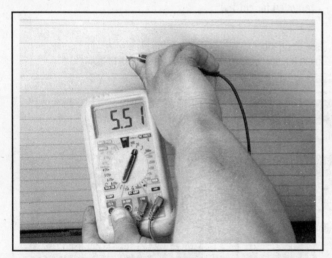

14.5 To determine if a heating element has broken, check the voltage at the center of each element - if the voltage is 5 or 6-volts, the element is unbroken - if the voltage is 10 or volts, the element is broken between the center and the ground side - if there is no voltage, the element is broken between the center and the positive side

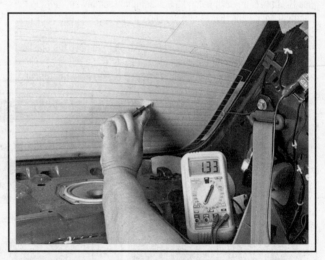

14.7 To find the break, place the voltmeter negative lead against the defogger ground terminal, place the voltmeter positive lead with the foil strip against the heating element at the positive terminal end and slide it toward the negative terminal end the point at which the voltmeter reading changes abruptly is the point at which the element is broken

11 Use masking tape to mask off the area being repaired.

12 Thoroughly mix the epoxy, following the instructions provided with the repair kit.

13 Apply the epoxy material to the slit in the masking tape, overlapping the undamaged area about 3/4-inch on either end (see illustration).

14 Allow the repair to cure for 24 hours before removing the tape and using the system.

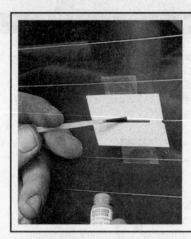

14.13 To use a defogger repair kit, apply masking tape to the inside of the window at the damaged area, then brush on the special conductive coating

15 Headlight bulb - replacement

▶ Refer to illustrations 15.1, 15.2, 15.3a and 15.3b

※※ WARNING:

Halogen gas filled bulbs are under pressure and may shatter if the surface is scratched or the bulb is dropped. Wear eye protection and handle the bulbs carefully, grasping only the base whenever possible. Do not touch the surface of the bulb with your fingers because the oil from your skin could cause it to overheat and fail prematurely. If you do touch the bulb surface, clean it with rubbing alcohol.

1 Open the hood. If you're replacing the right-side headlight, remove the windshield washer reservoir for access to the bulb. If you're removing the left-side headlight, remove the cover from the fuse/relay box for access to the bulb. If that doesn't give you enough working room you can unbolt the fuse/relay box which may give you a little more access. Otherwise, the headlight housing will have to be removed (see Section 17). Reach behind the headlight assembly and unplug the electrical connector, depressing the clip on the harness connector (see illustration).

2 Rotate the plastic cover counterclockwise to remove the plastic cover from the housing (see illustration).

3 Release the bulb retainer and remove the bulb from the housing

15.1 Unplug the wiring from the headlight bulb (headlight removed for clarity)

(see illustrations). Without touching the glass with your bare fingers, insert the new bulb assembly into the headlight housing.

4 Plug in the electrical connector.

15.2 Remove the plastic cover from the rear of the headlight

15.3a Release the bulb retainer . . .

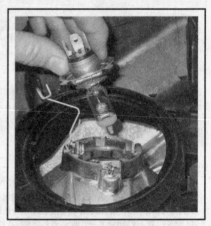

15.3b . . . then remove the bulb - don't touch the glass of the new bulb with your bare fingers

16 Headlights - adjustment

▶ **Refer to illustrations 16.1 and 16.3**

➡**Note: The headlights must be aimed correctly. If adjusted incorrectly they could blind the driver of an oncoming vehicle and cause a serious accident or seriously reduce your ability to see the road. The headlights should be checked for proper aim every 12 months and any time a new headlight is installed or front-end bodywork is performed. It should be emphasized that the following procedure is only an interim step, which will provide temporary adjustment until the headlights can be adjusted by a properly equipped shop.**

1   The vertical adjustment screws are located behind each headlight housing (see illustration). (There are no horizontal adjustment screws.)

2   There are several methods for adjusting the headlights. The simplest method requires masking tape, a blank wall and a level floor.

3   Position masking tape vertically on the wall in reference to the vehicle centerline and the centerlines of both headlights (see illustration).

4   Position a horizontal tape line in reference to the centerline of all the headlights.

➡**Note: It might be easier to position the tape on the wall with the vehicle parked only a few inches away.**

5   Adjustment should be made with the vehicle parked 25 feet from the wall, sitting level, the gas tank half-full and no heavy load in the vehicle.

16.1 Insert the end of a Phillips screwdriver into the headlight adjuster to turn it (left headlight shown)

6   Starting with the low beam adjustment, position the high intensity zone so it is two inches below the horizontal line. Adjustment is made by turning the adjusting screw clockwise to raise the beam and counter-clockwise to lower the beam.

7   With the high beams on, the high intensity zone should be vertically centered with the exact center just below the horizontal line.

➡**Note: It might not be possible to position the headlight aim exactly for both high and low beams. If a compromise must be made, keep in mind that the low beams are the most used and have the greatest effect on safety.**

8   Have the headlights adjusted by a dealer service department or service station at the earliest opportunity.

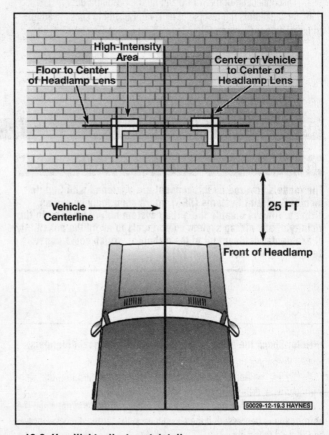

16.3 Headlight adjustment details

17 Headlight housing - replacement

❋❋ **WARNING:**

These vehicles are equipped with halogen gas-filled headlight bulbs that are under pressure and may shatter if the surface is damaged or the bulb is dropped. Wear eye protection and handle the bulbs carefully, grasping only the base whenever possible. Do not touch the surface of the bulb with your fingers because the oil from your skin could cause it to overheat and fail prematurely. If you do touch the bulb surface, clean it with rubbing alcohol.

➡**Note: Headlight housings are expensive to replace, but repair kits are available at Toyota dealerships that can save a headlight housing that has broken mounting tabs.**

2001 THROUGH 2003 MODELS

1   Remove the engine bottom cover and the front bumper cover (see Chapter 11).

2   Remove the two upper bolts and the nut at the bottom of the fender.

3   Disconnect the wiring and lift the headlight out.

4   Installation is the reverse of removal. Be sure to check headlight adjustment (see Section 16).

2004 AND LATER MODELS

▶ **Refer to illustration 17.6**

5   Remove the fender inner liners and the front bumper cover (see Chapter 11).

6   Remove the three fasteners from the headlight assembly (see illustration).

7   Disconnect all of the wiring and lift the headlight out.

8   Installation is the reverse of removal. Be sure to check headlight adjustment (see Section 16).

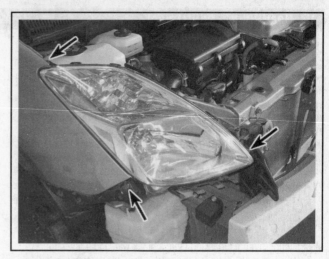

17.6 Headlight housing fasteners

18   Horn - check and replacement

✳✳ WARNING:

The models covered by this manual are equipped with Supplemental Restraint Systems (SRS), more commonly known as airbags. Always disable the airbag system before working in the vicinity of any airbag system components to avoid the possibility of accidental deployment of the airbag(s), which could cause personal injury (see Section 24).

CHECK

→**Note: Check the fuses before beginning electrical diagnosis.**

1   Disconnect the electrical connector from the horn.

2   To test the horn, connect battery voltage to the horn terminal with a jumper wire. If the horn doesn't sound, replace it.

3   If the horn does sound, check for voltage at the terminal when the horn button is depressed. If there's voltage at the terminal, check for a bad ground at the horn.

4   If there's no voltage at the horn, check the relay (see Section 5).

5   If the relay is OK, check for voltage to the relay power and control circuits. If either of the circuits is not receiving voltage, inspect the wiring between the relay and the fuse panel.

6   If both relay circuits are receiving voltage, depress the horn button and check the circuit from the relay to the horn button for continuity to ground. If there's no continuity, check the circuit for an open. If there's no open circuit, replace the horn button.

7   If there's continuity to ground through the horn button, check for an open or short in the circuit from the relay to the horn.

REPLACEMENT

2001 through 2003 models

8   There are two horns; one is behind the right headlight and the

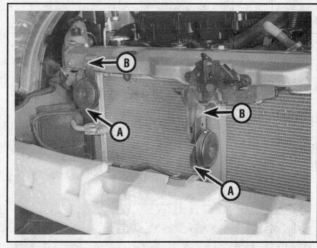

18.12 Disconnect the electrical connectors (A), then remove the mounting fasteners (B)

other is in the center of the front of the engine compartment. It is necessary to remove the front bumper cover to access the center horn (see Chapter 11).

9   To replace a horn, disconnect the electrical connector and remove its bracket bolt.

10   Installation is the reverse of removal.

2004 and later models

▶ **Refer to illustration 18.12**

11   Remove the front bumper cover for access to either horn (see Chapter 11).

12   To replace a horn, disconnect the electrical connector and remove its bracket bolt (see illustration).

13   Installation is the reverse of removal.

19 Bulb replacement

FRONT PARK/TURN SIGNAL LIGHTS

▶ **Refer to illustration 19.2**

1   The park/turn signal lights and side marker lights are all are part of the headlight housing. These bulbs are accessible from behind the headlight housing (in place), although with some difficulty. If you have trouble, refer to Section 17 and remove the headlight housing for access to these bulbs.

2   Rotate the bulb holder counterclockwise and pull the bulb out (see illustration). Remove the bulb from the holder. On some models, the side marker light is a separate unit mounted in the front fender. On these models, access to the bulb is from underneath the fender.

3   Installation is the reverse of removal.

REAR TAIL LIGHT/BRAKE LIGHT/TURN SIGNAL/SIDE MARKER/BACKUP

▶ **Refer to illustrations 19.4 and 19.5**

4   The taillight/brake/turn signal bulbs can be accessed by removing access panels in the luggage compartment (see illustration).

5   Rotate the bulb holders counterclockwise and pull the bulbs out to remove them. Remove the bulb from the holder (see illustration).

6   The backup lights in the tailgate are accessible only after opening a cover on the inside of the tailgate, using a screwdriver to release it. Twist the bulb holder counterclockwise to remove it.

7   Installation is the reverse of removal.

CENTER HIGH-MOUNTED STOP LIGHT

▶ **Refer to illustration 19.8**

8   Remove the fastners securing the center high-mounted stop light assembly (see illustration).

9   Pull the stop light assembly straight out, disconnect the electrical connector and remove it from the tailgate.

10 Installation is the reverse of removal.

INTERIOR LIGHT

▶ **Refer to illustrations 19.11, 19.12a and 19.12b**

11 Carefully pry the out the interior light housing (see illustration).
12 Detach the bulb from the terminals (see illustrations). It may be

19.2 The front turn signal bulbs can be removed easily; turn them counter-clockwise, then pull them out

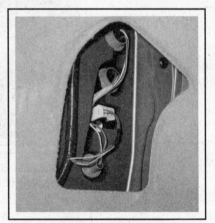

19.4 Remove the access panels to get to the rear lighting components

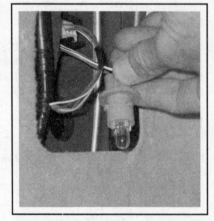

19.5 The bulb holders are removed by rotating them counterclockwise and then pulling

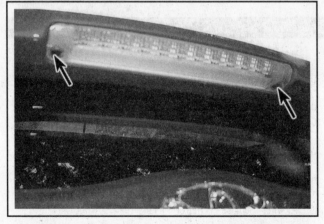

19.8 Remove the fastners securing the center high-mounted stop light assembly

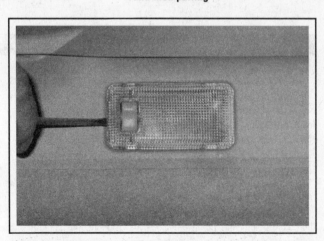

19.11 Pry the interior light housing from the trim panel

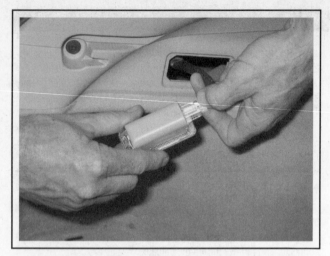

19.12a Disconnect the wiring from the socket

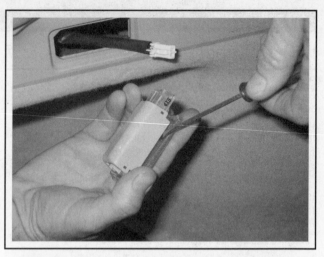

19.12b Pry the cover from the holder to remove the bulb

necessary to pry the bulb out - if this is the case, pry only on the ends of the bulb (otherwise the glass may shatter).

13 Installation is the reverse of removal.

LICENSE PLATE LIGHT

▶ **Refer to illustration 19.15**

14 Remove the tailgate trim panels (see Chapter 11)

15 Rotate the bulb holders counterclockwise and pull the bulbs out to remove them. Remove the bulb from the holder (see illustration).

16 Installation is the reverse of removal.

FOG LIGHT

17 Raise the vehicle and secure it on jackstands.

18 Remove the splash shield.

19 Twist the bulb holder from the housing and replace the bulb.

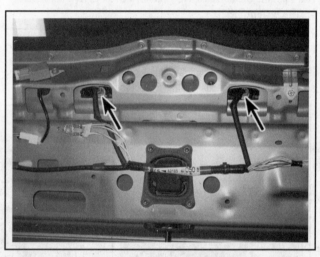

19.15 Remove the interior tailgate trim panel to access the license plate lamps

20 Electric side view mirrors - description

1 Most electric side view mirrors use two motors to move the glass; one for up and down adjustments and one for left-right adjustments.

2 The control switch has a selector portion that sends voltage to the left or right side mirror. With the ignition ON but the engine OFF, roll down the windows and operate the mirror control switch through all functions (left-right and up-down) for both the left and right side mirrors.

3 Listen carefully for the sound of the electric motors running in the mirrors.

4 If the motors can be heard but the mirror glass doesn't move, there's a problem with the drive mechanism inside the mirror.

5 If the mirrors do not operate and no sound comes from the mirrors, check the fuse (see Section 3).

6 If the fuse is OK, remove the mirror control switch from the dashboard. Have the switch continuity checked by a dealership service department or other qualified automobile repair facility.

7 If the mirror still doesn't work, remove the mirror and check the wires at the mirror for voltage.

8 If there's not voltage in each switch position, check the circuit between the mirror and control switch for opens and shorts.

9 If there's voltage, remove the mirror and test it off the vehicle with jumper wires. Replace the mirror if it fails this test.

21 Cruise control system - description

These models have an electrically controlled throttle body. The accelerator pedal communicates with the throttle body through the Powertrain Control Module (PCM). (See Chapters 4 and 6 for more information about the electronic throttle control system.) The PCM also controls the cruise control system, which is now an integral function of the electronic throttle control system. If the system malfunctions, begin diagnosis by checking to see if any trouble codes have been set (see Chapter 6). If that doesn't lead to the problem, take it to a dealer service department or other qualified repair shop for further diagnosis.

22 Power window system - description

1 The power window system operates electric motors, mounted in the doors, which lower and raise the windows. The system consists of the control switches, relays, the motors, regulators, glass mechanisms and associated wiring.

2 The power windows can be lowered and raised from the master control switch by the driver or by remote switches located at the individual windows. Each window has a separate motor that is reversible. The position of the control switch determines the polarity and therefore the direction of operation.

3 The circuit is protected by a fuse and a circuit breaker. Each motor is also equipped with an internal circuit breaker; this prevents one stuck window from disabling the whole system.

4 The power window system will only operate when the ignition switch is ON. In addition, many models have a window lockout switch at the master control switch that, when activated, disables the switches at the rear windows and, sometimes, the switch at the passenger's window also. Always check these items before troubleshooting a window problem.

5 These procedures are general in nature, so if you can't find the problem using them, take the vehicle to a dealer service department or other properly equipped repair facility.

6 If the power windows won't operate, always check the fuse and circuit breaker first.

7 If only the rear windows are inoperative, or if the windows only operate from the master control switch, check the rear window lockout switch for continuity in the unlocked position. Replace it if it doesn't have continuity.

8 Check the wiring between the switches and fuse panel for continuity. Repair the wiring, if necessary.

9 If only one window is inoperative from the master control switch, try the other control switch at the window.

→**Note: This doesn't apply to the driver's door window.**

10 If the same window works from one switch, but not the other, check the switch for continuity. Have the switch checked at a dealer service department or other qualified automobile repair facility.

11 If the switch tests OK, check for a short or open in the circuit between the affected switch and the window motor.

12 If one window is inoperative from both switches, remove the trim panel from the affected door and check for voltage at the switch and at the motor while the switch is operated.

13 If voltage is reaching the motor, disconnect the glass from the regulator (see Chapter 11). Move the window up and down by hand while checking for binding and damage. Also check for binding and damage to the regulator. If the regulator is not damaged and the window moves up and down smoothly, replace the motor. If there's binding or damage, lubricate, repair or replace parts, as necessary.

14 If voltage isn't reaching the motor, check the wiring in the circuit for continuity between the switches and motors. You'll need to consult the wiring diagram for the vehicle. If the circuit is equipped with a relay, check that the relay is grounded properly and receiving voltage.

15 Test the windows after you are done to confirm proper repairs.

23 Power door lock/smart key system - description

1 A power door lock system operates the door lock actuators mounted in each door. The system consists of the switches, actuators, a control unit and associated wiring. Diagnosis can usually be limited to simple checks of the wiring connections and actuators for minor faults that can be easily repaired.

2 Power door lock systems are operated by bi-directional solenoids located in the doors. The lock switches have two operating positions: Lock and Unlock. When activated, the switch sends a ground signal to the door lock control unit to lock or unlock the doors. Depending on which way the switch is activated, the control unit reverses polarity to the solenoids, allowing the two sides of the circuit to be used alternately as the feed (positive) and ground side.

3 Some vehicles may have an anti-theft system incorporated into the power locks. If you are unable to locate the trouble using the following general Steps, consult a dealer service department or other qualified repair shop.

4 Always check the circuit protection first. Some vehicles use a combination of circuit breakers and fuses.

5 Operate the door lock switches in both directions (Lock and Unlock) with the engine off. Listen for the click of the solenoids operating.

6 Test the switches for continuity. Remove the switches and have them checked by a dealer service department or other qualified automobile repair facility.

7 Check the wiring between the switches, control unit and solenoids for continuity. Repair the wiring if there's no continuity.

8 Check for a bad ground at the switches or the control unit.

9 If all but one lock solenoids operate, remove the trim panel from the affected door (see Chapter 11) and check for voltage at the solenoid while the lock switch is operated. One of the wires should have voltage in the Lock position; the other should have voltage in the Unlock position.

10 If the inoperative solenoid is receiving voltage, replace the solenoid.

11 If the inoperative solenoid isn't receiving voltage, check the relay for an open or short in the wire between the lock solenoid and the control unit.

➡**Note: It's common for wires to break in the portion of the harness between the body and door (opening and closing the door fatigues and eventually breaks the wires).**

KEYLESS ENTRY SYSTEM

12 The keyless entry system consists of a remote control transmitter that sends a coded infrared signal to a receiver that then operates the door lock system. On models so equipped, the transmitter may also engage the alarm system and provide a "panic" button that flashes the lights and blows the horn for emergencies.

13 Replace the transmitter batteries when the red LED light on the case doesn't light when the button is pushed. As the batteries deterio-rate with age, the distance at which the remote transmitter operates will diminish.

14 Use a coin or small screwdriver to carefully separate the case halves for battery replacement.

15 Replace the two lithium batteries with the same type as originally installed, observing the polarity diagram on the case.

16 Snap the case halves together.

SMART KEY SYSTEM

17 The smart key system is used on 2004 and later models. It has the same capabilities as the earlier systems with the addition of two-way communication between the key and the vehicle.

18 The certification ECU inside the car can "see" the smart key in several zones around it. When the smart key has been seen it can operate the door locks and also start the car.

19 The system uses several ECUs, transmitters and antennas as well as sensors, and switches. Because of this complexity, any problems must be referred to a dealer for diagnosis and repair.

24 Airbag system - general information

All models are equipped with a Supplemental Restraint System (SRS), more commonly known as airbags. This system is designed to protect the driver and the front seat passenger from serious injury in the event of a collision. On 2001 through 2003 models it consists of one impact sensor behind the front bumper, another in the dash and one on each side of the vehicle. There is an airbag module in the center of the steering wheel, in the right side of the instrument panel and in each front seat.

2004 and later models have airbag modules in the steering wheel, the passenger side of the instrument panel, in the front seats and side curtains along each side of the roof. There are pairs of sensors at the front bumper, the rear wheel areas and the sides of the vehicle. These later models also use seat position sensors and an occupant-classification computer.

AIRBAG MODULE

Driver's side

The airbag inflator module contains a housing incorporating the cushion (airbag) and inflator unit, mounted in the center of the steering wheel. The inflator assembly is mounted on the back of the housing over a hole through which gas is expelled, inflating the bag almost instantaneously when an electrical signal is sent from the system. A clockspring assembly on the steering column under the steering wheel carries this signal to the module.

This clockspring assembly can transmit an electrical signal regard-less of steering wheel position. The igniter in the airbag converts the electrical signal to heat and ignites the powder, which inflates the bag.

Passenger's side

The airbag is mounted above the glove compartment and designated by the letters SRS (Supplemental Restraint System). It consists of an inflator containing an igniter, a bag assembly, a reaction housing and a trim cover.

The airbag is considerably larger than the steering wheel-mounted unit and is supported by the steel reaction housing. The trim cover is textured and painted to match the instrument panel and has a molded seam that splits when the bag inflates.

Side impact airbags

Extra protection is provided with the addition of side-impact airbags. These are smaller devices located in the seat backs on the side toward the exterior of the vehicle. The impact sensors for the side-impact airbags are located at the bottom of the door pillars in the body, in the bottom of the driver and passenger seats or in the driver and passenger doors.

Side curtain airbags

Extra side-impact protection is provided on later models with the addition of side-curtain airbags (in addition to the side-impact airbags in the seatbacks). These are long airbags that, in the event of a side impact, come out of the headliner at each side of the car and come down between the side windows and the seats. They are designed to protect the heads of both front seat and rear seat passengers.

SENSING AND DIAGNOSTIC MODULE

The sensing and diagnostic module supplies the current to the airbag system in the event of the collision, even if battery power is cut off. It checks this system every time the vehicle is started, causing the "AIR BAG" light to go on then off, if the system is operating properly. If there is a fault in the system, the light will go on and stay on, flash, or the dash will make a beeping sound. If this happens, the vehicle should be taken to your dealer immediately for service.

DISARMING THE SYSTEM AND OTHER PRECAUTIONS

❊❊ WARNING:

Failure to follow these precautions could result in accidental deployment of the airbag and personal injury.

Whenever working in the vicinity of the steering wheel, steering column or any of the other SRS system components, the system must be disarmed. To disarm the system:

a) *Point the wheels straight ahead and turn the key to the Lock position (2003 and earlier models) or turn the Power button Off (2004 and later models).*

b) *Refer to Chapter 6 and disconnect the cable from the negative terminal of the auxiliary 12-volt battery. Be sure to perform the initialization procedure when reconnecting it. Make sure the cable is positioned so that it cannot come into contact with the battery terminal.*

c) *Wait at least two minutes for the back-up power supply to be depleted.*

Whenever handling an airbag module, always keep the airbag opening (the trim side) pointed away from your body. Never place the airbag module on a bench of other surface with the airbag opening facing the surface. Always place the airbag module in a safe location with the airbag opening facing up.

Never measure the resistance of any SRS component. An ohmmeter has a built-in battery supply that could accidentally deploy the airbag.

Never use electrical welding equipment on a vehicle equipped with an airbag without first disconnecting the yellow airbag connector, located under the steering column near the combination switch connector (driver's airbag) and behind the glove box (passenger's airbag).

Never dispose of a live airbag module. Return it to a dealer service department or other qualified repair shop for safe deployment and disposal.

COMPONENT REMOVAL AND INSTALLATION

Driver's side airbag module and clockspring

1   Refer to Chapter 10, *Steering wheel - removal and installation*, for the driver's side airbag module and clockspring removal and installation procedures.

Passenger's side airbag module

2001 through 2003 models

2   Refer to Chapter 11 and remove the lower cover panel from the instrument panel under the airbag module. It is secured by three screws and two bolts.

3   Disconnect the airbag wiring harness.

4   Remove the two bolts and carefully lift the airbag module out. Store it in a safe place with the finished side up.

2004 and later models

5   Disarm the airbag system as describes previously in this Section. Under the right side of the instrument panel, disconnect the yellow connectors for the passenger airbag.

6   Remove the glove box door (see Chapter 11). Be sure to heed the precautions outlined previously in this Section.

7   Carefully disconnect the airbag wiring harness.

8   Refer to Chapter 11 and remove the instrument panel safety pad.

9   Disconnect the wiring from the airbag module.

10 Release the ten claw-type clips that secure the airbag module to the instrument panel. Carefully lift it out and store it in a safe place with the finished side facing up.

11 Installation is the reverse of the removal procedure.

25 Wiring diagrams - general information

Since it isn't possible to include all wiring diagrams for every year covered by this manual, the following diagrams are those that are typical and most commonly needed.

Prior to troubleshooting any circuits, check the fuse and circuit breakers (if equipped) to make sure they're in good condition. Make sure the battery is properly charged and check the cable connections (see Chapter 1).

When checking a circuit, make sure that all connectors are clean, with no broken or loose terminals. When unplugging a connector, do not pull on the wires. Pull only on the connector housings themselves.

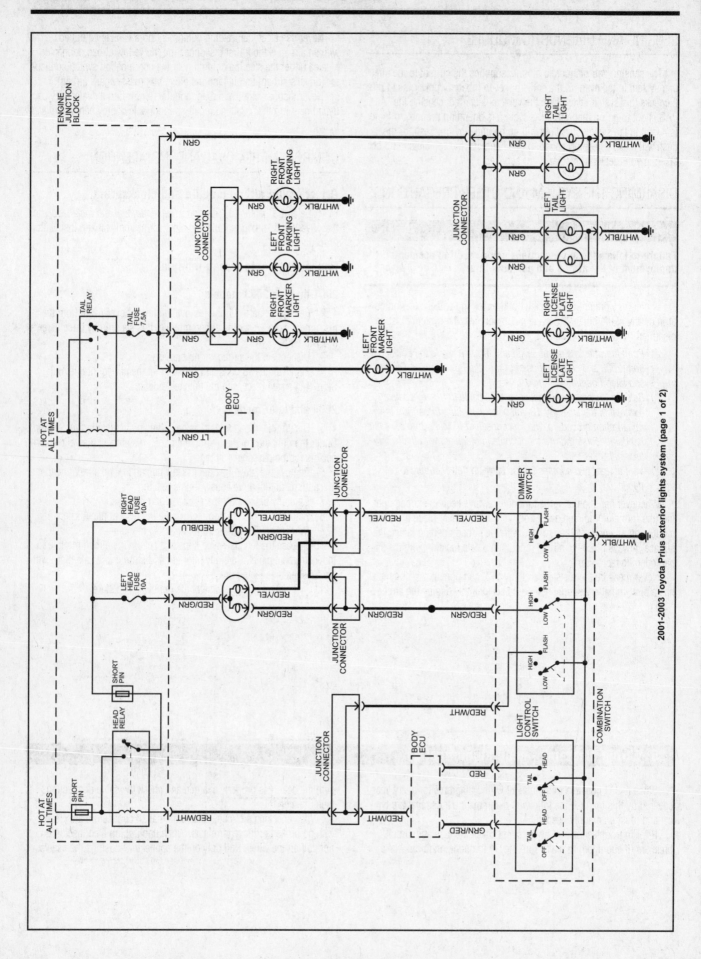

2001-2003 Toyota Prius exterior lights system (page 1 of 2)

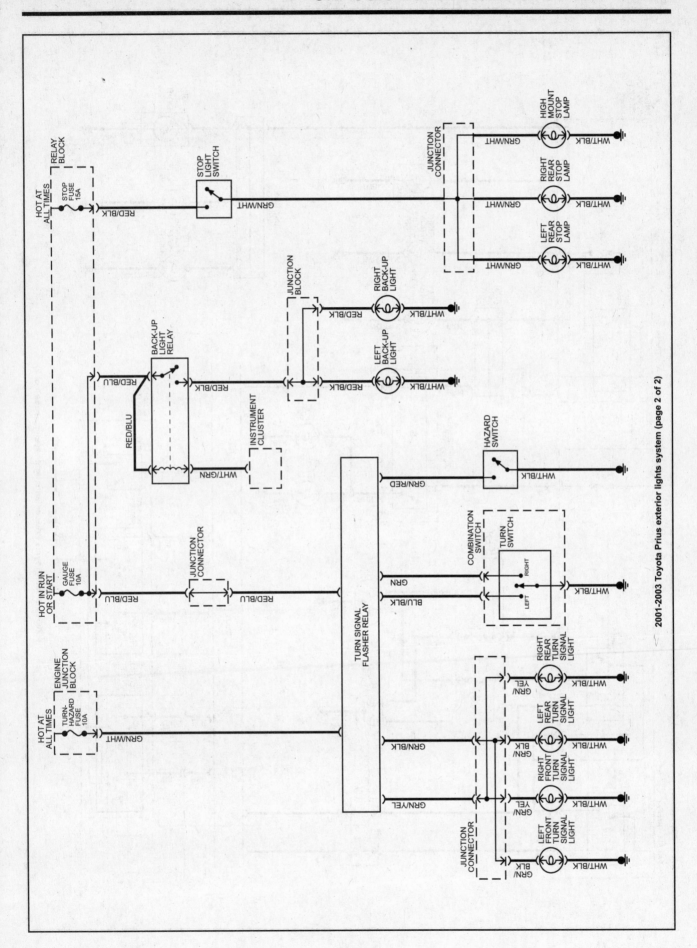

2001-2003 Toyota Prius exterior lights system (page 2 of 2)

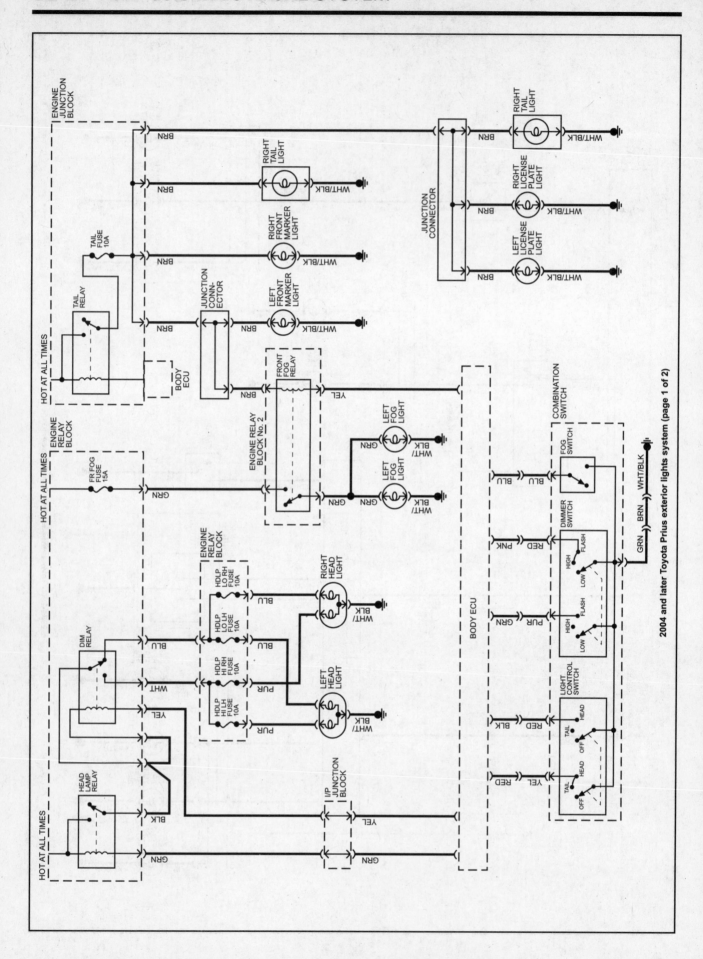

2004 and later Toyota Prius exterior lights system (page 1 of 2)

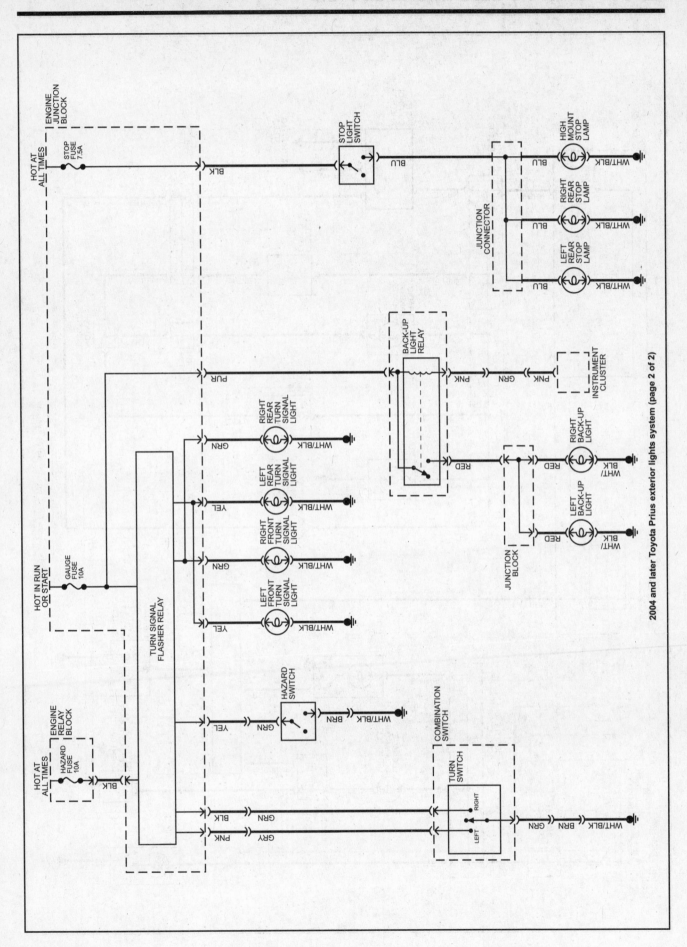

2004 and later Toyota Prius exterior lights system (page 2 of 2)

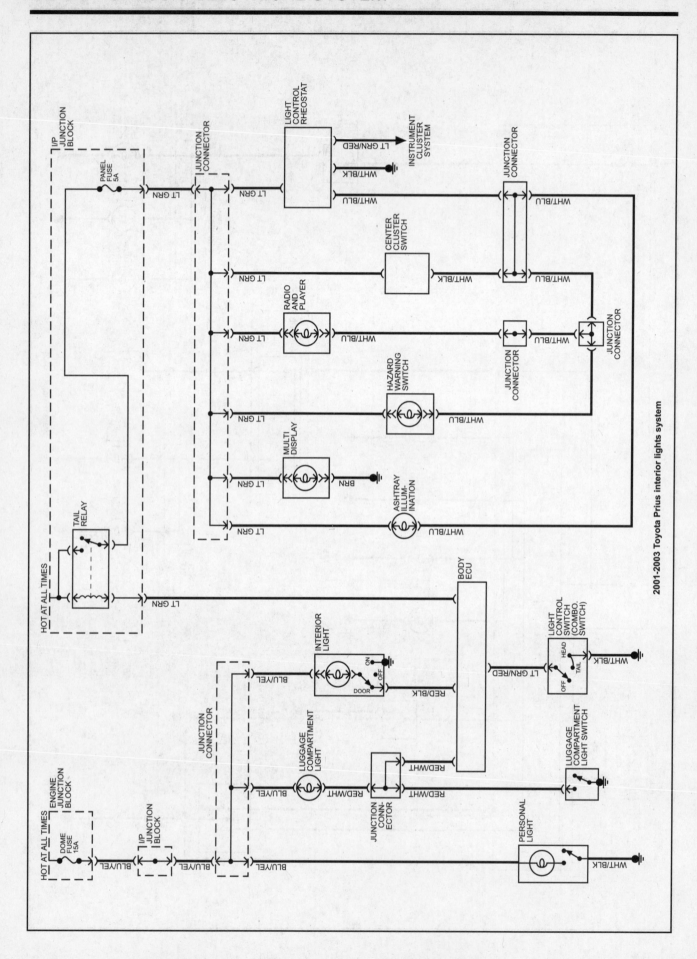

2001-2003 Toyota Prius interior lights system

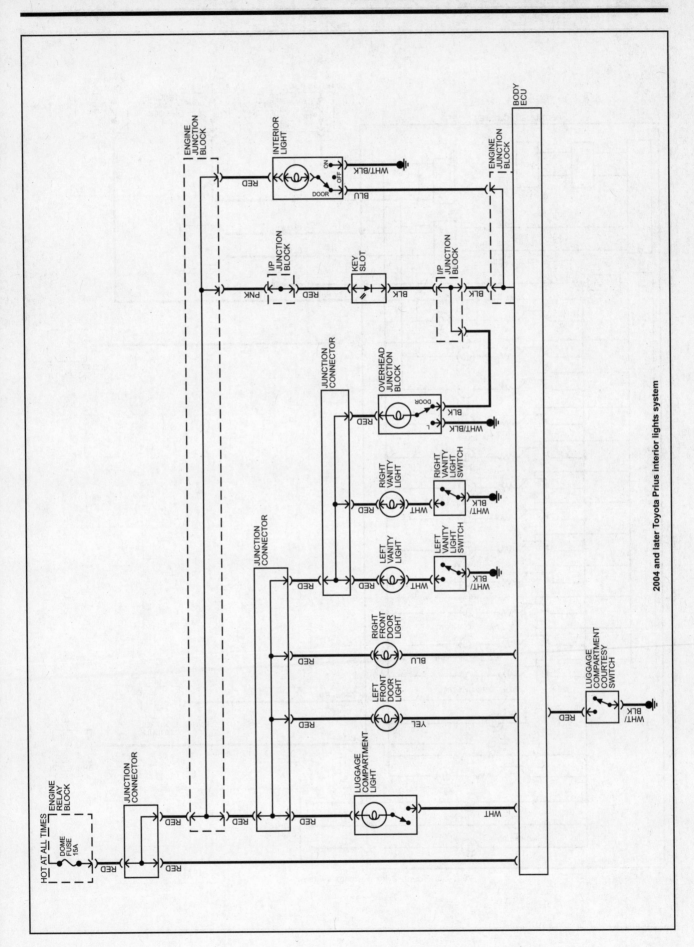

2004 and later Toyota Prius interior lights system

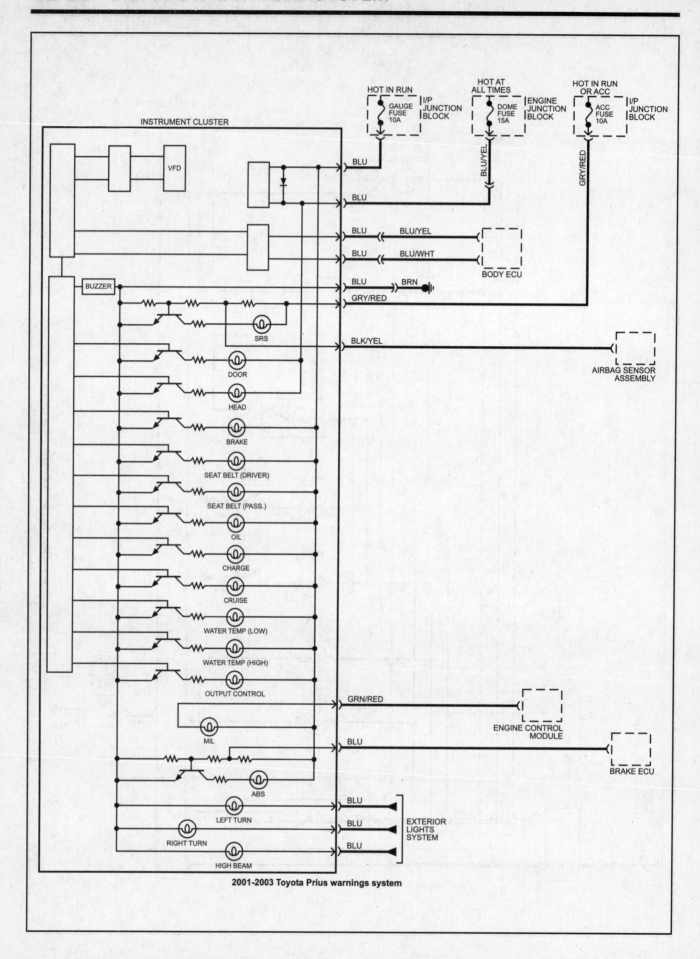

2001-2003 Toyota Prius warnings system

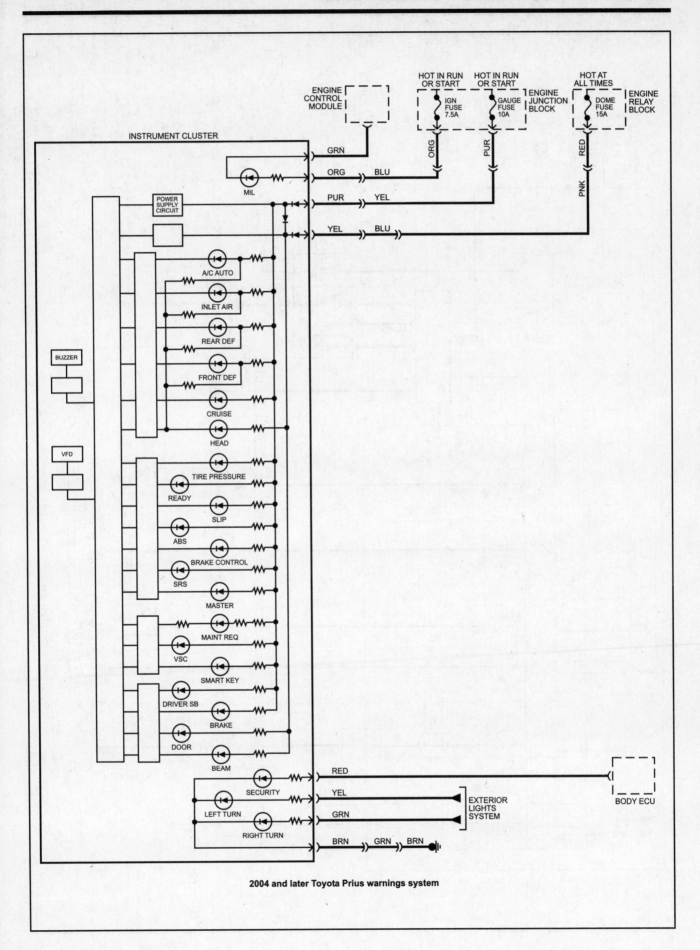

2004 and later Toyota Prius warnings system

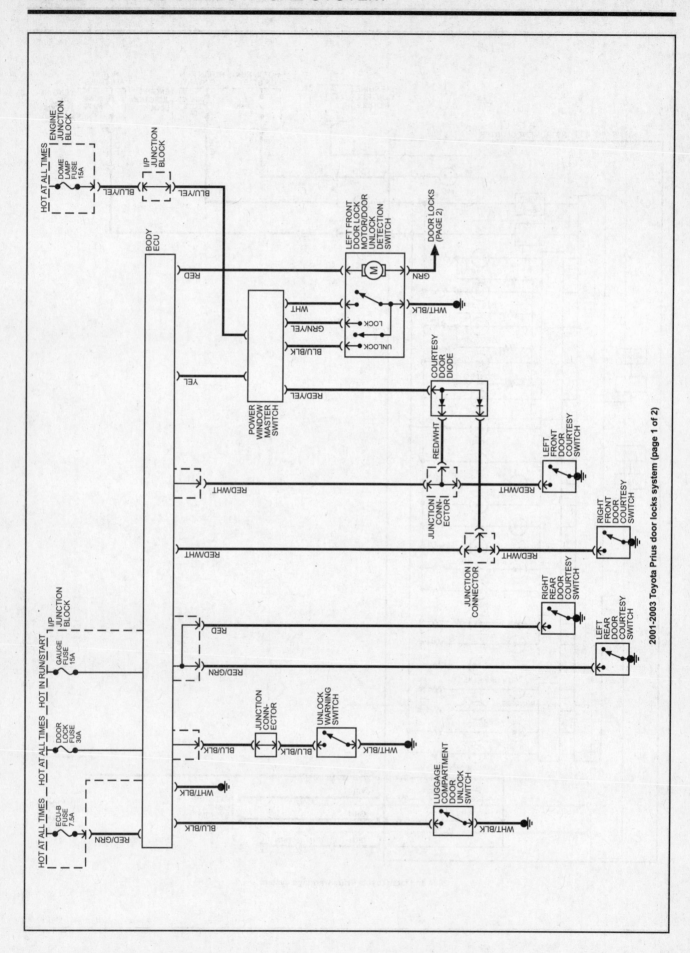

2001-2003 Toyota Prius door locks system (page 1 of 2)

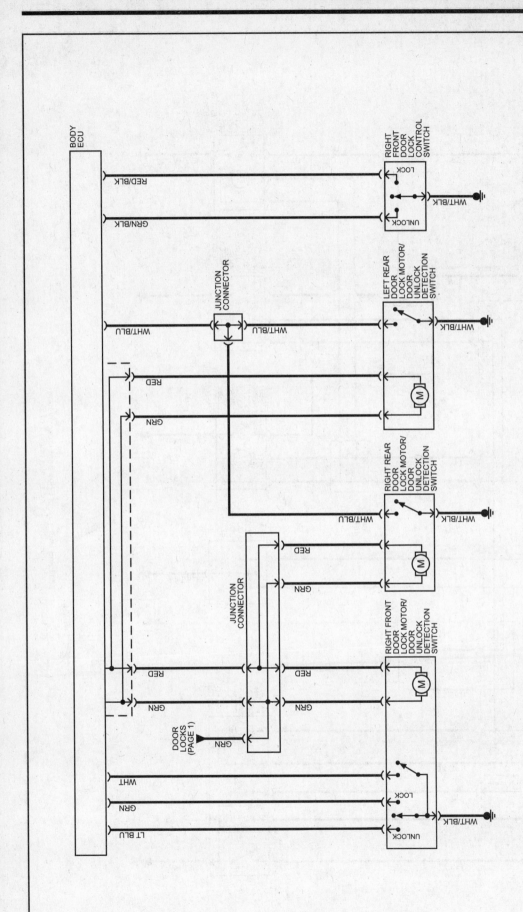

2001-2003 Toyota Prius door locks system (page 2 of 2)

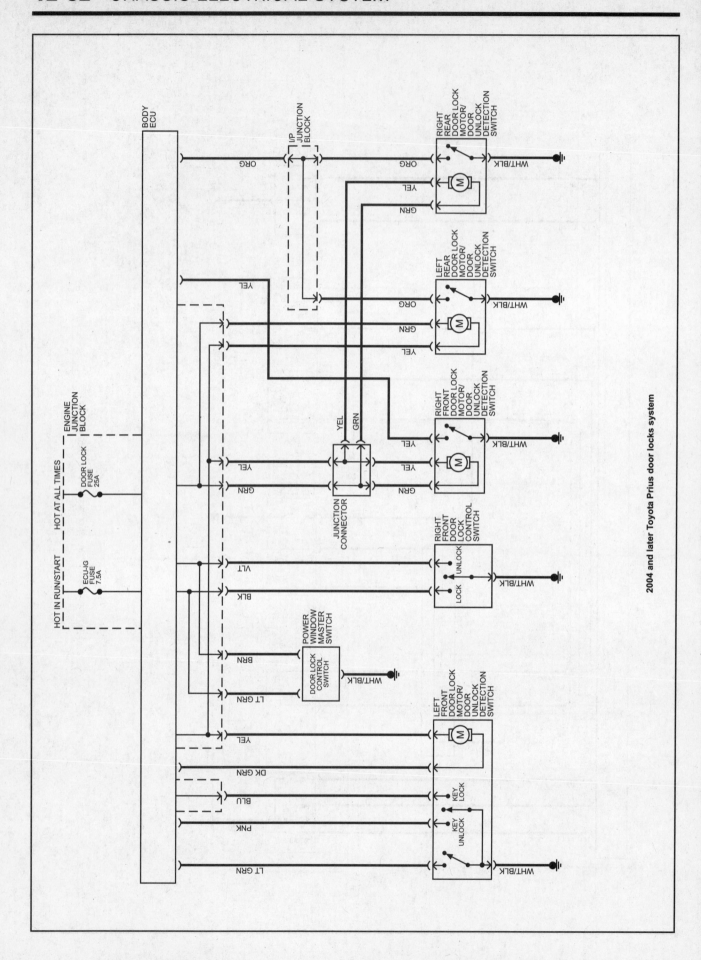

2004 and later Toyota Prius door locks system

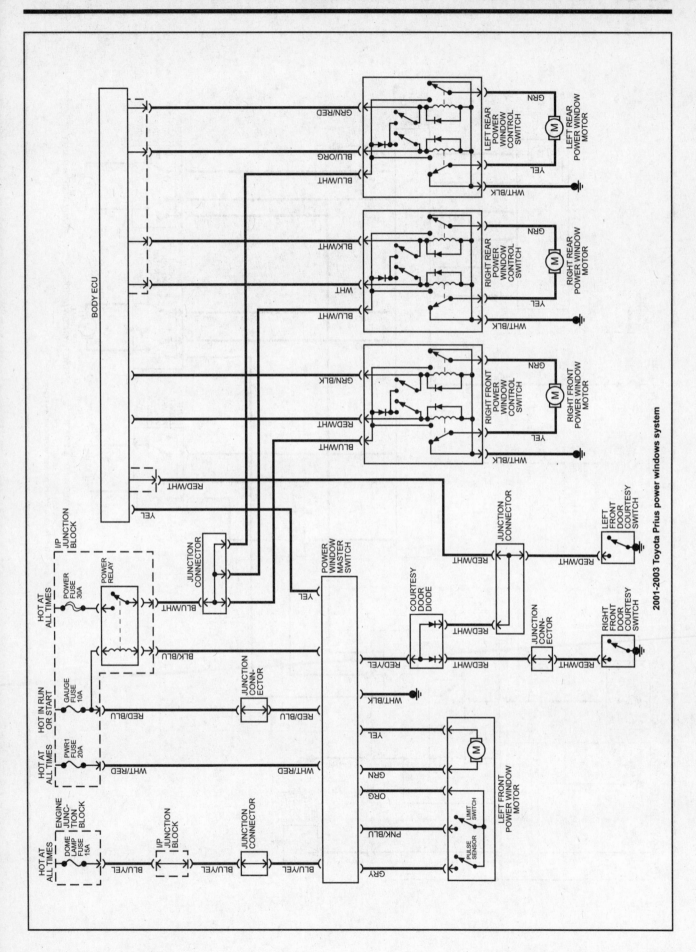

2001-2003 Toyota Prius power windows system

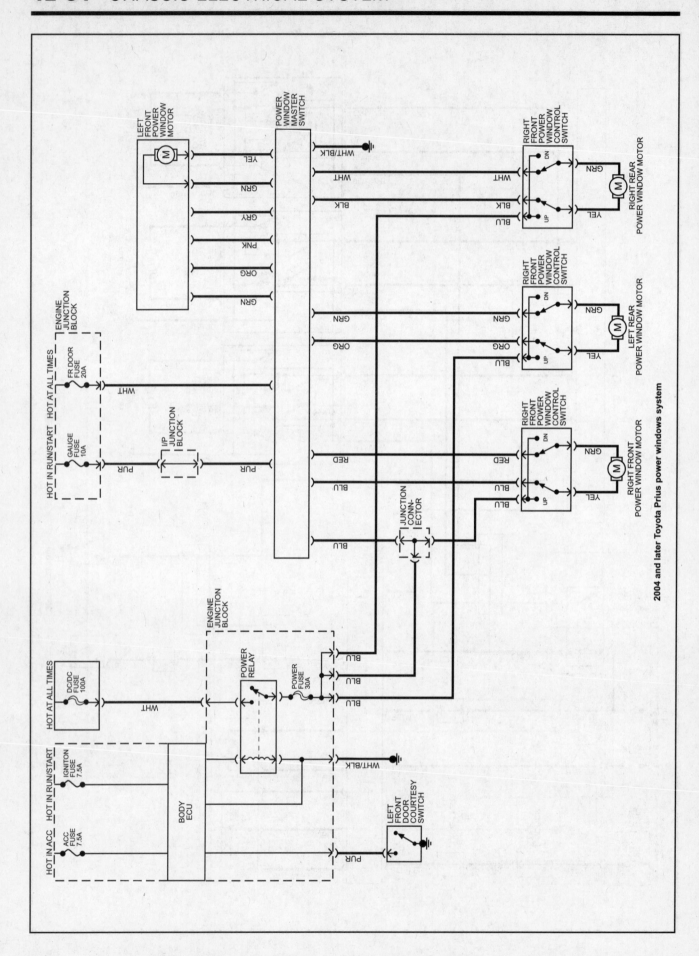

2004 and later Toyota Prius power windows system

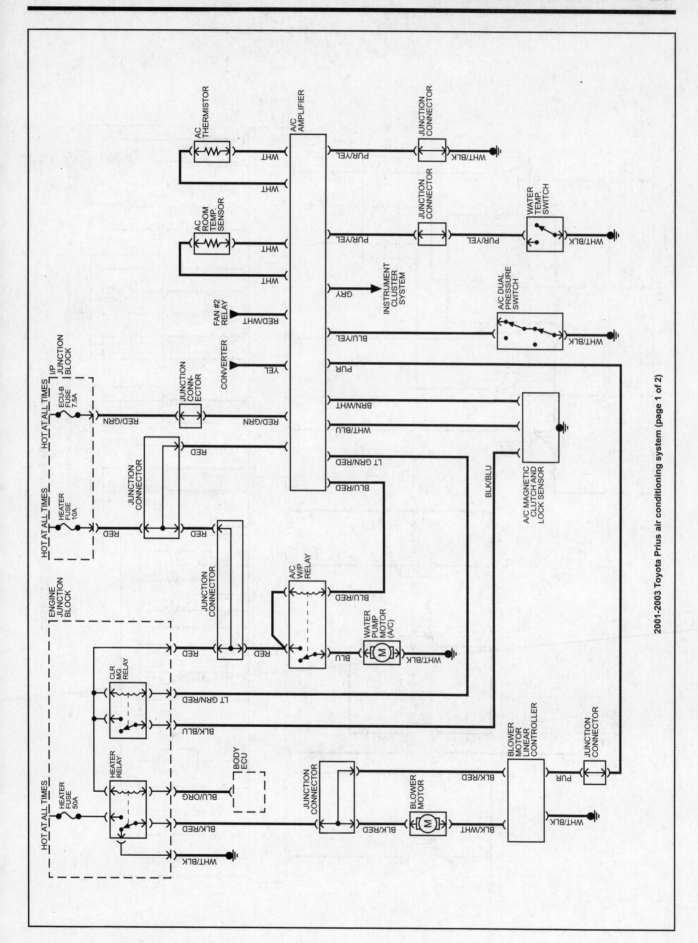

2001-2003 Toyota Prius air conditioning system (page 1 of 2)

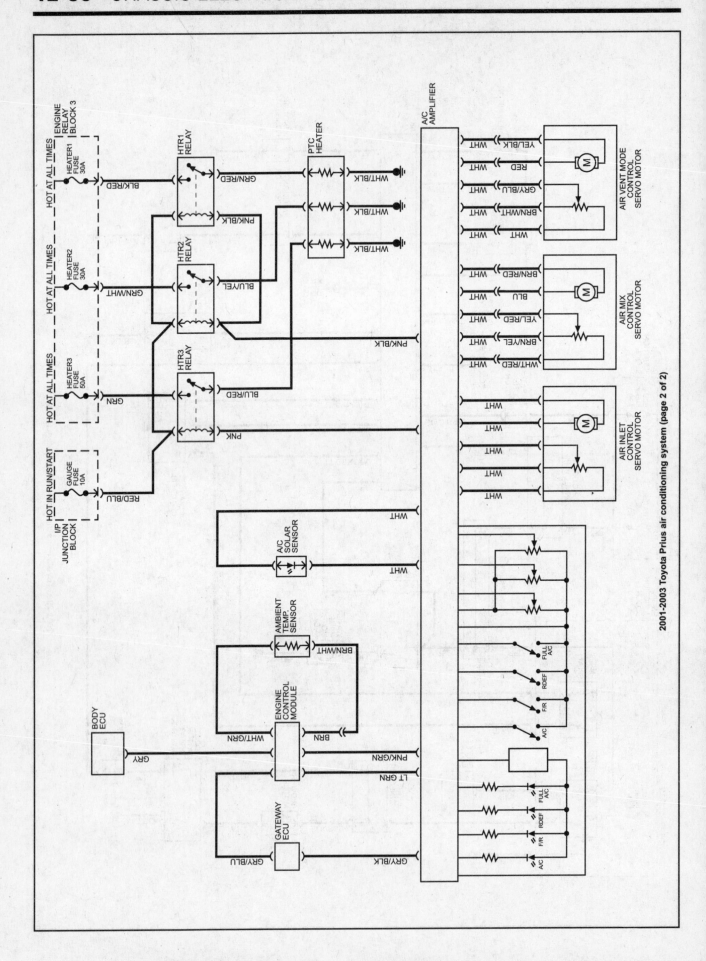

2001-2003 Toyota Prius air conditioning system (page 2 of 2)

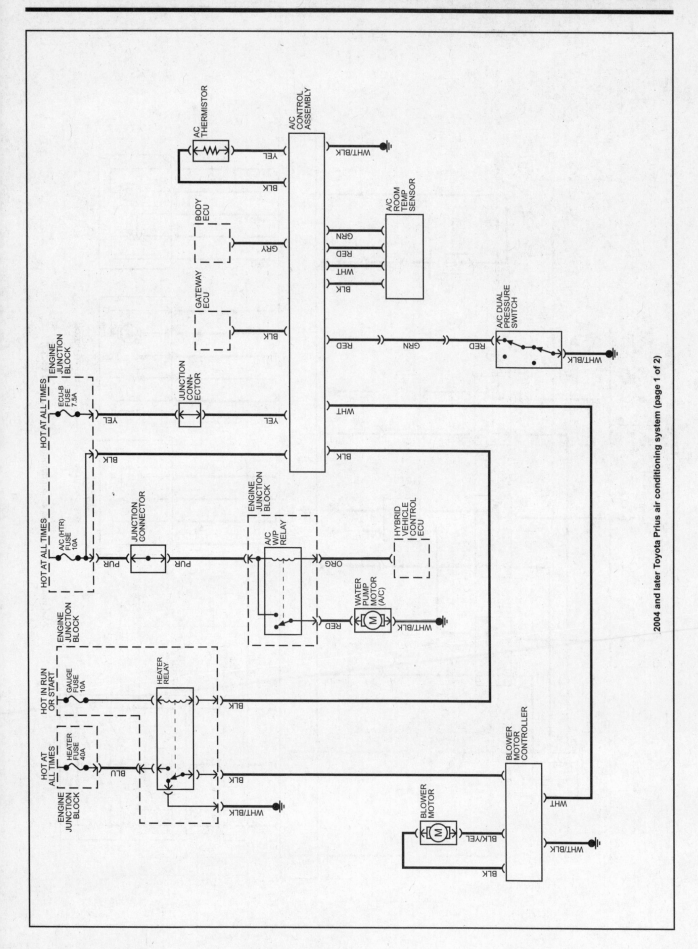

2004 and later Toyota Prius air conditioning system (page 1 of 2)

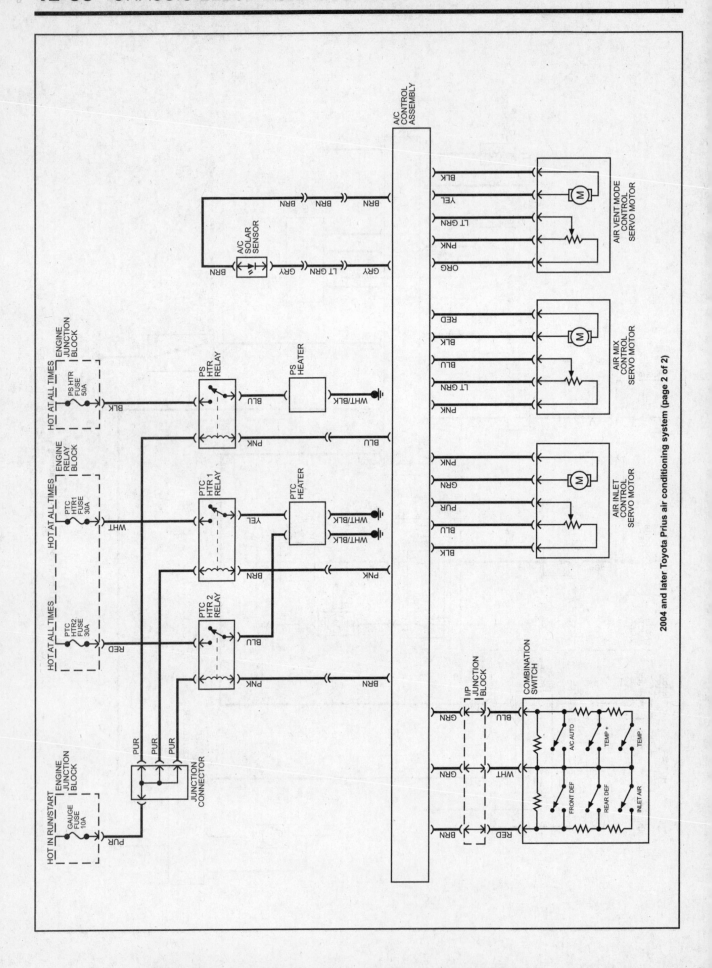

2004 and later Toyota Prius air conditioning system (page 2 of 2)

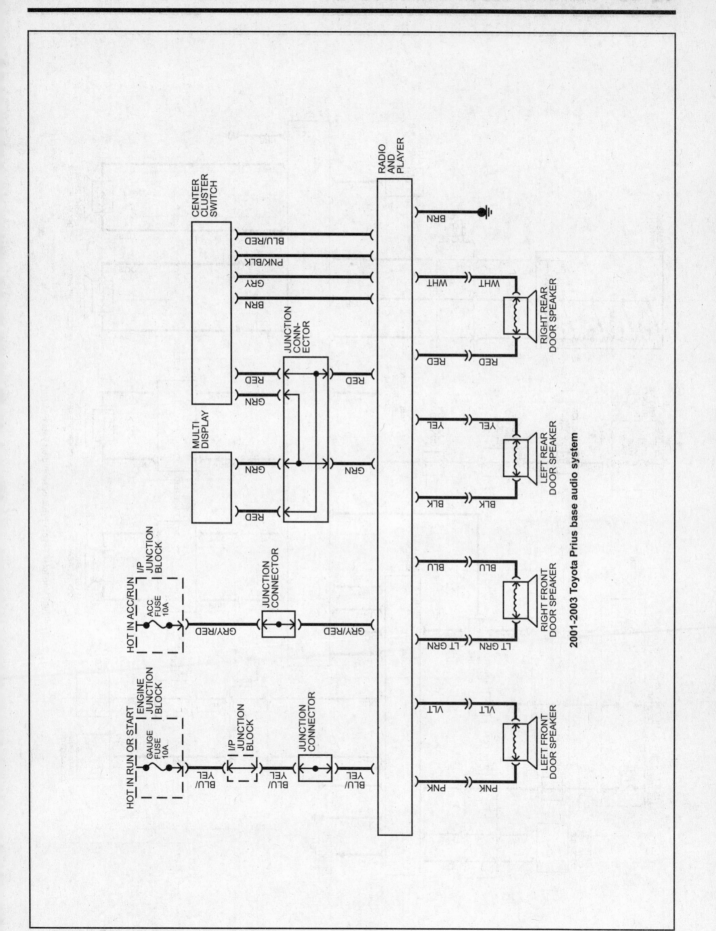

2001-2003 Toyota Prius base audio system

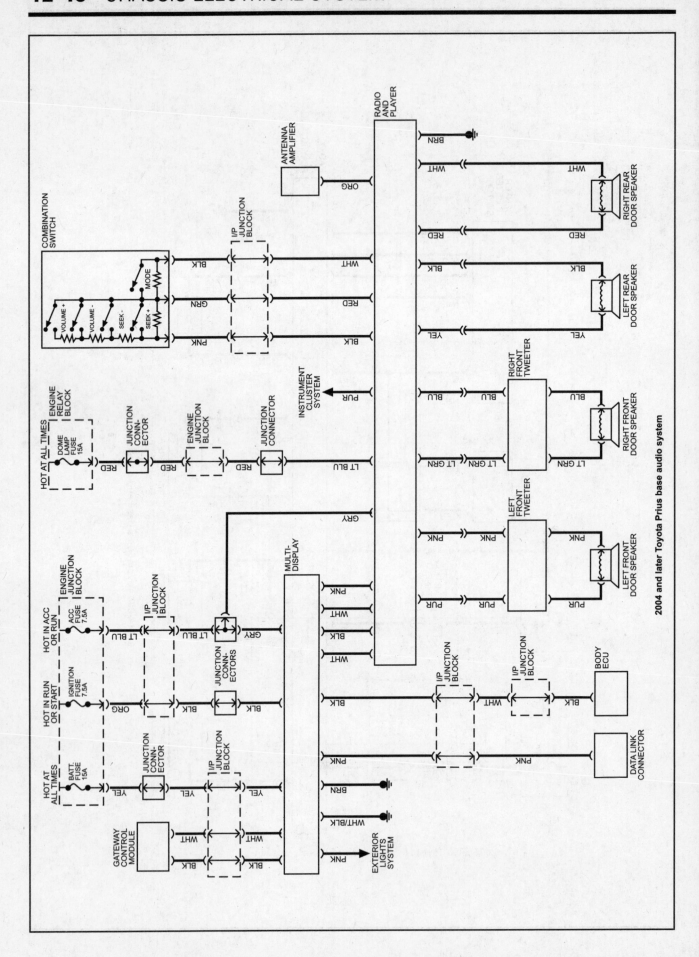

2004 and later Toyota Prius base audio system

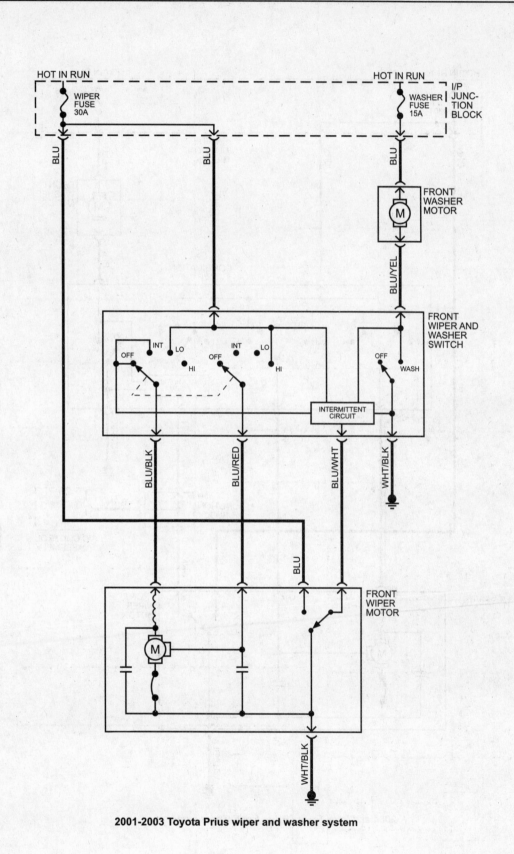

2001-2003 Toyota Prius wiper and washer system

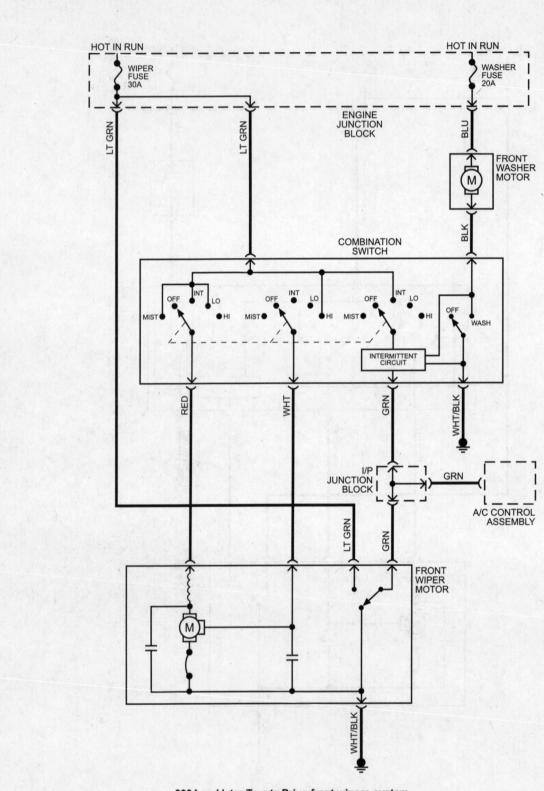

2004 and later Toyota Prius front wipers system

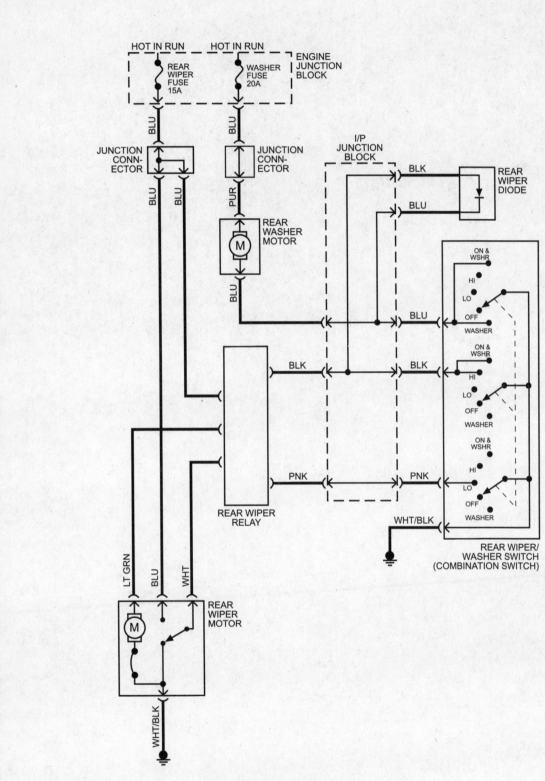

2004 and later Toyota Prius rear wipers system

Notes

GLOSSARY

AIR/FUEL RATIO: The ratio of air-to-gasoline by weight in the fuel mixture drawn into the engine.

AIR INJECTION: One method of reducing harmful exhaust emissions by injecting air into each of the exhaust ports of an engine. The fresh air entering the hot exhaust manifold causes any remaining fuel to be burned before it can exit the tailpipe.

ALTERNATOR: A device used for converting mechanical energy into electrical energy.

AMMETER: An instrument, calibrated in amperes, used to measure the flow of an electrical current in a circuit. Ammeters are always connected in series with the circuit being tested.

AMPERE: The rate of flow of electrical current present when one volt of electrical pressure is applied against one ohm of electrical resistance.

ANALOG COMPUTER: Any microprocessor that uses similar (analogous) electrical signals to make its calculations.

ARMATURE: A laminated, soft iron core wrapped by a wire that converts electrical energy to mechanical energy as in a motor or relay. When rotated in a magnetic field, it changes mechanical energy into electrical energy as in a generator.

ATMOSPHERIC PRESSURE: The pressure on the Earth's surface caused by the weight of the air in the atmosphere. At sea level, this pressure is 14.7 psi at 32°F (101 kPa at 0°C).

ATOMIZATION: The breaking down of a liquid into a fine mist that can be suspended in air.

AXIAL PLAY: Movement parallel to a shaft or bearing bore.

BACKFIRE: The sudden combustion of gases in the intake or exhaust system that results in a loud explosion.

BACKLASH: The clearance or play between two parts, such as meshed gears.

BACKPRESSURE: Restrictions in the exhaust system that slow the exit of exhaust gases from the combustion chamber.

BAKELITE: A heat resistant, plastic insulator material commonly used in printed circuit boards and transistorized components.

BALL BEARING: A bearing made up of hardened inner and outer races between which hardened steel balls roll.

BALLAST RESISTOR: A resistor in the primary ignition circuit that lowers voltage after the engine is started to reduce wear on ignition components.

BEARING: A friction reducing, supportive device usually located between a stationary part and a moving part.

BIMETAL TEMPERATURE SENSOR: Any sensor or switch made of two dissimilar types of metal that bend when heated or cooled due to the different expansion rates of the alloys. These types of sensors usually function as an on/off switch.

BLOWBY: Combustion gases, composed of water vapor and unburned fuel, that leak past the piston rings into the crankcase during normal engine operation. These gases are removed by the PCV system to prevent the buildup of harmful acids in the crankcase.

BRAKE PAD: A brake shoe and lining assembly used with disc brakes.

BRAKE SHOE: The backing for the brake lining. The term is, however, usually applied to the assembly of the brake backing and lining.

BUSHING: A liner, usually removable, for a bearing; an anti-friction liner used in place of a bearing.

CALIPER: A hydraulically activated device in a disc brake system, which is mounted straddling the brake rotor (disc). The caliper contains at least one piston and two brake pads. Hydraulic pressure on the piston(s) forces the pads against the rotor.

CAMSHAFT: A shaft in the engine on which are the lobes (cams) which operate the valves. The camshaft is driven by the crankshaft, via a belt, chain or gears, at one half the crankshaft speed.

CAPACITOR: A device which stores an electrical charge.

CARBON MONOXIDE (CO): A colorless, odorless gas given off as a normal byproduct of combustion. It is poisonous and extremely dangerous in confined areas, building up slowly to toxic levels without warning if adequate ventilation is not available.

CARBURETOR: A device, usually mounted on the intake manifold of an engine, which mixes the air and fuel in the proper proportion to allow even combustion.

CATALYTIC CONVERTER: A device installed in the exhaust system, like a muffler, that converts harmful byproducts of combustion into carbon dioxide and water vapor by means of a heat-producing chemical reaction.

CENTRIFUGAL ADVANCE: A mechanical method of advancing the spark timing by using flyweights in the distributor that react to centrifugal force generated by the distributor shaft rotation.

CHECK VALVE: Any one-way valve installed to permit the flow of air, fuel or vacuum in one direction only.

CHOKE: A device, usually a moveable valve, placed in the intake path of a carburetor to restrict the flow of air.

CIRCUIT: Any unbroken path through which an electrical current can flow. Also used to describe fuel flow in some instances.

CIRCUIT BREAKER: A switch which protects an electrical circuit from overload by opening the circuit when the current flow exceeds a predetermined level. Some circuit breakers must be reset manually, while most reset automatically.

COIL (IGNITION): A transformer in the ignition circuit which steps up the voltage provided to the spark plugs.

COMBINATION MANIFOLD: An assembly which includes both the intake and exhaust manifolds in one casting.

COMBINATION VALVE: A device used in some fuel systems that routes fuel vapors to a charcoal storage canister instead of venting them into the atmosphere. The valve relieves fuel tank pressure and allows fresh air into the tank as the fuel level drops to prevent a vapor lock situation.

COMPRESSION RATIO: The comparison of the total volume of the cylinder and combustion chamber with the piston at BDC and the piston at TDC.

CONDENSER: 1. An electrical device which acts to store an electrical charge, preventing voltage surges. 2. A radiator-like device in the air conditioning system in which refrigerant gas condenses into a liquid, giving off heat.

CONDUCTOR: Any material through which an electrical current can be transmitted easily.

CONTINUITY: Continuous or complete circuit. Can be checked with an ohmmeter.

COUNTERSHAFT: An intermediate shaft which is rotated by a mainshaft and transmits, in turn, that rotation to a working part.

CRANKCASE: The lower part of an engine in which the crankshaft and related parts operate.

CRANKSHAFT: The main driving shaft of an engine which receives reciprocating motion from the pistons and converts it to rotary motion.

CYLINDER: In an engine, the round hole in the engine block in which the piston(s) ride.

CYLINDER BLOCK: The main structural member of an engine in which is found the cylinders, crankshaft and other principal parts.

CYLINDER HEAD: The detachable portion of the engine, usually fastened to the top of the cylinder block and containing all or most of the combustion chambers. On overhead valve engines, it contains the valves and their operating parts. On overhead cam engines, it contains the camshaft as well.

DEAD CENTER: The extreme top or bottom of the piston stroke.

DETONATION: An unwanted explosion of the air/fuel mixture in the combustion chamber caused by excess heat and compression, advanced timing, or an overly lean mixture. Also referred to as "ping".

DIAPHRAGM: A thin, flexible wall separating two cavities, such as in a vacuum advance unit.

DIESELING: A condition in which hot spots in the combustion chamber cause the engine to run on after the key is turned off.

DIFFERENTIAL: A geared assembly which allows the transmission of motion between drive axles, giving one axle the ability to turn faster than the other.

DIODE: An electrical device that will allow current to flow in one direction only.

DISC BRAKE: A hydraulic braking assembly consisting of a brake disc, or rotor, mounted on an axle, and a caliper assembly containing, usually two brake pads which are activated by hydraulic pressure. The pads are forced against the sides of the disc, creating friction which slows the vehicle.

DISTRIBUTOR: A mechanically driven device on an engine which is responsible for electrically firing the spark plug at a predetermined point of the piston stroke.

DOWEL PIN: A pin, inserted in mating holes in two different parts allowing those parts to maintain a fixed relationship.

DRUM BRAKE: A braking system which consists of two brake shoes and one or two wheel cylinders, mounted on a fixed backing plate, and a brake drum, mounted on an axle, which revolves around the assembly.

DWELL: The rate, measured in degrees of shaft rotation, at which an electrical circuit cycles on and off.

ELECTRONIC CONTROL UNIT (ECU): Ignition module, module, amplifier or igniter. See Module for definition.

ELECTRONIC IGNITION: A system in which the timing and firing of the spark plugs is controlled by an electronic control unit, usually called a module. These systems have no points or condenser.

END-PLAY: The measured amount of axial movement in a shaft.

ENGINE: A device that converts heat into mechanical energy.

EXHAUST MANIFOLD: A set of cast passages or pipes which conduct exhaust gases from the engine.

FEELER GAUGE: A blade, usually metal, or precisely predetermined thickness, used to measure the clearance between two parts.

FIRING ORDER: The order in which combustion occurs in the cylinders of an engine. Also the order in which spark is distributed to the plugs by the distributor.

FLOODING: The presence of too much fuel in the intake manifold and combustion chamber which prevents the air/fuel mixture from firing, thereby causing a no-start situation.

FLYWHEEL: A disc shaped part bolted to the rear end of the crankshaft. Around the outer perimeter is affixed the ring gear. The starter drive engages the ring gear, turning the flywheel, which rotates the crankshaft, imparting the initial starting motion to the engine.

FOOT POUND (ft. lbs. or sometimes, ft.lb.): The amount of energy or work needed to raise an item weighing one pound, a distance of one foot.

FUSE: A protective device in a circuit which prevents circuit overload by breaking the circuit when a specific amperage is present. The device is constructed around a strip or wire of a lower amperage rating than the circuit it is designed to protect. When an amperage higher than that stamped on the fuse is present in the circuit, the strip or wire melts, opening the circuit.

GEAR RATIO: The ratio between the number of teeth on meshing gears.

GENERATOR: A device which converts mechanical energy into electrical energy.

HEAT RANGE: The measure of a spark plug's ability to dissipate heat from its firing end. The higher the heat range, the hotter the plug fires.

HUB: The center part of a wheel or gear.

HYDROCARBON (HC): Any chemical compound made up of hydrogen and carbon. A major pollutant formed by the engine as a byproduct of combustion.

HYDROMETER: An instrument used to measure the specific gravity of a solution.

INCH POUND (inch lbs.; sometimes in.lb. or in. lbs.): One twelfth of a foot pound.

INDUCTION: A means of transferring electrical energy in the form of a magnetic field. Principle used in the ignition coil to increase voltage.

INJECTOR: A device which receives metered fuel under relatively low pressure and is activated to inject the fuel into the engine under relatively high pressure at a predetermined time.

INPUT SHAFT: The shaft to which torque is applied, usually carrying the driving gear or gears.

INTAKE MANIFOLD: A casting of passages or pipes used to conduct air or a fuel/air mixture to the cylinders.

JOURNAL: The bearing surface within which a shaft operates.

KEY: A small block usually fitted in a notch between a shaft and a hub to prevent slippage of the two parts.

MANIFOLD: A casting of passages or set of pipes which connect the cylinders to an inlet or outlet source.

MANIFOLD VACUUM: Low pressure in an engine intake manifold formed just below the throttle plates. Manifold vacuum is highest at idle and drops under acceleration.

MASTER CYLINDER: The primary fluid pressurizing device in a hydraulic system. In automotive use, it is found in brake and hydraulic clutch systems and is pedal activated, either directly or, in a power brake system, through the power booster.

MODULE: Electronic control unit, amplifier or igniter of solid state or integrated design which controls the current flow in the ignition primary circuit based on input from the pick-up coil. When the module opens the primary circuit, high secondary voltage is induced in the coil.

NEEDLE BEARING: A bearing which consists of a number (usually a large number) of long, thin rollers.

OHM: (Ω) The unit used to measure the resistance of conductor-to-electrical flow. One ohm is the amount of resistance that limits current flow to one ampere in a circuit with one volt of pressure.

OHMMETER: An instrument used for measuring the resistance, in ohms, in an electrical circuit.

OUTPUT SHAFT: The shaft which transmits torque from a device, such as a transmission.

OVERDRIVE: A gear assembly which produces more shaft revolutions than that transmitted to it.

OVERHEAD CAMSHAFT (OHC): An engine configuration in which the camshaft is mounted on top of the cylinder head and operates the valve either directly or by means of rocker arms.

OVERHEAD VALVE (OHV): An engine configuration in which all of the valves are located in the cylinder head and the camshaft is located in the cylinder block. The camshaft operates the valves via lifters and pushrods.

OXIDES OF NITROGEN (NOx): Chemical compounds of nitrogen produced as a byproduct of combustion. They combine with hydrocarbons to produce smog.

OXYGEN SENSOR: Use with the feedback system to sense the presence of oxygen in the exhaust gas and signal the computer which can reference the voltage signal to an air/fuel ratio.

PINION: The smaller of two meshing gears.

PISTON RING: An open-ended ring with fits into a groove on the outer diameter of the piston. Its chief function is to form a seal between the piston and cylinder wall. Most automotive pistons have three rings: two for compression sealing; one for oil sealing.

PRELOAD: A predetermined load placed on a bearing during assembly or by adjustment.

PRIMARY CIRCUIT: the low voltage side of the ignition system which consists of the ignition switch, ballast resistor or resistance wire, bypass, coil, electronic control unit and pick-up coil as well as the connecting wires and harnesses.

PRESS FIT: The mating of two parts under pressure, due to the inner diameter of one being smaller than the outer diameter of the other, or vice versa; an interference fit.

RACE: The surface on the inner or outer ring of a bearing on which the balls, needles or rollers move.

REGULATOR: A device which maintains the amperage and/or voltage levels of a circuit at predetermined values.

RELAY: A switch which automatically opens and/or closes a circuit.

RESISTANCE: The opposition to the flow of current through a circuit or electrical device, and is measured in ohms. Resistance is equal to the voltage divided by the amperage.

RESISTOR: A device, usually made of wire, which offers a preset amount of resistance in an electrical circuit.

RING GEAR: The name given to a ring-shaped gear attached to a differential case, or affixed to a flywheel or as part of a planetary gear set.

ROLLER BEARING: A bearing made up of hardened inner and outer races between which hardened steel rollers move.

ROTOR: 1. The disc-shaped part of a disc brake assembly, upon which the brake pads bear; also called, brake disc. 2. The device

mounted atop the distributor shaft, which passes current to the distributor cap tower contacts.

SECONDARY CIRCUIT: The high voltage side of the ignition system, usually above 20,000 volts. The secondary includes the ignition coil, coil wire, distributor cap and rotor, spark plug wires and spark plugs.

SENDING UNIT: A mechanical, electrical, hydraulic or electromagnetic device which transmits information to a gauge.

SENSOR: Any device designed to measure engine operating conditions or ambient pressures and temperatures. Usually electronic in nature and designed to send a voltage signal to an on-board computer, some sensors may operate as a simple on/off switch or they may provide a variable voltage signal (like a potentiometer) as conditions or measured parameters change.

SHIM: Spacers of precise, predetermined thickness used between parts to establish a proper working relationship.

SLAVE CYLINDER: In automotive use, a device in the hydraulic clutch system which is activated by hydraulic force, disengaging the clutch.

SOLENOID: A coil used to produce a magnetic field, the effect of which is to produce work.

SPARK PLUG: A device screwed into the combustion chamber of a spark ignition engine. The basic construction is a conductive core inside of a ceramic insulator, mounted in an outer conductive base. An electrical charge from the spark plug wire travels along the conductive core and jumps a preset air gap to a grounding point or points at the end of the conductive base. The resultant spark ignites the fuel/air mixture in the combustion chamber.

SPLINES: Ridges machined or cast onto the outer diameter of a shaft or inner diameter of a bore to enable parts to mate without rotation.

TACHOMETER: A device used to measure the rotary speed of an engine, shaft, gear, etc., usually in rotations per minute.

THERMOSTAT: A valve, located in the cooling system of an engine, which is closed when cold and opens gradually in response to engine heating, controlling the temperature of the coolant and rate of coolant flow.

TOP DEAD CENTER (TDC): The point at which the piston reaches the top of its travel on the compression stroke.

TORQUE: The twisting force applied to an object.

TORQUE CONVERTER: A turbine used to transmit power from a driving member to a driven member via hydraulic action, providing changes in drive ratio and torque. In automotive use, it links the driveplate at the rear of the engine to the automatic transmission.

TRANSDUCER: A device used to change a force into an electrical signal.

TRANSISTOR: A semi-conductor component which can be actuated by a small voltage to perform an electrical switching function.

TUNE-UP: A regular maintenance function, usually associated with the replacement and adjustment of parts and components in the electrical and fuel systems of a vehicle for the purpose of attaining optimum performance.

TURBOCHARGER: An exhaust driven pump which compresses intake air and forces it into the combustion chambers at higher than atmospheric pressures. The increased air pressure allows more fuel to be burned and results in increased horsepower being produced.

VACUUM ADVANCE: A device which advances the ignition timing in response to increased engine vacuum.

VACUUM GAUGE: An instrument used to measure the presence of vacuum in a chamber.

VALVE: A device which control the pressure, direction of flow or rate of flow of a liquid or gas.

VALVE CLEARANCE: The measured gap between the end of the valve stem and the rocker arm, cam lobe or follower that activates the valve.

VISCOSITY: The rating of a liquid's internal resistance to flow.

VOLTMETER: An instrument used for measuring electrical force in units called volts. Voltmeters are always connected parallel with the circuit being tested.

WHEEL CYLINDER: Found in the automotive drum brake assembly, it is a device, actuated by hydraulic pressure, which, through internal pistons, pushes the brake shoes outward against the drums.

Notes

MASTER INDEX

Notes